MEDIUM ÆVUM MONOGRAPHS

SERIES EDITORS

K. P. Clarke, S. Huot, A. J. Lappin,
N. F. Palmer, C. Saunders

MEDIUM ÆVUM
MONOGRAPHS XXX

HUMANISM

IN FIFTEENTH-CENTURY

EUROPE

edited by

DAVID RUNDLE

THE SOCIETY FOR THE STUDY OF MEDIEVAL
LANGUAGES AND LITERATURE

OXFORD · MMXII

The Society for the Study of Medieval Languages
and Literature
Oxford, 2012
http://mediumaevum.modhist.ox.ac.uk/

Chapters: © 2012 The Authors
Appendix & all prefaratory material: © 2012 SSMLL

ISBN-13:
978-0-907570-63-9 (pb)
978-0-907570-74-5 (hb)
978-0-907570-40-0 (e-bk)

British Library Cataloguing in Publication Data
A catalogue record for this book is available
from the British Library

This reprint, with minor revisions, published 2016

CONTENTS

List of Abbreviations and Conventions   vii

List of Contributors   ix

Introductory Note to Paperback Edition (2016)   xii

Foreword   xiii

The Italian Peninsula: Reception and Dissemination   1
    Stephen J. Milner

The Greeks and Renaissance Humanism   31
    John Monfasani

Humanism in the German-speaking Lands during the Fifteenth Century   79
    John L. Flood

Fifteenth-Century Humanism in Poland: Court and Collegium   119
    Jacqueline Glomski

The Power of the Book and the Kingdom of Hungary during the Fifteenth Century   147
    Cristina Neagu

Humanism and the Court in Fifteenth-Century Castile   175
    Jeremy Lawrance

The Ambivalent Influence of Italian Letters and the Rediscovery of the Classics in Late Medieval France   203
    Craig Taylor

The Development of Humanism in Late-Fifteenth-Century Scotland   237
    Tom Rutledge

England: Humanism beyond Weiss   265
    Daniel Wakelin

Humanism across Europe: The Structures of Contacts   307
    David Rundle

Biographical Appendix of Italian Humanists of the Fifteenth Century   337
    Oren Margolis & David Rundle

Index   381

LIST OF ABBREVIATIONS AND CONVENTIONS

In each chapter, the name of any Italian humanist who appears in the Biographical Appendix is placed in small caps at its first mention.

BAV   Vatican City: Biblioteca Apostolica Vaticana

BL   London: British Library

BnF   Paris: Bibliothèque nationale de France

CE   P. G. Bietenholz & T. B. Deutscher ed., *Contemporaries of Erasmus. A Biographical Register of the Renaissance and Reformation*, 3 vols (Toronto, 1985–87)

CTC   P. O. Kristeller, F. E. Cranz & V. Brown ed., *Catalogus Translationum et Commentariorum: mediaeval and Renaissance Latin translations and commentaries*, 8 vols to date (Washington D. C., 1960–)

IMU   *Italia medioevale e umanistica*

ISTC   British Library Incunabula Short Title Catalogue, available on-line at: http://www.bl.uk/catalogues/istc/index.html

ITRL   I Tatti Renaissance Library

ÖNB   Vienna: Österreichische Nationalbibliothek

T&T   L. D. Reynolds et al., *Texts and Transmission. A Survey of the Latin Classics* (Oxford, 1983).

Weiss[4]   R. Weiss, *Humanism in England during the Fifteenth Century*, 4th edn, ed. D. Rundle and A. J. Lappin (Oxford, 2010), available on-line at: http://aevum.space/OS4

INTRODUCTORY NOTE TO REVISED EDITION (2016)

This is a reprint of the original hardback edition with changes confined to minor corrections. John Monfasani's article in this volume has been reprinted in a Variorum collection of his essays: *Greek Scholars between East and West in the Fifteenth Century* (Farnham, 2016), ch. I and the author there provides some further addenda.

LIST OF CONTRIBUTORS

JOHN L. FLOOD is Emeritus Professor of German in the University of London. A past president of the Bibliographical Society, he has published widely, particularly on the history of the book in early modern Germany. In addition to many contributions to German, French, British and American handbooks and scholarly journals, his publications include *Die Historie von Herzog Ernst. Die Frankfurter Prosafassung des 16. Jahrhunderts* (Berlin, 1991), *The German Book 1450–1750* (London, 1995), *Johannes Sinapius (1505–1560): Hellenist and Physician in Germany and Italy* (Geneva, 1997), and, in four volumes, *Poets Laureate in the Holy Roman Empire. A Bio-bibliographical Handbook* (Berlin and New York, 2006).

JACQUELINE GLOMSKI is an Honorary Research Fellow in the History Department at King's College London. She is a specialist in neo-Latin literature, and has published over a dozen articles and one book – *Patronage and Humanist Literature in the Age of the Jagiellons* (Toronto, 2007) – on early humanism at Cracow.

JEREMY LAWRANCE is Professor of Golden Age / Early Modern Studies at the University of Nottingham and Fellow of the British Academy. He has written extensively on Hispanic cultures from the *Poema de mio Cid* to Cervantes. He is the editor, with Brian Tate, of the *Gesta Hispaniensia ex annalibus suorum dierum collecta* of Alfonso de Palencia (Madrid, 1998–99).

OREN MARGOLIS is a Junior Researcher at the Ludwig Boltzmann Institute for Neo-Latin Studies (Vienna). Educated at the University of Southern California, King's College London, and Jesus College, Oxford, he has written on the politics of culture in the Italian network of King René of Anjou (d. 1480); his current research is on the 'hyper-literate' class at the heart of humanist and diplomatic cultures as they grew up and then spread across Renaissance Europe. He is also editor of an on-line collection of essays marking the 150th anniversary of *The Civilization of the Renaissance in Italy* by Jacob Burckhardt.

STEPHEN J. MILNER is Serena Professor of Italian at the University of Manchester. His research focuses on Italian late medieval and Renaissance cultural history especially in Florence and its territorial state. He has published on vernacular rhetoric, space and the city, artistic patronage and the Medici. He has edited and co-edited a number of volumes including *The Erotics of Consolation: Distance and Desire in the Middle Ages* (Basingstoke, 2008), *At the Margins: Minority Groups in Premodern Italy* (Minneapolis, MN, 2005), and *Artistic Exchange and Cultural Translation in the Italian Renaissance City* (Cambridge, 2004).

JOHN MONFASANI is Distinguished Professor in the History Department at the University at Albany, State University of New York. He publishes on Greek and Latin humanists in Renaissance Italy and is presently working on the Plato–Aristotle Controversy of the Fifteenth Century. His latest volume is *Bessarion Scholasticus: a Study of Cardinal Bessarion's Latin Library* (Turnhout, 2012).

CRISTINA NEAGU holds a doctorate from the University of Oxford and specialises in the literature and arts of the Renaissance. The fields in which most of her work has been conducted include neo-Latin literature, rhetoric and the history of the book. Among her research interests are Central and East European humanism, illuminated manuscripts and Albrecht Dürer as theoretician and reformer of the image. Her publications include *Servant of the Renaissance: The Poetry and Prose of Nicolaus Olahus* (Bern, 2003). She is currently in charge of Special Collections at Christ Church Library, Oxford.

DAVID RUNDLE is a member of Corpus Christi College and the History Faculty, University of Oxford; he is also Executive Officer of the Society for the Study of Medieval Languages and Literature. His research interests focus on late medieval and

Renaissance intellectual culture, often using the palaeographical and codicological evidence of manuscripts to trace the history of the ownership and reading of texts. He is completing a volume on *England and the Identity of Italian Renaissance Humanism*, and another on *English Humanist Scripts up to c. 1509*.

THOMAS RUTLEDGE is a lecturer in the School of Literature, Drama, and Creative Writing at the University of East Anglia; his work focuses on the reception of classical and Italian literature in fifteenth- and sixteenth-century Scotland. He has written on the vernacular humanism of Robert Henryson, Gavin Douglas and John Bellenden, and is currently working on the Scottish translation of Ariosto and Rabelais.

CRAIG TAYLOR is Senior Lecturer in the Department of History at the University of York. He works on the political cultures of late medieval France and England. He is the editor of *Debating the Hundred Years War: Pour ce que plusieurs (La loi salicque) & A declaracion of the trew and dewe title of Henrie VIII* which appeared in the Camden Series in 2007, and of *Joan of Arc, La Pucelle* (Manchester, 2006). He has a volume forthcoming on *Chivalry, Honour and Martial Culture in Late Medieval France* (Cambridge).

DANIEL WAKELIN is Jeremy Griffiths Professor of Medieval English Palaeography at the University of Oxford, having formerly been a Fellow and University Lecturer in English at Christ's College, Cambridge. He is author of *Humanism, Reading and English Literature, 1430–1530* (Oxford, 2007) and co-editor of *The Production of Books in England, 1350–1500* (Cambridge, 2011).

FOREWORD

DAVID RUNDLE

The volume you have in your hands is the third part of a project that began in the virtual world of on-line publishing and continued in the face-to-face context of a conference. The project developed from a suggestion of Anthony Lappin, Monographs Editor of the Society for the Study of Medieval Languages and Literature, to digitize and make freely available on the internet some of the early Medium Ævum Monographs. It was decided that the first work to receive this treatment should be Roberto Weiss's *Humanism in England during the Fifteenth Century*, which originally appeared in 1941 and then was re-published, with addenda, in 1957 and 1967. The volume was digitized by Tony Lappin himself, with new addenda and corrigenda, as well as an historiographical introduction and appendix of original texts, by myself.[1]

As work on the digitization of the monograph progressed, the Committee of the Society decided it would be appropriate to celebrate its fourth edition of *Humanism in England* by organising a conference that would put the subject in a broader geographical context, considering the influence of Italian Renaissance humanism in different parts of Europe during the Quattrocento. It must be said that in his monograph, his first published book, Roberto Weiss himself paid little attention to comparisons, or even potential connexions forged by humanists who travels took them between European lands; that broader narrative was one to which he turned in later work.[2] What

---

[1] The edition is on-line at http://aevum.space/OS4 and will be published in hard copy in 2016.

[2] R. Weiss, 'Italian Humanism in Western Europe' in E. F. Jacob ed., *Italian Renaissance Studies. A tribute to the late Cecilia M. Ady* (London,

Humanism in England provided was the tale of a dialogue, more like, as it were, a two-way phone conversation (and that rather one-sided) than a conference call. It can certainly be paralleled by other narratives, often nationally defined, of conversations happening simultaneously between Italy and other parts of Europe. Narratives of humanism in various countries of Europe have also, on occasion, been brought together into collections of essays – but rarely with the same chronological focus that Weiss set himself in his work.[3] His span, from the 1410s to 1485, has little traction outsides the confines of English history, and even in that context those chronological limits are of questionable value. However, broadened slightly to take in the full extent of the fifteenth century and there is a time-period which may merit consideration for the engagement of scholars and patrons across Europe with humanism in its Italian heyday.

The conference which had this rationale took place at Corpus Christi College, Oxford, on 17th October 2009. It should be emphasised that this book is by no means simply the proceedings of that conference. On the minus side, circumstances forced one of the day's speakers, Arjo Vanderjagt, to withdraw from the project; his masterly comparison of the development of humanism in Burgundy and the Low Countries is irreplaceable. Counter-balancing that, we are delighted to be able to include two papers from scholars not present that autumn Saturday: John Monfasani and Tom Rutledge provided discussions which extend the reach of this volume in highly important ways. In addition, to assist the reader in tracing the activities of particular humanists, many of whom

---

1960), pp. 69–93; id., *The Spread of Italian Humanism* (London, 1964).

[3] H. A. Oberman and T. A. Brady ed., *Itinerarium Italicum: the profile of the Italian Renaissance in the mirror of its European transformations* (Leiden, 1975); A. Goodman and A. Mackay ed., *The Impact of Humanism on Western Europe* (London, 1990); J. Helmrath et al. ed., *Diffusion des Humanismus: studien zur nationalen Geschichtsschreibung europäischer Humanisten* (Göttingen, 2002); also relevant are the special issue of *Studi francesi*, li (2007) and R. Porter and M. Teich ed., *The Renaissance in National Context* (Cambridge, 1992).

appear at disparate points in the volume, a biographical appendix of quattrocento Italian humanists mentioned in the essays, much of which was compiled by Oren Margolis, closes the contents.

The resulting collection of essays is a demonstration of how much not only our knowledge of details but our perception of humanism as a whole has changed since Weiss was first active. The definition of the concept that Weiss presented in the first pages of *Humanism in England* reads as outdated – indeed, it seemed so to some of his earliest readers.[4] Any sense that humanism was a new intellectual system defining the worldview of the Renaissance was already open to doubt and has become all the harder to sustain. That is the case, in large part, because of the enduring influence of Paul Oskar Kristeller (1905–1999), who pointed out that 'humanismus' was a German coinage of the nineteenth century, intended to signify an educational programme centred on the classics such that the *humanistae* of the later fifteenth and sixteenth centuries would have promoted; the term 'humanist' was in turn derived from the revived Ciceronian phrase, *studia humanitatis*.[5] As Stephen Milner explains early in his opening chapter for this volume, a consensus has developed that sees humanism as a set of shared activities centring on respect for and imitation of ancient Latin and Greek texts – activities that did not themselves add up to a particular philosophy, though they were often practised in relation to ancient philosophies. The chapters that follow are also testimony to the desire to re-conceptualise humanism by detecting its edges: its chronological limits, its diffusion (to use Daniel Wakelin's term) into non-humanist writings, and, of course, its geographical extent.

[4] See D. Rundle, 'Editor's Introduction' to Weiss⁴, pp. v–xliv at pp. xii, xxiii–xxiv.

[5] For a mature statement of his views, see P. O. Kristeller, 'Humanism' in C. B. Schmidt et al. ed., *The Cambridge History of Renaissance Philosophy* (Cambridge, 1988), pp. 113–37. On Kristeller, see J. Monfasani ed., *Kristeller Reconsidered: essays on his life and scholarship* (New York, 2006).

The basic division of the chapters is geographical – though without intending to privilege the nation as the unit for response to humanist influences. The essays are presented without an attempt to channel them all into one interpretation. Indeed, as some of the contributors emphasise, what can be immediately most noticeable is how the experience of humanism in a different land contrasted with its history in England, as it was described by Roberto Weiss. Of course, the contribution of Daniel Wakelin here and the addenda to the fourth edition of *Humanism in England* should alert us to how far the narrative which receives its classic presentation in Weiss's work needs revising. Yet, however much transformation that undergoes, it will still present a rather different story from the multi-centred engagement with Italian influences fuelled particularly by a self-identification with the re-found text of Tacitus' *Germania* that is described here by John Flood for the German-speaking lands, or even from the court-centred practices that Jeremy Lawrance describes in his discussion of Castile. It is also the case that such histories have come to have contrasting uses for nation-states' cultural mythologies – with, for instance, Hungarian nostalgia for the heyday of its Corvinian glory (lovingly reconstructed here by Cristina Neagu) or Polish perceptions of the preparation for a Golden Age (Jacqueline Glomski) or French claims for an indigenous tradition of learning defiantly independent of Italian influence (dispassionately reviewed by Craig Taylor) while, indeed, for the identity-formation of Scotland (Tom Rutledge) or England (Wakelin) fifteenth-century engagement with humanism has been all but forgotten.

At the same time, there are both links and similarities that can bind these individual tales into a broader shared history. The final chapter of this volume considers the patterns of communication that underlie the various discussions and so elucidates some of the themes that run through the volume. Its particular approach is to suggest that, faced with the evidence gathered in this book, we should revise our understanding of how intellectual ideas spread, thinking of quattrocento humanism not so much in terms of a centre and peripheries but rather as, from the outset, an international enterprise. This suggests one thread which could guide us; readers are welcome to find others.

It is a pleasure to end this opening with acknowledgements to those who have been involved in this project. They include all the participants at the conference, in particular the speakers, and Martin McLaughlin, who ably led the final round-table discussion. They must also include the Series Editors of Medium Ævum Monographs from among whom it cannot be invidious to single out one for special thanks since Tony Lappin was the first originator of this project. I do not mind admitting both that I was originally sceptical of the endeavour and that I am pleased to have been persuaded that I was wrong.

THE ITALIAN PENINSULA: RECEPTION AND DIS-SEMINATION

STEPHEN J. MILNER

Italy has traditionally been cast as the birthplace of Renaissance humanism, the cradle and nursery of the humanists who not only travelled in search of new texts in foreign lands but also attracted others to visit the multiple centres of cultural activity and learning found within the peninsula itself.[1] Yet, in considering both the historiography and future directions of the study of humanism from multiple regional perspectives, a differentiation needs to be made at the outset between Italy understood as nation and Italy as a geographic entity. Given Italy's relatively recent unification as a nation-state during the third quarter of the nineteenth century, humanistic activity during the Renaissance was resolutely 'pre'-national and manifested itself in different guises within the many political and regional centres of the peninsula each of which provided a specific and differing reception context.[2] The use of the term 'peninsula' in the title of the current study, therefore, deliberately privileges a geographic formation over the nation as a political entity and social fiction. In this way a differentiation is maintained between the many political forms and centres that

---

[1] Such a teleology is apparent in the three-volume set edited by Albert Rabil Jr. in 1988 in which volume one is entitled 'Humanism in Italy', volume two 'Humanism beyond Italy', and the final volume eschews geography in favour of examining the 'disciplines'. See A. Rabil Jr ed., *Renaissance Humanism: foundations, forms, and legacy*, 3 vols (Philadelphia, 1988).

[2] For a discussion of the multiplicity of reception contexts see S. J. Campbell and S. J. Milner ed., *Artistic Exchange and Cultural Translation in the Italian Renaissance City* (Cambridge, 2004).

constituted the pre-national landscape of late medieval and Renaissance Italy with its amalgam of republics, *signori*, papal-states, and kingdoms. That a specifically 'Italian Renaissance' was subsequently promoted by the Fascists as part of their triumphalist nationalism in the 1930s and 1940s can be read as another, albeit more contemporary, instance of cultural appropriation which purposively overlooked the complexity of the peninsula's late medieval and Renaissance political ordering in foregrounding the Roman, and largely imperial, destiny of the Italian nation.[3]

Seeking to assess and account for Renaissance humanism as a cultural phenomenon is an endeavour that has given rise to an extensive scholarly literature that dates back to the writings of the humanists themselves and is now the subject of its own historiography.[4] Whether understood as a concern with the rediscovery and imitation of classical literary forms or the emergence of a new 'modern' philosophy of man, the tension between the philological practices and educational programme of the humanists, on the one hand, and the ideological ends to which their activities were directed, on the other, continues to animate critical debate. Whilst a broad consensus has been reached that humanism as a substantive philosophical or ideological position did not emerge until the nineteenth century, it has also been recognised that humanists did share certain traits which included a knowledge and interest in classical languages, a philological approach to towards textual criticism, an interest in the imitation of classical literary style and

---

[3] D. M. Lasansky, *The Renaissance Perfected: architecture, spectacle, and tourism in Fascist Italy* (Pennsylvania, 2004) and C. Lazzaro and R. J. Crum ed., *Donatello among the Blackshirts: history and modernity in the visual culture of Fascist Italy* (Ithaca, NY, 2005).

[4] See P. Burke, *The Renaissance Sense of the Past* (London, 1969) and M. McLaughlin, 'Humanist concepts of Renaissance and Middle Ages', *Renaissance Studies*, ii (1988), pp. 131–42. For surveys of the history of humanistic scholarship see, for example, J. Woolfson ed., *Renaissance Historiography* (Basingstoke, 2005) and A. Mazzocco ed., *Interpretations of Renaissance Humanism* (Leiden, 2006).

a sense of partaking in a revival of learning with a moral purpose.⁵ As this collection amply demonstrates, this critical orientation and set of scholarly practices had a major impact upon numerous fields of learning across early modern Europe and beyond. Yet, nevertheless, the words 'Renaissance' and 'humanism' still seem to overwhelm scholars, who often add a qualifying adjective in order to render the scope of study more manageable: civic humanism; curial humanism, literary humanism, Christian humanism; Venetian humanism; even Italian humanism. Notwithstanding such attempts at containment, however, the fact remains that both the Renaissance and humanism constantly escape and exceed the definitions that seek to confine them.

In what follows the aim is to furnish an indicative account of the emergence of the humanists as agents of the classical revival, showing how the textual cultures from which they evolved, and the socio-political and cultural contexts within which they grew up, conditioned their readings and representations of an ancient past whose form they helped define through their textual discoveries, philological analysis, and creative imitation. Such an account can in no way be exhaustive, but in pointing out what rendered the Italian peninsula susceptible to revived classicism, and in focusing on the mobility of Renaissance humanism as movement, rather than *a* movement, the aim is to furnish a platform for the reading of the following essays all of which demonstrate just how intellectual exchange ebbed and flowed both within and beyond the Italian peninsula.⁶

---

5   See P. O. Kristeller, 'Studies on Renaissance Humanism during the last Twenty Years', *Studies in the Renaissance*, ix (1962), pp. 7–30 and G. M. Logan, 'Substance and form in Renaissance humanism', *The Journal of Medieval and Renaissance Studies*, vii (1977), pp. 1–34. On humanism as a 'critical idiom', see T. Davies, *Humanism* (London and New York, 1998).

6   See the classic essay by E. H. Gombrich, 'The Renaissance: Period or Movement?' in J. B. Trapp ed., *Background to the English Renaissance: introductory lectures* (London, 1974), pp. 9–30.

Humanism as contagion

In characterising humanism as a form of transmission and dissemination the intention is to present it in terms of epidemiology, namely as a cultural phenomenon which was transmitted through contact and exchange.[7] Tracing the roots and routes of such cultural contagion, charting the clustering of its outbreaks and its mutations, involves tracing an increasingly complex and subtle web of associations, collaborations, and exchanges that criss-cross boundaries and frontiers: geographical; political; temporal; and disciplinary. Mapping these relationships necessarily requires the identification of the agents of such transmission and the multiple media that were used by these cultural go-betweens in a manner commensurate with the Renaissance's own increasingly sophisticated engagement with both cartography and epidemic biology.[8] It also requires an understanding of the extent to which successful transmission depended on the receptivity of the host to infection by the carrier. For, more often than not, such infection was actively sought, as receiving cultures were less passive victims than active hosts who sought out a particular strain of the classical virus. Petrarch's account of how the ancient authors became 'absorbed into my being and implanted not only in my memory but in the marrow of my bones' is indicative.[9] For humanism not only sought to reconnect with, and make sense of, ancient cultures but also transmitted its knowledge and skills as it went viral in the fifteenth century, the analogy cohering with the notion of humanists as citizens of a virtual republic of letters that

---

[7] On the epidemiology of representation see D. Sperber, *Explaining Culture: a naturalistic approach* (Oxford, 1996).

[8] On Renaissance mapping see F. Fiorani, *The Marvel of Maps: srt, vartography and politics in Renaissance Italy* (New Haven, CT, 2005). A scientific germ theory of disease was first proposed by Girolamo Fracastoro in his *De contagione* (1546): see C. Pennuto, *Simpatia, fantasia e contagio: il pensiero medico e il pensiero filosofico di Girolamo Fracastoro* (Rome, 2008).

[9] Petrarch, *Rerum familiarium. Letters on familiar matters*, trans. Aldo S. Bernardo, 3 vols (Baltimore and London, 1975-85), i, p. 45.

extended above and beyond any specific political form. And if the humanists were the carriers, then texts were the virus. As Martin Davies has put it, 'there was no humanism without books', whether they were manuscript or incunables.[10]

The most comprehensive attempt to offer an itinerary of the intellectual migration of humanism is the multi-volume *Iter Italicum* project initiated by Paul Oskar Kristeller (1905–1999) in 1963 which, as its sub-title indicates, serves as 'a finding list of uncatalogued or incompletely catalogued humanistic manuscripts of the Renaissance in Italian and other libraries.'[11] Whilst the first two volumes survey Italy, the subsequent four volumes cover other routes, 'alia itinera', identifying humanist manuscripts found in libraries from Australia to Sweden (plus 'Utopia'). Even more systematic are the annotated lists and guides contained in another brain-child of Kristeller, the multi-volume and on-going *Catalogus translationum et commentariorum*.[12] As successive volumes are published, an increasingly nuanced account of the transmission and reception histories of individual classical authors over the late medieval and Renaissance period is emerging through the charting of their Latin translation and commentary traditions. As anyone who has searched their pages will testify, both works facilitate our following in the footsteps of the ancients. The fact that we are still at the listing stage of predominantly Latin works, let alone material in the vernacular, indicates the enormous scale of humanistic activity and the sheer complexity of the web of humanistic interaction even prior to the advent of printing.

---

[10] M. Davies, 'Humanism in script and print in the fifteenth century' in J. Kraye ed., *The Cambridge Companion to Renaissance Humanism* (Cambridge, 1996), pp. 47–62.

[11] P. O. Kristeller et al. ed., *Iter Italicum: a finding list of uncatalogued or incompletely catalogued humanistic manuscripts of the Renaissance in Italian and other libraries*, 6 vols (London, 1963–1997).

[12] V. Brown et al. ed., *Catalogus Translationum et Commentariorum: Mediaeval and Renaissance Latin translations and commentaries. Annotated lists and guides,* 8 vols to date (Washington, 1960–).

A convenient starting point in seeking to understand the scope of humanism is the coinage of the term humanist itself. In the mid-1940s two influential interventions were published by Kristeller and Augusto Campana which proved foundational for conditioning subsequent scholarship. Both scholars independently sought to identify the origins of humanism by charting the emergence of the word *humanista* during the Renaissance.[13] Their conclusions were broadly similar: that the term emerged in the late fourteenth and early fifteenth centuries to identify a specific group of teachers who offered an educational programme, either publicly or privately, known as the *studia humanitatis*, the humanities or what we might now broadly refer to as the 'arts'. The phrase has subsequently been traced back to Cicero who used it in a judicial oration, the *Pro Archia*, in which he defended the citizenship of a Greek poet resident in Rome and, by association, the value of poetry itself. Significantly, the speech was rediscovered by Petrarch in 1333 and has recently been described as the 'charter of foundation' of classical scholarship in the Renaissance.[14] The *humanista* was therefore differentiated from other well-established figures found within the late medieval university sector, such as the *legista*, *sophista*, *canonista*, *summista*, or *artista*. In contrast to the other disciplines, the focus of study was on a literary programme that drew extensively on texts from classical antiquity to provide instruction in grammar, rhetoric, poetry, history and moral philosophy. Emphasis was therefore placed on the liberal arts rather than the disciplines traditionally associated with scholasticism – philosophy, theology, law (Roman and canon) and medicine. In addition, rhetoric was granted precedence over the other two components within the medieval *trivium*, namely logic and dialectic. This orientation was sufficiently well defined

---

[13] P. O. Kristeller, 'Humanism and Scholasticism in the Italian Renaissance', *Byzantion*, xvii (1944–45), pp. 346–74 and A. Campana, 'The Origin of the Word "Humanist"', *Journal of the Warburg and Courtauld Institutes*, ix (1946), pp. 60–73.

[14] See M. D. Reeve, 'Classical Scholarship' in Kraye ed., *Cambridge Companion to Renaissance Humanism*, pp. 20–46 at pp. 22–24.

as a critical and educational platform to enable the likes of LEO-
NARDO BRUNI and POGGIO BRACCIOLINI to self-consciously
identify themselves as promoters of the *studia humanitatis* by
the early fifteenth century.[15]

Yet knowledge of the work of classical authors – some Greek,
as well as many more Latin – was a given well before the
designation of the humanist as an identifiable type.[16] Previous
Renaissances in scholarly activity, in the eighth to ninth century
during the so-called Carolingian Renaissance initiated by the
edicts of the Emperor Charlemagne (d. 814), and again during
the twelfth-century Renaissance, saw classical learning undergo
marked revivals in response to the Catholic programme of
educating its clergy and to the need to train layman as lawyers,
doctors and officials to serve the courts and chanceries of major
European centres.[17] The monastery and cathedral schools of
northern France, Spain, Sicily and northern Italy, many of
which subsequently became universities, offered instruction
which drew on the works of classical authors and maintained
extensive libraries and scriptoria which produced fine
manuscript versions of classical works.[18] Just as Kristeller sought

[15] B. G. Kohl, 'The changing concept of the *studia humanitatis* in the early Renaissance', *Renaissance Studies*, vi (1992), pp. 185–209 and R. Black, 'Humanism' in *The New Cambridge Medieval History*, 8 vols (Cambridge, 1995–2005), vii, ed. C. Allmand (1998), pp. 243–77.

[16] For one strand of Greek interest before the quattrocento, see R. Weiss, *Medieval and Humanist Greek* (Padua, 1977).

[17] C. D. Lanham, 'Writing Instruction from Late Antiquity to the Twelfth Century' in J. J. Murphy ed., *A Short History of Writing Instruction: from Ancient Greece to Modern America*, 2nd edn (Davis, CA, 2001), pp. 79–121. See also the classic studies of C. H. Haskins, *The Renaissance of the Twelfth Century* (Cambridge, MA, 1927); R. W. Southern, *Medieval Humanism and other Studies* (Oxford, 1970) and id., *Scholastic Humanism and the Unification of Europe*, 2 vols to date (Oxford, 1995–), and the essays in R. L. Benson et al. ed., *Renaissance and Renewal in the Twelfth Century* (Cambridge, MA, 1982).

[18] See L. D. Reynolds and N. G. Wilson, *Scribes and Scholars: a guide to the transmission of Greek and Latin literature*, 3rd edn (Oxford, 1991), pp. 70–107.

to map the locations of humanistic manuscripts, scholars such as Munk Olsen and Reynolds have mapped the late antique and medieval manuscript attestations of classical authors.[19] The humanist recovery of the classical tradition was largely, therefore, the recovery of the classical texts copied during the Carolingian Renaissance, a fact reflected in the adoption of Caroline minuscule, which the humanists called *littera antiqua*, as the model for Italian humanistic bookhand in the early fifteenth century.[20] The task remains to account for the particular cultural factors that facilitated the classical revival and the prevailing textual cultures from which humanism incrementally emerged.

Law and poetry: medieval textual sensitivities and the classics

The origins of Italian humanist textual sensitivities date back to the final decades of the twelfth century. Although manuscript evidence is scarce, it now appears that the indigenous grammar and rhetorical instruction based on classical authors received a major boost after the Investiture Controversy from the increasing traffic of students and teachers between the centres of learning in northern France and the Rhineland, resulting in a marked acceleration in the authoring of precept literature.[21]

---

[19] B. Munk Olsen, *L'Étude des auteurs classiques latins aux XI et XII siècles: catalogue des manuscripts classiques latins copiés du IXe au Xiie siècle*, 3 vols (Paris, 1982–87) and *T&T*.

[20] See B. L. Ullman, *The Origin and Development of Humanistic Script* (Rome, 1960), and A. C. de la Mare, *The Handwriting of Italian Humanists*, i / 1 (Oxford, 1973). For further discussion of humanist scribes, see pp. 319–21 below.

[21] On the correlation between French and Italian rhetorical commentaries in the late twelfth century see K. M. Fredborg, 'Petrus Helia's *Summa* on Cicero's *De Inventione*', *Traditio*, lxiv (2009), pp. 139–82, and the discussion of the two late twelfth-century Italian rhetorical commentaries in G. C. Alessio, 'Due trattati di retorica nell'Italia centro-settentrionale' in L. Calboli Montefusco ed., *Papers on Rhetoric V. Atti del convegno internazionale 'Dictamen, Poetria and Cicero: Coherence and Diversification'* (Rome, 2003), pp. 1–20. For a discussion of indigenous Italian grammar instruction in the late twelfth century see

Manuscript evidence shows that the study and commentary on Latin authors in the French and northern European schools and monasteries was more extensive than in Italy and no doubt contributed to what Ronald Witt has described somewhat polemically as 'the French cultural invasion of 1180–1230'.[22] The seeds of revived Latin literacy, therefore, lay in the growth of professional training associated with the legal and notarial sectors in centres such as Bologna, Arezzo, Padua, Siena and the many other communes which established *studia* at this time.[23] Moving away from the ideal of an integrated curriculum, the Italian schools offered differentiated instruction in specific skills within a highly competitive educational marketplace. The turf wars in Bologna between masters like Boncompagno da Signa (c. 1170–c. 1240) and Guido Fava (c. 1190–c. 1243), offering juridical, dictaminal, notarial, rhetorical, and grammar teaching are well documented and to some extent illustrate the extent of overlap in the content of instruction.[24] Commentaries on rhetorical texts such as the Cicero's *De inventione* were as relevant as Boethius' more dialectical *De topicis differentiis* in the teaching of topical invention, whilst poetry, as a sub-division of the *ars grammatica*, involved both rhetorical and grammatical elements, as evidenced in Geoffrey of Vinsauf's preceptive

---

R. Black, *Humanism and Education in Medieval and Renaissance Italy: tradition and innovation in Latin schools from the twelfth to the fifteenth century* (Cambridge, 2001), pp. 185–91.

[22] R. Witt, 'The French cultural invasion, 1180–1230' in Calboli Montefusco ed., *Papers on Rhetoric*, pp. 229–59 and id., *'In the Footsteps of the Ancients'. The origins of humanism from Lovato to Bruni* (Leiden, 2000), pp. 31–80. For a critique of Witt's thesis see R. Black, 'The origins of humanism, its educational context and its early development: a review article of Ronald Witt's *In the Footsteps of the Ancients*', *Vivarium*, xl (2002), pp. 272–97, esp. pp. 275–86.

[23] On Italian *studia* see P. Nardi, 'Dalle *Scholae* allo *Studium generale*: la formazione delle università medievali' in F. Liotta ed., *Studi di storia del diritto medioevo e moderno* (Bologna, 1999), pp. 1–32.

[24] See the comments in E. H. Kantorowicz, 'An "Autobiography" of Guido Faba', *Mediaeval and Renaissance Studies*, i (1943), pp. 253–80.

grammar.[25] Similarly whilst the *dictamina* of the period contained specifically medieval instruction on the cursus, they also drew extensively on Book Four of the *Ad Herennium* in identifying rhetorical figures and took the five parts of the classical oration as the template for epistolary composition.[26]

The specialisation and utilitarian orientation of instruction was a direct response to the urban expansion of the self-determining communes of Italy that witnessed a marked growth in lay literacy and an explosion of documentary production associated with the increasingly complex bureaucratic structures they generated.[27] The evolution of a specific *ars notaria* as well as the collating of exemplary speeches under the title of the *ars arigandi* or *ars concionandi* led to further specialisation in instruction due to the need to witness contracts and to offer guidance to podestà and other itinerant judicial officials who combined the roles of rectors and rhetors within the communes.[28] Under these cultural pressures, the controversial and disputational aspects of scholastic dialectical argumentation were adapted to the civic contexts of the law court, public piazza and council chamber and given a rhetorical makeover

---

[25] On the interrelation of the medieval *artes* in this period, see S. Reynolds, *Medieval Reading: grammar, rhetoric and the classical Text* (Cambridge, 1996) and R. Copeland & I. Sluiter ed., *Medieval Grammar and Rhetoric: language arts and literary theory, AD 300–1475* (Oxford, 2009), pp. 544–50 and 684–98. On the *Poetria nova* in Italy during the thirteenth century see M. Curry Woods, *Classroom Commentaries: teaching the* Poetria nova *across Medieval and Renaissance Europe* (Columbus, OH, 2010), pp. 94–162.

[26] M. Carmargo, *Ars dictaminis. Ars dictandi* (Turnhout, 1991).

[27] For a comprehensive treatment of the origins of the Italian communes and their relation to classical forms of social ordering, see P. Jones, *The Italian City-State: from commune to signoria* (Oxford, 1997). On literacy and the explosion of documentary production see W. Robins ed., *Textual Cultures of Medieval Italy* (Toronto, 2011).

[28] See the foundational studies of G. Orlandelli, 'Genesi dell'*ars notariae* nel secolo XIII', *Studi medievali*, vi (1965), pp. 329–66 and E. Artifoni, 'I podestà professionali e la fondazione retorica della politica comunale', *Quaderni storici*, lxiii (1986), pp. 687–719.

within a social world governed by consultation and deliberation.[29] The adoption of a more controversial *stilus rhetoricus* within epistolary exchanges between rival chanceries as well as the deployment of invective in inter-communal disputes, reflected the localised and antagonistic political world of early communal Italy and the respective allegiances to Papal and Imperial claims to sovereignty over the *Regnum Italicum*.[30] Consequently, the professional and practical orientation of such instruction in Italy differed markedly from the more belletristic approach to the language arts found in France. This is reflected in the numerous references to factional disputes in the classically informed precept literature produced in Italy in the late Due and early Trecento.

On the literary front, the French influence was evident in the quantity of chivalric and troubadour texts and verses which migrated south in the early 1200s, finding a ready reception amongst the knightly class of *milites* and feudal nobles, many of whom were moving away from the land and taking up residence in the burgeoning urban centres.[31] The cohabitation of an urban aristocracy and guild-based *popolo* in a shared social space saw chivalric and communal values overlapping and often in tension. The result was an incredibly complex generic and linguistic commixing that reflected the shifting social constitution of the major urban centres of the peninsula and which involved both classical and romance material. Whilst French and

---

[29] S. J. Milner, 'Communication, Consensus and Conflict: Rhetorical principals, the *ars concionandi* and social ordering in late medieval Italy' in V. Cox and J. O. Ward ed., *The Rhetoric of Cicero in its Medieval and Renaissance Commentary Tradition* (Leiden, 2006), pp. 411–60.

[30] L. Shepherd, *Courting Power: persuasion and politics in the early thirteenth century* (New York, 1999), pp. 137–56 and N. Rubinstein, 'Political Rhetoric in the Imperial Chancery during the Twelfth and Thirteenth Centuries', *Medium Ævum*, xiv (1945), pp. 22–43.

[31] See S. Gasparri, *I 'milites' cittadini: studi sulla cavalleria in Italia* (Rome, 1992); J.-C. Maire Vigueur, *Cavalieri e cittadini: guerra, conflitti e società nell'Italia comunale* (Bologna, 2004) and the essays collected in F. Cardini, I. Gagliardi and G. Ligato ed., *Cavalieri e città* (Pisa, 2009).

the variants of Franco-Italian, Occitan and Provençal were acknowledged as the languages of romance and chivalry associated with the dynastic aristocracy, Latin was the language of law, the clergy, education, and high-level diplomacy, and the vernaculars the languages of everyday business and communal deliberation. Often these languages and discourses literally overlapped in texts. For example, the transcription of love lyrics, themselves modelled on the troubadour poetry of feudal southern France which was written in *langue d'oc*, are found in the margins of communal registers, as is the case with the so-called *Memoriali bolognesi* produced by the notaries of the Bolognese commune from 1265 onwards.[32] Similarly, one of the most studied manuscripts of duecento Provençal poetry from the Veneto was written on a palimpsest of an earlier precept text on law or logic.[33] Brunetto Latini's *Li Livres dou trésor* (1262–66) was written in French, was clearly modelled on the French encyclopaedic tradition, and drew on the French medieval *florilegia* that combined classical with romance and chivalric literature, in his case *Li Fait des romains* (1213–14) which proclaimed itself as a collation of work by Lucan, Sallust and Suetonius.[34] Yet Latini's text was clearly addressed to an Italian reception context as it was written by a notary who championed the mastery of rhetoric and law as the pillars of political order whilst defining the duties of the podestà in administering communal justice.

---

[32] See A. Stussi, 'Versi d'amore in volgare tra la fine del secolo XII e l'inizio del XIII', *Cultura neolatina*, xlix (1999), pp. 1–68; S. Orlando, '*Best sellers* e notai: la tradizione estravagante delle rime fra Due e Trecento in Italia' in F. Brugnolo and G. Peron ed., *Da Guido Guinizzelli a Dante: nuove prospettive sulla lirica del Duecento* (Padua, 2004), pp. 257–70, and the discussion in J. Steinberg, *Accounting for Dante: urban readers and writers in Late Medieval Italy* (Notre Dame, IN, 2007), pp. 17–60.

[33] See M. Careri, *Il canzoniere provenzale H (Vat. Lat. 3207): struttura, contenuto e fonti* (Modena, 1990).

[34] See L.-F. Flutre and K. Sneydens de Vogel, *Li Fet des Romains compilé ensemble de Saluste, et de Suetoine et de Lucan*, 2 vols (Paris, 1938).

This fluidity was further witnessed by the speed with which texts were rendered into the vernacular. Both the *Li Fait des romains* and the *Trésor* were quickly translated into the vernacular, reflecting the growing demand for such literature on the part of the communal laity.[35] From the mid-Duecento onwards a raft of translations were produced by what we might term 'vernacular humanists', from Latini himself who translated several Ciceronian orations into Tuscan to the likes of Taddeo Alderotti (1215–1295), Bono Giamboni (c. 1240–c. 1292), Bartolomeo da San Concordio (1262–1347), Domenico Cavalca (c. 1270–1342) and Filippo Ceffi (1280s–1340s).[36] Works and vernacular paraphrases of texts by Ovid, Valerius Maximus, Orosius, Sallust, Livy, Cicero, Aristotle, Boethius, and even near-contemporaries such as the judge and civil commentator Albertano da Brescia (c. 1200–c. 1270) were rendered in the *volgare*, especially in the environs around Florence and Tuscany.[37]

Not surprisingly, therefore, many of the leading scholarly and literary figures of late medieval Italy were not only capable of writing in multiple literary registers, and languages, but also had a vested interest in the translation, reception and transmission of classical authors and texts. Dante (c.1265–1321) was not untypical in his plurilingualism, even if he was largely addressing and voicing fictive audiences.[38] It is significant that as

---

[35] S. Marroni, *'I fatti dei romani': saggio di edizione critica di un volgarizzamento fiorentino del duecento* (Rome, 2004).

[36] See A. Cornish, *Vernacular Translation in Dante's Italy: illiterate literature* (Cambridge, 2011) and S. J. Milner, '"*Le sottili cose non si possono bene aprire in volgare*": vernacular oratory and the transmission of classical rhetorical theory in the late medieval Italian communes', *Italian Studies*, lxiv (2009), pp. 221–44.

[37] See the ENAV initiative (Edizione Nazionale degli antichi volgarizzamenti dei testi latini nei volgari italiani) which is a strand of the larger project Il ritorno dei Classici nell'Umanesimo: www.ilritornodeiclassici.it [accessed 1st March 2012].

[38] See M. Gragnolati, J. Trabant and S. Fortuna ed., *Dante's Plurilingualism: authority, knowledge and subjectivity* (Oxford, 2010).

a wandering exile he took the poet Virgil as his guide as far as *Paradiso* whilst Latini, his own master, adopted Cicero as his mentor given his own role as communal chancellor to the first popular regimes of Florence.[39] Such wholesale identifications with classical authors are highly telling as is the multilingualism of the literary, epistolary, political and philosophical works produced from the mid-Duecento onwards. Whilst their respective literary formations were recognisably medieval in drawing on the various *artes* as well as the poetic and encyclopaedic traditions imported from France, they mark a significant moment in the piecemeal emergence of an author-based and ultimately Latin-centred humanistic textual culture.

Given the formal sensitivities and attention to lexis and metre required in reading and composing a variety of literary forms in a variety of languages, from *langue d'oïl* and *langue d'oc* to regional vernaculars and Latin, it is no surprise that attempts were eventually made to imitate systematically classical literary forms through bypassing the precepts of the various medieval *artes* and *florilegia* and turning directly to the classical texts themselves, *ad fontes*. The increased critical attention afforded to the actual texts of classical authors as repositories of classical literary and poetic forms was not solely an aesthetic choice, however, but also a recognition that they addressed the shared realities of civic debate, social conflict and political exile, as well as the affective realm which was conditioned by friendship, social life, the vagaries of fortune and the concomitant need for philosophical and literary consolation.

---

[39] On Latini, see J. Bolton Holloway, *Twice-Told Tales: Brunetto Latino and Dante Alighieri* (New York, 1993) and the essays collected in I. Maffia Scariati ed., '*A scuola con ser Brunetto*': *indagini sulla ricezione di Brunetto Latini dal Medioevo al Rinascimento* (Florence, 2008). That Dante left a pagan guide behind and adopted Bernard of Clairvaux in the *Paradiso* anticipates Petrarch's wholesale adoption of Augustine in his Christian Latin humanism. See M. Picone, 'Dante and the Classics' in A. A. Iannucci ed., *Dante: contemporary perspectives* (Toronto, 1997), pp. 51–73.

Where the humanists would later seek to distance themselves from the legal profession and the universities, in this first phase such net distinctions were more difficult to establish. Although Witt has consistently sought to differentiate lawyers from humanists, describing those with literary interests as 'humanist sympathisers', he has more recently noted that it was the predominant rhetorical and legal culture in Italy in the twelfth and early thirteenth century which was instrumental in furnishing a grounding in critical reading and compositional practices.[40] For, instruction in legal commentary, grammar, rhetoric and letter writing were key components of the required skill-set for those serving in chanceries or leading the increasingly complex municipal governments of the urban centres of the peninsula. The revival of interest in Roman, and classical, culture, therefore was not initially a literary phenomenon but rather rooted in a growing recognition of the socio-political similarities between Roman and late medieval Italian cultural life and the applicability of large parts of Roman legal writing and precept literature to their own institutional and political landscape.[41]

Roberto Weiss: a latter-day humanist

And so to Roberto Weiss (1906–1969) whose work is the catalyst for the current collection and whose career mirrored those of the humanists he studied. Weiss was himself a displaced scholar, an exile who chose to stay in England rather than return to Mussolini's Italy. Born in Milan of a Czech family, Weiss

---

[40] R. Witt, 'Rhetoric and Reform during the Eleventh and Twelfth Centuries' in Robins ed., *Textual Cultures*, pp. 53–79.

[41] On the twelfth-century revival of Roman law and Bologna see J. A. Brundage, *The Medieval Origins of the Legal Profession: canonists, civilians and courts* (Chicago, 2008), pp. 75–125 and on students coming to Bologna to study law see A. Sorbelli, *Storia della Università di Bologna*, 2 vols (Bologna, 1944–47), i, pp. 31–87. On early communal genealogies of *Romanitas* see R. L. Benson, 'Political *Renovatio*: two models from Roman Antiquity', in Benson ed., *Renaissance and Renewal*, pp. 339–86.

came to England in 1926. Like Petrarch, Salutati and Bruni before him he initially studied law as an undergraduate, prior to taking a doctorate in the humanities at Oxford which was awarded in 1934. Two years previously he had taken British citizenship and decided to stay in the United Kingdom, initially working in the manuscript room of the Bodleian Library. From 1946 to his death in August 1969 he held the Chair in Italian at University College, London (UCL).[42] As if such a profile was not suggestive enough in terms of the parallels with the careers of the humanists he chose to study, in the archive of his working papers held at the Warburg Institute are thirteen small notebooks which span 1955–1969, each entitled 'Iter Italicum' and relating to a specific research trip to Italy. Inside, his notes record the manuscripts consulted in the various Italian libraries he visited as well as his transcription of Latin inscriptions found on numerous buildings and monuments, testimony to his own scholarly itinerary when following in the footsteps of the humanists.[43]

Weiss's concern with the revival and spread of Renaissance humanism and its Italian origins is apparent from the developmental narrative evidenced in the titles of his works, from his Inaugural Lecture at UCL in 1947 entitled *The Dawn of Humanism in Italy* to his study of three early pioneers of humanism – Geremia da Montagnone, Geri d'Arezzo and Petrarch – in *Il primo secolo dell'umanesimo: studi e testi*, published in 1949. Subsequent volumes included *The Spread of Italian Humanism* of 1964 and finally *The Renaissance*

---

[42] For a brief overview of his career and cultural milieu, particularly as it relates to his first work, see D. Rundle, 'Editor's Introduction' to Weiss[4], pp. vi–xliv at pp. ix–xii.

[43] The notebooks are contained in a box file entitled 'Roberto Weiss: *Itinera italica* + Miscellaneous Notebooks'. I would like to thank François Quiviger, librarian at the Warburg Institute, for allowing me to consult this material.

Discovery of Classical Antiquity published in 1969.⁴⁴ Throughout his career Weiss also published articles and chapters on the Italian reception of Greek classicism and was one of the most important scholars of this aspect of the spread of humanism.⁴⁵ The incremental widening of humanism's horizons, therefore, could not be more clearly charted, with Italy witnessing its first 'dawning' light.

What is striking given the subsequent scholarship on the origins and spread of humanism is both the concision and perspicacity of Weiss's Inaugural Lecture in 1947, published in the same years as Kristeller's and Campana's essays mentioned above. In it Weiss modestly states his intention to show the gradual passage from 'medieval to more modern methods of scholarship, which brought about the Renaissance,' adding that 'In all probability the medieval approach to Roman law, the use of rhetoric, and the study of grammar all had their share in it.' Significantly he also stressed the role of the lawyers in 'the launching of humanist activities', beginning with the Paduan circle of Lovato dei Lovati (c.1240–1309), his nephew Rolando da Piazzola (d. 1325), the aforementioned Geremia da Montagnone (1255–1321), and the notary Albertino Mussato (1261–1329).⁴⁶ Weiss showed how Lovato was able to draw on the rich holdings of classical material held at the Abbey of Pomposa near Ferrara, which included Carolingian copies of works by Horace, Virgil, Juvenal, Persius, Quintilian, Terence, Cicero and Livy, to establish a circle of like-minded friends and

---

⁴⁴ R. Weiss, *The Dawn of Humanism in Italy* (London, 1947), id., *The Spread of Italian Humanism* (London, 1964) and id., *The Renaissance Discovery of Classical Antiquity* (Oxford, 1969).

⁴⁵ See Weiss, *Medieval and Humanist Greek*.

⁴⁶ Weiss, *The Dawn of Humanism*, pp. 5–11 and *The Spread*, pp. 14–17. Specifically on Lovato, see R. Weiss, 'Lovato Lovati (1241–1309)', *Italian Studies*, vi (1951), pp. 3–28. This grouping formed the basis of the study by G. Billanovich, 'Il preumanesimo padovano', in *Storia della cultura veneta*, 6 vols (Vicenza, 1976–), ii, pp. 19–110.

correspondents with whom he discussed and shared his scholarly interests.[47]

As with Latini and the Florentines, much of the literary endeavour of the Paduan circle was preoccupied with the analysis and discussion of political discord and communal conflict, Lovato authoring a now lost work *De conditionibus urbis Padue et peste Guelfi et Gibolengi nominis*. Similarly, the poetic epistles exchanged with Mussato and their respective historical works were also animated by concerns for civic peace and liberty. Yet unlike Latini and the Florentines, these works were written in Latin and deliberately written in imitation of classical literary models. Moreover, unlike Latini, the critical orientation of the Paduan circle was more grammatical than rhetorical in its approach to literary form.[48] For, it was in Padua that Weiss noted 'humanist activities were mainly directed towards bringing back to life the classical spirit' through the editing and analysis of texts such as Seneca's *Tragedies*, and the circulation of works long lost to the classical canon such as Martial's *Epigrams* and Ovid's *Ibis*. Weiss granted a foundational role in the Renaissance of literary humanism to these Paduan scholars, and to their specific concern with classical poetic forms as found in Catullus, Statius, Lucretius and Propertius.[49]

---

[47] See G. Billanovich, 'La lettera di Enrico a Stefano: altri classici a Pomposa (ca. 1093)', *Medioevo e umanesimo padovano*, xliv (1981), pp. 141–65.

[48] The differences between Florentine and Paduan early humanism are noted by R. Weiss, 'Lineamenti per una storia del primo umanesimo fiorentino', *Rivista storica italiana*, lx (1948), pp. 349–66 where he states of Latini (p. 351): 'I suoi scritti e le sue attività mostrano però che i classici non venivano considerati da lui dal punto di vista filologico e che egli non sentiva un distacco netto tra i suoi tempi e l'antichità classica.'

[49] Weiss, *The Dawn*, p. 15. Weiss's thesis has been reasserted and further consolidated by Ronald Witt in his more recent comprehensive study of the origins of Italian humanism. See Witt, *'In the Footsteps of the Ancients'*, esp. pp. 81–173. In place of 'classical spirit', Witt describes

Weiss's mapping of the increasing dissemination, critical reading and imitation of classical authors from the mid-thirteenth century and early fourteenth century encompassed Padua, Verona, Vicenza, Venice, Milan, Bologna, Florence and Naples, a geographical range not matched in many later studies.[50] In addition, the two conclusions Weiss reached still hold sway within the critical literature on Italian humanism: namely that an early form of humanism was in existence before Petrarch and Boccaccio, and that 'this early humanism was not the result either of a reaction against an aspect of philosophical speculation or of a conscious desire for a "renovatio studiorum" and hopes of a new golden age, but that it was a spontaneous and natural development of classical studies as pursued during the Middle Ages.'[51] This stress on continuity over rupture, on the combined impact of medieval styles of reading and learning to the treatment of classical texts through the cross-fertilization between scholastic commentary practices and lecturing on *auctores*, on the role of chancery officials, notaries and lawyers in transmitting classicizing literary imitations, and on the centrality of grammar instruction – all remain the key building blocks in more recent readings of the advent of humanism.[52]

Christian humanism and civic humanism: *studia humanitatis* and *studia divinitatis*

how the Paduan poetry 'evoked the presence' of the classical models imitated (p. 260).

[50] On the pre-humanists beyond Padua see his two studies: R. Weiss, 'La cultura preumanistica veronese e vicentina nel tempo di Dante' in V. Branca and G. Padoan ed., *Dante e la cultura veneta* (Florence, 1966), pp. 263–72 and id., 'Benvenuto Campensani (1250/55?–1323)', *Bolletttino del Museo civico di Padova*, xliv (1955), pp. 129–44.

[51] Weiss, *The Dawn*, p. 21. See also Weiss, *The Renaissance Discovery*, pp. 16–29.

[52] In addition to the works of Kristeller see also Black, *Humanism and Education* and P. F. Gehl, *A Moral Art: grammar, society and culture in trecento Florence* (Ithaca, NY, 1993).

If Petrarch's discovery of Cicero's *Pro Archia* can be read as furnishing the 'charter of foundation' for classical scholarship, then the 'familiar' letters Petrarch addressed to Cicero and the ancients can similarly be characterised as an *incipit* for the Renaissance. For they established a literal and metaphorical correspondence whereby not only ancients and moderns but also Christians and Pagans became what A. J. Minnis has suggestively termed 'familiar authors'.[53] As we have seen, however, this process of cultural and stylistic proximation was already underway. One of Petrarch's contributions was to address the ancients in recognisably classicised prose through the emulation of Seneca and Cicero's epistolary style, shunning the conventions of the *ars dictaminis*. Yet he also dramatically shifted the nascent humanism's focus, on the one hand disentangling it from local political and jurisdictional concerns and on the other interweaving it with the textual corpus of the Christian fathers. Although he recognised the alterity of pagan antiquity, he still sought to marshal the classical authors in support of his own brand of Christian humanism. Unlike Latini and Dante, therefore, Petrarch chose a Christian author versed in the classics as his mentor rather than a pagan one: namely Augustine.[54] Consequently his classical corpus included patristic as well Roman sources. Yet, while his work of textual recovery and philological emendation — especially on Livy — sought to bring the ancients closer to the moderns, it also admitted their distance and separateness. One of the legacies of his pioneering

---

[53] See S. Hinds, 'Defamiliarizing Latin Literature, from Petrarch to Pulp Fiction', *Transactions of the American Philological Association*, cxxxv (2005), pp. 49–81 at pp. 49–63. Both Latin and vernacular dialogue with the ancients, however, predates Petrarch. See the section entitled 'Di conversare cogli antichi' in the early trecento *Ammaestramenti degli antichi Latini e Toscani raccolti e volgarizzati per Fra Bartolomeo da San Concordio Pisano*, ed. V. Nannucci (Florence, 1840), III.10.i–xiii. On 'familiar authors', see A. J. Minnis, *Medieval Theory of Authorship: scholastic literary attitudes in the Later Middle Ages*, 2nd edn (Aldershot, 1988), pp. 211–17.

[54] See C. Trinkaus, *"In Our Image and Likeness": humanity and divinity in Italian humanist thought*, 2 vols (London, 1970), i, pp. 3–50.

scholarship, therefore, was an increasingly nuanced historical consciousness of the gap between past and present.[55]

Petrarch was equally important in establishing certain operational parameters for humanistic activity, or at least the terms around which subsequent discussions would circulate. In self-consciously fashioning himself as a man of letters he simultaneously sought to distance himself from the practices and arenas of his contemporaries. His marked antipathy towards legal studies, scholasticism and universities, his shunning of the political realm and the textual culture of communal and curial chanceries saw him privilege the study and library over the council chamber, the exchange of private over public letters, the salvation of the individual soul over the securing of the common good, and the patronage of a protective patron over the vagaries of salaried employment as *magister* or communal notary within an institution demanding accountability. His peripatetic youth as the son of an exiled Florentine notary, the formative years spent at the papal court at Avignon where his father secured work in the curia, and his fractured law studies at Montpellier and Bologna meant Petrarch never really identified with a specific city or region. Such a lacuna was filled, however, by his intellectual and literary affiliation to Rome as both classical and Catholic capital, an association which reached its apotheosis in 1341 when he was crowned poet laureate on the Capitol for his work on a Latin epic which sought to emulate Virgil's *Aeneid*. Significantly, his one moment of political activism involved his support of Cola di Rienzo in attempting to refound the *Res publica romana* in the late 1340s. Though unsuccessful, this moment of excitement can be read as a nostalgia-induced attempt to recreate a classical *Romanitas* which looked beyond

---

[55] The literature on Petrarch is vast. See G. Billanovich, *Petrarca e il primo umanesimo* (Padua, 1996); N. Mann, *Petrarch* (Oxford, 1984); Witt, *In the Footsteps*, pp. 230–91; T. Barolini and H. W. Storey ed., *Petrarch and the Textual Origins of Interpretation* (Leiden, 2007); V. Kirkham and A. Maggi ed., *Petrarch: a critical guide to the complete works* (Chicago, 2009), and G. Zak, *Petrarch's Humanism and the Care of the Self* (Cambridge, 2010).

the particularities of communal identification to establish a pre-national, but post-classical, Italy.⁵⁶

If Petrarch built on the work begun over the previous seventy years by the first generations of humanists, his successors often referred to him in paternalistic terms when acknowledging their own humanistic genealogy. As self-confessed *litteratus* Petrarch actively sought to eschew the compromises that came with involvement in civic affairs, but the careers of both Coluccio Salutati (1331–1406) and Leonardo Bruni as successive Chancellors of Florence saw humanistic activity thrust back into the contested political realm.⁵⁷ Salutati's more dialectical and disputational style manifested itself in both his philosophical works and his chancery output and he was more accommodating towards the medieval textual traditions and less afraid than Petrarch to draw on scholastic authors. His philological method was clearly influenced by the grammarian's interest in etymology and his letter-writing informed by the more combative *stilus rhetoricus* of the late thirteenth century. As Chancellor of Florence his letters on behalf of the republic were semi-public missives. They were disseminated far and wide and cast him as postmaster at the centre of a network of chancellors and scholars with whom he corresponded and exchanged both texts and private letters, as witnessed by his *Epistolario*.⁵⁸ His *De nobilitate legum et medicine* of the 1390s laid out a clear manifesto for the moral benefits of the engaged civic life, the *vita activa*, in which those who instituted laws to regulate and govern the social realm were to be praised above

---

[56] See the texts collected in *Petrarch. The revolution of Cola di Rienzo*, ed. M. E. Cosenza, 2nd edn (New York, 1986).

[57] On Salutati, see D. de Rosa, *Coluccio Salutati: il cancelliere e il pensatore politico* (Florence, 1980) and R. G. Witt, *Hercules at the Crossroads: the life, work and thought of Coluccio Salutati* (Durham, NC, 1983) and id., *In the Footsteps*, pp. 292–337 and, on Bruni, pp. 392–442.

[58] *Epistolario di Coluccio Salutati*, ed. F. Novati, 4 vols. (Rome, 1891–1911).

those who followed the speculative disciplines of the *vita contemplativa*.⁵⁹

Both Salutati and Bruni, as inheritors of Latini's Florentine mantle, drew on further textual discoveries, some of which they made themselves, and their own philological and orthographical researches to articulate a specifically Florentine version of *Romanitas* in an increasingly classicised Latin. The republican virtue of liberty was clearly set against the supposedly tyrannical ambition of the Church and successive Dukes of Milan.⁶⁰ Bruni in particular overwrote the vernacular Brunetto Latini, creating a palimpsest of which the upper text was his own pure Latin Ciceronianism. In the oligarchic social world of late fourteenth- and early fifteenth-century Florence, Latini's antipathy towards the noble class which threatened the institutions of the nascent commune was transformed into a collaborative rapprochement through which the patrician élite actively engaged in the sponsorship and pursuit of the new learning led by the notaries of the city's chancery. Salutati's circle was frequented not only by a young Leonardo Bruni but also by the sons of the élite such as Lorenzo Ridolfi (b. 1362) and Palla Strozzi (1372–1462) who were destined to assume major political and diplomatic roles in the early decades of the 1400s and who provided a form of patronage for the *studia humanitatis*.⁶¹ The

---

⁵⁹ Coluccio Salutati, *De nobilitate legum et medicine: De verecundia*, ed. E. Garin (Florence, 1947). In the latter stage of his life Salutati's work showed a marked preference for Christian texts over pagan ones. See Witt, *In the Footsteps*, pp. 334–37.

⁶⁰ See the classic study by H. Baron, *The Crisis of the Early Italian Renaissance: civic humanism and republican liberty in an age of classicism and tyranny*, 2 vols (Princeton, 1955) and the essays collected in J. Hankins ed., *Renaissance Civic Humanism: reappraisals and reflections* (Cambridge, 2000).

⁶¹ On Salutati's role as mediator between scholastic and the new humanistic practices, see T de Robertis et al. ed., *Coluccio Salutati e l'invenzione dell'umanesimo* (Florence, 2008). On Palla Strozzi's patronage of the Florentine Studio see J. Davies, *Florence and its University during the early Renaissance* (Leiden, 1998), pp. 79–83, 86, 110–12.

vogue for the sons of the city's patricians to receive an education in the classics led to the establishment of schools beyond the level of grammar instruction but below that of university study. Giovanni Malpaghini (b. 1346–c.1420), Roberto de' Rossi (c.1355–1417) and Cino Rinuccini (c. 1350–1417) all serviced this emerging market, often simultaneously occupying posts within the Florentine *studio*.[62]

Migration and new media

The adoption of humanist fashions by patricians and chancery officials, as well as the gradual migration of its disciplines into the classroom, marked a significant acceleration in the transmission and dissemination of classical learning and textual scholarship.[63] In 1440, LORENZO VALLA, often cited as the father of modern philology, established its political significance with his devastating exposé of the Donation of Constantine as a fraud, thereby undermining the legitimacy of papal claims to authority over the temporal realms of the West.[64] More generally, philological practice and textual emendation became the battleground of humanist disputation and argument and the arena in which reputations were made and destroyed and scholarly rivalries performed.[65] Yet it was the educated moneyed

[62] On this cultural milieu, see the foundational study of L. Martines, *The Social World of the Florentine Humanists, 1390–1460* (London, 1963) and G. Tanturli, 'Cino Rinuccini e la scuola di Santa Maria in Campo', *Studi medievali*, xvii (1976), pp. 625–74.

[63] On philological advances see S. Rizzo, *Il lessico filologico degli umanisti*, 2nd edn (Rome, 1984) and ead., 'Il latino nell'Umanesimo', in A. Asor Rosa ed., *Letteratura italiana*, 6 vols (Turin, 1986), v, pp. 379–408. On humanist practice in relation to imitation, see M. McLaughlin, *Literary Imitation in the Italian Renaissance* (Oxford, 1995).

[64] See Lorenzo Valla, *On the Donation of Constantine*, trans. G. W. Bowersock [ITRL, xxiv] (Cambridge, MA, 2007) and R. Black, 'The Donation of Constantine: A New Source for the Concept of the Renaissance' in A. Brown ed., *Languages and Images of Renaissance Italy* (Oxford, 1995), pp. 51–85.

[65] See M. Davies, 'An Emperor without clothes?: Niccolò Niccoli under attack', *IMU*, xxx (1987), pp. 95–148, and A. Grafton, 'Quattrocento

class and enlightened patrons who provided the contacts and the finance to facilitate the importation, copying and collection of texts in the first wave of what nineteenth-century book collectors termed *bibliofilia*. Salutati and Palla Strozzi were instrumental in getting the Byzantine scholar Manuel Chrysoloras (c. 1349–1415) to Florence in 1397 where he taught (among others) Leonardo Bruni his Greek, enabling a lifetime's work in translating Greek works into Latin including Plato's dialogues and Aristotle's *Politics*, *Economics* and *Ethics*.[66] And with migration came further discoveries and a renewed interest in translation. The itineraries of humanists likes of FRANCESCO FILELFO and GUARINO DA VERONA passed through republics and courts from Florence and Ferrara to Venice and Milan working their passage by offering instruction in both Latin and Greek to the sons of rulers and patricians. Both Guarino and Filelfo spent five years studying Greek in Constantinople with Manuel and his nephew John Chrysoloras, and both were instrumental in bring Greek texts back to the Italian peninsula as well as translating parts of works by Aristotle, Isocrates, Strabo, Plutarch, Xenophon and Lysias. GIOVANNI AURISPA, a Sicilian scholar who studied in Bologna and went to Greece as tutor to a Genoese merchant family, famously brought 238 Greek codices to Italy in 1423 containing classical Greek works including almost a complete corpus of works by Plato, Plotinus, Proclus and many works by Iamblichus and Pindar in addition to the plays of Aeschylus and Sophocles.[67] The early fifteenth century also saw significant discoveries of classical Latin texts.

Humanism and Classical Scholarship' in Rabil ed., *Renaissance Humanism*, iii, pp. 23–66.

[66] See J. Hankins, *Plato in the Renaissance*, 2 vols (Leiden, 1991) and P. Botley, *Latin Translation in the Renaissance* (Cambridge, 2004). On Bruni's translation theory, see his 'De interpretatione recta', in Leonardo Bruni, *Opere letterarie e politiche*, ed. P. Viti (Turin, 1996), pp. 150–93.

[67] See the collected essays of J. Monfasani, *Greeks and Latins in Fifteenth-Century Italy: Renaissance philosophy and humanism* (Aldershot, 2004), and pp. 31–78 below.

Poggio Bracciolini discovered a complete text of Quintilian's *Institutio oratoria* and works by Valerius Flaccus and Silius Italicus whilst attending the Council of Constance (1414–18). Late in life, he too undertook to learn Greek and attempted translations of works by Diodorus Siculus, Lucian and Xenophon.[68]

From the 1400s the itinerant pedagogue became a feature of the cultural landscape within the peninsula, moving between patrons and centres of learning in search of work and environments conducive to study. Eventually the figure of the pedant was sufficiently well-known to be satirised and added to the pantheon of stock characters that peopled the classically informed *commedia erudita*.[69] Simultaneously, the emergence of collectors and book traders like NICCOLÒ NICCOLI and Vespasiano da Bisticci (1421–1498) coincided with the ambition of patricians and princes to form their own libraries of classical texts.[70] The invention of printing with moveable metal type and the raft of print workshops which opened in Italy in the 1470s marked a further acceleration in the transmission and dissemination of both Latin and Greek classical works, as humanism moved into the mechanical age of mass reproduction through new media.[71] From this point on, both the virus and its carriers spread exponentially as it was carried across frontiers,

---

[68] On the rediscovery of classical texts see the classic study R. Sabbadini, *Le scoperte dei codici latini e greci ne'secoli XIV e XV*, 2 vols (Florence, 1905–14), and M. D. Reeve, 'The rediscovery of classical texts in the Renaissance' in O. Pecere ed., *Itinerari dei testi antichi* (Rome, 1991), pp. 115–57.

[69] A. Stäuble, 'Una ricerca in corso: il personaggio del pedante nella commedia cinquecentesca' in M. de Panizza Lorch ed., *Il teatro italiano del Rinascimento* (Milan, 1980), pp. 85–101.

[70] See for example F. Ames-Lewis, *The Library and Manuscripts of Piero di Cosimo de'Medici* (New York, 1984).

[71] See B. Richardson, *Printing, Writers and Readers in Renaissance Italy* (Cambridge, 1999) and see pp. 330–34 below.

translated into numerous vernaculars and imported into an ever-wider variety of genres and forms of cultural production.[72]

Evaluations of the significance of the humanistic rhetorical revival and the impact of the educational programme of the *studia humanitatis* in the Italian peninsula have varied extensively, to the point where it has almost become a latter-day *disputatio* in its own right. While some more philosophically orientated scholars have expressed scepticism concerning the sincerity of humanistic rhetoric produced by hired pens, some historians of education have depicted the revised educational programme as designed to produce pliant bureaucrats for the emerging nation states rather than critically engaged and morally upright citizens.[73] The implication of women within the movement has also been the subject of extensive discussion and analysis in the context of establishing a parallel female Renaissance canon.[74] Yet, when understood as the shared culture of a virtual republic of letters, *res publica litterarum*, and when read as an allegory or synecdoche – a figure or fragment through which a familiar past serves to imagine a plausible present – the history and historiography of Renaissance humanism can be seen for what it is, less a history of controversy and disputation than a history of cultural correspondence. For the rebirth em-

---

[72] See the studies in C. W. Kallendorf ed., *A Companion to the Classical Tradition* (Chichester, 2007).

[73] See, for example, J. Seigel, '"Civic humanism" or "Ciceronian Rhetoric"? The Culture of Petrarch and Bruni', *Past & Present*, xxxiv (1966), pp. 3–48 and the reply of H. Baron, 'Leonardo Bruni: "Professional Rhetorician" or "Civic Humanist"?, *Past & Present*, xxxvi (1967), pp. 21–37. For a similar dialogue on education see A. Grafton and L. Jardine, *From Humanism to the Humanities: education and the liberal arts in fifteenth- and sixteenth-century Europe* (London, 1986) and the review article by Robert Black, 'Italian Renaissance Education: changing perspectives and continuing controversies', *Journal of the History of Ideas*, lii (1991), pp. 315–34.

[74] J. Kelly Gadol, 'Did Women have a Renaissance?' in R. Bridenthal and C. Koonz ed., *Becoming Visible: women in European history* (Boston, MA, 1977), pp. 137–64, and V. Cox, *Women's Writing in Italy, 1400–1650* (Baltimore, MD, 2008).

bedded within the term 're-naissance' involved the conjuring of spectres, the reanimation of figures, the unearthing of sculptural and literary bodies or *corpora* which were then displayed and voiced by the cultural mediums of their day and made to speak to the various presents of those calling them forth.[75]

That contemporary thinking on the humanist movement has largely been shaped by an exiled community of itinerant scholars escaping the reduction of politics to aesthetics under fascism and National Socialism is, by way of conclusion, worthy of comment. The list is formidable: Kristeller, Baron, Panofsky, Wittkower, Cassirer, Rubinstein, Gilbert, Saxl, Auerbach, and, as we have seen, Weiss himself. There is little doubt the experiences of this generation of scholars conditioned their reading and representation of the Renaissance in Italy as well as the translation of humanistic critical practices to the Anglophone academic community.[76] Rejecting the earlier more benign characterisation of humanists as flighty free-literates peddling their wares across the courts of Europe to the highest bidder (Monnier's thesis), they added political urgency to their readings of the humanist movement and the revival of the classical tradition, specifically in their focus upon the revival of rhetorical republicanism.[77] They also moved beyond the

---

[75] On the excavation of ancient artworks and their role in the invention of the Renaissance see L. Barkan, *Unearthing the Past: archaeology and aesthetics in the making of Renaissance culture* (New Haven, 1999). On allegory and personification, see the editors' introduction to R. Copeland and P. Stuck ed., *The Cambridge Companion to Allegory* (Cambridge, 2011), pp. 1–11 and E. Petersen, '"The Communication of the Dead". Notes on *Studia humanitatis* and the nature of Humanist Philology' in A.C. Dionisotti et al. ed., *The Uses of Greek and Latin: historical essays* (London, 1988), pp. 57–69.

[76] See, for example, the essays in E. Timms and J. Hughes ed., *Intellectual Migration and Cultural Transformation: refugees from National Socialism in the English-speaking world* (Vienna, 2003), esp. D. McEwan, 'Mapping the Trade Routes of the Mind: the Warburg Institute', pp. 37–47.

[77] M. Monnier, *Histoire générale de la littérature moderne*, 2 vols. (Paris, 1884–85), i (La Renaissance de Dante à Luther).

nineteenth-century Burckhardtian narratives of Renaissance individualism, genius and great men that only granted the revival of antiquity a secondary role in the Renaissance as cultural phenomenon and which aligned all too easily with the construction of personality cults. By contrast, much of the work undertaken by this generation of scholars was precisely directed towards the development of the sort of critical philology, rhetorical critique and reading of texts and images, which enabled the discerning evaluation of the situated use to which symbols and words can be put and the powerful instrumentality of symbolic practices. In the face of narratives of nation they continued to map the flow of texts and images across landscapes and ages, flows that they themselves as a generation embodied. Exiled within his own country, Ernst Robert Curtius penned his *European Literature and the Latin Middle Ages* as part of what he termed a 'plea for a new Humanism' in the face of 'the barbarization of education and the nationalistic frenzy' that were the forerunners of the Nazi regime.[78] Edward Said has more recently noted that today's canons were formed by yesterday's radicals and that the scholars now often held responsible for Eurocentric humanism were in fact critics of National Socialism and supporters of free speech and the freedom of learning. His last collection of essays published a year after his death, and entitled *Humanism and Democratic Criticism*, was a call for a new philology in America to revitalise the humanities by establishing dialogue between multiple cultural traditions and further teach the skills of critical reading, interrogation and debate through the intervention of public intellectuals.[79] The call to extend the practices of humanism ever wider to encompass different cultures, different Renaissances and different media is, I would argue, simply the most recent manifestation of the humanist virus whose origins

---

[78] Curtius expressed these sentiments in his 1932 pamphlet *Deutscher Geist in Gefahr* and again in his 'Author's Foreward to the English Translation': see E. R. Curtius, *European Literature and the Latin Middle Ages* (Princeton, 1953), pp. vii–viii.

[79] E. W. Said, *Humanism and Democratic Criticism* (Basingstoke, 2004).

lie in the political world of the medieval Italian peninsula.[80] And Roberto Weiss stands squarely, and proudly, within the illustrious ranks of the carriers and agents of humanism's continuing transmission.

---

[80] J. Goody, *Renaissances: the one or the many?* (Cambridge, 2010) sets the Italian Renaissance in the context of multiple Renaissances as conceptualised within other cultures. C. S. Celenza, *The Lost Italian Renaissance: humanists, historians and Latin's legacy* (Baltimore, MD, 2004) calls for a reanimation of the humanistic critical legacy through renewed translation activity and the exploitation of new media and digital content to disseminate knowledge of the movement and its literary heritage.

THE GREEKS AND RENAISSANCE HUMANISM

JOHN MONFASANI

Introduction: A Question of Perspective

Friedrich Nietzsche remarks in the *Genealogy of Morals* that all seeing is perspective.[1] To that I would add that some perspectives give a more comprehensive view than others. This is certainly true as far as Greeks in the Renaissance are concerned.[2] In the seventeenth century great scholars such as the sieur du Cange (Charles du Fresne, 1610–88), Philippe Labbe (1607–67), and Michel Lequien (1661–1733) laid the foundations of Byzantine studies.[3] As late as 1728, Johann

---

[1] *Zur Genealogie der Moral* in F. Nietzsche, *Werke. Kritische Gesamtausgabe*, ed. G. Colli and M. Montinari, 41 vols to date (Berlin, 1967–), vi/2 (1968), p. 383: 'Es giebt nur ein perspektivisches Sehen'.

[2] It is a mistake to speak of Greek refugees *tout court* since many Greeks came to the Latin West before and after the fall of Constantinople freely seeking greater opportunity. On the movement of Greeks into Western Europe in general, see J. Harris, *Greek Émigrés in the West, 1400–1520* (Camberley, 1995); my 'Greek Renaissance Migrations', *Italian History and Culture*, viii (2002), pp. 1–14 [reprinted as Essay I in J. Monfasani, *Greeks and Latins in Renaissance Italy: studies on humanism and philosophy in the 15th century* (Aldershot, 2004)]; and several books of Deno Geanakoplos: *Greek Scholars in Venice: studies in the dissemination of Greek learning from Byzantium to western Europe* (Cambridge, MA, 1962); id., *Interaction of the 'Sibling' Byzantine and Western Cultures in the Middle Ages and Italian Renaissance (330–1600)* (New Haven, CT, 1976), and id., *Constantinople and the West: essays on the Late Byzantine (Palaeologan) and Italian Renaissances and the Byzantine and Roman Churches* (Madison, WI, 1989).

[3] See G. Ostrogorsky, *History of the Byzantine State*, revised ed., trans. J. Hussey (New Brunswick, NJ, 1969), pp. 3–4; O. Mazal, *Manuel*

Albert Fabricius (1668–1736) tacitly assumed the continuity of Hellenic high culture into the Middle Ages by fully integrating Byzantine authors into the final volumes of his monumental encyclopaedia of Greek literature, the *Biblioteca Graeca*.[4] But soon, in 1742, reflecting the Enlightenment sense that the West needed rescuing from medieval barbarism, *On the Illustrious Greeks who Restored the Greek Language and Humane Letters* by Humphrey Hody (1659–1709) was published posthumously and, a few years later, in 1750, Christian Friedrich Boerner (1683–1753) followed with a similarly titled work: *On the Learned Greeks who Restored Greek Letters in Italy*.[5] Thus, the Greek émigrés were seen as worthy of study because they abetted – if they did not outright instigate – the revival of Greek letters in the Latin West.[6] The intellectual incoherence contained in this new view

    d'études byzantines, trans. Claude Detienne (Turnhout, 1995), pp. 15–16, and J.-M. Spieser, 'Du Cange and Byzantium' in R. Cornmack and E. Jeffreys ed., *Through the Looking Glass: Byzantium through British eyes* (Aldershot, 2000), pp. 199–210.

[4] *Bibliotheca Graeca: sive notitia scriptorum veterum graecorum quorumcunque monumenta integra, aut fragmenta edita exstant, tum plerorumque è MSS. ac deperditis*, 14 vols (Hamburg, 1706–28). Starting with the tenth volume, Fabricius dealt, as his subtitle put it, 'maxime vero de scriptoribus mediae et infimae Graeciae'.

[5] Hody's work was put through the press by Samuel Jebb: *De Graecis illustribus linguae Graecae literarumque humaniorum instauratoribus, eorum vitis, scriptis, et elogiis libri duo* (London, 1742); C. F. Boerner, *De doctis hominibus Graecis litterarum Graecarum in Italia instauratoribus liber* (Leipzig, 1750). The classic statement of the West's need to be rescued from its barbarism is, of course, Edward Gibbon's *Decline and Fall of the Roman Empire* (1776–88). For Gibbon's reading of Hody's book, see W. K. Ferguson, *The Renaissance in Historical Thought: five centuries of interpretation* (Cambridge, MA, 1958), pp. 104–05; and for his attitude towards Byzantium, F. K. Haarer, 'Writing Histories of Byzantium: the Historiography of Byzantine History' in L. James ed., *A Companion to Byzantium* (Chichester, 2010), pp. 9–21 at pp. 11–12.

[6] For the myth that Greek refugees from the fall of Constantinople started the Italian Renaissance, see Ferguson, *Renaissance in Historical Thought*, pp. 71–72, 76, 91, 97, 105, and 162. For the progress of

did not seem especially to bother the Enlightenment. On the one hand, Byzantium was the 'triumph of barbarism and religion', in the memorable phrase of Edward Gibbon (1737–94), but on the other its émigrés were assumed to have jump-started the Italian Renaissance.[7] Be that as it may, the Italian humanists themselves, beginning with Petrarch and Boccaccio, saw their Greek teachers exclusively as carriers of classical culture.[8] Such a classicist attitude towards Byzantine scholars continues up to today.[9] To be sure, it was natural for Italian humanists to see learned Greek émigrés as kindred spirits. Traditional Byzantine education stressed rhetoric and classical literature, just as the Italian humanists prescribed.[10] The best of

Greek studies in the Renaissance, see N. G. Wilson, *From Byzantium to Italy* (London, 1992), and J. Hankins, 'The Study of Greek in the Renaissance' in id., *Humanism and Platonism in the Italian Renaissance*, 2 vols (Rome, 2003–04), i, pp. 273–91.

[7] E. Gibbon, *Decline and Fall of the Roman Empire*, 6 vols (London, 1994), vi, p. 624 [ch. lxxi].

[8] See A. Pertusi, *Leonzio Pilato fra Petrarca e Boccaccio. Le sue versioni omeriche negli autografi di Venezia e la cultura greca del primo umanesimo* (Rome, 1964), and F. Pontani, '*Odissea* di Petrarca e gli scoli di Leonzio' in M. Feo and A. Rollo ed., *Petrarca e il mondo greco. Atti del Convegno internazionale di studi, Reggio Calabria 26–30 novembre 2001*, 2 vols (Florence, 2007), i, pp. 295–328.

[9] See the critiques of N. G. Wilson's learned *Scholars of Byzantium*, revised edn (London, 1996) and *From Byzantium to Italy* [now to be read in the revised edition: *Da Bizanzio all'Italia*, trans. B. Sancin (Alessandria, 2000)] by K. Alpers in *Classical Philology*, lxxxiii (1988), pp. 342–60 at p. 343: 'dessen Byzanzbild noch immer entscheidend durch Edward Gibbons *Decline and Fall of the Roman Empire* geprägt ist [whose idea of Byzantium is still decidedly shaped by Edward Gibbon's *Decline and Fall* ...]' and Anna Pontani in *Thesaurismata*, xxv (1995), pp. 83–123. In *Aevum*, lxxvi (2002), pp. 853–67, Pontani also warns against a much less learned book, J. C. Saladin, *La bataille du grec à la Renaissance* (Paris, 2000).

[10] On late Byzantine education, see S. Mergiali, *L'enseignement et les lettrés pendant l'époque des Paléologues (1261–1453)* (Athens, 1996). For the earlier period, see S. Efthymiadis, 'L'enseignement secondaire à Constantinople pendant les XIe et XIIe siècles: modèle éducatif pour la terre d'Otrante au XIIIe siècle', *Nea Rhome*, ii (2005), pp. 259–75.

the émigré scholars arrived with a training Italian humanists found admirable.[11] Humanists could also make common cause with the Greek émigrés in calling for a crusade against the Turk to rescue the classical homeland.[12] Most of all, Greek scholars, scribes, printers, and book collectors unquestionably and significantly contributed to the growth of classical Greek learning in the Renaissance. For instance, in Appendix I below, I give a far from complete list of more than 170 émigrés and visitors to the Latin West whose activity as copyists of Greek manuscripts modern scholarship can pinpoint in quite exact ways.[13] Émigré scholars demonstrably exercised an important influence as teachers of Greek, and in the case of Manuel Chrysoloras at Florence in 1397–1400, one should say a pivotal influence as the first great teacher of Greek in the Renaissance (for a list of émigré teachers, see Appendix II

---

[11] But this preparation was not enough to spare them from modern criticism: see, e.g., Pertusi, *Leonzio Pilato*, p. 506, where a sclerotic Byzantine classicism is contrasted with a vital Italian humanist classicism: 'L'umanista bizantino ... legge gli antichi unicamente per rendere più erudite le proprie opere ...; l'umanista italiano e occidentale legge non solo per apprendere e documentarsi ... ma anche per trarre motivo da esse di nuove riflessioni morali, estetiche, politiche ... anche per trarre da essa [l'antichità] ispirazione per nuove opere, cioè infondere in esse uno spirito nuovo'.

[12] See J. Hankins, 'Renaissance Crusaders: Humanist Crusade Literature in the Age of Mehmed II', *Dumbarton Oaks Papers*, xlix (1995), pp. 111–207 [reprinted in his *Humanism and Platonism*, i, pp. 293–424]; M. Meserve, 'Patronage and Propaganda at the First Paris Press: Guillaume Fichet and the First Edition of Bessarion's *Orations against the Turks*', *The Papers of the Bibliographical Society of America*, xcvii (2003), pp. 521–88, and J. Wittaker, 'Janus Lascaris at the Court of the Emperor Charles V', *Thesaurismata*, xiv (1977), pp. 76–107.

[13] The émigrés are included in the great modern survey of E. Gamillscheg and D. Harlfinger, *Repertorium der griechischen Kopisten 800–1600*, 9 vols to date (Vienna, 1981–) [hereafter *RGK*]. The *Repertorium* is not exhaustive since thus far it only covers collections in three geographic areas, but it has certainly captured the majority of the copyists 800–1600 whose activity can be documented in the extant manuscripts.

below);[14] and as translators of Greek classical and patristic texts (see Appendix III below), the émigrés shaped Renaissance culture in ways that we are only now beginning adequately to grasp.[15] The influence of some émigrés extended far beyond even these activities; Cardinal Bessarion, for instance, several times almost became pope and at his death left to the Republic of Venice a great library that became the historic core of the modern Biblioteca Marciana.[16] To take another example, Janus Lascaris enjoyed a brilliant career as a diplomat for the French crown after having played a significant role in the creation of the Greek manuscript collection of what is today the Biblioteca Laurenziana in Florence.[17] Nonetheless, it needs to be said that

[14] See the articles in R. Maisano and A. Rollo ed., *Manuele Crisolora e il ritorno del greco in Occidente. Atti del Convegno Internazionale (Napoli, 26–29 giugno 1997)* (Naples, 2002); and Wilson, *From Byzantium to Italy*, pp. 8–12. One émigré whose dynamic influence in encouraging Greek instruction has hitherto not been fully understood is Janus Lascaris; see S. Pagliaroli, 'Giano Lascari e il ginnasio greco', *Studi medievali e umanistici*, ii (2004), pp. 215–93.

[15] See, for instance, E. Berti, 'La traduzione umanistica' in M. Cortesi ed., *Tradurre dal greco in età umanistica. Metodi e strumenti* (Florence, 2007), pp. 3–15 and the literature cited there.

[16] The classic study of this bequest is L. Labowsky, *Bessarion's Library and the Biblioteca Marciana: six early inventories* (Rome, 1979); see also C. Bianca, 'La formazione della biblioteca latina del Bessarione', now to be read in ead., *Da Bisanzio a Roma. Studi sul cardinale Bessarione*, (Rome, 1999), pp. 43–106; useful, though not always accurate in his identifications, is E. Mioni, 'Bessarione scriba e alcuni suoi collaboratori' in *Miscellanea Marciana di studi bessarionei (a coronamento del V Centario della donazione nicena)* (Padua, 1976), pp. 263–318. In addition to the standard L. Mohler, *Kardinal Bessarion als Theologe, Humanist und Staatsmann*, 3 vols., (Paderborn, 1923–42 [reprint Aalen–Paderborn, 1967]), also most useful is G. Fiaccadori ed., *Bessarione e l'Umanesimo* (Naples, 1994).

[17] See B. Knös, *Un ambassadeur de l'Hellenisme – Janus Lascaris – et la tradition greco-byzantine dans l'humanisme français* (Uppsala, 1945), and E. B. Fryde, *Greek Manuscripts in the Private Llibrary of the Medici, 1469–1510*, 2 vols (Aberystwyth, 1996). But see now concerning Lascari's early career in Italy, S. Gentile, 'Lorenzo e Giano Lascaris. Il fondo greco della biblioteca medicea privata' in G. C.

all this scholarship is also in a way distortive because it fails to put the Greek-Latin cultural dynamic into a comprehensive perspective. Though it concentrates on the Greeks, it does not, in fact, sufficiently take into account the motives and outlook of the Greeks themselves; it leaves out a great deal which one can best capture by turning from the literature on the classical tradition and humanism to the literature on Byzantine culture *qua* Byzantine culture. The late Byzantine figure of Demetrius Cydones and the rise of Byzantine Thomism are cases in point.

Byzantium and Latin Scholasticism

One of the most stunning cultural developments of what has been called the Palaeologan Renaissance of late Byzantium was the growing admiration and appropriation by Greek intellectuals of Latin scholasticism and especially of Thomism.[18]

Garfagnini ed., *Lorenzo il Magnifico e il suo mondo* (Florence, 1994), pp. 177–94, and Pagliaroli, 'Giano Lascari e il ginnasio greco'.

[18] See A. Fyrigos, 'Tomismo e antitomismo a Bisanzio (con una nota sulla *Defensio S. Thomae adversus Nilum Cabasilam* di Demetrio Cidone)' in A. Molle ed., *Tommaso d'Aquino († 1274) e il mondo bizantino* (Venafro, 2004), pp. 27–72; J. A. Demetracopoulos, 'Georgios Gemistos-Plethon's Dependence on Thomas Aquinas' *Summa contra Gentiles* and *Summa Theologiae*', *Archiv für mittelalterliche Philosophie und Kultur*, xii (2006), pp. 276–341; and G. Podskalsky, *Theologie und Philosophie in Byzanz: Der Streit um die theologische Methodik in der spätbyzantinischen Geistesgeschichte (14./15. Jh.), seine systematischen Grundlagen und seine historische Entwicklung* (Munich, 1977). For Latin influences more generally, see also A. Garzya, 'Sul latino a Bisanzio nei secoli XIII e XIV' in M. Cortesi ed., *Padri greci e latini a confronto (secoli XIII–XV)* (Florence, 2004), pp. 143–52, and E. V. Maltese, 'Massimo Planude interprete del *De Trinitate* di Agostino' in Cortesi ed., *Padri greci*, pp. 207–19. A valuable scholarly tool that has statistical value here is R. E. Sinkwicz and W. M. Hayes, *Manuscript Listings for the Authored Works of the Palaeologan Period* (Toronto, 1989), which lists over 16,000 items for 289 authors; see also E. B. Fryde, *The Early Palaeologan Renaissance (1261–c. 1360)* (Leiden, 2000), who nicely expressed the traditional Enlightenment bias by offering a negative judgment on Byzantine scholarship after the mid-fourteenth century (p. 374) – that is, on the period of Byzantine enthusiasm for Latin scholasticism.

Central to that movement was Demetrius Cydones (1324/25–1397), the imperial chancellor who took up the study of Latin in the 1350s for reasons of diplomacy and ended up falling in love with Thomas Aquinas' *Summa contra gentiles* and *Summa theologiae*; he translated both of them into Greek and converted to Catholicism.[19] Cydones stands at the head of a broad current of Byzantine Thomism and also of philo-Latinism that ran from the mid-fourteenth to the later fifteenth century.[20] This is not the place to trace out the history of these currents, but their connexion to the Byzantine émigrés is worth noting. Cydones was not only a good friend and sometimes companion in Italy of the first great Byzantine teacher in Italy, Manuel Chrysoloras, who inherited some of Cydones' library, but also, it would seem, a teacher of the Platonist George Gemistus Pletho, whose influence the great Renaissance Platonist MARSILIO FICINO would acknowledge.[21] After leaving Florence for the court of Milan,

---

[19] For his life and works, see F. Tinnefeld, *Kydones, Demetrius. Briefe*, 5 vols (Stuttgart, 1981–2003), i, pp. 4–74; J. R. Ryder, *The Career and writings of Demetrius Kydones: a study of fourteenth-century Byzantine politics, religion and society* (Leiden, 2010). On the date of his death, see T. Ganchou, 'Démétrios Kydônes, les frères Chrysobergès et la Crète (1397–1401) de nouveaux documents' in C. A. Maltezou and P. Schreiner ed., *Bisanzio, Venezia e il mondo franco-greco (XIII–XV secolo)* (Venice, 2002), pp. 435–93 at pp. 476–79.

[20] Even Petrarch's and Boccaccio's Greek teacher, Leontius Pilatus, took an interest Latin scholasticism: D. Harlfinger and M. Rashed, 'Leonzio Pilato fra Aristotelismo bizantino e scolastica latina. Due nuovi testimoni postillati' in Feo and Rollo, *Petrarca e il mondo greco*, i, pp. 277–93.

[21] On Chrysoloras' friendship with Cydones, see A. Rollo, 'Problemi e prospettive della ricerca su Manuele Crisolora' in *Manuele Crisolora*, pp. 31–85 at pp. 37–40, and for his bequest, see Niccolò Zorzi, 'I Crisolora: personaggi e libri' in *Manuele Crisolora*, pp. 87–131 at pp. 118–22. On the relationship with Pletho, see the argument of J. Mamalakis, Γεώργιος Γεμιστὸς-Πλήθων (Athens, 1939), pp. 43–45, accepted by Demetracopoulos, 'Georgios Gemistos-Plethon's Dependence', p. 279. Ficino's acknowledgement is in his 1492 preface to Lorenzo the Magnificent for his translation of Plotinus' *Enneads*;

Chrysoloras was in contact with his old friend, Manuel Calecas, a Catholic convert and disciple of Demetrius Cydones, also resident at the time in Milan, who eventually entered the Dominican Order and translated, *inter alia*, Boethius' *De trinitate* and Anselm's *Cur deus homo*.[22] Calecas himself, in turn, became friends with another Greek Catholic, Demetrius Scaranos, who, having migrated to Italy, entered AMBROGIO TRAVERSARI's monastery of S. Maria degli Angeli in Florence as an oblate and spent his later years as a Greek copyist.[23] Scaranos also wrote a now lost defence of the medieval Latin translations of Aristotle against the criticisms of one of the foremost quattrocento humanists, LEONARDO BRUNI.[24] The Cretan émigré George of Trebizond had no direct connexion with Cydones, but once he had arrived in Italy, he became a fervent advocate of Latin scholasticism and Thomas Aquinas.[25] As we have already seen, his great opponent in the Plato-Aristotle controversy, Cardinal Bessarion, created a library of historic importance. But what is not appreciated is that scholastic texts dominated Bessarion's Latin collection. He had more volumes of Thomas Aquinas than any other Latin

---

for a modern edition of this preface, see D. O'Meara, 'Plotinus' in *CTC*, vii (1992), pp. 55–73 at pp. 68–70.

[22] For his life and works, see the introduction in R. J. Loenertz, *Correspondance de Manuel Calecas* [Studi e testi, clii] (Vatican City, 1950).

[23] Loenertz, *Correspondance de Manuel Calecas*, pp. 86–89 provides an excellent profile. For Scaranos as a Greek copyist, see his listing in Appendix I below. See also G. T. Dennis, *The Letters of Manuel II Palaeologus. Text, translation, and notes* (Washington, D. C., 1977), p. lvii, and L. Thorn-Wickert, *Manuel Chrysolora (ca. 1350–1415). Eine Biographie des byzantinischen intellektuellen vor dem Hintergrund der hellenistischen Studien in der italienische Renaissance* (Frankfurt am Main, 2006), pp. 31–32.

[24] Loenertz, *Correspondance de Manuel Calceas*, p. 89.

[25] See J. Monfasani, *George of Trebizond: a biography and a study of his rhetoric and logic* (Leiden, 1976), pp. 152–229.

author, including Cicero or Augustine.²⁶ Indeed, he owned nearly three times the number of copies of the writings of Thomas Aquinas than he did of all the writings of the Italian humanists combined. Bessarion conceded nothing to George of Trebizond in his admiration of Thomas and the scholastic tradition. I am convinced that another opponent of George of Trebizond, Theodore Gaza, came to Italy to obtain a degree in medicine from an Italian university, therefore to be trained as a Latin scholastic, though he deserted his studies at Ferrara to take up a more lucrative career in Rome as a translator for Pope Nicholas V.²⁷ Another well-known Greek émigré, John Argyropoulos, did in fact earn a doctorate from the University of Padua in 1444 and, despite modern assumptions about his Platonism, proved himself a Latin Averroist when he lectured on Aristotle's *De anima* in Florence in 1460–61.²⁸ Finally, to end this string of examples, George Scholarius, the first Patriarch after the fall of Constantinople in 1453, was a translator of Thomas Aquinas and also the most competent Byzantine student of Latin scholasticism since Demetrius Cydones.²⁹ In short, in the last hundred years of Byzantium,

---

[26] See J. Monfasani, *Bessarion Scholasticus: a study of Cardinal Bessarion's Latin Library* (Turnhout, 2012), and A. Rigo, 'Bessarione tra Costantinopoli e Roma' in Bessarion, *Orazione dogmatica sull'unione dei greci e dei latini*, trans. G. Lusini (Naples, 2001), pp. 19–68.

[27] See J. Monfasani, 'L'insegnamento di Teodoro Gaza a Ferrara' in M. Bertozzi ed., *Alla corte degli Estensi: filosofia, arte e cultura a Ferrara nei secoli XV e XVI* (Ferrara, 1994), pp. 5–17 [reprinted as Essay III in Monfasani, *Greeks and Latins*].

[28] See J. Monfasani, 'The Averroism of John Argyropoulos and His *Quaestio utrum intellectus humanus sit perpetuus*', *I Tatti Studies*, v (1993), pp. 157–208 [reprinted as Essay II in id., *Greeks and Latins*].

[29] In general, see M.-H. Blanchet, *Georges-Gennadios Scholarios (vers 1400–vers 1472): un intellectual orthodoxe face à la disparition de l'empire byzantin* (Paris, 2008), and F. Tinnefeld, 'George Gennadios Scholarios' in C. G. & V. Conticello ed., *La théologie byzantine et sa tradition*, only vol. ii to date (Turnhout, 2002), pp. 477–549; but specifically for his Thomism, see J. A. Demetracopoulos, 'Georgios Gennadios II-Scholarios' *Florilegium Thomisticum*: his early abridg-

what a significant portion of the best and brightest of the Greeks found most attractive and compelling in Latin culture was not emerging humanism, but traditional Latin scholasticism. A narrative that does not take this fact into account distorts the picture of how the Greek émigrés related to Renaissance Italy.

Byzantine Intellectuals and Catholicism

One other element of Latin culture entered the equation: Catholicism. The incidence of Greek admirers of Latin scholasticism who converted to Catholicism was so high from the fourteenth century on that expressions of interest in Latin culture could and did lead to accusations of being a Latinophrone, that is, a Catholic Latinophile apostate from Orthodoxy.[30] Contrary to what was thought just a few decades ago, it is now clear that one of the earliest of these converts, the controversial Barlaam of Calabria (1290--1348) was not a Thomist interloper among the Greeks. Nor was he a Latin nominalist. He had little knowledge of Latin scholasticism

---

ment of various chapters and *Quaestiones* of Thomas Aquinas' *Summae* and his anti-Plethonism', *Recherches de Théologie et Philosophie Médiévales*, lxix (2002), pp. 117–71; id., 'Georgios Gennadios II-Scholarios', *Florilegium Thomisticum I (De Fato) and its anti-Plethonic Tenor*', *Recherches de Théologie et Philosophie Médiévales – Forschungen zur Theologie und Philosophie des Mittelalters*, lxxiv (2007), pp. 301–76; G. Podskalsky, 'Die Rezeption der thomistischen Theologie bei Gennadios II. Scholarios (ca. 1403–1472)', *Theologie und Philosophie*, xlix (1974), pp. 305–23, and C. J. G. Turner, 'The Career of George-Gennadius Scholarius', *Byzantion*, xxxix (1969), pp. 420–55. See also K. Ierodiakonou, *Byzantine Philosophy and its Ancient Sources* (Oxford 2002) ch. 11.

[30] For conversions, see C. Delacroix-Besnier, 'Conversions constantinopolitaines au XIVe siècle', *Mélanges de l'École Française de Rome*, cv (1993), pp. 715–61, and T. M. Kolbaba, 'Conversion from Greek Orthodoxy to Roman Catholicism in the Fourteenth Century', *Byzantine and Modern Greek Studies*, xix (1995), pp. 120–34. For an example of the suspicions, see M. Trizio, '"Un uomo sapiente ed apostolico". Agostino a Bisanzio: Gregorio Palamas lettore del *De trinitate*,' *Quaestio*, vi (2006), pp. 131–89 at p. 148.

when he became embroiled in his famous quarrel with Gregory Palamas concerning Hesychasm. Indeed, he was a staunch opponent of Latin scholastics in his early years in Greece and only converted to Catholicism after he returned to the West.[31] The same can be said of Simon Atumanos (1310/18–1383/86), the other Greek who played a role in early humanism and who also eventually became a Catholic bishop.[32] Even the high patriarchal official and head of the monastery of the Pantocrator in Constantinople, Macarios Macres (1386–1431), could not escape accusations of Latinophilia after having had long and fruitful discussions concerning union with Latin theologians in Rome in 1430.[33] Similarly, Maximus Planudes (c. 1260–c. 1305), the first major Byzantine translator of Latin texts, could not escape such accusations, nor could George Scholarius (c. 1400–c. 1468), the eventual leader of the opponents of union with Rome, but

---

[31] See A. Fyrigos, 'Barlaam Calabro e la Rinascenza italiana,' *Il Veltro*, xxxi (1987), pp. 395–403; id., 'Tomismo e antitomismo a Bisanzio', pp. 30–31, and R. Sinkewicz, 'The Doctrine of the Knowledge of God in the Early Writings of Barlaam the Calabrian,' *Medieval Studies*, xliv (1982), pp. 181–242 at pp. 194–96 (p. 195, n. 56: 'A careful reading of the *Antilatin Treatises* leaves little doubt that Barlaam's acquaintance with the works and theology of Thomas Aquinas was minimal and restricted entirely to what was provided for him by his Latin (and Dominican) opponents.'). On Greek culture in southern Italy in the later Middle Ages, see G. Cavallo, 'La cultura italo-greca nella produzione libraria' in *I bizantini in Italia* (Milan, 1983), pp. 497–612. For a survey of classical interests in Southern Italy into the sixteenth century, see G. Fiaccadori's 'Nota introduttiva' in G. Fiaccadori and P. Eleuteri ed., *I Greci in Occidente: la tradizione filosofica, scientifica e letteraria dalle raccolte della Biblioteca Nazionale Marciana* (Venice, 1996), pp. xii–lxxv.

[32] See G. Fedalto, *Simone Atumano. Monaco di Studio arcivescovo latino di Tebe, secolo XIV*, 2nd ed. (Brescia, 2007).

[33] See A. Argyriou, *Macaire Makrès et la polémique contre l'Islam* [Studi e testi, cccxiv] (Vatican City, 1986), pp. 8–9. Macres' treatise in defence of virginity borrows greatly from Thomas Aquinas' *Summa Contra Gentiles*, III, c. 136, though it is not clear that Macres himself knew that Thomas was the source.

early in his career an acknowledged expert in Latin.[34] For the Greeks, familiarity with Latin educated culture suggested sympathy with Catholicism, and Latin educated culture in all these instances meant Latin scholasticism. In the event, all the most influential Greek émigrés did convert to Catholicism: Manuel Chrysoloras,[35] George of Trebizond,[36] Cardinal Bessarion,[37] John Argyropoulos,[38] Theodore Gaza,[39] just to

[34] See C. J. G. Turner, 'George-Gennadius Scholarius and the Union of Florence', *Journal of Theological Studies*, new ser., xviii (1967), pp. 83–103 at p. 87, and Giovanni Mercati, 'Un' autoapologia di Giorgio Scolario' in id., *Opere minori*, 6 vols [Studi e testi, lxxvi–lxxx & ccxcvi] (Vatican City, 1937–84), iv (1937), pp. 72–84.

[35] See G. Cammelli, *I dotti bizantini e le origini dell'umanesimo*. I. *Manuele Crisolora* (Florence, 1941), pp. 141, 178–79, and Thorn-Wickert, *Manuel Chrysolora*, pp. 69–70. Note that the treatise on the procession of the Holy Spirit ascribed to Chrysoloras by G. Cammelli and H. Laemmer, *Melematon Romanorum Mantissa* (Regensburg, 1875), pp. 114–121 has now been shown to have been written by Nil Cabasilas, an opponent of the *Filioque*; see A. Spourlacou, 'Εἶναι ὁ Μανουὴλ Χρωσολωρᾶς ὁ συγγραφεὺς τοῦ ἔργου <<Κεφάλαια ὅτι καὶ ἐκ τοῦ Ψίοῦ τὸ "Αγιον Πνεῦμα ἐκπορεύεται>>', *Thesaurismata*, ii (1963), pp. 83–117. For the papal indult granting Chrysoloras permission to proceed to holy orders and say mass in Greek according to the Latin rite, see A. Mercati, 'Una notiziola su Manuele Crisolora' in id., *Saggi di storia e letteratura* (Rome, 1982), pp. 227–30.

[36] See Monfasani, *George of Trebizond*, pp. 21–22.

[37] See Mohler, *Kardinal Bessarion*, pp. 179–324; Rigo, 'Bessarione tra Costantinopoli e Roma.'

[38] See Argyropoulos' treatise defending the *Filioque* in S. P. Lampros, 'Ἀργυροπούλεια (Athens, 1910), pp. 107–28; and in J. P. Migne ed., *Patrologia Graeca*, 161 vols (Paris, 1857–1912), clviii (1866), col. 991–1010. G. Cammelli, *I dotti bizantini e le origini dell'umanesimo*. II: *Argiropulo*, (Florence, 1941), pp. 37–38, dates the treatise to 1448–49. On his participation in the declaration of union with Rome in Constantinople in December 1452, see J. Gill, *The Council of Florence* (Cambridge, 1961), p. 387.

[39] He was clearly a unionist from the moment he first arrived in Italy in 1440; see C. Bianca, 'Gaza, Teodoro', *Dizionario biografico degli italiani*, 74 vols to date (Rome, 1960–), lii (1999), pp. 737–46. For

mention the five best known, and to pass over other important figures with less impact in Italy, such as the Gregory III Mammas, Patriarch of Constantinople, and Isidore, Metropolitan of Kiev, who were forced to spend their final years in Rome because of their adherence to union with the Catholic Church.[40] In other words, serious Greek-Latin interchange could and did have far more serious personal consequences for Greeks than it did for Latins. The emigration of Greek scholars to the Latin West in the Renaissance forms an important chapter in the history of Uniate Catholicism just as it does of the classical tradition.[41]

The declaration of union between the Greeks and Latins on 6 July 1439 at the Council of Florence might have been the realization of what the Greek Latinophiles had wanted but, in point of fact, political needs – not theological or cultural imperatives – had driven the Byzantine emperor John VIII to bring the Greek delegation to Italy, and in the end the union

---

his letter to his brothers in support of the union in 1451, see P. L. Leone, 'In margine al Concilio: a proposito di una lettera di Teodoro Gaza' in P. Viti ed., *Firenze e il Concilio del 1439*, 2 vols (Florence, 1994), ii, pp. 921–29.

[40] For Mammas see Gill, *Council of Florence, ad indicem*; and G. Mercati, *Scritti d'Isidoro, il cardinale ruteno, e codici a lui appartenuti che si conservano nella Biblioteca Apostolica Vaticana* (Rome, 1926), pp. 132–38. For Isidore see Mercati, *Scritti d'Isidoro, il cardinale ruteno*; J. Gill, *Personalities of the Council of Florence and other Essays* (Oxford, 1964), pp. 65–78; Isidor of Kiev, *Sermones inter Concilium Florentium Conscripti*, ed. G. Hofmann and E. Candal (Rome, 1971), and P. Schreiner, 'Ein byzantinischer Gelehrter zwischen Ost und West. Zur Biographie des Isidor von Kiew un seinem Besuch in Lviv (1436)', *Bollettino della Badia Greca di Grottaferrata*, 3rd ser., iii (2006), pp. 215–28.

[41] The word 'uniate,' meaning a church of a non-Roman rite in union with Rome, seems to have entered into usage only after the Union of Brest in 1595–96 which joined the Ruthenian Church with Rome: A. Fortescue and G. D. Smith, *The Uniate Eastern Churches: the Byzantine rite in Italy, Sicily, Syria and Egypt* (London, 1923), pp. 1–4.

failed.[42] The clergy and populace back in Greece rejected it, and the disastrous defeat of the Latin crusading army at Varna near the Black Sea in Bulgaria on 10 November 1444 put paid to the political promise implicit in the agreement of union. Greek scholars had been coming to Italy for generations before the Council and would continue to do so for generations after, but the dream of a union of churches died within fifteen years of the Council of Florence.

The Fall of Constantinople and the Renaissance

The fall of Constantinople to the Turks in 1453 did not trigger the Renaissance by driving learned Greeks to Italy, as once believed,[43] but it did terminate the two phenomena that we have been talking about: the appropriation of Latin scholasticism and the conversion to Catholicism of leading Byzantine intellectuals. Philo-latinism became dangerous under the Ottomans. Even the Aristotelian philosopher George Amiroutzes (c.1400–c.1470), an erstwhile supporter of union with Rome and, it would seem, a student of the works of Thomas Aquinas, gave up all expressions of Latin sympathy and ended his days as an obedient member of Mehmed the Conqueror's official family. I suspect that if it had not been for the fall of Constantinople, and despite the failure of the union of the Council of Florence, the spread of Latin scholasticism among the Greek educated élite would have continued apace. So, the real effect of the fall was not to jump-start the Italian Renaissance under Greek influence, but to bring down the curtain on the Greek Renaissance which had been under way in late Byzantium partly under Latin influence. Thereafter, cultural interchange essentially flowed one way, as Greeks in the Latin West necessarily adapted their

---

[42] The literature on the Council is large, but as a start, see Gill, *Council of Florence*; Viti ed., *Firenze e il Concilio del 1439*; and J.-L. van Dieten, 'Die Streit in Byzanz um die Rezeption der Unio Florentina', *Ostkirchliche Studien*, xxxix (1990), pp.160–80.

[43] See note 6 above.

learning and skills to satisfy the wants and needs of their new environment.

Although learned Greeks themselves had little need of Italian humanism, humanists in and outside of Italy were in fact their best customers; and so, first and foremost, starting with Leontius Pilatus and Manuel Chrysoloras, educated émigré Greeks in the Latin West became teachers, translators, and copyists of Greek.

Teaching

The Greek émigrés were products of a long tradition of literary-rhetorical education in Byzantium.[44] So, as far as the Italian humanists were concerned, the émigrés were a cultural match.[45] But in point of fact some émigrés resisted when they could and taught instead what primarily interested them. John Argyropoulos in Florence and Andronicus Callistus in Bologna taught philosophy, but late in life they too ended up teaching Greek.[46] George of Trebizond claimed that he never taught Greek but concentrated on Latin and rhetoric.[47] Trebizond's choice, I would contend, was driven more by market forces

---

[44] See note 10 above.

[45] The most comprehensive attempt to cover the great teachers is G. Cammelli, *I dotti bizantini e le origini dell'Umanesimo*. I: *Manuele Crisolora*; II: *Giovanni Argiropulo*; III: *Demetrio Calcondila* (Florence, 1941–54), to which should be added his article, 'Andronico Callisto', *La Rinascita*, v (1942), pp. 104–21, 174–214.

[46] See in general my 'L'insegnamento universitario e la cultura bizantina in Italia nel Quattrocento' in L. Avellini et al. ed., *Sapere e/è potere. Discipline, dispute e professioni nell'Università medievale e moderna* (Bologna, 1990), pp. 43–65 [reprinted as Essay XII in J. Monfasani, *Byzantine scholars in Renaissance Italy: Cardinal Bessarion and other émigrés* (Aldershot, 1995)]. By the end of his career, Callistus gave up philosophy to teach literature and language exclusively; see G. Resta, 'Andronico Callisto, Bartolomeo Fonzio e la prima traduzione umanistica di Apollonio Rodio' in E. Livrea and G. A. Privitera ed., *Studi in onore di Anthos Ardizzoni*, 2 vols (Rome, 1978), ii, pp. 1055–1131 [reprinted as *Apollonio Rodio e gli umanistici* (Rome, 1980)].

[47] See Monfasani, *George of Trebizond*, p. 22.

than intellectual predilection. For, though a small number of Greek émigrés had brilliantly successful careers as teachers of Greek, most of the Greek émigrés teaching Greek had a hard go of it. In the 1480s, Constantine Lascaris, while he himself was teaching at Messina, far away from the major centres of Renaissance culture, famously lamented the fate of his fellow émigrés: Theodore Gaza, scorned in Rome, died in provincial Policastro in Calabria; Andronicus Callistus died after leaving Italy while seeking his fortune in England; Demetrius Castrenus returned to Greece in desperation; and John Argyropoulos eked out a living in his last days in Rome by selling books from his library.[48] The limited market for their product, their own less than perfect command of Latin, and the growing competition of Latin Hellenists made the services of the émigrés as teachers of Greek only marginally profitable.[49]

[48] See T. Martínez Manzano, *Konstantinos Laskaris: Humanist, Philologe, Lehrer, Kopist* (Hamburg, 1994), pp. 161–62; see also Monfasani, 'L'insegnamento universitario', pp. 45–46.

[49] Note the relatively small number of Greek teachers in Appendix II compared to the large number of Greek copyists. To be successful as a teacher, an émigré had to have good Latin, which was not a skill they normally could acquire in Greece. The Latinity of the literal translations Leontius Pilatus made for Petrarch and Boccaccio could be appalling (see note 8 above). Even though the first Greek teacher, Manuel Chrysoloras, preached the translation of sense, not words, he himself never attempted a literary translation and the translation of Plato's *Republic* made by Uberto Decemberio under his tutelage justly came under severe criticism; see J. Hankins, 'A Manuscript of Plato's *Republic* in the Translation of Chrysoloras and Uberto Decembrio with Annotations of Guarino Veronese (Reg. lat. 1131)' in J. Hankins, J. Monfasani and F. Purnell Jr. ed., *Supplementum Festivum: studies in honor of Paul Oskar Kristeller* (Binghamton, NY, 1987), pp. 149–88 [reprinted in Hankins, *Humanism and Platonism*, ii, pp. 51–90]. Even Cardinal Bessarion, while his Latin was quite correct, felt the need to have his secretary NICCOLÒ PEROTTI revise his Latin texts to bring them up to contemporary humanist standards of Latinity; see J. Monfasani, 'Bessarion Latinus', *Rinascimento*, 2nd ser., xxi (1981), pp.165–209; and id., 'Still more on Bessarion Latinus,' *Rinascimento*, 2nd ser., xxiii (1983), pp. 217–35 [reprinted as Essays II and III in id., *Byzantine Scholars*]. The reason George of Trebizond and Theodore

Janus Lascaris had tried to establish a Greek academy in Florence as a refuge of Greek learning which would enroll promising students from Greece, and he finally succeeded with his plans in 1514 in Rome; but this academy did not outlast the death of its Medici patron, Pope Leo X, in 1521.[50] Only in 1576, under the patronage of Pope Gregory XIII, did the Greek College in Rome begin life anew, but this time as a religious foundation meant to foster the conversion of Greeks to Roman Catholicism.[51] No wonder so many educated émigrés sought out more lucrative careers in the church, the state, or business.[52] After Manuel Chrysoloras' transformative three years in Florence from 1397 to 1400, the most important didactic achievement of the Greek émigrés was not their classroom teaching, but the three extraordinarily successful textbooks that they left behind, namely, Chrysoloras' *Erotemata*, Theodore Gaza's Greek *Grammar*, and Con-

Gaza became such successful translators was because their Latinity matched their command of Greek.

[50] Pagliaroli, 'Giano Lascari e il ginnasio greco'; V. Fanelli, 'Il Ginnasio Greco di Leone X a Roma', *Studi Romani*, ix (1961), pp. 379–93.

[51] See Z. N. Tsirpanlis, 'Il primo e secondo Collegio Greco di Roma', *Il Veltro*, xxvii (1983), pp. 507–21; id., Τὸ Ἑλληνικὸ Κολλέγιο τῆς Ῥώμης καὶ οἱ μαθητές του *(1576–1700)* (Athens, 1980), and the various articles in A. Fyrigos ed., *Il Collegio Greco di Roma. Richerche sugli alunni, la direzione, l'attivita* (Rome, 1983).

[52] See Harris, *Greek Émigrés*, *passim*. Two émigré members of Bessarion's household who had very successful ecclesiastical careers were Athanasius Chalceopoulos and Alexius Celadenus. On the latter, see J. Monfasani, 'Alexius Celadenus and Ottaviano Ubaldini: an epilogue to Bessarion's relationship with the court of Urbino', *Bibliothèque d'humanisme et Renaissance*, xlvi (1984), pp. 95–110 [reprinted as Essay IX in idem, *Byzantine Scholars*]. For the former, see M. Manoussacas, 'Calceopulo, Attanasio', *Dizionario biografico degli italiani*, xvi (1973), pp. 515–17, and M.-H. Laurent and A. Guillou, *Le 'Liber Visitationis' d'Athanase Chalkéopoulos (1457–1458)* [Studi e testi, ccvi] (Vatican City, 1960), pp. xviii–xxxiii.

stantine Lascaris' Greek *Grammar*. Into the mid-sixteenth century, these works were inescapable to students of Greek.[53]

Translations

Translation was another obvious way Greek émigrés could satisfy the wants of their Latin patrons. Yet, even here, the opportunities and successes of the émigrés were limited. The émigrés translated a wide range of Greek literature, as the listing in Appendix III below shows. Nonetheless, the translations produced by the émigrés that enjoyed wide success were clustered overwhelmingly in science, philosophy, and patristics. Some of these translations, such as Theodore Gaza's versions of the Aristotelian *De animalibus* and *Problemata* and Bessarion's version of Aristotle's *Metaphysics*, enjoyed enormous success into modern times.[54] Even if the miserably poor literal translation of *Iliad* by Leontius Pilatus in the fourteenth century was not widely known in the fifteenth, there seems to have been an unstated understanding on the part of Latins and Greeks that the Greeks had a competitive advantage in rendering difficult Greek technical texts while Latins would be more capable of scaling the stylistic heights demanded by the neo-classical standards of contemporary humanists and expected for works of oratory, history, poetry, drama, and

---

[53] See P. Botley, *Learning Greek in Western Europe, 1396–1529: Grammars, Lexica, and Classroom Texts* (Philadelphia, 2010), pp. 7–12, 14–31. Botley also treats the grammar of Demetrius Chalcondyles (pp. 34–36).

[54] For Gaza, see J. Monfasani, 'The Pseudo-Aristotelian *Problemata* and Aristotle's *De Animalibus* in the Renaissance' in A. Grafton and N. Siraisi ed., *Natural Particulars: Nature and the disciplines in Renaissance Europe* (Cambridge, MA, 1999), pp. 205–47 [reprinted as Essay VI in id., *Greeks and Latins*]. For Bessarion's translation of the *Metaphysics*, see F. E. Cranz and C. B. Schmitt, *A Bibliography of Aristotle Editions, 1501–1600*, 2nd ed. (Baden-Baden, 1984), p. 180, where 34 editions are listed up to 1600. As Mohler, *Kardinal Bessarion*, p. 345, points out, Immanuel Bekker's edition of Aristotle's works for the Berlin Academy in 1831 included in its Volume 3 Bessarion's translation of the *Metaphysics*.

belletristic essays. One could question these assumptions, but even in the case of a distinguished Latin stylist such as George of Trebizond, who had established himself as a teacher of Latin rhetoric and who bragged that he was more eloquent in Latin than Greek, his most successful translations in terms of popularity, other than his rendering of Aristotle's *Rhetoric*, clustered in philosophy, science and patristic texts, just as was true for the translations of the other émigrés. It should also be pointed out that it really was not Greek translation, but knowledge of Greek that the émigrés taught. As Ernesto Berti put it, the dynamics behind the drive for new artistic translations of the Greek classics, starting with Chrysoloras' instruction in Florence, were 'tutte latine.'[55] The humanists extracted from the émigrés what they needed for themselves to translate the classics into worthy Latin.

Copying and Printing

Of the three services the émigré scholars could perform to earn their keep in the Latin West, copying may have been the humblest, but it was also the most common, especially if one counts printing as a high-tech form of copying. The data in Ernst Gamillscheg's and Dieter Harlfinger's *Repertorium der Griechischen Kopisten 800–1600* suggest the numbers involved.[56] I estimate that about 170 of the copyists in these volumes can be categorized as Renaissance émigrés or visitors (see Appendix I below). Since many important collections remain to be systematically probed, the number of émigré and visiting copyists will certainly rise well beyond 170; and since the *Repertorium* reports high numbers of manuscripts for professional scribes such as Andreas Darmarius (115),[57] John

---

[55] E. Berti, 'Manuele Crisolora, Plutarco e l'avviamento delle traduzioni umanistiche', *Fontes*, i (1998), pp. 80–99 at p. 92.

[56] See note 13 above.

[57] I take into account the repetition in *RGK*, iA and iiiA of Rome: Biblioteca Casanatense, MS. 1357, Rome: Biblioteca Vallicelliana, MSS B. 22 & R. 32, and BAV, MS. Vat. Gr. 231.

Rhosus (65),[58] and Michael Apostolis (69),[59] we may safely assume that many of the 170 or so copyists produced well over 100 and more probably well over 200 manuscripts in the course of their careers (if a scribe produced, say, 15 manuscripts a year for 20 years, that would result in 300 manuscripts). We have no way of fixing even approximately how many manuscripts the circa 170 listed copyists actually did produce, but clearly it was a very large number, and consequently the scribal activity of the émigrés may well have been their most substantial contribution to the Hellenization of Renaissance culture. And if we add to this their work as printers, editors, and correctors of printed texts, including for the most illustrious of Renaissance printers, Aldus Manutius,[60] their importance only grows.[61] Émile Legrand's classic *Biographie hellénique des XVe et XVIe siècles* missed a large number of relevant editions (balanced by the fact that it

---

[58] I take into account the repetition in *RGK,* iA and iiiA of Rome: Biblioteca Casanatense, MS. 197, Rome: Biblioteca Vallicelliana, MS. A. 25 and BAV, MS. Pal. Gr. 276.

[59] I take into account the repetition in *RGK,* iiiA of the eleven Roman and Vatican MSS listed in *RGK,* iA.

[60] For Manutius and his Greek collaborators, see Geanakopolos, *Greek Scholars in Venice*, pp. 256–67, and M. Lowry, *The World of Aldus Manutius: business and scholarship in Renaissance Venice* (Oxford, 1979), *passim*. Short but penetrating is M. Davies, *Aldus Manutius, Printer and Publisher of Renaissance Venice* (London, 1995). Though technical, there is useful information about Manuzio's Greek collaborators in N. Barker, *Aldus Manutius and the Development of Greek Script & Type in the Fifteenth Century* (New York, 1992).

[61] For the fifteenth century, now see K. S. Staikos, *Charta of Greek Printing: the contribution of Greek editors, printers, and publishers in Italy and the West.* I: *Fifteenth Century* (Cologne, 1998). For the sixteenth century, one may consult E. Layton, *The Sixteenth Century Greek Book in Italy: printers and publishers for the Greek world* (Venice, 1994), whose range is limited, focusing on editions produced in Italy in modern Greek and editions meant for liturgical and other religious purposes, but Layton's coverage of printers and printing types is extensive and of a fundamental nature, superseding Legrand in the material covered.

includes works in Greek not produced by Greeks), but the sheer number of editions it describes – 1,102 – remains a telling reflection of the contribution of the Greek émigrés to the Renaissance.[62]

Interestingly enough, Appendix I highlights the fact that we can identify more sixteenth-century than fifteen-century émigré scribes. The fifteenth century marked an explosion of Greek scribes in Europe compared to the fourteenth, but the proliferation of Greek scribes in the sixteenth, quite apart from the production of prolific non-Greek scribes such as Camillus Venetus and his father Bartolomeo Zanetti, proves how successfully Greek studies had taken root in the Latin West.[63] Into the late Renaissance not even the printing press could satisfy the growing demand for Greek texts of all sorts and of varying degrees of rarity and scholarly value.

The manuscripts and editions produced by the émigrés also highlight the difference between how the Renaissance Latins viewed the émigrés and how the émigrés viewed themselves. If we take as a representative sample the manuscripts listed in the first volume of the *Repertorium der griechischen Kopisten* for six well-known fifteenth-century émigré copyists (Andronicus Callistus, Demetrius Trivolis, George Trivizias, Immanuel Rhousotas, John Rhosus, and Michael Apostolis), we have a sum total of 140 manuscripts, of which 116, or 83%, contain classical or patristic texts and 24, or 17%, contain Byzantine texts. If we were in a position to survey all the manuscripts copied by the émigrés, the percentages might change, but I do

---

[62] The title of Legrand's works continues: *ou description raisonnée des ouvrages publiés en grec par des Grecs aux XVe et XVIe siècles*, 4 vols, (Paris, 1885–1906); the reprint of Paris, 1962, added a bracketed precision '... *ouvrages publiés en grec [ou] par des Grecs ...*'. 290 editions are described in vols i and ii and 868 in vol. iii and iv. For 69 fifteenth-century editions missed by Legrand, see Staikos, *Charta of Greek Printing*, pp. 42–47.

[63] For literature on Camillus Venetus and Zanetti, see M. L. Sosower, *A Descriptive Catalogue of Greek Manuscripts at St John's College, Oxford* (Oxford, 2007), pp. 20–27.

not think they would shift radically. If we survey, however, the 1,102 editions listed in Émile Legrand's *Bibliographie hellénique* and discard editions of liturgical texts and the works meant to help Latins master Greek (that is, grammars), as well as translations of Cicero into Greek, we shall discover that only 21 editions of Byzantine texts were printed in the whole of the fifteenth and sixteenth centuries, which amounts to a mere 2% of the editions in Legrand.[64] Even in the Latin West the émigrés as copyists had maintained their Byzantine identity for themselves and their patrons who paid for the manuscripts, but the broader market of printed books had scant interest in medieval Greek texts. Byzantine studies is a post-Renaissance phenomenon, taking rise especially in later seventeenth-century France.[65] For the Renaissance, the émigrés remained for their Latin public essentially vehicles to Greek antiquity.

'Critical Spirit'

A theme commonly associated with the Greek émigrés since the Enlightenment is the belief that they brought with them a new critical spirit.[66] But the evidence points to the émigrés

---

[64] Half of these editions were of works of George Gemistus Pletho. The 21 editions are as follows: Barlaam of Calabria (iv, no. 867), Demetrius Cydones (iv, no. 797), George Gemistus Pletho (iii, nos 389, 393, 403, 406; iv, nos 577, 699, 705–707, 718, 743), George Scholarius (ii, no. 205; iv, nos 580, 738), Nicholas Cabasilas (ii, no. 209), Psellus (i, no. 88; iii, nos 411, 463), Thomas Magister (i, no. 52).

[65] See note 3 above.

[66] Ferguson, *Renaissance in Historical Thought*, pp. 71 (Pierre Bayle) and 97 (Condorcet). Modern scholars take a more measured approach. E. Garin, *L'Umanesimo italiano. Filosfia e vita civile nel Rinascimento* (Bari, 1968 [first edition 1947 in German; first Italian 1952]), p. 98, recognized the Greeks as instruments of Italian humanism ('un carattere sopratutto strumentale'), but he also still believed in some sort of amorphous spiritual influence, providing intellectuals 'in crisis' a new spiritual force through Platonic escapism ('offrirono in un momento opportune a delle coscienze in crisi le vie dell'evasione platonica') and a fresh vision of intellectual contemplation ('con gli

actually being no more advanced in this regard than the Italian humanists and not even substantially more sophisticated than the medieval scholastics in understanding how to determine the correct original text.[67] At the Council of Florence, the Greeks and Latins argued about what was the authentic text of Basil the Great's *Adversus Eunomium*,[68] but this textual problem had already been noticed in the previous century by the Catholic convert Demetrius Cydones and by a Dominican friar resident in Greece, Fra Philip of Pera.[69] After the Council, the leading Greek resident in Italy, Cardinal Bessarion, wrote a treatise on detecting errors in the text of Scripture.[70] The main source for the principles he laid down, however, as he himself acknowledged, was the twelfth-century Latin Hebraist Nicolò

occhi fissi a quella finale esaltazione dell'intelletto contemplante e separato ove si riversava tutto il più puro platonismo'). P. O. Kristeller, in his 'Italian Humanism and Byzantium', which I have consulted in id., *Renaissance Thought and its Sources*, ed. M. Mooney (New York, 1979), pp. 137–50 [for other editions, see T. Gilbhard, *Bibliographia Kristelleriana* (Rome, 2006), no. 288], did not attribute any new intellectual vision to the Greeks, but concentrated instead on the more concrete aspects of their influence, namely, the acquisition of new texts and manuscripts as well as new translations of classical texts.

[67] A useful survey of Italian humanist criticism, though it makes some unwarranted assumptions about the Greek contribution, is W. Speyer, *Italienischen Humanisten als Kritiker der Echtheit antiker und christlicher Literatur* [Akademie der Wissenschaften under Literatur, Mainz. Abhandlungen der geistes- und sozialwissenschaftlichen Klasse, Jahrgang 1993, no. 3] (Stuttgart, 1993).

[68] See Gill, *Council of Florence*, pp. 195–206, 211–12.

[69] See C. Delacroix-Besnier, *Les dominicains et la chrétienté grecque aux XIVe et XVe siècles* (Rome, 1997), pp. 227–28 (for Fra Philip of Pera and Demetrius Cydones) and pp. 346, 350, 402–03 (for the renewal of the issue at the Council of Florence). See also Gill, *Council of Florence*, pp. 195–206, for the Council; and Bessarion, *De Spiritus Sancti processione ad Alexium Lascarin Philanthropinum*, ed. E. Candal (Rome, 1961), pp. 8–9, for how he discovered in Constantinople after the Council a manuscript of Basil in which Demetrius Cydones had noted the surreptitious deletion in the manuscript of the passage favourable to the Latin position.

[70] Mohler, *Kardinal Bessarion*, i, pp. 399–403, and iii, pp. 70–87.

Maniacutia.⁷¹ Also, Bessarion's faith in the Byzantine recension of the New Testament made him fail to see the cogency of the argument of his fellow émigré George of Trebizond, who was deeply influenced by his Latin sources and had argued for the critical value of the *Itala*, the pre-Vulgate Latin version of the Bible.⁷² George did not fully understand that he had swum into philological deep waters, but impressed as he was with the Latin tradition, he had stumbled onto the modern insight that the *Itala* reflected a pre-Byzantine text of the New Testament. Furthermore, Bessarion's insistence on the *veritas Graeca* merely replicated the insistence of the medieval Latin Hebraists on the *veritas Hebraica*, and it had been already anticipated and put methodically into practice by the Italian humanist LORENZO VALLA perhaps as much as a decade earlier.⁷³ For all their copying of manuscripts and editing of texts for printed editions, no Greek anticipated POLITIAN's brilliant insights on the filiation of manuscripts.⁷⁴ Even on the question of the pronunciation of ancient Greek, it is worth noting that the Spanish humanist Antonio de Nebrija and the Dutchman Erasmus of Rotterdam took the lead in the correction of the pronunciation taught by contemporary Greek teachers.⁷⁵

---

⁷¹ V. Peri, 'Nicola Maniacutia: un testimone della filologia romana del XII', *Aevum*, xli (1967), pp. 67–90.

⁷² See Monfasani, *George of Trebizond*, pp. 92–99, and id., 'Criticism of Biblical Humanists in Quattrocento Italy' in E. Rummel ed., *Biblical Humanism and Scholasticism in the Age of Erasmus* (Leiden, 2008), pp. 15–38, at pp. 19–20, 28–30.

⁷³ See J. H. Bentley, *Humanists and Holy Writ: New Testament scholarship in the Renaissance* (Princeton, 1983), pp. 32–69; Monfasani, 'Criticism of Biblical Humanists', pp. 19–28.

⁷⁴ See A. Grafton, 'The Scholarship of Poliziano and Its Context' now most readily available in id., *Defenders of the Text: traditions of scholarship in an age of science, 1450–1800* (Cambridge, MA, 1991), pp. 47–75.

⁷⁵ See I. Bywater, *The Erasmian Pronunciation of Greek and its Precursors* (Oxford, 1908), and D.-C. Hesseling and H. Pernot, 'Erasme et les origines de la pronounciation érasmienne', *Revue des études grecques*, xxxii (1919), pp. 278–301.

The most intellectually daring of the émigrés was Theodore Gaza. Against the firm belief of his patron, Cardinal Bessarion, he denied the authenticity of the writings of Dionysius the Areopagite.[76] But so did Lorenzo Valla, and Valla did so more boldly and explicitly than did Gaza.[77] Gaza's boldness also had a bizarre side to it. In translating Aristotle's *Problemata*, he radically reordered the text without informing the reader.[78] Furthermore, in this translation and also in that of Aristotle's *De animalibus*, he often arbitrarily imposed meaning by adding words, phrases and passages not found in the Greek.[79]

[76] See J. Monfasani, 'Pseudo-Dionysius the Areopagite in Mid-Quattrocento Rome' in Hankins et al. ed., *Supplementum Festivum*, pp. 189–219 [reprinted as Essay IX in id., *Language and Learning in Renaisance Italy* (Aldershot, 1994)].

[77] Monfasani, 'Pseudo-Dionysius' in Hankins et al. ed., *Supplementum Festivum*; G. Makris, 'Zwischen Hypatios von Ephesos und Lorenzo Valla. Die areopagitische Echtheitsfrage im Mittealter' in T. Boiadjiev, G. Kapriev and A. Speer ed., *Die Dionysius-Rezeption im Mittelalter. Internationales Kolloquium in Sofia vom 8. bis 11 April 1999 unter der Schirmherrschaft der Société Internationale pour l'Étude de la Philosophie Médiévale* (Turnhout, 2000), pp. 3–39, who shows that, though the Byzantines firmly believed in the authenticity of Pseudo-Dionysius, initially there was some resistance because of opposition to sixth-century Monophysites, who favoured this author. These doubts about Dionysius survived in the literature and could have influenced fifteenth-century doubters such as Gaza and Valla.

[78] Monfasani, 'The Pseudo-Aristotelian *Problemata* '.

[79] Monfasani, 'The Pseudo-Aristotelian *Problemata*'. As David Rundle reminds me, Italian humanists could treat the texts they translated just as wantonly. He points to Bruni's changing of the gender of Hiero's lover in his translation of Xenophon's *Hiero*, and GIOVANNI AURISPA's giving a new ending to Lucian's *Dialogue* XII of his *Dialogues of the Dead*. One could also cite as examples Bruni's expunging of the overt homosexuality in Plato's *Symposium* when translating this work (see J. Hankins, *Plato in the Renaissance*, 2 vols (Leiden, 1990), i, pp. 80, ii, pp. 399–400); POGGIO BRACCIOLINI's notoriously free paraphrasing (in part surely because, unlike Bruni and Aurispa, his Greek was not especially good) when translating Xenophon (see P. Botley, *Latin Translation in the Renaissance: the theory and practice of Leonardo Bruni, Giannozzo Manetti and*

Some modern critics, flustered by the difference between what they found in the manuscripts and in Gaza, have even supposed that Gaza had access to some now lost extraordinary manuscripts. Gaza's arbitrariness was not unique in late Byzantium. We now know that George Gemistus Pletho simply deleted passages in Plato that did not agree with his own understanding of how the pagan gods related to each other.[80] Like Gaza with Aristotle, Pletho thought he could issue a new redaction of the text of Plato by imposing on the text his own view of what Plato should have said. It should also be noted that Pletho's influential recension of Chaldaean Oracles was in fact also another act of philological arbitrariness, as he picked and chose among the *logia* he found in Psellus and adapted them to the fictive Zoroastrian authorship that he created for them.[81] In short, the critical thinking and philological innovations of fifteenth-century Byzantines were not necessarily anticipations of sound historical method or in advance of the practice in the Latin West.

Summation

Educated Greek émigrés helped shape the Renaissance. They also adapted to serve it. Trained in a Greek environment, the best many could do was to function as copyists either professionally or on occasion. In the case of teachers and translators, however, not only market conditions, but also the high level of Latinity required to be a successful translator kept

    Desiderius Erasmus (Cambridge, 2004), pp. 47–48), and, I would add, Diodorus Siculus. It would not be hard to multiple these examples.

[80] See F. Pagani, 'Un nuovo testimone della *recensio* pletoniana al testo di Platone: il Marc. gr. 188 (K^a)', *Res Publica Litterarum*, new ser., xxix (2006), pp. 5–20; id., '*Damnata Verba*: Censure di Pletone in alcuni codici platonici', *Byzantinische Zeitschrift*, cii (2009), pp. 167–202, and id., 'Filosofia e teologia in Giorgio Gemisto Pletone: la testimonianza dei codici platonici', *Rinascimento*, 2nd ser., xlix (2009), pp. 3–45.

[81] See B. Tambrun-Krasker ed., *Oracles chaldaïque. Recension de Georges Gémiste Pléthon* (Athens, 1995), pp. 37–156, and M. Tardieu, 'Pléthon lecteur des Oracles', *Métis*, ii (1987), pp. 141–64.

their number relatively low. On the other hand, the demand for Greek copyists, especially for writings that were not yet in print, encouraged Greeks to work as copyists to a surprisingly large extent through the sixteenth century. In contrast, as Appendices II and III show, Greek teachers of Greek and translators peaked in the fifteenth century and declined rapidly as the sixteenth century progressed. The enthusiasm for Latin scholasticism, so characteristic of many of the leading fourteenth- and fifteenth-century émigrés and visitors, also declined in significance in the sixteenth century. Humanism, and not scholasticism, was the disciplinary area in which the émigrés would make their mark. The one constant throughout was the acceptance of Roman Catholicism. Indeed, at the end of the sixteenth century, this was the purpose of the revived Greek College in Rome.[82] This religious emphasis no doubt contributed to the continuation into the seventeenth century of the pro-Latin scholastic and pro-uniate attitudes of the fourteenth- and fifteenth-century émigrés. To take an illustrious example, one of the College's students, Leone Allacci of Chios (Leo Allatius, 1587–1669), not only made major contributions to the new field of Byzantine studies, but also was a trained scholastic (he had degrees in philosophy, theology and medicine), a distinguished classicist and an ardent scholarly promoter of union between the Orthodox and Roman churches.[83] Intellectually and religiously, Allacci had kept faith with Demetrius Cydones, Manuel Chrysoloras, Cardinal Bessarion, George of Trebizond, and the other early émigrés of the Renaissance.

---

[82] See Tsirpanlis, 'Il primo e secondo Collegio Greco', pp. 512, 515, 520. From 1625 on, the requirement that the students profess the 'fede cattolica' was strictly enforced.

[83] See T. Cerbu, *Leone Allacci, 1587–1669: the fortunes of an early Byzantinist*, (unpublished PhD dissertation, Harvard University, Cambridge, MA, 1986), and K. Hartnup, *'On the Beliefs of the Greeks': Leo Allatios and popular Orthodoxy* (Leiden, 2004), pp. 53–74.

APPENDIX I

Partial List of Émigré and Visiting Greek Copyists in the Renaissance

This list is extracted from Ernst Gamillscheg's and Dieter Harlfinger's *Repertorium der griechischen Kopisten 800–1600*, with a small number of names added from other sources. Hence, it is far from comprehensive since the three volumes of the *Repertorium* published thus far cover only collections in Rome, Paris, and Great Britain. The *Repertorium* freely cites manuscripts in collections outside these three locations, but it does not list scribes who happen not to have any manuscripts in a collection in these locations. The locations surveyed to date no doubt contain examples of manuscripts copied by the majority of Greek copyists active in the Renaissance, but how many other copyists wait to be captured in this great scholarly enterprise remains to be seen. I include Greek visitors as well as émigrés because visitors not only copied manuscripts in the Latin West, but were also providers of manuscripts copied in Greece by themselves and others. I have omitted scribes who clearly produced manuscripts for the European market, such as those in Venetian-ruled Crete, but, as far as I could tell, never travelled to the West. I probably omitted some scribes who did in fact visit Europe; but, by the same token, I may have included some who were neither visitors nor émigrés. I can only hope that my mistakes on either side of the ledger have cancelled each out in reaching the resulting figure of circa 170 scribes.

The list is ordered by century; before the name of each copyist appear both their number within this list and, in square brackets, their number within their chronological section. The numbers in square brackets following their name are the sequential numbers the copyists have in volumes i-iii of the *Repertorium*.

In addition to the short titles as employed in the footnotes to the main body of the article above, the following abbreviations are used:

Canart, 'Addition'	P. Canart, 'Additions et corrections au *Repertorium der griechischen Kopisten 800–1600*, 3¹' in J. M. Martin, B. Martin-Hisard and A. Paravicini-Bagliani ed., *Vaticana et medievalia. Études en l'honneur de Louis Duval-Arnould* (Florence, 2008), pp. 41–63.
Eleuteri-Canart	P. Eleuteri and P. Canart, *Scrittura greca nell'Umanesimo italiano* (Milan, 1996).
Patrinelis	C. G. Patrinelis, '"Ελληνες κωδικογράφοι τῶν χρόνων τῆς ἀναγεννήσεως', *Epeteris tou Mesaionikou Archeiou*, viii–ix (1958–59), pp. 63–124.
RGK	E. Gamillscheg and D. Harlfinger, *Repertorium der griechischen Kopisten 800–1600*, 9 vols to date (Vienna, 1981–).
VG	Marie Vogel and Victor Gardthausen, *Die griechischen Schriber des Mittelalters und der Renaissance* (Leipzig, 1909).
Wiesner-Victor	J. Wiesner and U. Victor, 'Griechische Schreiber der Renaissance. Nachträge zu den Repertorien von Vogel-Gardthausen, Patrinelis, Canart, de Meyier,' *Rivista di studi bizantini e*

neoellenici, new ser., viii–ix (1971–72), pp. 51–66.

In addition, I consulted but, in the event, did not cite P. Canart, 'Scribes grec de la Renaissance. Additions et corrections aux répertoires de Vogel-Gardthausen et de Patrinélis', *Scriptorium*, xvii (1963), pp. 56–82, and K. A. de Meyier, 'Scribes grecs de la Renaissance. Additions et corrections aux répertoires de Vogel-Gardthausen, Patrinélis et de Canart', *Scriptorium*, xviii (1964), pp. 258–66.

Fourteenth Century

1. [1.]   Demetrius Cydones [iii, no. 164]
2. [2.]   Leontius Pilatus [Eleuteri-Canart, no. 81][1]

Fourteenth / Fifteenth Century

3. [1.]   Manuel Calecas [ii, no. 346]
4. [2.]   Manuel Chrysoloras [Canart, 'Addition,' p. 56]
5. [3.]   Maximus Chrysoberges [iii, no. 428]

Fifteenth Century

6. [1.]   Alphonsus Doursos Athenaios, OP [i, no. 9; ii, no. 16; iii, no. 20]
7. [2.]   Andronicus Callistus [i, no. 18; ii, no. 25; iii, no. 31][2]

---

[1] Rollo, *Leonzio lettore*, argues that he was from Greece and not from Southern Italy.

[2] *RGK* corrects the error of attributing to 'Georgios Cretensis' manuscripts copied by Callistus made by, e.g., Wiesner-Victor, pp. 53–54.

GREEKS

8. [3.]   Andronicus Galiziotes [VG, p. 30][3]
9. [4.]   Antonius Athenaios [ii, no. 29]
10. [5.]   Antonius Logothetes [Harris, *Greek Émigrés*, p. 124][4]
11. [6.]   Athanasius Chalceopoulos [ii, no. 7; iii, no. 7]
12. [7.]   Bessarion (Cardinal) [i, no. 41; ii, no. 61; iii, no. 77]
13. [8.]   Caesar Strategos [ii, no. 292]
14. [9.]   Charitonymus Hermonymos [i, no. 380; ii, no. 523]
15. [10.]   Constantine Lascaris [i, no. 223; ii, no. 313; iii, no. 362]
16. [11.]   Cosmas (Trapezuntios) of Crete, hieromonachos [i, no. 218]
17. [12.]   Demetrius Cantactuzenos [ii, no. 129]
18. [13.]   Demetrius Castrenus [VG, p. 103]
19. [14.]   Demetrius Chalcondyles [i, no. 96]
20. [15.]   Demetrius Leontares [ii, no. 130]
21. [16.]   Demetrius Rhaoul Cavaces [i, no. 95; ii, no. 128e; iii, no. 162]
22. [17.]   Demetrius Scaranos [Canart, 'Addition,' p. 47]
23. [18.]   Demetrius Sgouropoulos [i, no. 101; ii, no. 134; iii. no. 168]
24. [19.]   Demetrius Trivolis [i, no. 103; ii, no. 135; iii, no. 169]
25. [20.]   Demetrius Xanthopoulos [i, no. 98; ii, no. 132; iii, no. 166]
26. [21.]   Dositheos (Dramas) [iii, no. 182]
27. [22.]   Emmanuel Atramyttinos [i, no. 112; ii, no. 144; iii, no. 187]
28. [23.]   Emmanuel of Constantinople [i, no. 115; ii, no. 147]

---

[3] See F. Piñero, 'Andronico Galesiotes: un copista griego en la Mesina del siglo XV', *Erytheia*, x (1989), pp. 309–15.

[4] É. Legrand, *Cent-dix lettres grecques de François Filelfe* (Paris, 1892), pp. 9–12.

29. [24.] George Alexandros of Crete [i, no. 54; ii, no. 72; iii, no. 89], perhaps only worked in Crete
30. [25.] George Balsamon [iii, no. 92]
31. [26.] George Bembaines [ii, no. 76; iii, no. 95]
32. [27.] George Calophonos [iii, no. 104]
33. [28.] George Calophrenas [i, no. 63; ii, no. 83; iii, no. 103]
34. [29.] George Disypatos Galesiotes [i, no. 59; ii, no. 79; iii, no. 99]
35. [30.] George Gemistos Pletho [Patrinelis, p. 73; VG, p. 83][5]
36. [31.] George Scholarius [i, no. 71; ii, no. 92; iii, no. 119]
37. [32.] George of Trebizond [iii, no. 122]
38. [33.] George Trivizias [i, no. 73; ii, no. 93; iii, no. 123]
39. [34.] George Tzangaropoulos [i, no. 72; ii, no. 93; iii, no. 121]
40. [35.] Gerardus of Patras [i, no. 80; ii, no. 107; iii, no. 144]
41. [36.] Harmonius Athenaios [iii, no. 47][6]
42. [37.] Isidore of Kiev [i, no. 155; ii, no. 205; iii, no. 258]
43. [38.] Immanuel Rhousotas [i, no. 154; ii, no. 203; iii, no. 255]
44. [39.] John Argyropoulos [i, no. 158; ii, no. 212; iii, no. 263]
45. [40.] John Chalceopulos [ii, no. 249]
46. [41.] John Eugenicos [ii, no. 217; iii, no. 270]

---

[5] For more recent bibliography, see S. Martinelli Tempesta, 'Nuove ricerche su Giorgio Gemisto Pletone e il codice platonico Laur. 80, 19 (ß)', *Studi medievali e umanistici*, ii (2004), pp. 309–26, and the articles of Pagani cited in note 80 above.

[6] See M. Papanicolaou, "Ἁρμόνιος ὁ Ἀθηναῖος. Bibliofilo e copista, maestro di greco e diplomatico,' in Ὀπώρα. *Studi in onore di mgr. Paul Canart per il LXX compleanno*, 3 vols. [*Bollettino della Badia Greca di Grottaferrata*, new ser., li–liii] (Grottaferrata, 1997–99), ii, pp. 283–301.

47. [42.]   John Papulas [iii, no. 289]
48. [43.]   John Plousiadenos [i, no. 176; ii, no. 234; iii, no. 294]
49. [44.]   John Rhosos [i, no. 178; ii, no. 237; iii, no. 298]
50. [45.]   John Scoutariotes, s. XV [i, no. 183; ii, no. 242; iii, no. 302]
51. [46.]   John Serbopoulos [i, no. 180; ii, no. 240]
52. [47.]   John Sophopoulos [iii, no. 303]
53. [48.]   Leo Atrapes [ii, no. 328; iii, no. 383]
54. [49.]   Leo Calciopoulos [i, no. 237]
55. [50.]   Manuel Atrapes [i, no. 246; ii, no. 338; iii, no. 407]
56. [51.]   Manuel Rhaul Palaiologus [VG, p. 280]
57. [52.]   Manuel, student of Constantine Lascaris [i, no. 256 bis]
58. [53.]   Matthaius Lampoudes [ii, no. 366; iii, no. 441]
59. [54.]   Matthew Camariotes [i, no. 269; ii, no. 365][7]
60. [55.]   Michael Apostolis [i, no. 278; ii, no. 379; iii, no. 454]
61. [56.]   Michael Damescenos [i, no. 279; ii, no. 381; iii, no. 457]
62. [57.]   Michael Tribolis [i, no. 287; ii, no. 395; iii, no. 469]
63. [58.]   Nicholas Secundinus [i, no. 316]

---

[7] As Botley, *Learning Greek*, pp. 13–14 argues, Camariotes visited Italy. The ownership note, presumably by Giorgio Valla, in Modena: Biblioteca Estense, MS. II A 10 suggests this ('Liber hic scriptus est manu doctissimi viri domini Matthei Camarioti Constantinopolitani, quem mihi dono dedit, anno domini MCCCCLXXXIIII. [*a second hand adds*: praeceptor ille optimus]': C. Samberger, *Catalogi Codicum Graecorum qui in minoribus bibliothecis italicis asservantur*, 2 vols (Leipzig, 1965), i, p. 304). Camariotes must have been in Italy at the time, as Giorgio Valla never travelled to Greece (J. L. Heiberg, *Beiträge zur Geschichte Georg Valla's und seiner Bibliothek* (Leipzig, 1896), p. 10, presumes that Camariotes gave Valla the manuscript in Pavia). Camariotes must have returned to Greece since he died there in 1490, as Janus Lascaris reported in a letter from Constantinople in 1491 (Legrand, *Bibliothèque hellénique*, ii, p. 322).

64. [59.]   Nicodemos [i, no. 307 bis]
65. [60.]   Peter of Crete [ii, no. 352]
66. [61.]   Silvester Syropoulos [ii,no. 490; iii, no. 574]
67. [62.]   Theodore Gaza [i, no. 128; ii, no. 165; iii, no. 211]
68. [63.]   Theodorus [ii, no. 175; iii, no. 226]

Fifteenth – Sixteenth Century

69. [1.]   Andreas Donos [i, no. 14; ii, no. 22, iii, no. 23]
70. [2.]   Antonius Damilas [i, no. 22; ii, no. 30; iii, no. 34]
71. [3.]   Antonius Eparchos [i, no. 23; ii, no. 32; iii, no. 36]
72. [4.]   Aristobolus (Arsenius) Apostolus [i, no. 27; ii, no. 38; iii, no. 46]
73. [5.]   Demetrius Chalcondyles [i, no. 105; iii, no. ii, 138; iii, no.171]
74. [6.]   Demetrius Damilas [i, no. 93; ii, no. 127; iii, no. 160]
75. [7.]   Demetrius Moschos [i, no. 97; ii, no. 131; iii, no. 165]
76. [8.]   Emmanuel Zacharides [i, no. 114; ii, no. 146; iii, no. 189]
77. [9.]   George Hermonymos [i, no. 61; ii, no. 80; iii, no. 102]
78. [10.]   George Moschos [i, no. 67; ii, no. 88; iii, no. 111]
79. [11.]   Janus Lascaris [i, no. 197; iii, no. 245]
80. [12.]   John Gregoropoulos [Patrinelis, p. 74]
81. [13.]   Manuel Cabaces [iii, no. 412]
82. [14.]   Marcus Musurus [i, no. 265; ii, no. 265; iii, no. 433]
83. [15.]   Michael Souliardos [i, no. 286; ii, no. 392]
84. [16.]   Nicholas (Byzantios?) [i, no. 330; ii, no. 447]
85. [17.]   Nicholas Blastos [ii, no. 424]
86. [18.]   Nicholas Petreius [i, no. 314 ter]

87. [19.]   Paulus [i, no. 342; ii, no. 460; iii, no. 539]
88. [20.]   Peter Hypselas [i, no. 349; ii, no. 478; ii, no. 558]
89. [21.]   Phanourios Carabelos [iii, no. 595?][8]
90. [22.]   Philippos Rhodios [Martínez Manzano, *Konstantinos Laskaris*, p. 299]
91. [23.]   Zacharia Callierges [i, no. 119; ii, no. 156; iii, no. 197]

Sixteenth Century

92. [1.]   Alexander Lascaris [iii, no. 13]
93. [2.]   Alexios [ii, no. 15; iii, no. 18]
94. [3.]   Andreas Darmarius [i, no. 13; ii, no. 21; iii, no. 22]
95. [4.]   Andronicus Nouccios [i, no. 20; ii, no. 27; iii, no. 32]
96. [5.]   Angelus Bergicius [i, no. 3; ii, no. 3; iii, no. 3]
97. [6.]   Antonius Calosunas [i, no. 25]
98. [7.]   Antonius Dizomaios [i, no. 31; iii, no. 35]
99. [8.]   Antonius Episkopopoulos [i, no. 24; ii, no. 33; iii, no. 37]
100. [9.]   Antonius Ischadianos [iii, no. 38]
101. [10.] Basil Baleris [i, no. 34; ii, no. 50; iii, no. 66]
102. [11.] Benedictus Episcopopoulos [i, no. 38]
103. [12.] Bernardinus Sandros [i, no. 39; ii, no. 59; iii, no. 75]
104. [13.] Christopher Contoleon [i, no, 383; ii, no. 526; iii, no. 615]
105. [14.] Constantine, collaborator of Demetrius Zenos [i, no. 233; ii, no. 322; iii, no. 377]

[8] See B. Shailor, *Catalogue of Medieval and Renaissance Manuscripts in the Beinecke Rare Book and Manuscript Library, Yale University*, 4 vols (Binghamton, NY, 1984), ii, pp. 67–68, and Botley, *Greek Learning*, p. 63, for Yale University: Beinecke Library, MS. 291, written in Italy in 1489.

106. [15.] Constantine Mesobotes [i, no. 224; ii, no. 315; iii, no. 363]
107. [16.] Constantine Palaiolocappas [i, no. 225; ii, no. 316; iii, no. 364]
108. [17.] Constantine Rhesinos [i, no. 227; ii, no. 227; iii, no. 365]
109. [18.] Constantine, collaborator of Demetrius Zenos [i, no, 233; ii, no. 322]
110. [19.] Demetrius Zenos [i, no. 94; ii, no. 128; iii, no. 161]
111. [20.] Emmanuel Bembaines [i, no. 113; ii, no. 145; iii, no. 188]
112. [21.] Franciscus Clados [iii, no. 602]
113. [22.] Franciscus Graecus [iii, no. 607]
114. [23.] Franciscus Syropoulos [iii, no. 605]
115. [24.] George Basilicos [i, no. 56; ii, no. 75; iii, no. 93]
116. [25.] George Cocolos [i, no. 65; ii, no. 84; iii, no. 107]
117. [26.] George Mpoucer (i.e. Boucer) [iii, no. 112]
118. [27.] George Tryphon [i, no. 74]
119. [28.] Hieronymos Tragoudistes [ii, no. 201; iii, no. 253]
120. [29.] Hippolytus Bareles [iii, no. 256]
121. [30.] Iacobus Diassorinos [i, no. 143; ii, no. 191; iii, no. 241]
122. [31.] Iacobus Episcopopoulos [i, no. 144; ii, no. 192; iii, no. 242]
123. [32.] John Catelos [ii, no. 220; iii, no. 278]
124. [33.] John Choniates (Chonianos) [i, no. 192; ii, no. 254; iii, no. 316]
125. [34.] John Damascenos [ii, no. 213; iii, no. 268]
126. [35.] John Dracopoulos [ii, no. 216; iii, no. 269]
127. [36.] John Eurippiotes [i, no. 163; iii, no. 271]
128. [37.] John Franciscus Graecus [i, no. 188]
129. [38.] John Malaxos [i, no. 170; ii, no. 226; iii, no. 282]
130. [39.] John Mauromates [i, no. 171; ii, no. 229; iii, no. 283]

GREEKS

131. [40.] John Mourmouris [i, no. 172; ii, no. 230]
132. [41.] John Nathanael [i, no. 173; ii, no. 231; iii, no. 285]
133. [42.] John Phroulas [i, no. 189; ii, no. 248]
134. [43.] John Pizanos [i, no. 175; iii, no. 293], possibly the Italian Gian Giacomo Pisani
135. [44.] John Severos Lacedaimenos [i, no. 181; ii, no. 241; iii, no. 300]
136. [45.] Leontius Eustratios [ii, no. 325]
137. [46.] Manuel Glynzounos [i, no. 248; ii, no. 341; iii, no. 410]
138. [47.] Manuel Malaxos [i, no. 250; ii, no. 347; iii, no. 415]
139. [48.] Manuel Moros [i, no. 252; ii, no. 348]
140. [49.] Manuel Probatares [i, no. 254; ii, no. 350; iii, no. 418]
141. [50.] Matthew Debares [ii, no. 364; iii, no. 440]
142. [51.] Maximus Margounios [i, no. 259; ii, no. 356; iii, no. 427]
143. [52.] Michael [iii, no. 475]
144. [53.] Michael Contaleon [ii, no. 383]
145. [54.] Michael Maleas [VG, p. 315]
146. [55.] Michael Murokephalites [i, no. 284; ii, no. 389; iii, no. 466]
147. [56.] Michael Rhosaitos [ii, no. 391; iii, nos 467
148. [57.] Michael Sophianos [ii, no. 393; and iii, no. 468e]
149. [58.] Nicetas Corogonas [i, no. 298; iii, no. 486]
150. [59.] Nicholas Choniates [i, no. 321; ii, no. 439; iii, no. 521]
151. [60.] Nicholas Cocolos [i, no. 310; ii, no. 429]
152. [61.] Nicholas Malaxos [i, no. 312, ii, no. 432; iii, no. 502]
153. [62.] Nicholas Mourmouris [i, no. 314 bis; ii, no. 434; iii, no. 507]
154. [63.] Nicholas Pachys [ii, no. 435; iii, no. 511]
155. [64.] Nicholas Sophianos [i, no. 318; ii, no. 437; iii, no. 517]

156. [65.] Pachomius Rhousanos [VG, p. 380]
157. [66.] Pantaleon Mamoukas [ii, no. 455]
158. [67.] Peter Bergicios [i, no. 344; ii, no. 470; iii, no. 547]
159. [68.] Peter Carnabacas [i, no. 346–47; ii, no. 474–75; iii, no. 551]
160. [69.] Peter Carnedes [i, no. 347]
161. [70.] Peter Coletes [iii, no. 552]
162. [71.] Petrus Debares [iii, no. 548]
163. [72.] Philippos [iii, no. 597]
164. [73.] Sophianus Melissenos [i, no. 362]
165. [74.] Theodore Rhentios [iii, no. 215]
166. [75.] Theoleptus [i, no. 135; ii, no. 178; iii, no. 135]
167. [76.] Thomas Trebizanos [iii, no. 238]
168. [77.] Zacharia Scordulios [ii, no. 157]

Sixteenth – Seventeenth Century

169. [1.] John Alexios [iii, no. 262]
170. [2.] John Matthaios Caryophyllos [iii, no. 277]
171. [3.] John Sanctamauras [i, no. 179; ii, no. 238; iii, no. 299]
172. [4.] Nicholas Tourrianos [i, no. 319; ii, no. 438; iii, no. 520]

APPENDIX II

Émigré Teachers of Greek in the Renaissance

I have not included in this listing the graduates of the *Collegio Greco* after its refounding in 1576, a very high number of whom went on to become teachers for part or all of their subsequent careers. For these graduates, see Tsirpanlis, 'Il primo e secondo Collegio Greco,' pp. 516–20, and id., *Τὸ Ἑλληνικὸ Κολλέγιο*, pp. 249–708 [see note 52 in the main body of the article]. In addition to short titles and abbreviations employed above, the following is used:

PLP   E. Trapp, R. Walter and H.-V. Beyer ed., *Prosopographisches Lexikon der Palaiologenzeit*, 14 vols (Vienna, 1976–96). I cite entry numbers, not pages.

Fourteenth Century
1. Leontius Pilatus [Pertusi, *Leonzio Pilato*][1]

Fourteenth – Fifteenth Century
2. Manuel Chrysoloras [*PLP* 31165; see Appendix I, no. 4]

Fifteenth Century
3. Andronicus Callistus [*PLP* 10484; see Appendix I, no.

---

[1] For the argument that Pilatus was born in Greece and not Southern Italy, see Appendix I, no. 1.

7]
4. Andronicus Contoblacas [*PLP* 13053][2]
5. Andronicus Galiziotes [*PLP* 3526; Piñero, 'Andronico Galesiotes'; see Appendix I, no. 8]
6. Constantine Lascaris [*PLP* 14540; see Appendix I, no. 15]
7. Demetrius Castrenus [*PLP* 11393; see Appendix I, no.18]
8. Demetrius Chalcondyles [*PLP* 30511; see Appendix I, no.19]
9. Emmanuel Adramyttenos [*PLP* 306; see Appendix I, no. 22]
10. George of Trebizond [*PLP* 4120; see Appendix I, no. 37]
11. Harmonius Athenaios [see Appendix I, no. 41]
12. Theodore Gaza [*PLP* 3449; see Appendix I, no. 67]

Fifteenth – Sixteenth Century

13. Alexander Cretensis[3]
14. Aristobulus (Arsenius) Apostolus [Geanakoplos, *Greek Scholars*, pp. 167–200]
15. Demetrius Moschos [see Appendix I, no. 75]
16. George Hermonymos [*PLP* 6125; see Appendix I, no. 77]
17. John Argyropoulos [*PLP* 1267; see Appendix I, no. 44]
18. Janus Lascaris [*PLP* 14536; see Appendix I, no. 79]

---

[2] See also J. Monfasani, 'In Praise of Ognibene and Blame of Guarino: Andronicus Contoblacas' Invective against Niccolò Botano and the Citizens of Brescia', *Bibliothèque d'humanisme et Renaissance*, lii (1990), pp. 309–21 [reprinted as Essay XI in id., *Byzantine Scholars*]. Note that the invective edited by Hankins, 'Renaissance Crusaders', pp. 203–04 [reprinted in id., *Humanism and Platonism*, pp. 417–19], is not against Andronicus Callistus, but against Andronicus Contoblacas.

[3] See M. Cosenza, *Biographical and Bibliographical Dictionary of the Italian Humanists and of the World of Classical Scholarship in Italy, 1300–1800*, 6 vols (Boston, 1962), i, p. 122 and v, p. 14.

19. John Gregoropoulos [see Geanakoplos, *Greek Scholars, ad indicem*][4]
20. Marcus Musurus [see Appendix I, no. 82]

Sixteenth Century
21. Demetrius Ducas [Geanakoplos, *Greek Scholars*, pp. 223–55].

Sixteenth – Seventeenth Century
22. John Matthaios Caryophyllos [see Appendix I, no. 170]

---

[4] For his lecturing on Aristophanes in Venice, see H. D. Saffrey, 'Un humaniste dominicain, Jean Cuno de Nuremburg, precurseur d'Erasme à Bale', *Bibliothèque d' humanisme et Renaissance*, xxxiii (1971), pp. 19–62, at p. 28 [reprinted in id., *Recherches sur la tradition platonicienne au Moyen Âge et à la Renaissance* (Paris, 1987), pp. 203–48].

APPENDIX III

Émigré Greek Translators and Their Translations in the Renaissance

Many of these translations have a large scholarly literature attached to them. The purpose of my references is only to document the existence of these translations and to point the reader to some bio-bibliographical sources for the translators, and not to give a full bibliography of the translators or the translations.

1. Angelus Bergecius (s. XV)[1]
   Pseudo-Plutarch, *De fluviorum et montium nominibus*[2]

2. Anonymous Bishop (s. XV)[3]
   Basil the Great, *Encomium in Gordium martyrem*

---

[1] Legrand, *Bibliographie hellénique*, iv, pp. 60–66.

[2] See Plutarch, *Fiumi e monti*, ed. E. C. Dorda, A. De Lazzer and E. Pellizer (Naples, 2003).

[3] See J. Monfasani, 'Some Quattrocento Translators of St. Basil the Great: Gaspare Zacchi, Episcopus Anonymus, Pietro Balbi, Athanasius Chalkeopoulos, and Cardinal Bessarion' in C. Maltezou, P. Schreiner and M. Losacco ed., *ΦΙΛΑΝΑΓΝΩΣΤΗΣ. Studi in onore di Marino Zorzi* (Venice, 2008), pp. 249–64.

3.   Andronicus Callistus (s. XV)[4]
Apollonius of Rhodes, *Argonautica*
Aristotle, *De generatione et corruptione*

4.   Athanasius Chalceopoulos (s. XV)[5]
Basil the Great, *Homilia in principium Proverbiorum*
    Homilia in illud: Attende tibi
    Homiliae duae de ieiunio
Pseudo-Crates Cynicus, *Epistolae*
Gregory of Nyssa, *Homiliae quintae de oratione dominica*
Lucian, *De saltatione*
Lysis Pythagoricus, *Epistola ad Hipparchum*[6]

5.   Bessarion (s. XV)
Aristotle, *Metaphysica*[7]
Basil the Great, *Homilia in illud: Attende tibi*[8]
Demosthenes, *First Olynthiac Oration*[9]
Theophrastus, *Metaphysics*[10]

---

[4] E. Bigi, 'Andronico Callisto,' *Dizionario biografico degli italiani*, iii (1961), pp. 162–63; G. Resta, 'Andronico Callisto'; M. Rashed, 'La "translatio callistiana" du *De generatione et corruptione* d'Aristote. Edition princeps' in J. Ducos and V. Giacomotto-Charra ed., *Lire Aristote au Moyen Âge et à la Renaissance: Réception du traité* Sur la génération et la corruption (Paris, 2011), pp. 201–48; Legrand, *Bibliographie hellénique*, i, p. lvii.

[5] See G. de Gregorio, 'Manoscritti greci patristici fra ultima età bizantina e umanesimo italiana. Con un'appendice sulla traduzione latina di Atanasio Calceopulo dell'Omelia In principium Proverbiorum di Basilio Magno' in M. Cortesi and C. Leonardi ed., *Tradizioni patristiche nell'Umanesimo* (Florence, c. 2000), pp. 317–96 at pp. 386–96; M. Manoussacas, 'Calceopulo, Attanasio,' *Dizionario biografico degli italiani*, xvi (1973), pp. 515–17, and Monfasani, 'Some Quattrocento Translators'.

[6] See R. Hercher ed., *Epistolographi Graeci* (Paris, 1873), pp. 601–03.

[7] See Mohler, *Kardinal Bessarion*, i, pp. 341–45.

[8] See Monfasani, 'Still More on *Bessarion Latinus*' and id., 'Some Quattrocento Translators,' pp. 252–55 and 262–63.

[9] See Meserve, 'Patronage and Propaganda.'

Xenophon, *Memorabilia*[11]

6.   George Hermonymos (s. XV-XVI)[12]
Anonymous, *Vita Machometi*
Pseudo-Aristotle, *De virtutibus*
Demetrius of Phalerum, *Septem sapientium apophthegmata*
Gennadius II-George Scholarius, *Confesio fidei*
Pseudo-Gennadius II-George Scholarius, *De via salutis hominum*
Plato, *Letter to Axiochus*
Menander, *Sententiae*
Sententiae gnomicae ex sanctis patribus et auctoribus Graecis
Sosipiades, *Septem sapientium praecepta*
Themistocles, *Letter to Chrysippus*

7.   George of Trebizond (s. XV)[13]
Anonymous: Two Greek Inscriptions
Aristotle, *De anima*
  De animalibus (*De historia animalium*, *De partibus animalium*, *De generatione animalium*)
  De caelo
  De generatione et corruptione
  Physica
  Problemata
  Rhetorica
Basil the Great, *Adversus Eunomium*
  De Spiritu Sancto

---

[10] See C. B. Schmitt, 'Theophrastus' in *CTC*, ii (1971), pp. 239–322 at pp. 305–06.

[11] See D. Marsh, 'Xenophon' in *CTC*, vii (1992), pp. 75–196 at pp. 166–68.

[12] See M. P. Kalatzi, *Hermonymos. A study in scribal, literary and teaching activities in the fifteenth and early sixteenth centuries* (Athens, 2009), pp. 102–06.

[13] See J. Monfasani, *Collectanea Trapezuntiana: texts, documents, and bibliographies of George of Trebizond* (Binghamton, NY, 1984), pp. 698–754.

Cyril of Alexandria, *Thesaurus*
    Commentaria super Evangelium Ioannis
Demosthenes, *Oratio de Corona*
Eusebius of Caesaria, *Praeparatio Evangelica*
Gregory Nazianzenus, *Oratio de laudibus S. Athanasii*
    Oratio de laudibus S. Basilii
Gregory of Nyssa, *De perfecta hominis vita, sive de vita Moysis*
John Chrysostom, *Homiliae XC in Matthaeum*, homilies 26–88
Plato, *Parmenides*
    Laws
    Epinomis
Ptolemy, *Almagest*
Pseudo-Ptolemy, *Centiloquium*

8.   Janus Lascaris (s. XV-XVI)
Polybius, *De militia Romanorum*[14]

9.   John Argyropoulos (s. XV)[15]
Aristotle, *Analytica priora et posteriora*
    De anima
    De interpretatione
    Ethica Nicomachea
    Letter to Alexander the Great
    Physica
    Praedicamenta
Porphyry, *Isagoge*
Basil the Great, *Hexameron*

---

[14] *De Romanorum militia et castrorum metatione*, which is an excerpt of Book 6 of Polybius' *Histories*; see Polybius, *Histoires. Livre VI*, ed. R. Weil and C. Nicolet (Paris, 1977), p. 59. Legrand, *Bibliothèque hellénique*, iii, pp. 367–68, reports the Basel 1537 edition, but omits the Venice 1529 *editio princeps*.

[15] See Cammelli, *Argiropulo*, pp. 183–84.

10. Leontius Pilatus (s. XIV)[16]
Pseudo-Aristotle, *De mirabilibus auscultationibus*[17]
Euripides, *Hecuba*[18]
Homer, *Iliad*[19]
   Odyssey

11. Manuel Chrysoloras (s. XIV-XV)
Plato, *Res publica*[20]

12. Michael Sophianos (s. XVI)[21]
Aristotle, *De anima*

13. Nicholas Petreius (s. XV-XVI)[22]
Diocles of Carystus, *Epistola ad Antigonum regem de tuenda Valetudine*[23]
Gregory Nazianzenus, *Orationes* (translation not extant)[24]

---

[16] For his being Greek, not Southern Italian by birth, see App. I, no. 1.

[17] See M. Pastore Stocchi, *Tradizione medievale e gusto umanistico nel «De montibus» del Boccaccio* (Padua, 1963), pp. 80–85, and G. Billanovich, 'Il Petrarca e i *retori latini minori*', *IMU*, v (1967), pp. 103–64 at pp. 119–22.

[18] See Rollo, *Leonzio lettore*.

[19] See Pertusi, *Leonzio Pilato*, and M. Pade, 'The *Fortuna* of Leontius Pilatus' Homer, with an edition of Piero Candido Decembrio's 'Why Homer's Greek verse are rendered in Latin prose" in F. T. Coulson and A. A. Grotans ed., *Classica et Beneventana. Essays presented to Virginia Brown* (Leiden, 2008), pp. 149–72.

[20] See Hankins, 'A Manuscript of Plato's *Republic*'.

[21] See A. Meschini, *Michele Sofianòs* (Padua, 1981), pp. 35–43.

[22] Legrand, *Bibliographie hellénique*, ii, pp. 183–87 & iv, p. 30.

[23] This text survives in Paulus Aegineta, *Epitomae Medicae*, ed. J. L. Heiberg, 2 vols (Leipzig, 1921–24), i, pp. 68.25–72.12 (= § 100); see P. J. van der Dijk, *Diocles of Carystus. A collection of the fragments with translation and commentary*, 2 vols (Leiden, 2000–01), i, pp. 310–21, frag. 183a.

[24] See A. C. Ware, 'Gregorius Nazianzenus' in *CTC*, ii, pp. 43–192 at pp. 169–70, who calls the translation attributed to Petreius 'doubtful.'

Hippocrates, *De hominis structura*[25]
Melampus, *De naevis corporis*[26]
Meletius Monachus, *De natura hominis*[27]
Philoponus (*sic*; really Michael of Ephesus),[28] *Commentaria in Aristotelis De generatione animalium*
Polemon Periegetes[29], *Fragmenta*

14. Nicholas Secundinus (s. XV)[30]
Acta of the Council of Florence
Arrian, *Anabasis*
Demosthenes, *De corona*
  First Olynthiac Oration
  On the Chersonese
Oraculum super Corinthiaco Isthmo[31]
Osiander, *Strategicon*
Plato, excerpt: *Sententia pulcherrima Socratis, verbis celebrata Platonis*[32]

---

[25] This is really Pseudo-Hippocrates' letter *ad Ptolemaeum regem de hominis fabrica*; see G. Fichtner, *Corpus Hippocraticum. Verzeichnis der hippokratischen und pseudohippokratischen Schriften* (Tübingen, 1989), p. 71, no. 79; and P. Kibre, *Hippocrates Latinus. Repertorium of Hippocratic writings in the Latin Middle Ages*, rev. edition (New York, 1985), p. 153, no. 7.

[26] See J. G. F. Franz, *Scriptores Physiognomoniae Veteres* (Altenburg, 1780), pp. 501–08.

[27] The Greek text is available in J. Migne, *Patrologia Graeca*, lxiv (Paris, 1862), col. 1075–1310.

[28] See M. Hayduck ed., *Ioannis Philoponi (Michaelis Ephesii) in libros De generatione animalium commentaria* [Commentaria in Aristotelem Graeca, XIV/iii] (Berlin, 1903), p. vi.

[29] See L. Preller ed., *Polemonis Periegetae fragmenta* (Leipzig, 1938 [reprint Chicago, 1967]).

[30] Panagiotis Mastrodimitris, Νικόλαος Σεκουνδινός *(1402–1464). Βίος καὶ ἔργον* (Athens, 1970), pp. 203–23.

[31] See F. Stok, 'Niccolò Sagundino traduttore dell' *Oraculum de isthmo*', *Studi umanistici piceni*, xxviii (2008), pp. 227–38.

[32] See Hankins, *Plato in the Italian Renaissance*, ii, p. 798.

Plutarch, *Praecepta gerendae reipublicae*

15.   Simon Atumanos (s. XIV)
Plutarch, *De cohibenda iracundia*[33]

16.   Ioannes Sophianos (s. XV)[34]
(philosophical) *Apopthegmata*
Pseudo-Aristotle, *De virtutibus et vitiis*
Demosthenes, *Funeral Oration (on the Dead of Chaironea)*
George Gemistus Pletho, *De fato*
   De virtutibus
Hero Byzantius, *Poliorcetica*

17.   Theodore Gaza (s. XV)
Aristotle,[35] *De animalibus* (*Historia animalium*)
   Problemata
Dionysius of Halicarnassus, *Praecepta nuptialia, Natalicia, Epithalamia*[36]
Plutarch,[37] *Maxime cum principibus philosopho esse disserendum*
   Theophrastus, *De plantis*[38]

---

[33] See Fedalto, *Simone Atumano*, pp. 127, 152–57.

[34] See P. O. Kristeller, 'A Latin Translation of Gemistos Plethon's *De Fato* by Johannes Sopianos dedicated to Nicholas of Cusa' in id., *Studies in Renaissance Thought and Letters*, 4 vols (Rome, 1956–96), iii (1993), pp. 21–38.

[35] See Monfasani, 'The Pseudo-Aristotelian *Problemata*.'

[36] See R. Santoro, 'La prima traduzione latina di Teodoro Gaza', *Studi umanistici*, iii (1992), pp. 165–84.

[37] M. Papanicolaou, 'Teodoro Gaza e Plutarco', *Rendiconti della Accademia Nazionale dei Lincei. Classe di scienze morali, storiche e filologiche*, ser. 9, viii (2007), pp. 363–428.

[38] See Schmitt, 'Theophrastus' in *CTC*, ii, 266–68.

HUMANISM IN THE GERMAN-SPEAKING LANDS DURING THE FIFTEENTH CENTURY

JOHN L. FLOOD

No one coming from Roberto Weiss's account of humanism in fifteenth-century England can fail to be struck by the contrast with the situation found in Germany.[1] The range of interests of German humanists but above all the pluricentric landscape of German humanism contrast markedly with the relative narrowness of everything in England.[2] In Weiss's interpretation, English humanistic stirrings were to be found chiefly in Oxford, with more limited activity in Cambridge, London, St Albans and Canterbury – a kind of 'golden pentangle'. At the same time, the German-speaking lands of the Holy Roman Empire already boasted a strikingly large number of universities: Prague (founded by Emperor Charles IV in 1348),[3] Vienna (1365), Heidelberg (1386), Cologne

---

[1] Throughout this chapter 'Germany' refers not only to the area within the borders of today's Federal Republic of Germany, but to the much more extensive German-speaking territories of the Holy Roman Empire which ceased to exist in 1806. For details see G. Köbler, *Historisches Lexikon der deutschen Länder*, 6th revised edn (Darmstadt, 1999).

[2] Even such important areas as Greek and Hebrew studies, mathematical and scientific humanism, and humanistic writings in the vernacular cannot adequately be addressed here. For these topics see the list of Further Reading.

[3] Signs of early humanism at Prague under Charles IV (1316–1378), Holy Roman Emperor since 1346, were limited. The most important personality at the court from the intellectual point of view was Charles's chancellor, Johann von Neumarkt (c. 1315–80). Although not a creative writer – his principal achievement was the reform of the administration of the imperial chancery, the correspondence of which

(1388), Erfurt (1392), Würzburg (1402), Leipzig (1409)[4], Rostock (1419), Greifswald (1456), Freiburg (1457), Basel (1460), Ingolstadt (1472), Tübingen and Mainz (both 1477), and Graz (1486), soon to be followed by Wittenberg (1502) and Frankfurt an der Oder (1506). To be sure, by no means may all of these be accounted as hotbeds of humanist endeavour – as Conrad Celtis' scathing poem about Cologne shows:

> [...] in urbe tecum condidici vagas
> inferre fraudes per συλλογιστικοὺς
>   nexus, quod et contentioso
>   tradiderat dialexis ore.
>
> primaeque tecum hac prendideram sacros
> libros sophiae, tunc mihi cognitum
>   Albertus et quid Thomas alti
>   in physicis docuere rebus.
>
> nemo hic Latinam grammaticam docet,
> nec expolitis rhetoribus studet,
>   mathesis ignota est, figuris
>   quidque sacris numeris recludit.
>
> nemo hic per axem candida sidera
> inquirit, aut quae cardinalibus vagis
>   moventur, aut quid doctus alta
>   contineat Ptolomaeus arte.

was not untouched by humanist style – he was receptive to intellectual and cultural ideas. He accompanied the Emperor to Italy in 1354/55 and 1368/69. Petrarch corresponded both with him and the Emperor. Although Charles himself remained unaffected by Petrarch, Johann von Neumarkt admired him greatly, both for his style and his rhetoric. In 1362 he asked him to send him copies of his *De viris illustribus* and the *Remedia utriusque fortunae*. One of the people whom Johann von Neumarkt influenced was Johann von Tepl (c. 1342/50–c. 1414), the author of *Der Ackermann aus Böhmen* (c. 1400) which may be accounted the first work of German prose influenced by humanist style.

[4] Recent accounts of scholarly activity at Leipzig include: H. Nickel, 'Inkunabeln als Quellen der Leipziger Universitätsgeschichte', *Leipziger Jahrbuch zur Buchgeschichte*, xviii (2009), pp. 11–31, and E. Bünz et al., *Geschichte der Universität Leipzig 1409–2009*, I: *Spätes Mittelalter und Frühe Neuzeit 1409–1830/31* (Leipzig, 2009).

> ridentur illic docta poemata
> Maronianos et Ciceronios
>   libros verentur tanquam Apella
>   carne timet stomacho suilla. [...]⁵

In this city [Cologne] I have learned with you how to make false syllogistic connexions and to employ dubious dialectical methods. Here with you I have read the holy books of philosophy; here I have learned what Albertus Magnus and Thomas Aquinas taught about the nature of the world. But nobody teaches Latin grammar here or makes a study of elegant style; what mathematics can teach about numbers and shapes is unknown here. No one here is curious about the stars or about how they move, or about what the learned Ptolemy teaches with his sublime skill. Learned poems are ridiculed there, and the works of Virgil and Cicero are loathed in the same way as pork turns Apella's stomach.

Nonetheless, the universities were important. Although widely scattered, they were linked together through the wanderings of peripatetic scholars, many of whom had studied in Italy also. For instance, Peter Luder (c. 1410–1472) who, after studying at Heidelberg in 1430/31, went to Italy, Macedonia and Greece before further studies in Verona and Padua, becoming an imperial notary and serving in the retinue of Francesco Foscari, Doge of Venice, in 1444. Returning to Heidelberg, he was appointed to teach Latin, lecturing on Valerius Maximus, Horace, Seneca, Terence, Cicero and Ovid. In the early 1460s he went to Erfurt, lecturing on Virgil, Ovid and Terence, and then to Leipzig where one of his students was the Nuremberg humanist Hartmann Schedel (1440–1514). In his inaugural

---

[5] Conrad Celtis, 'Ad Wilhelmum Mummerlochum civem Coloniensem et philosophum', ll. 5–24 (cited after H. C. Schnur, *Lateinische Gedichte deutscher Humanisten* (Stuttgart, 1967), p. 44). Apella was the proverbial Jew, referred to in Horace, *Satires*, 1, 5, 100. The unfavourable image of Cologne may reflect Petrarch's impression: 'Quid inepta Colonia tantis/una nocet titulis, fulvi cui gratia nummi,/ventris amor, studiumque gule somnusque quiesque/esse solet potior sacre quam cura poesis? (*Epistolae metricae*, II, 11; 'How foolish is Cologne, where people delight only in gold coins, gorging themselves, sleeping and taking it easy, and have no care for poetry?')

lectures at Heidelberg and Erfurt, Luder emphasised history as an important aspect of rhetoric, and everywhere he went he aroused interest in newly fashionable literature. Luder's wanderlust soon took him to Italy again; he obtained a doctorate in medicine at Padua in 1464. Later that year we find him at Basel, described as *poeta et medicinae doctor*; he lectured on poetry and was also municipal physician there. Later, in 1472, he is found lecturing on Cicero at Vienna.[6] Another wandering scholar was the aspiring poet Samuel Karoch (c. 1448–1492), who enrolled at Leipzig in 1462. In an address there in 1469 he lauded Cicero's oratory and praised the Italians for their devotion to learning. Following a brief visit to Venice he is found at Erfurt in 1470 announcing lectures on the orator and historian AGOSTINO DATI. In 1472 Karoch appeared as *magister* at the newly founded University of Ingolstadt, then in 1473 at Basel, in 1480 at Tübingen and in 1485 at Cologne. His letters tell also of a stay in Heidelberg, four years in Italy, and a final sojourn in Vienna.[7]

In the opening chapters of his *Humanism in England*, Weiss emphasised the role played by the various activities of papal officialdom in England and Englishmen back from Italy, of book-loving patrons such as Humfrey, duke of Gloucester, of the various Italians who found employment here, and of the growing appreciation of the style of polite literature. To some extent such considerations apply to Germany also; after all, German links with Italy were inevitably stronger than those between England and Italy since Germany not only physically borders on Italy but there were also political ties between the

---

[6] On him see R. Kettemann, 'Peter Luder (um 1415–1472). Die Anfänge der humanistischen Studien in Deutschland' in P. G. Schmidt ed., *Humanismus im deutschen Südwesten* (Sigmaringen, 1993), pp. 13–34; also M. Steinmann, 'Die humanistische Schrift und die Anfänge des Humanismus in Basel', *Archiv für Diplomatik*, xxii (1976), pp. 376–437.

[7] On him see H. Entner, *Frühhumanismus und Schultradition in Leben und Werk des Wanderpoeten Samuel Karoch von Lichtenberg* (Berlin, 1968).

Empire and parts of Italy. One of the most important figures stimulating German humanism, to be discussed more fully presently, was ÆNEAS SYLVIUS PICCOLOMINI, who became Latin secretary to Emperor Frederick III (1415–93, reg. 1440–93). Frederick himself, though no scholar in his own right, encouraged contacts with Italian scholars who were to be found in increasing numbers at princely and episcopal courts. The many Germans who went to study at Italian universities brought back knowledge and books, and some of them tried to make German courts imitate Italian ones. Various individuals made themselves the centre of humanist circles, for example, the merchant Sigmund Gossembrot (1417–1493) at Augsburg and Johannes von Dalberg (1445–1503), bishop of Worms, at Heidelberg. Gossembrot, who studied at Vienna in the mid-1430s, came from a patrician family; he built up a distinguished collection of manuscripts.[8] Dalberg, who had studied at Erfurt and taken his doctorate in laws at Ferrara, was instrumental in bringing the University of Heidelberg to the pinnacle of its reputation. Through him Rudolf Agricola (1443/44–1485) came to be appointed to the chair of Greek there.[9] An excellent illustration of the way humanism could develop locally is provided by four generations of the Pirckheimer family of Nuremberg who all studied in Italy. Franz Pirckheimer the Elder (1388–1449), who is said to have enjoyed some kind of humanist education himself, had three sons: Franz the Younger (d. 1462), Thomas (1418–1473) and Hans (c. 1415–1492). Franz and Thomas are found studying Roman law at Pavia in 1438, and Franz was also at

[8] See K. Schädle, *Sigmund Gossembrot, ein Augsburger Kaufmann, Patrizier und Frühhumanist* (Augsburg, 1938).

[9] See K. Morneweg, *Johann von Dalberg, ein deutscher Humanist und Bischof* (Heidelberg, 1887); D. Mertens, 'Bischof Johann von Dalberg (1455–1503) und der deutsche Humanismus' in K. Andermann ed., *Ritteradel im alten Reich: die Kämmerer von Worms genannt von Dalberg* (Epfendorf, 2009), pp. 35–50. On Agricola, see F. Akkerman and A. Vanderjagt ed., *Rodolphus Agricola Phrisius (1444–1485)* (Leiden, 1988).

Padua from 1457–60. He is known to have studied Greek, but of particular importance is that we find him turning from law to ancient legal writers, which necessarily involved an engagement with history and poetry. Thomas studied in Bologna, Perugia, Pavia and Padua, obtaining his doctorate in laws at Perugia.[10] Supplementing practical studies of the law with the finer ones of the humanities, he formed an enormous collection of letters, speeches and invectives of Italian humanists (including Petrarch, GUARINO, PANORMITA, POGGIO BRACCIOLINI and LEONARDO BRUNI) and works of classical authors including Cicero, Plutarch, and Lucian.[11] The third brother, Hans, who studied at Bologna and Padua, similarly assembled a collection of 218 treatises, speeches and letters by Italian humanists in the late 1440s. He copied a Virgil manuscript and wrote a commentary on it five times the length of the original, with extensive notes on history, geography, topography and especially mythology. Hans's son

---

[10] For some indication of the number of Germans studying at Italian universities in the later Middle Ages, see G. C. Knod, *Deutsche Studenten in Bologna 1289–1562* (Berlin, 1899). See also the various studies by A. Sottili, especially his *Studenti tedeschi e umanesimo italiano nell'Università di Padova durante il Quattrocento* (Padua, 1971); *Università e cultura: studi sui rapporti italo-tedeschi nell'età dell'Umanesimo* [Bibliotheca eruditorum: internationale Bibliothek der Wissenschaften, vol. v] (Goldbach, 1993); and *Humanismus und Universitätsbesuch: die Wirkung italienischer Universitäten auf die studia humanitatis nördlich der Alpen. Renaissance Humanism and University Studies: Italian universities and their influence on the studia humanitatis in Northern Europe* [Education and Society in the Middle Ages and Renaissance, vol. xxvi] (Leiden, 2006); and further the volume S. Negruzzo ed., *Università, umanesimo, Europa: giornata di studio in ricordo di Agostino Sottili (Pavia, 18 novembre 2005)* [Fonti e studi per la storia dell'Università di Pavia, vol. xlvii] (Milan, 2007).

[11] See G. Strack, *Thomas Pirckheimer (1418–1473): Gelehrter Rat und Frühhumanist* (Husum, 2010) and id., 'Thomas Pirckheimer (1418–1473). Studien und Tätigkeitsfelder eines gelehrten Juristen und Frühhumanisten' in F. Fuchs ed., *Medizin, Jurisprudenz und Humanismus in Nürnberg um 1500* (Wiesbaden, 2010) [= *Pirckheimer Jahrbuch*, xxiv (2009/2010)], pp. 315–38.

Johann (c. 1440–1501) followed family tradition in studying law in Italy, obtaining his doctorate at Padua in 1465. His father had made him copy out the whole of Virgil when he was a teenager, between 1455 and 1457. After his return from Italy he took pains to develop the family library. Though practising as a lawyer, he expended much energy on studying the ancient poets and historians. He was one of the first Germans to have a good knowledge of Greek. But the most renowned member of this family was Johann's son, Willibald Pirckheimer (1470–1530), who, after spending seven years studying in Padua and Pavia, served as a member of the Nuremberg council for twenty-seven years and as counsellor to Emperors Maximilian I and Charles V. He became a leading figure among the group of Nuremberg humanists who included Celtis, Dürer, Hartmann Schedel, Christoph Scheurl, Lazarus Spengler, and, as a Greek scholar, he edited and translated numerous Greek, Byzantine and patristic writers, among them Plato, Aristotle, Galen, Xenophon, Lucian, Aristophanes, Demosthenes, Isocrates, Plutarch, and Gregory of Nazianzus.[12]

Rather as in England, early German humanism was primarily receptive in nature, influenced by Italians such as Petrarch, Poggio, Bruni, LORENZO VALLA and others. The elder PIER PAOLO VERGERIO had served Emperor Sigismund in various capacities from 1418 to 1437, bringing to bear his expertise in Latin and Greek.[13] Of particular importance, though, was Æneas Sylvius Piccolomini, who did not just have contacts with humanists, he actively promoted humanist

---

[12] See N. Holzberg, *Willibald Pirckheimer: Griechischer Humanismus in Deutschland* [Humanistische Bibliothek, Reihe 1, Abhandlungen, vol. xli] (Munich 1981). On Willibald Pirckheimer's library see D. Paisey, 'Searching for Pirckheimer's Books in the Remains of the Arundel Library at the Royal Society', *Pirckheimer Jahrbuch*, xxii (2007), pp. 159–218.

[13] See J. M. McManamon, *Pierpaolo Vergerio the Elder. The humanist as orator* (Tempe AZ, 1996), esp. ch. 10, and, for further discussion of his career, see pp. 150–1, 197–8, 218, 308–10, 362, and 371 below.

scholarship. In 1445 he gave an address before the Emperor and the nobility in which he spelt out the value of philosophy and poetry, jurisprudence and education generally as the basis of a new ideal of living. Æneas Sylvius had first appeared in 1432 as secretary to the Bishop of Fermo at the Council of Basel. He was admired not only for his diplomatic skills but especially for the elegance of his Latin which led to his appointment as Latin secretary to the Emperor in 1443. Altogether he spent twenty-three years in German-speaking territory, eleven of them as a central figure at the imperial chancery at Vienna and Wiener Neustadt, where Frederick had his residence. Feeling impelled to mediate the literary and rhetorical values of Italy to the north, he wrote prolifically, encouraged translations, developed personal contacts, and wrote the influential novella *Historia de duobus amantibus* (1444) of which, alongside its popularity in manuscript, at least seventy-three editions, including twenty-one in Germany alone, would be printed before 1500. His combination of history and geographical description in works such as his *Commentaries*, *De situ, ritu, moribus et conditione Germaniae descriptio* (c. 1458) and *Historia Austrialis*, an account of the doings of Emperor Frederick III (which includes a fine account of Vienna), strongly influenced German historiographical writing.[14] He promoted humanist ideas with the Emperor, amongst the nobility, the church, the universities and amongst his professional colleagues in Germany, Austria, Bohemia, Hungary and Poland. Just as Petrarch appeared to the Italians

---

[14] Editions of his historical writings include: *Pii II commentarii rerum memorabilium que temporibus suis contigerunt*, ed. A. van Heck, 2 vols (Vatican City, 1984); *Pius II: Commentaries*, ed. M. Meserve and M. Simonetta, 2 vols to date [ITRL, xii, xxix] (Cambridge, MA, 2003–7); *Enea Silvio Piccolomini: De situ, ritu, moribus et conditione Germaniae descriptio*, ed. G. Paparelli (Florence, 1949); *Aeneas Silvius de Piccolomini, Historia Austrialis. Österreichische Geschichte*, ed. J. Sarnowsky [Freiherr vom Stein Gedächtnisausgabe, series A, vol. xliv], (Darmstadt, 2005) and *Historia Austrialis*, ed. M. Wagendorfer, 2 vols [Monumenta Germaniae Historica. Scriptores rerum Germanicarum, xxiv] (Hannover, 2009).

as a teacher of new ideas, so too Æneas Sylvius seemed to the Germans to embody new ideas coupled with an imported elegance of style and diction.

Æneas Sylvius was something of an exception among Italians in Germany. Whereas others may have generally felt themselves to be Roman citizens in barbaric lands,[15] he was prepared to recognise merit wherever it was found. Thus he complimented Gregor Heimburg (d. 1472), town clerk of Nuremberg and a pupil of Lorenzo Valla, on having brought eloquence from Italy to Germany just as once Cicero had brought it from the Greeks to the Romans.[16] Similarly he complimented Niklas von Wyle (c. 1410–1478/79), town clerk of Reutlingen and translator of his *Historia de duobus amantibus*, on his humanistic hand. Niklas von Wyle was so appreciative of Ciceronian style that he encouraged the scribes working under him to model their German on Latin style in the 1470s.[17]

Æneas Sylvius apart, the Germans often perceived Italian humanists to be arrogant, and this only served to harden prejudices against them. Rudolf Agricola, in a remark that neatly encapsulates how an insult can be used both to submerge a compliment and to serve as a goad to self-improvement, had expostulated:

> Summam in spem adducor, fore aliquando, ut priscam insolenti Italiae et propemodum occupatam benedicendi gloriam

---

[15] Compare Weiss's interpretation of the experiences of men like Poggio Bracciolini and PIETRO DEL MONTE in England: Weiss[4], p. 45.

[16] Heimburg, who had got to know Æneas Sylvius at Basel, later became locked in controversy with him. See R. Kemper, *Gregor Heimburgs Manifest in der Auseinandersetzung mit Pius II* (Mannheim, 1984), and K. Stadtwald, *Roman Popes and German Patriots* (Geneva, 1996).

[17] J. L. Flood, 'Niklas von Wyle' in J. Hardin and M. Reinhart ed., *German Writers of the Renaissance 1280–1580* [Dictionary of Literary Biography, clxxix] (Detroit, 1997), pp. 332–37. On Niklas' German translation of the *Historia de duobus amantibus* see E. J. Morrall ed., *Aeneas Silvius Piccolomini (Pius II) and Niklas von Wyle: the tale of two lovers, Eurialus and Lucretia* (Amsterdam, 1988).

extorqueamus vindicemusque nos, et ab ignominia qua nos barbaros indoctosque et elingues, et si quid est his incultius, esse nos jactitant, exsolvamus, futuramque tam doctam et literatam Germaniam nostram ut non Latinius vel ipsum sit Latium.[18]

I sincerely hope that the time will come when we shall succeed in wresting from the conceited Italians their long-held reputation for eloquence which they have in a manner of speaking taken to themselves, lay claim to it on our own account and free ourselves from the reproach of being called ignorant and inarticulate barbarians or worse; and that our Germany may rise so high in learning and literature that Latium itself shall not speak better Latin.

There was in any case a long history of tension and antagonism between Germans and Italians, and this only spurred the Germans on to imitate and emulate Italian achievements, encouraged nationalistic sentiments among them, and in particular provoked them to point out the deficiencies and corruption within the Roman Church, which would culminate in Luther's break with Rome in the 1520s.[19]

Some of these issues can be particularly well observed in the case of Conrad Celtis. The importance of Æneas Sylvius' *De situ ... Germaniae descriptio* for the development of German historiography has already been mentioned. Even more momentous was the discovery of Tacitus' *Germania*. Indeed, one thing that is striking about Weiss's account of humanism in England is the apparent absence here of any interest in

---

[18] Rudolphus Agricola, *Lucubrationes*, ed. Alardus Amstelredamus (Cologne: J. Gymnich, 1539), p. 178.

[19] An early instance is found in the ninth-century Kassel glosses where the sentence 'Stulti sunt Romani, sapienti sunt Paioari, modica est sapientia in Romana, plus habent stultitia quam sapientia' is given in Old High German translation as 'Tole sint Uualhā, spāhe sint Peigira; luzīc ist spāhi in Uualhum, mēra hapēnt tolaheitī denne spahī' (The Romans [= Italians] are stupid, the Bavarians are wise; there is little wisdom among the Romans, they have more stupidity than wisdom). See W. Braune, *Althochdeutsches Lesebuch*, 15th edn, ed. E. A. Ebbinghaus (Tübingen, 1969), p. 9. For examples from a later period see J. L. Flood, 'Nationalistic currents in early German typography', *The Library*, 6th ser., xv (1993), pp. 125–41.

Tacitus – Weiss mentions him only once *en passant*, in connexion with a manuscript of his *Dialogus de oratoribus* in the library of John Tiptoft, Earl of Worcester.[20] For Germany, and for Celtis in particular, the discovery of the *Germania* in the mid-fifteenth century was of seminal significance.

It may be helpful briefly to recall the history of the discovery of the *Germania*. In November 1425 Poggio Bracciolini wrote to Niccolò Niccoli of the discovery in a German monastery of *aliqua volumina* including *aliqua opera Cornelii Taciti nobis ignota*, 'some works of Cornelius Tacitus unknown to us'.[21] By 1431 Niccolò was able to catalogue as at the imperial abbey at Hersfeld (midway between Kassel and Fulda) a book comprising *Germania*, *Agricola* and other texts. A manuscript answering to this description was seen by PIER CANDIDO DECEMBRIO at Rome in 1455, it apparently having been brought from Germany that year.[22] This, the Codex Hersfeldensis, had perhaps been written at Fulda c. 830–850, possibly during the abbacy of the great scholar Hrabanus Maurus. However, the part containing the *Germania* no longer survives; the text is now known to us only through several fifteenth-century copies of which a manuscript in the Vatican may be the closest to the original.[23] From the early 1470s on, the *Germania* came out regularly in print, both in collected editions of Tacitus' works (the earliest seems to have

---

[20] Now London: British Library, MS. Harl. 2639. In addition, Tiptoft owned Oxford: Jesus College, MS. 109 (Tacitus' *Historiae*): see Weiss[4], p. 180.

[21] Poggio Bracciolini, *Lettere*, ed. Helene Harth, 3 vols (Florence, 1984–87), i, p. 166.

[22] See E. Koestermann ed., *P. Cornelii Taciti libri qui supersunt*, ii/2: *Germania, Agricola, Dialogus de oratoribus* (Leipzig, 1962), and *T&T*, pp. 410–11.

[23] BAV, MS. Vat. lat. 1862. Thus, at any rate, R. Much, *Die Germania des Tacitus*, 2nd edn, revised by R. Kienast (Heidelberg, 1959), p. xiv. The Codex Aesinus (Rome: Biblioteca Nazionale Centrale, MS. Vitt. Eman. 1631), so known as it is from the library of Count Aurelio Guglielmo Balleani at Iesi, is said to be oldest surviving copy directly made from the Codex Hersfeldensis.

been Vindelinus de Spira's Venice edition of c. 1471–2 or c. 1473), coupled with the works of Diodorus Siculus (at Bologna in 1472 and in two Venice editions in 1476/77 and 1481), and also on its own.[24] The two earliest separate editions are those printed in Nuremberg by Friedrich Creussner in 1473–74 and the Rome edition, perhaps printed by Johannes Schurener de Bopardia, which is variously dated between 'about 1473' and 'about 1477'.[25] It is difficult to determine what precise role these early editions played in the reception of Tacitus in Germany. Creussner's seems to have had precious little impact; indeed, as we shall see, it was apparently through encountering various Italian humanists' mentions of the *Germania* that Germans first began to take notice of it. The first really significant edition was the one prepared by Conrad Celtis under the title *De origine et situ Germanorum*, printed by Johann Winterburg at Vienna around or shortly before 1500.[26] Celtis was the first person to give lectures on the subject at the University of Vienna that year. His contribution to the exploration of Germany's past laid the foundation of historical research in the early modern period, notably influencing Beatus Rhenanus (1485–1547), who himself produced an edition of the *Germania* (Basel: Froben, 1519) and would write the standard work on early German history, *Rerum Germanicarum libri tres* (1531).[27] The earliest

---

[24] These are, respectively, ISTC, nos it00006000, id00210000, id00211000, and id00212000.

[25] These are, respectively, ISTC, nos it00010000 and it00009000.

[26] ISTC, no. it0001500. A second Vienna edition was printed by Johannes Singriener for Leonhart Alantsee in January 1515, after Celtis' death. Others were published at Leipzig in 1502 and 1509, the latter prepared by Johannes Aesticampianus who also lectured on Tacitus. For a summary list of early and modern editions see M. Landfester ed., *Geschichte der antiken Texte. Autoren- und Werklexikon* [Der neue Pauly. Supplement 2] (Stuttgart, 2007), pp. 573–77.

[27] See J. S. Hirstein, *Tacitus' 'Germania' and Beatus Rhenanus, 1485– 1547: a study of the editorial and exegetical contribution of a sixteenth century scholar* (Frankfurt am Main, 1995), and F. Mundt, *Beatus*

translation of the *Germania* into German was made by the Lutheran preacher Johann Eberlin von Günzburg (c. 1470–1533) who probably worked from Beatus Rhenanus' 1519 edition.[28] Another early translation was made by Jakob Moltzer (Micyllus, 1503–1558) and published at Mainz in 1535.

Whatever Tacitus' own aim in writing the *Germania* may have been – whether it was intended as an excursus supplementing his histories, or whether he was holding up a mirror to his contemporaries in which the Romans might perceive the contrast between the purity and simplicity of the German tribes' life-style with the luxury and corruption of their own – among the German humanists the discovery of the *Germania* engendered an enormous sense of pride in the Germans with their growing national awareness and at the same time confirmed their traditional prejudices.[29] This was

    Rhenanus: *Rerum Germanicarum libri tres (1531). Ausgabe, Übersetzung, Studien* (Tübingen, 2008).

[28] See A. Masser ed., *Johann Eberlin von Günzburg, Ein zamengelesen buochlin von der Teutschen Nation gelegenheit, Sitten vnd gebrauche, durch Cornelium Tacitum vnd etliche andere verzeichnet (1526)* (Innsbruck, 1986). Since Eberlin's translation seems never to have progressed beyond a draft, Hans Rupprich's claim (*Die deutsche Literatur vom späten Mittelalter bis zum Barock. 2. Teil: Das Zeitalter der Reformation, 1520–1570* (Munich, 1973), p. 122) that it made the *Germania* 'widely known' is totally unfounded.

[29] The countless studies of the reception and long-term influence of Tacitus' *Germania* in Germany include: P. Joachimsen, 'Tacitus im deutschen Humanismus', *Neue Jahrbücher für das klassische Altertum, Geschichte und deutsche Literatur*, xiv (1911), pp. 697–717; H. Tiedemann, *Tacitus und das Nationalbewußtsein der deutschen Humanisten Ende des 15. und Anfang des 16. Jahrhunderts* (Berlin, 1913); R. Kuehnemund, *Arminius or the Rise of a National Symbol in Literature* (Chapel Hill, NC, 1953); E.-L. Etter, *Tacitus in der Geistesgeschichte des 16. und 17. Jahrhunderts* (Basel, 1966); K. von See, *Deutsche Germanen-Ideologie vom Humanismus bis zur Gegenwart* (Frankfurt am Main, 1970); J. Ridé, *L'Image du Germain dans la pensée et la littérature allemandes: de la redécouverte de Tacite à la fin du XVIe siècle. Contribution à l'étude de la genèse d'un mythe* (Paris, 1977); L. Krapf, *Germanenmythus und Reichsideologie. Frühhumanistische Rezeptionsweisen in der taciteischen 'Germania'* (Tübingen, 1979); M. Fuhrmann,

bolstered still further by pride in the German invention of printing at about the same time. This technological advance naturally gave a tremendous boost to humanist endeavours, reinforcing still further the notion of humanism as a movement characterized by the primacy of the book, not only in Germany but throughout fifteenth-century Europe. It is worth remembering that it was German printers who introduced the technology everywhere: in Italy, France, Spain, Scandinavia, indeed everywhere except England (but even William Caxton learnt the technique in Cologne).[30] Both these themes, the pride in German achievements in culture and

---

Brechungen: Wirkungsgeschichtliche Studien zur antik-europäischen Bildungstradition (Stuttgart, 1982), pp. 113–28 ('Die Germania des Tacitus und das deutsche Nationalbewußtsein'); D. R. Kelly, '*Tacitus Noster*: The *Germania* in the Renaissance and Reformation' in T. J. Luce and A. J. Woodman ed., *Tacitus and the Tacitean Tradition* (Princeton, 1993), pp. 152–67; H. Münkler et al. ed., *Nationenbildung. Die Nationalisierung Europas im Diskurs humanistischer Intellektueller in Italien und Deutschland* (Berlin, 1998); D. Mertens, 'Die Instrumentalisierung der "Germania" des Tacitus durch die deutschen Humanisten' in H. Beck et al. ed., *Zur Geschichte der Gleichung "germanisch–deutsch". Sprache und Namen, Geschichte und Institutionen* [Reallexikon der germanischen Altertumskunde, Ergänzungsbände, xxxiv] (Berlin, 2004), pp. 37–101; U. Goerlitz, *Literarische Konstruktion (vor-)nationaler Identität seit dem 'Annolied'* (Berlin, 2007), and C. B. Krebs, 'A dangerous book: The reception of Tacitus' *Germania*' in A. J. Woodman ed., *The Cambridge Companion to Tacitus* (Cambridge, 2010), pp. 280–99.

[30] For a useful (if somewhat dated) survey see F. Geldner, *Die deutschen Inkunabeldrucker*, 2 vols (Stuttgart, 1968–70), the first volume of which is devoted to German printers in Germany and the second to German printers in other countries. The rapid growth of printing led to the emergence of the Frankfurt book fair by the end of the fifteenth century as the centre of the international book trade; see J. L. Flood, '*Omnium totius orbis emporiorum compendium*: The Frankfurt Fair in the Early Modern Period' in R. Myers, M. Harris and G. Mandelbrote ed., *Fairs, Markets and the Itinerant Book Trade* (London, 2007), pp. 1–42 [repr. in I. Gadd ed., *The History of the Book in the West*, vol. II: *1455–1700* (Farnham, 2010), pp. 321–62].

technology, come together in Celtis, dubbed 'the German archhumanist'.[31]

Conrad Celtis, whose German name was Conrad Bickel, was born the son of a wine-grower at Wipfeld in Franconia on 1 February 1459. He died at Vienna on 4 February 1508 and was buried in St Stephen's Cathedral. After studying at Cologne, Heidelberg, Erfurt, Rostock and Leipzig, he went to Italy where he came under the influence of POMPONIUS LAETUS at Rome, heard lectures on Homer at Bologna, encountered the poetry of Tito Vespasiano Strozzi at Ferrara, and experienced court festivals with their theatrical interludes, all of which influenced the direction of his own future work. Returning from Italy via Hungary, he first spent a couple of years at Cracow, improving his knowledge of mathematics and astronomy, before moving to Ingolstadt, where in his celebrated inaugural lecture on 31 August 1492 he outlined his plans for a synthesis of poetics, rhetoric, philosophy, historiography, geography, mathematics and music, all this against a background of a strongly patriotic, national, political system of ideas.[32] He envisioned a Roman Empire of the German Nation in cultural terms.

The Germans soon came to identify themselves with Tacitus' *Germani* and the Italians with his *Romani*, though in fact it was not the Germans but rather Italian humanists who had established this equation. Perhaps the first to invoke a continuum between the Germanic tribes of old and the contemporary Germans was GIOVANNI ANTONIO CAMPANO, bishop of Teramo, who, having been charged by the Papal

---

[31] 'Der deutsche Erzhumanist' – the phrase was coined by David Friedrich Strauß. See F. von Bezold, *Konrad Celtis, 'der deutsche Erzhumanist'* (Darmstadt, 1959) [originally published in *Historische Zeitschrift*, xlix (1883), 1–45]; L. W. Spitz, *Conrad Celtis: the German Arch-Humanist* (Cambridge, MA, 1957).

[32] On his time in Cracow, see see pp. 121-2, 131, 138-40 below. For a full discussion of his system of ideas, see J. Robert, *Konrad Celtis und das Projekt der deutschen Dichtung. Studien zur humanistischen Konstitution von Poetik, Philosophie, Nation und Ich* (Tübingen, 2003).

Legate with the task of encouraging the German princes to counter the growing danger from the Turks, prepared an address for the Imperial Diet at Regensburg in 1471 in which he sought to shame the princes into action by reminding them of how, according to Tacitus, the Germans had always been a courageous people. He concluded:

> Imploro & appello te Cesar & vos principes oro: per gloriosissimas umbras patrum vestrorum: erigite mentem intendite nobis dum est tempus: Facite ut Germania Germania sit et eos nunc habent propugnatores quos olim habuit.[33]
>
> I implore and appeal to you, Emperor, and I beg you princes, for the sake of the most glorious shades of your forefathers, turn your mind and listen to us while there is time. Act so that Germany may be Germany and that it might have now the warriors that it used to have.

Although the German princes for whom the speech was intended never heard it since it was not actually delivered (though it was later printed), it came to the attention of German humanists, foremost amongst them Celtis, as also Jakob Wimpheling, Heinrich Bebel and others. Thus from this equating of 'Germanic' with 'German' there arose the notion of the 'German nation' which depended on the contrast between 'then' and 'now', a great and glorious past contrasting with an unease about the political, social and moral circumstances of the present.

For an understanding of Celtis' attitude to the Italians his letter of 1491 to the Ingolstadt law professor Sixtus Tucher von Simmelsdorf (1459–1507) is instructive. Celtis was sending him some of his own poems and wrote:

---

[33] Johannes Antonius Campanus, *Oratio ad principes Germanorum contra Turcos in conventu Ratisponensi anno 1471 habita* (Rome: Stephan Plannck, before 1487) [ISTC, no. ic00075000], fol. 12ʳ. On this text see J. Blusch, 'Zur Rezeption der Germania des Tacitus bei Gianantonio Campano und Enea Silvio Piccolomini', *Humanistica Lovaniensia*, xxxii (1983), pp. 75–106, and, more generally, Mertens, 'Die Instrumentalisierung der "Germania"'.

Ipse nostra legens non ad ingenii ostentationem missa putabis, quandoquidem incocta adhuc et cruda quaedam sint, longam limam et amicorum censuram exposcentia, sed ut intelligeres me nulli parcere vigiliis, ut aliquid excuderem, quod, etsi Italicis ingeniis impar foret, Germanos tamen nostros, qui me doctrina et ingenio et multum haec duo fulcientibus opibus praestarent, impellerem expergefaceremque, quo Itali in suam gloriam effulsissimi fateri cogerentur non solum Rhomanum imperium et arma, sed et litterarum splendorem ad Germanos commigrasse.[34]

When you read my products you will not gain the impression that I am sending them to you as proud evidence of my abilities for they are the work of a mere beginner that need to be refined and improved by friends, but so that you can see that I am striving to produce something that, even though it does not match the achievements of the Italians, yet will spur on and stimulate our Germans who exceed me in learning and intellectual ability so that the Italians who are so wrapped up in their own fame finally admit that not only Roman rule and military might but also the splendour of its learning have passed to the Germans.

Celtis sought to counter the overweening arrogance of the Italians by declaring that not only were the Germans the legitimate heirs of Rome by virtue of the fact that the imperial dignity had passed to them but also by asserting that their ancestors had been civilized and had instituted religion not thanks to the Romans but – bizarrely – thanks to the Celtic druids whom the Romans had driven out of Gaul.[35]

Whenever Celtis speaks of Italy it is now half-admiringly, now half-jealously. We see this again in his Ingolstadt inaugural address in 1492, directed to the *nobiles viri et adolescentes generosi [...] ad quos avita virtute et Germano illo invicto robore Italiae imperium commigravit* (the 'distinguished men and well-born youths, to whom by virtue of the courage of [their] ancestors and the unconquerable strength of Germany

---

[34] H. Rupprich, *Der Briefwechsel des Konrad Celtis* (Munich, 1934), p. 29.

[35] See W. Goez, *Translatio imperii* (Tübingen, 1958). On Celtis' view of the druids see G. M. Müller, *Die 'Germania generalis' des Conrad Celtis* (Tübingen, 2001), pp. 418–24.

the Italian empire [had] passed', §25).³⁶ His aim was to inspire his audience to fame and 'virtue' which, he said, was to be found at the fountainhead of philosophy and eloquence (§17). By philosophy Celtis meant not narrow speculation but a broader generic concept embracing the theory and practice of the arts and sciences. Learning and literature (i.e. ancient literature) were aids to the understanding of philosophy, virtue the practical living of it, eloquence its outward expression, immortal fame its ultimate reward. He, and like-minded humanists, were urging a system of secular ethics independent of the Church – here, indeed, though Celtis could not be aware of it, lay the seeds of the Reformation's demand for direct interpretation of the Scriptures and its rejection of the traditions of the Church and, ultimately, of the modern debate about science versus religion. For Celtis philosophy was the foundation of statecraft: it was small wonder that Germany's condition was so lamentable when so little attention was paid to true philosophy and learning. The Germans, he believed, bore a particular responsibility because the Holy Roman Empire was the heir of ancient Rome (§25, 43, 78); it was their duty to maintain the cultural traditions of the past: *Ita et vos accepto Italorum imperio exuta foeda barbarie Romanarum artium affectatores esse debebitis* ('In the same way you who have taken over the empire of the Italians should cast off repulsive barbarism and seek to acquire Roman culture', §29). He attributed 'the ever-flourishing condition of Italy' (*semper florentis Italiae causam*) solely to the fact that 'they surpass us in no blessing other than the love of literature and its cultivation (*quod illi nos non alia felicitate quam litterarum amore et earum studio antecedunt*). Thus it was that the Italians could overawe other nations as if by force of arms, and win their admiration for their genius and industry (§71, 72).

---

³⁶ For the following account I am heavily indebted to the edition, translation and commentary in L. Forster, *Selections from Conrad Celtis* (Cambridge, 1948; repr. 2011), pp. 36–65 and 96–111. An old, but still useful, account of humanism at Ingolstadt is G. Bauch, *Die Anfänge des Humanismus in Ingolstadt* (Munich, 1901).

But this admiration for Italian achievements was coupled with severe criticism (§6):

> Ita nos Italicus luxus corrupit et saeva in extorquendo argento pernicioso crudelitas, ut plane sanctius et sacrius fuisset nos agere rudi illa et silvestri vita, dum inter continentiae fines vivebamus, quam tot gulae et luxus instrumenta, quibus nihil unquam satis est, invexisse peregrinosque mores induisse.

> To such an extent are we corrupted by Italian sensuality and by fierce cruelty in exacting filthy lucre, that it would have been far more holy and reverent for us to practise that rude and rustic life of old, living within the bounds of self-control, than to have imported the paraphernalia of sensuality and greed which are never sated, and to have adopted foreign customs.

Salvation lay in the Germans' own hands if only they could see it. Their strength lay in the Holy Roman Empire which was their direct link with the ancient world. They should not forget 'that unconquerable strength' of their ancestors through which they had inherited 'the Italian empire' (§25). Celtis repudiated historians' disparagement of 'barbarian' Germans. He continued:

> [...] tantum potuit vetus et inexpiabile inter nos odium et antiqua discordia numinum, quam nisi provida natura Alpibus et elatis in sidera scopulis diremisset, a mutuis caedibus pro hostili utrinque spiritu nunquam temperaretur.

> Such has been the power of that long-standing and irreconcilable hatred between the protecting deities of our two nations, which would, in view of the hostile spirit on both sides, inevitably have led to mutual slaughter, had not prudent Nature separated us by the Alps and by rocks towering to the stars (§37).

This is a direct reference to Petrarch who had written:

> Ben provide Natura al nostro stato
> Quando de l'Alpi schermo
> Pose fra noi e la tedesca rabbia.[37]

---

[37] In the canzone 'Italia mia', in Francesco Petrarca, *Canzoniere*, ed. U. Dotti, 2 vols (Rome, 2004), ii, p. 387, ll. 33–5. On the Italians' view

> Nature dealt well by our realm when she placed the barrier of the Alps between ourselves and the frenzy of the Germans.

It is precisely the *tedesca rabbia*, the *furor teutonicus*, that Celtis wishes to see revived. He envisaged a strong, united Germany worthy of its historical roots. Thus he appealed to his Ingolstadt audience:

> Induite veteres illos animos, viri Germani, quibus totiens Romanis terrori et formidini fuistis, et ad angulos Germaniae oculos convertite limitesque eius laceros et distractos colligite!

> Assume, O men of Germany, that ancient spirit of yours, with which you so often confounded and terrified the Romans, and turn your eyes to the frontiers of Germany; collect together her torn and broken territories! (§41)

But this reassumption of the 'ancient spirit' requires the cultivation of philosophy and letters; on this will depend the glory and prestige of Germany in the political as well as the cultural sphere. This necessitated formation of a national consciousness through study of German history, geography and antiquities. It should, he said, be

> super omnem impudentiam regionis nostrae et terrae nescire situm, sidera, flumina, montes, antiquitates, nationes, denique quae peregrini homines de nobis ita scite collegere

> the height of shame to be ignorant of the topography, the climate, the rivers, the mountains, the antiquities and the peoples of our own region and our own country, in short all those facts which foreigners have so cleverly collected concerning us (§31)

– among the 'foreigners' first and foremost Tacitus was meant. The lack of German historiography inevitably meant that the events of the past were recorded only by foreign chroniclers, notably Italians, who as often as not were bent on decrying German achievements. Celtis was thinking in particular of MARCANTONIO SABELLICO, author of *Historiae rerum Venetarum ab urbe condita libri xxiii* (Venice, 1487), whom

of the Germans see P. Amelung, *Das Bild der Deutschen in der Literatur der italienischen Renaissance, 1400–1559* (Munich, 1964).

he had met in Venice. The Venetians apparently considered German princes barbarians.

It was precisely as part of this historiographical programme that Celtis set about editing Tacitus' *Germania* as a priceless source of German history, geography and antiquities to boost national consciousness and German self-confidence, for the 'ancient spirit' Celtis wished to see revived was just what Tacitus had praised and Petrarch abhorred. The *Germania* – a unique document among Roman writing, focusing as it does on a foreign people – answered many of Celtis' needs, for it described the boundaries of Germania and the nature of the land (c. 1–5), aspects of public (c. 6–15) and private life (c. 16–27), and finally the individual tribes (c. 28–46). Other historiographical works Celtis undertook included his *Norimberga*, an account of Nuremberg, which gives us just a taste of what his planned, but unrealised, *Germania illustrata* would have been like – the *Germania illustrata* was intended to be a direct counterpart to FLAVIO BIONDO's *Italia illustrata*, written in the early 1450s and printed in 1474.[38] Celtis' *Germania generalis*, issued in 1500 and intended as a complement to and corrective of Tacitus' *Germania*, was a poetic draft of the whole plan.[39] He also edited one of the principal monuments of medieval drama, the Latin plays of the Benedictine nun Hrotswitha of Gandersheim (c. 935–c. 1002) (whom he calls 'the German Sappho'), to counter the

---

[38] On the *Norimberga* see A. Werminghoff, *Conrad Celtis und sein Buch über Nürnberg* (Freiburg im Breisgau, 1921).

[39] For an exhaustive study of this work see Müller, *Die 'Germania generalis' des Conrad Celtis*. On the *Germania generalis* as a corrective to Tacitus see P. Luh, *Kaiser Maximilian gewidmet: die unvollendete Werkausgabe des Conrad Celtis und ihre Holzschnitte* (Frankfurt am Main, 2001), pp. 407–11. Johann Eberlin, the first translator of the *Germania*, similarly sought to correct Tacitus by omitting anything that reflected badly on the Germans, for example, the reference in c. 4 to their fierce wild eyes and red hair and the claim that they cannot sustain hard work, and the assertion in c. 20 that the children run around naked and dirty. See Masser ed., *Johann Eberlin von Günzburg*, p. 19.

claims of the 'conceited' Italians that Italy was the only country favoured by the Muses.[40] A further undertaking to demonstrate German achievements was his edition, completed shortly before his death, of the Latin epic *Ligurinus* by the Cistercian Gunther of Pairis (in Alsace), written in 1186–7, based on Otto of Freising's *Gesta Friderici I. Imperatoris* and describing the deeds of Frederick I Barbarossa from his accession in 1152 up to 1160. Celtis had discovered the manuscript in the Franconian monastery of Ebrach, near Bamberg, in (probably) 1502 and arranged publication through his friends at Augsburg.[41] The preface tells us how one of Celtis' reasons for publishing it was *amor patriae*, 'the love of his homeland'. According to the colophon of the 1507 edition, printed by Erhard Oeglin, the work was

> per vniversam Germaniam & eius publici gymnasia iam notus: & iuuentuti germanicae ad legendum & enarrrandum prebitus primo Vienne per C. C. Friburgi per Hieronimum Baldung: Dubingi per Henricum Bebelium Ingolstadi per Iacobum Philomusum Lipsi per Hermannum Bostium [Boscium] qui in praedictis gymnasiis publico stipendio Romanas litteras foeliciter profitentur,

> already known throughout Germany and her universities and given to the youth of Germany through lectures and interpretations, first at Vienna by C[onrad] C[eltis], in Freiburg by Hieronymus Baldung, in Tübingen by Heinrich Bebel, in Ingolstadt by Jacob [Locher] Philomusus and in Leipzig by Hermann Buschius who are successfully teaching Latin on a professional basis at these universities,

a remark which well illustrates how Celtis' example inspired others. Thus at Augsburg the patrician Conrad Peutinger collected Roman inscriptions as a source of information about

---

[40] *Opera Hrosvite illustris virginis et monialis Germane Gente Saxonica orte nuper a Conrado Celte inventa* (Nuremberg, 1501). See E. H. Zeydel, 'The reception of Hrotsvitha by the German humanists after 1493', *Journal of English and Germanic Philology*, xliv (1945), pp. 239–49. See also Rupprich, *Briefwechsel*, pp. 468–71.

[41] On this see F. P. Knapp (ed.), *Der 'Ligurinus' des Gunther von Pairis. In Abbildung des Erstdrucks von 1507* (Göppingen, 1982).

the ancient Germans, and owned the road map of the ancient world, now known as the *Tabula Peutingeriana*, which Celtis himself had discovered at Worms and bequeathed to Peutinger in his will.[42] Celtis and Peutinger were quickly established as models; they are respected as prime authorities already in *Germaniae exegesis* (Hagenau, 1518), the twelve-book survey of Germany by Franciscus Irenicus (1494/5–1553). Other writers indelibly influenced by Celtis were Beatus Rhenanus, already mentioned, and Ulrich von Hutten (1488–1523) who, in his dialogue *Arminius* (written in the early 1520s, printed in 1529), drew on Tacitus and established Arminius (c. 16 B.C. – 21 A.D.) as a national hero, fighting for German freedom against Roman repression (interpreted on the threshold of the Reformation as the tyranny of the Papacy). Celtis' interest in exploring Germany's past encouraged many others, including Heinrich Bebel (1472–1518), author of *Oratio ad regem Maximilianum de laudibus et amplitudine Germaniae* (Pforzheim, 1504), the Bavarian chronicler Johannes Turmair Aventinus (1477–1534), author of *Annales ducum Boiariae* (published 1554, and in German as *Bayerische Chronik* in 1556), the Swiss humanist Joachim von Watt (Vadianus) (1484–1551), and the Hebrew scholar Sebastian Münster (1488–1552), compiler of the hugely successful *Cosmographia*.[43]

---

[42] On Peutinger's interest in Roman epigraphy see M. Ott, 'Konrad Peutinger und die Inschriften des römischen Augsburg' in G. M. Müller ed., *Humanismus und Renaissance in Augsburg* (Berlin, 2010), pp. 275–89. The *Tabula Peutingeriana* is now ÖNB, MS. 324; see R. J. A. Talbert, *Rome's World: the Peutinger Map reconsidered* (Cambridge, 2010). For Peutinger's extensive library see H.-J. Künast and H. Zäh, *Die Bibliothek Konrad Peutingers. Edition der historischen Kataloge und Rekonstruktion der Bestände*, 2 vols (Tübingen, 2003–5).

[43] On Bebel, see H. Tiedemann, *Tacitus und das Nationalbewußtsein der deutschen Humanisten Ende des 15. und Anfang des 16. Jahrhunderts* (Berlin, 1913); on Aventinus, G. Strauss, *Historian of an Age of Crisis: the life and work of Johannes Aventinus 1477–1534* (Cambridge, MA, 1963), and K. Bosl, 'Johann Turmair, gen. Aventinus aus Abensberg in seiner Zeit', *Zeitschrift für bayerische Landesgeschichte*, xl (1977), pp.

Yet Celtis was not a particularly original thinker; his forte was networking. When he dedicated his *Ars versificandi et carminum* (Leipzig, 1486) to Frederick the Wise (1463–1525), the youthful Elector of Saxony, the latter commended him to the Emperor, Frederick III, who laureated him as a poet at Nuremberg in April 1487.[44] Celtis was exceedingly proud of this: in his autograph collection of letters, he arranged the contents according to the years of his laureateship: *Primus annus laureae ... Quartus decimus annus laureae.*[45] All the early laureates had been Italians and indeed Petrarch, who had re-established the tradition of laureation in 1341 and who scorned the very notion that poets might be found anywhere other than in Italy, was – like Boccaccio – appalled when the German Emperor Charles IV laureated Zanobi da Strada at Pisa in 1355.[46] The first man created *poeta laureatus* on German soil had been an Italian, none other than Æneas Sylvius Piccolomini, at Frankfurt in 1442. Now the fact that a German, Celtis, wore the laurel (as the first of, eventually, many hundreds) signalled to him and to the world that German scholarship had 'arrived'. His new-found status stood him in good stead when in 1493 Frederick III died and was

325–40; on Vadianus, E. Götzinger, *Joachim Vadian, der Reformator und Geschichtsschreiber von St. Gallen* (Halle, 1895); and on Münster, see M. McLean, *The 'Cosmographia' of Sebastian Münster: describing the world in the Reformation* (Aldershot, 2007).

[44] For the letter of dedication see Rupprich, *Briefwechsel*, p. 1. For his praise of Frederick III for the grant of the laurel see Celtis' *Proseuticum ad divum Fridericum tertium pro laurea Appollinari* (Nuremberg: Friedrich Creussner [after 25 April 1487]) [ISTC, no. ic00373000].

[45] Rupprich, *Briefwechsel*, pp. vi–vii. Celtis' letters are in ÖNB, MS. 3448.

[46] Petrarch, *Opera quae extant omnia* (Basel: S. Henricpetri, 1581), p. 1087: 'Ante alios Coenobius noster uir doctus, & quem Ausonijs armatum Musis, barbarica nuper laurus ornauit, deque nostris ingenijs, mirum dictu, iudex, censorque Germanicus ferre sententiam non expauit.' For details, see J. L. Flood, *Poets Laureate in the Holy Roman Empire: a bio-bibliographical handbook*, 4 vols (Berlin, 2006), i, pp. lxxiii–lxxiv.

succeeded by Maximilian I. In 1492 Celtis dedicated his *Epitoma in utramque Ciceronis Rhetoricam* (Ingolstadt, 1492) to Maximilian, whom he saw as a symbolic focus for his own aspirations.[47] Maximilian, who was exactly the same age as Celtis, was receptive to his ideas and later involved him in many of his grandiose plans, summoning him on 7 March 1497 to be Professor of Eloquence and Poetry at Vienna. When Celtis arrived there in September 1497, he was welcomed by the historian and physician Johannes Cuspinian (1473–1529) who declared that, just as Aesculapius was supposed to have swum up the Tiber in the form of a serpent to deliver Rome from the plague, so now Celtis had arrived down the Danube to put an end to barbarism.[48] One of Celtis' first acts as professor was to give his lectures on the *Germania* and publish his edition of it.

One of the most curious joint enterprises involving Maximilian and Celtis was the Collegium poetarum et mathematicorum at Vienna, which the Emperor announced his intention of establishing on 31 October 1501. It was in effect a fifth faculty beside the traditional ones of Theology, Law, Medicine, and Philosophy, and served the purpose of underlining the independence of poetry as a discipline. It was precisely through the laureation of poets by the Emperor that Poetry itself had acquired its status as a quasi-imperial discipline. The college, inaugurated on Celtis' forty-third birthday, was to comprise four professors, one each for Poetry and Rhetoric and two for Mathematics, and the Professor of Poetry – Celtis himself – was to be the principal of the whole, with the right to laureate poets on behalf of the Emperor.[49] The designation and constitution of the institution reflect the two principal concerns of German humanism: on the one hand language and style, on the other mathematics and science. Mathematical and scientific studies at Vienna were

---

[47] For the dedication see Rupprich, *Briefwechsel*, pp. 42–45.
[48] See Cuspinian's poem, cited in Rupprich, *Briefwechsel*, pp. 302–3.
[49] See Flood, *Poets Laureate in the Holy Roman Empire*, i, pp. xcii–c.

already very well established.⁵⁰ Building on the foundations laid by the theologian and astronomer Heinrich von Langenstein (1325–1397), who had spent the years 1360–82 at the University of Paris and later played a major role in reorganising the University of Vienna, and the mathematician Johann von Gmunden (c. 1384–1442)⁵¹, Georg von Peuerbach (1423–1461), who would be appointed court astronomer to Emperor Frederick III, had begun lecturing on the Latin classics and on mathematics at Vienna in 1454.⁵² Out of these lectures grew his *Theoricae novae planetarum*, which was edited by his pupil and friend Johannes Regiomontanus (Johnnes Müller from Königsberg, 1436–1476) in 1473 and went through fifty-six editions in the next two hundred years. Regiomontanus continued Peuerbach's work, seeing his edition of Ptolemy's *Epitoma Almagesti* through the press and himself editing various ancient mathematicians. He was in touch with many leading scholars of the age, especially in Italy. The *Epitoma Almagesti* was a work that Copernicus and Galileo would still be studying. After Peuerbach died in 1461 Regiomontanus, whose interests included the application of mathematics for research and discovery and for artistic theory too, left Vienna, and went to Italy at the invitation of Cardinal Bessarion before spending four years at the court of Matthias Corvinus, King of Hungary.⁵³ In 1471 he moved to Nuremberg where the merchant Bernhard Walther (1430–1504) gave him an observatory, a workshop for building scientific instruments (Regiomontanus improved the astrolabe) and a printing shop. In 1475 he died at Rome where he had gone to advise Pope Sixtus IV on calendar

---

⁵⁰ For humanism at Vienna, see G. Bauch, *Die Rezeption des Humanismus in Wien* (Breslau, 1903).

⁵¹ See R. Simek and K. Chlench ed., *Johannes von Gmunden (ca. 1384–1442), Astronom und Mathematiker* (Vienna, 2006).

⁵² See F. Samhaber, *Höhepunkte mittelalterlicher Astronomie. Georg von Peuerbach und die Folgen* (Raab, 2000).

⁵³ See p. 151 below.

reform.[54] An interesting feature of the edition of Peuerbach's *Theoricae novae planetarum* is the impressive publishing programme Regiomontanus sets out in an advertisement: it lists twenty-nine works by various authors, sundry translations, adaptations and excerpts, and twenty-two works by Regiomontanus himself, as well as collections of maps, descriptions and guides to the use of various instruments – all in all, a telling indication of what German humanism believed itself to be capable. Through the application of mathematics to astronomy and geography Peuerbach and Regiomontanus laid the foundations of surveying, which would be so essential to the Portuguese and the Spanish on their voyages of discovery. The principles of mathematics were also important for art, for instance, in regard to the geometrical representation of the human form in Dürer and for the understanding of perspective.

To return to Celtis, not the least significant manifestation of his pride in the German nation lay in his pride in the German invention of printing, though he was not the first to put it into words – already the colophon of the Mainz *Catholicon* dated 1460 (possibly printed by Gutenberg himself) is effusive in its praise:

> Altissimi presidio cuius nutu infantium lingue fiunt diserte. Qui que numerosepe paruulis reuelat quod sapientibus celat. Hic liber egregius. catholicon. Dominice incarnacionis annis Mccclx Alma in urbe maguntina nacionis inclite germanice. Quam dei clemencia tam alto ingenij lumine. dono que gratuito. ceteris terrarum nacionibus preferre illustrareque dignatus est. Non calami. stili aut penne suffragio. sed mira

---

[54] On Regiomontanus and Walther, see E. Zinner, *Leben und Wirken des Joh. Müller aus Königsberg, gen. Regiomontanus*, 2nd revised edn (Osnabrück, 1968) [translated as *Regiomontanus: his life and work* (Amsterdam, 1990)].

patronarum formarum que concordia proporcione et modulo. impressus atque confectus est. [...]⁵⁵

With the help of the Most High at whose will the tongues of infants become eloquent and who often reveals to the lowly what he hides from the wise, this noble book *Catholicon* has been printed and accomplished without the help of reed, stylus or pen but by the wondrous agreement, proportion and harmony of punches and types, in the year of the Lord's incarnation 1460 in the noble city of Mainz of the renowned German nation, which God's grace has deigned to prefer and distinguish above all other nations of the earth with so lofty a genius and liberal gifts. [...]

Even in Italy German eminence in this field had been acknowledged at an early date: in 1468 (the year of Gutenberg's death) GIOVANNI ANDREA BUSSI had written: *Digne honoranda saeculisque omnibus magnificacienda profecto Germania est, utilitatem inventrix maximarum* ('Germany deserves fame for all time for having brought forth this invention').[56] The ready availability of books was a benefit welcomed by LUDOVICO CARBONE, in his preface to Pliny, *Epistolae* (Venice, 1471):

---

[55] Translation from S. H. Steinberg, *Five Hundred Years of Printing*, new edition, revised by John Trevitt (London, 1996), p. 5, where the original colophon is also reproduced.

[56] In the preface to vol. I of the Letters of St Jerome (Rome: Conrad Sweynheym and Arnold Pannartz, 1468) [ISTC, no. ih00161000]. M. Giesecke, *Der Buchdruck in der frühen Neuzeit* (Frankfurt am Main, 1991), p. 193, also cites Baptista Fulgosus as saying that the invention of printing surpassed all other mechanical achievements. It is worth remembering also that, in March 1455, Piccolomini reported that while attending the Imperial Diet at Frankfurt the previous October, he had seen samples of a printed Bible 'that could be read without glasses', produced for inspection by 'a marvellous man' (whether this was Gutenberg himself or, perhaps more likely, his associate Peter Schöffer, we do not know): see M. Davies, 'Juan de Carvajal and Early Printing', *The Library*, 6th ser., xviii (1996), pp. 193–215. On Italian praise of the German invention, see also p. 330 below.

... adeo late pateat Romana et Graeca facundia ut iam et Galli et Britanni bonos oratores et poetas habere videantur, ad quam quidem rem commodissimum adiumentum praestiterunt nobilissima Germanorum ingenia, qui artificiosissimas imprimendorum librorum formas excogitarunt, ut sapientissimorum auctorum plurima simul eodem temporis momento volumina in promptu essent, omnesque utilissimi codices et in magna copia et leviore sumptu parari possent.[57]

What is more, Roman and Greek eloquence had been spread so widely that even the French and English are seen to have good orators and poets, which the outstanding genius of the Germans has most conveniently assisted by devising exceedingly clever means of printing books so that many volumes of the most learned authors may easily be available at the same time and all of the most useful books can readily be obtained in large quantity.

Celtis himself lost no opportunity to praise German printing. Thus already around the time of his laureation he lauded Frederick III for having ushered in a golden age in which German printing ensured the dissemination of the knowledge of the past:

> Te vivo Latiis gloria litteris
> Antiquumque decus iam redit artibus,
> In lucem veniunt cum modo singula,
> Quae Grai et Latii condiderant viri
> Et qui Nialico littore sederant
> Quique Euphratis habent conflua flumina.
> Hinc caelum omne patet terraque cognita est
> Et, quid quadrifidis continet angulis,
> In lucem veniunt artem arte Alemanica,
> Quae pressis docuit scribere litteris.[58]

Under your rule honour accrues to us through our mastery of the writings of the Romans; the arts and sciences, the pride and renown of the ancients are returning, for little by little is being

---

[57] ISTC, no. ip00804000. See B. Botfield, *Praefationes et epistolae editionibus principibus auctorum veterum praepositae* (London, 1861), p. 132.

[58] Conradus Celtis, *Libri odarum quattuor. Liber epodon, Carmen saeculare*, ed. F. Pindter (Leipzig, 1937), p. 1 (Bk I, no. 1, ll. 19–28).

brought to light what the Greeks and Romans, and those dwelling on the Nile and Euphrates once achieved. The starry heaven is a mystery for us no more, we know the earth, and through that German skill which taught us to use printed letters we are discovering what the four corners of the world contain.

It remains a recurrent theme. Witness:

> Rhene pater, debent tibi singula numina coeli,
>   Et quidquid tellus salsus et humor alit,
> Per tua scriptorum cum sunt inventa labores
>   Sublati, et cunctis utile crevit opus,
> Scilicet in parvo dum scribunt aera labore,
>   Mille prius numquam quod potuere manus.[59]

Father Rhine, the gods and all that earth and sea have brought forth owe you thanks for your invention that has relieved scribes of their labours and has created an art useful to all, namely, that metal letters now write with little effort what formerly not even a thousand hands could achieve.

> Iamque Moguntiacum vastus te flectis ad urbem,
>   quae prima impressas tradidit aere notas.
> Qualem ego te memorem, talem qui inveneris artem,
>   Italicis, Graiis plus memorande viris.[60]

And now, great river, you bend towards the city of Mainz which was the first to produce printed letters in metal, the like of which neither Italians nor Greeks have matched with anything comparable or more memorable.

> Quae docuit spretis Germanos scribere pennis,
> Cernitur ut pulchris littera pressa notis.[61]

---

[59] *Fünf Bücher Epigramme von Konrad Celtes*, ed. K. Hartfelder (Berlin, 1881) [repr. Hildesheim, 1963], p. 35 (Bk II, no.56) (written c. 1489).

[60] Conradus Celtis, *Quattuor libri Amorum. [...] Germania generalis*, ed. F. Pindter (Leipzig, 1934), p. 72 (*Amores*, Bk III, no. 13, ll. 39–42) (written 1491, printed 1502).

[61] *Quattuor libri Amorum*, ed. Pindter, p. 54 (Bk III, no. 1, ll. 11–12).

[The city, Mainz] which taught the Germans to write with despised quills is now recognised for the beauty of its printed letters.

> Qui sculpsit solidos aere characteres,
> Et versis docuit scribere litteris,
> Quo nasci utilius non poterat magis
>   Cunctis, credite, saeculis.
>
> Iam tandem Italici non poterunt viri
> Germanos stolida carpere inertia,
> Cum nostris videant crescere ab artibus
>   Romanis saecula litteris.[62]

He cut letters from metal and taught how to write with reversed type. Surely nothing more useful could have been invented in the centuries! No longer will the Italians be able to accuse the Germans of stupid inactivity, for now they can see that our skills outdo the centuries of Roman literature.

This emphasis on German industriousness is important, because Tacitus had claimed in chapter 15 of the *Germania* that, when not fighting, the Germans were prone to be idle.

Celtis' theme was taken up by other humanists. For instance, the Münster schoolmaster Johannes Murmellius (1480–1517), in a poem addressed to the book-lover Heinrich Morlage, canon at Münster, says it is not her military might that makes Germany worthy of praise, but rather her invention of printing which has made inexpensive books readily available:

> Inclyta laudetur merito Germania claris
>   artibus, eximio carmine digna cani;
> non tam Mavorti quod gentes ducet aptas,
>   quas olim populus Romuleus timuit;
> aut quia tormentis dederit reboantibus uti,
>   bellica quae diro fulmine castra terunt:
> quam quod chalcotypam solers invenerit artem,

---

[62] Text following Nuremberg: Stadtbibliothek, Cod. Cent. V. Ms. App. 3. The 1513 Strasbourg edition reads 'Qui sculpsit solidas aere citus notas.' Cf. *Libri odarum quattuor*, ed. Pindter, p. 74 (Bk III, no. 9, ll. 9–16).

> qua recipit cultos mens studiosa libros.
> o felix tellus, felix inventor et auctor
>   muneris et quisquis vivit, Apollo, tibi!
> nunc pretio parvo divina volumina constant
>   omnibus, et late Pallados arma patent;
> obruta quae densis quondam latuere tenebris,
>   in lucem redeunt accipiuntque decus [...][63]

It is right that the praise of famous Germany, renowned for its arts, should resound in song, not so much because it nourishes peoples skilled in war whom the people of Romulus [= the Romans] once feared, or because they invented the cannon that smashes an enemy camp with a terrible lightning flash. No, rather because by their genius they invented the art of printing which furnishes the curious mind with informative books. O happy land, happy discoverer and originator of this gift and happy man who lives for you, Apollo. Now everyone can obtain holy books for little cost, and Minerva's tools are accessible to the whole world. What once was hidden in deep obscurity has now come to light again and receives due recognition.

Then there is Sebastian Brant (1458–1521) who, in his poem for the Basel printer Johannes Bergmann de Olpe 'de praestantia artis impressoriae a Germanis nuper inventae', not only reinforces the pro-German, anti-Italian sentiment but also introduces an anti-French element:

> gratia diis primum, mox impressoribus aequa
>   gratia, quorum opera haec prima reperta via est.
> quae doctos latuit Graecos Italosque peritos,
>   ars nova, Germano venit ab ingenio.
> dic age, si quid habes, Latialis cultor agelli,
>   quod tali invento par sit et aequivalens?
> Gallia tuque adeo recta cervice superbam
>   quae praefers frontem: par tamen exhibe opus!
> dicite si posthac videatur barbara vena
>   Germanis, quorum hic prodiit arte labor?
> crede mihi, cernes (rumparis, Romule, quamvis)
>   pierides Rheni mox colere arva sui,
> nec solum insigni probitate excellere et armis

---

[63] Johannes Murmelius, 'De librorum amatore ad Henricum Morlagium' (excerpt), cited after Schnur, *Lateinische Gedichte deutscher Humanisten*, pp. 300–03.

Germanos: orbis sceptra tenere simul.
quin etiam ingenio, studiis, musisque beatis
 praestare et cunctos vincere in orbe viros. [...][64]

Thanks first to the gods, then to the printers whose works have first shown us the way. German genius has discovered that new art that remained unknown to the learned Greeks and was hidden from the clever Italians. Tell me, tiller of Italian soil, what you have that can be compared with this invention? France, with your head held so proud, what have you to compare with it? Can you henceforth still call the Germans barbarians who have invented this art? Believe me, you will soon see (explode, little Roman, with envy) how the Muses take up residence on the Rhine, and how the Germans will excel not only in loyalty and valour, but how at the same time they will rule the world, and how through their cleverness, scholarship and their devotion to the Muses they will have conquered the whole world.

As already noted, in his *Germania generalis*, Celtis was at pains to correct Tacitus. When, in that poem, he emphasises that the *Germani* are a *gens invicta*, 'an unconquered people' (*Germania generalis*, 56), living where they have always lived, accustomed to heat, cold and hard work, eschewing idleness, and bearing a name which the nobility still today revere (56–65), we detect not only a pointed rebuttal of Tacitus' assertion that when not engaged in warfare, the Germans spent most of their time 'idling, abandoning themselves to sleep and gluttony' (*Germania*, c. 15), but – more important – a barbed criticism of the Romans: by emphasising that the *Germani* were still called *Germani*, he is implicitly deploring the fact that the descendants of the *Romani* now call themselves *Itali*, which weakens any case they might have for regarding themselves as the heirs of the Roman empire.[65] Another correction concerns Tacitus' claim that, among the Germans, men and women were equally ignorant of letters (*litterarum*

---

[64] Cited after Schnur, *Lateinische Gedichte deutscher Humanisten*, pp. 16–21.

[65] On this see Müller, *Die 'Germania generalis' des Conrad Celtis*, pp. 126–27.

secreta viri pariter ac feminae ignorant: Germania, c. 19).[66] What Tacitus precisely meant by this is uncertain, but some commentators, old and recent, seem to think he was implying a lack of culture. With that past state of affairs Æneas Sylvius contrasts the present when he says the arts are flourishing in Germany and there are many towns with universities in which the law, medicine and the liberal arts are fostered.[67] In the *Germania generalis*, Celtis also stresses how studious the Germans are. Interestingly, this very passage from Tacitus is cited as late as 1640 by a group of Strasbourg printers celebrating the bicentenary of printing in the course of their claim that Germany excelled all other nations by dint of having invented this art:

> Vnd ob schon wir Teutschen etwas spaat darzu gelanget/ auch deßwegen von Tacito in German. 19,1 hören müssen/ literarum secreta viros pariter ac feminas ignorare: Es verstehe vnder den Teutschen weder Mann noch Weib die geheimnuß deß Schreibens: So ist doch/ Gottlob/ seithero dise langdaurige Vnwissenheit nicht allein gantz außgetrieben; sondern auch durch die glückseligste Erfindung der Buchtrucker-Kunst (so alle der alten Schreibereyen weit vbertrifft) stattlich ersetzet worden: daß also die Italiäner nicht mehr gelusten wird/ die Teutschen als grobe/ Barbarische/ vnverständige vnd wilde Völcker zuschelten: Sintemal die Gelehrheit [!]/ seit Erfindung gedachter Kunst/ in Teutschland so hoch gestiegen/ daß man sich darmit auch gegen die gantze Welt darff hervorthun; Doch were zu wünschen es hetten die Teutschen eher dieses grosse Glück gehabt; so würden nicht allein die streitbare [!] Thaten der dapffern Helden Ariouisti, Arminii, vnd anderer/ besser

---

[66] Text after Koestermann ed., *P. Cornelii Taciti libri qui supersunt*, ii / 2, p. 16. What this passage means is disputed. Much, *Die Germania des Tacitus*, p. 197, says that *litterarum secreta* must refer to clandestine affairs conducted by means of love-letters since the chapter concerned deals with the sanctity of marriage and the virtues of German women. Much's opinion is shared by several modern translators.

[67] *Littere quoque et omnium bonarum artium studia apud vos florent. Scolas quoque, in quibus et iura et medicina et liberales traduntur artes, in Germania plures urbes habent* (Germania Eneae Silvii [...], (Strasbourg: R. Beck, 1515), 2, 27 (p. 65)).

auffgezeichnet seyn/ vnd gewiß mehr Sieg als Niderlag/ von jhnen gelesen werden; sondern auch das Liecht deß H. Evangelij bey den VorEltern eher geschinnen haben.[68]

Although we Germans got this far rather late [i.e. we learned about writing later than ancient peoples such as the Egyptians, Greeks and Etruscans] and consequently have to listen to Tacitus saying in *Germania*, 19, 1 *literarum secreta viros pariter ac feminas ignorare* 'among the Germans neither man nor woman understands the mysteries of writing',[69] since then, God be praised, this long enduring ignorance has not only been expelled but been admirably replaced by the most happy invention of the art of printing (which is far superior to all the old ways of writing), so that the Italians will no longer delight in deriding the Germans as coarse, barbaric, ignorant and wild tribes, for learning has advanced so much in Germany since the invention of the aforementioned art that we may hold our heads up before the whole world. But one could wish that the Germans had had this great good fortune earlier, for then not only would the valorous deeds of the brave warriors Ariovistus, Arminius and others be better recorded, and surely we should read more of their victories than defeats, but also the light of the Holy Gospel would have shone earlier amongst our ancestors.

This claim of German superiority, coupled with the allusions to the ancient Germanic heroes Ariovistus and Arminius, is all the more interesting for coming from a group of Strasbourg printers; it may be interpreted as an instance not only of the long-term influence of Celtis' 'take' on Tacitus but also of anti-French feeling superimposed on anti-Italian sentiment; this anti-French feeling we noted already in the poem by the Strasbourg humanist Sebastian Brant. Like Mainz, Strasbourg was intimately associated with Gutenberg's early experiments in printing. Pro-German sentiments were prominent in the thinking of another Strasbourg humanist, too: Jakob

---

[68] J. A. Schrag, *Bericht von Erfindung der Buchtruckerey in Straßburg* (Strasbourg: M. Carle, 1640), fol. 2^v–3^r.

[69] Interestingly, Eberlin renders this as *Es send weder man noch weiber jn den gschriften gelert* (Masser ed., *Johann Eberlin von Günzburg*, p. 59), perhaps meaning 'neither men nor women are skilled at reading'.

Wimpheling (1450–1528).[70] In 1501 Wimpheling resigned his appointment as Professor of Rhetoric and Poetics at Heidelberg and came to teach in Strasbourg. His time here was marked by the publication of various pieces designed to bolster German patriotism and counter French influences. Of particular importance was his assertion that the left bank of the Rhine, with Alsace, had been German since the days of Caesar.[71] After Basel had transferred its allegiance in 1501 from the Empire to the Swiss Confederation, Wimpheling proposed to despatch preachers to the city to bring home to them the grievousness of their sin. For Wimpheling the Empire was a Holy Empire indeed and the Emperor God's instrument whom it was impious to disobey. In his *Germania* (1501) Wimpheling exhorts the council of Strasbourg not to allow themselves to be misled by the Francophiles in their midst into believing that the left bank of the Rhine, together with Strasbourg and Alsace, had once been French. Many of the

---

[70] Jakob Wimpheling, from Sélestat, studied at the universities of Freiburg, Erfurt and Heidelberg. He entertained ideas of church reform, combining with them ideas for improving teaching, especially Latin. His *Elegantiarum medulla* (1493) was indebted to Lorenzo Valla, but his most important publication of the time was his *Isidoneus germanicus* (1496) in which he set out his views on the upbringing and education of German youth. For his views on the German heritage of Alsace see E. Martin, *Germania von Jakob Wimpfeling* (Strasbourg, 1885).

[71] For knowledge of Caesar in medieval and early modern Germany see A. Suerbaum, 'The Middle Ages' in M. Griffin ed., *A Companion to Julius Caesar* (Oxford, 2009), pp. 317–34. The earliest edition published in Germany was *Libri commentariorum de bello gallico* (Esslingen: C. Fyner, 1473) [ISTC, no. ic00027000], to which is prefixed the life of Caesar extracted from Petrarch's *De viris illustribus*. The first German translation of Caesar's writings was that by Matthias Ringmann Philesius, *Julius der erst Römisch Kaiser von seinen Kriegen* (Strasbourg: J. Grüninger, 1507), which combines Caesar's *De bello Gallico* and *De bello civile*. During the summer of 1492 Celtis wrote to Sixtus Tucher listing books he needed for his work: *Opus habeo pro studio meo Herodoto, Suetonio, Bocacio, commentario C. Caesaris* (Rupprich, *Briefwechsel*, p. 62).

reasons he adduces to support his belief that this area had always been German are less than convincing, but one worth noting is his observation that Tacitus (*Germania*, c. 28) accounts the Triboci, Nemetes, Vangiones and Ubii as German tribes dwelling on the left bank of the Rhine, that is, as the ancestors of the inhabitants of Strasbourg, Speyer, Worms and Cologne respectively.[72] The Franciscan polemicist Thomas Murner (1475–c. 1537) dismissed some of these 'proofs' as patently absurd in his *Germania nova* (1502). Wimpheling, highly offended, succeeded in having Murner's book suppressed and issued a counterblast in his *Declaratio ad mitigandum adversarium* (1502) and in the *Epithoma rerum Germanicarum* (1505), the basic idea of which is that German history and culture are worthy to be compared with the achievements of antiquity.[73]

Wimpheling, like Celtis and Brant, was proud of the German invention of printing. In his *Germania*, he speaks of Strasbourg being famous for its genius in inventing printing even though it was perfected at Mainz, and in the *Epithoma rerum Germanicarum* he expands this as follows:

> Anno xpi. Mcccc.xl. Friderico tertio romanorum imperatore regnante Magnum quoddam ac pene diuinum beneficium collatum est uniuerso terrarum orbi a Ioanne gutenbergk Arge]. nouo scribendi genere reperto. Is enim primus artem impressoriam [...] in urbe Arge]. inuenit. Inde Maguncia veniens eandem feliciter compluit. Interea Ioannes mentel id opificij genus inceptans multi volumina castigate ac polite Argentinae imprimendo factus et breui opulentissimus.[74]

---

[72] This is his '*testis septimus*'. See E. von Borries, *Wimpfeling und Murner im Kampf um die ältere Geschichte des Elsasses* (Heidelberg, 1926), p. 104: this book includes the Latin text and translation of Wimpheling's *Declaratio* and of Murner's *Germania nova*, as well as a complete facsimile of the latter. See the commentary in Much, *Die Germania des Tacitus*, pp. 267–8.

[73] Wimpheling, *Epithoma rerum Germanicarum usque ad nostra tempora* (Strasbourg: J. Prüss, 1505), especially fol. 12^r.

[74] Wimpheling, *Epithoma*, fols. 38^v–39^r.

In the year of Our Lord 1440, in the reign of the Roman Emperor Frederick III, a great, almost divine benefit was granted to the whole earth by Johannes Gutenberg at Strasbourg who invented a new way of writing. For he was the first to invent the art of printing at Strasbourg. Going thence to Mainz he happily perfected it there. Meanwhile Johannes Mentel had begun to practise this kind of work, having produced and finished many volumes by printing them at Strasbourg and having become very wealthy in a short time.

One of the books Mentelin published at Strasbourg, in 1466, was the first German Bible, the very first vernacular Bible ever printed – but that is another story.

Further Reading

In addition to the specialist studies detailed in the footnotes, the following more general treatments are recommended. Items marked with an asterisk offer sound guidance to the current state of research.

A. Aurnhammer ed., *Francesco Petrarca in Deutschland. Seine Wirkung in Literatur, Kunst und Musik* [Frühe Neuzeit, cxviii] (Tübingen, 2006).

I. Bennewitz and U. Müller ed., *Von der Handschrift zum Buchdruck: Spätmittelalter–Reformation–Humanismus 1320–1572* [Deutsche Literatur: Eine Sozialgeschichte, ii] (Reinbek, 1991).

E. Bernstein, *Die Literatur des deutschen Frühhumanismus* [Sammlung Metzler, clxviii] (Stuttgart, 1978).

E. Bernstein, *German Humanism* (Boston, 1983).

S. Füssel ed., *Deutsche Dichter der frühen Neuzeit (1450–1600): Ihr Leben und Werk* (Berlin, 1993).

P. Grendler ed., *Handbuch der deutschen Bildungsgeschichte, I: 15. bis 17. Jahrhundert* (Munich, 1996).

M. S. Grossmann, *Humanism in Wittenberg, 1485–1517* (Nieuwkoop, 1975).

N. Hammerstein ed., *Bildung und Wissenschaft vom 15. bis zum 17. Jahrhundert* [Enzyklopädie deutscher Geschichte, lxiv] (Munich, 2003).

E. Keßler and H. C. Kuhn ed., *Germania latina–Latinitas teutonica: Politik, Wissenschaft, humanistische Kultur vom späten Mittelalter bis in unsere Zeit*, 2 vols (Munich, 2003).

A. Noe, *Der Einfluß des italienischen Humanismus auf die deutsche Literatur vor 1600* (Tübingen, 1993).

J. H. Overfield, *Humanism and Scholasticism in Late Medieval Germany* (Princeton, 1984).

J. Overfield, 'Germany' in R. Porter and M. Teich ed., *The Renaissance in National Context* (Cambridge, 1992), pp. 92–122.

D. H. Price, *Johannes Reuchlin and the Campaign to Destroy Jewish Books* (New York, 2011).

*M. Reinhart ed., *Early Modern German Literature 1350–1700* (Columbia SC, 2007).

*K. Ruh, B. Wachinger et al. ed., *Die deutsche Literatur des Mittelalters. Verfasserlexikon*, 2nd revised edn, 14 vols (Berlin and New York, 1977–2008).

H. Rupprich, *Die deutsche Literatur vom späten Mittelalter bis zum Barock. 1. Teil: Das ausgehende Mittelalter, Humanismus und Renaissance, 1370–1520*, 2nd edn, revised by H. Heger, [Geschichte der deutschen Literatur von den Anfängen bis zur Gegenwart, ed. H. de Boor and R. Newald, iv / 1] (Munich, 1994), esp. pp. 425–729 and the bibliography on pp. 836–86.

P. G. Schmidt, *Humanismus im deutschen Südwesten: Biographische Profile*, 2nd edn (Stuttgart, 2000).

F.-J. Worstbrock, *Deutsche Antikerezeption 1450–1550* (Boppard, 1976).

*F.-J. Worstbrock ed., *Deutscher Humanismus 1480–1520. Verfasserlexikon*, 2 vols (Berlin and New York, 2005–).

FIFTEENTH-CENTURY HUMANISM IN POLAND: COURT AND COLLEGIUM

JACQUELINE GLOMSKI

In a letter to ÆNEAS SILVIUS PICCOLOMINI, the future Pope Pius II, of September 1453, Cardinal Zbigniew Oleśnicki, the bishop of Cracow, praised Piccolomini's writing style.[1] A refined Latin style, the cardinal commented, was not necessarily the elegance of the ancient Romans but instead, that of the present-day writers of Italy.[2] Oleśnicki's remarks indicate his awareness of the Italians' superiority in international communications and diplomacy. Moreover, his admission that he wished to imitate Piccolomini's writing style hints at his desire, as a statesman of an emerging European power, to play a recognized role in pan-European affairs.

Due to its position as the country's capital, with its conjunction of court (both royal and ecclesiastical) and

---

[1] On Oleśnicki, see T. Ulewicz, 'Polish Humanism and its Italian Sources: Beginnings and Historical Development' in S. Fiszman ed., *The Polish Renaissance in its European Context* (Bloomington, IN, 1988), pp. 215–35 at 219–20. See also Ulewicz's later article, which covers much the same ground: id., 'Przed przyjściem Kallimacha. Pierwsze zwiastuny humanizmu w złotej jesieni polskiego średniowiecza' in I. Opacki, A. Wilkoń and J. Żurawska ed., *Studia slavistica et humanistica in honorem Nullo Minissi* (Katowice, 1997), pp. 59–74. On Oleśnicki's correspondence with Piccolomini, see I. Zarębski, *Stosunki Eneasza Sylwiusza z Polską* [Polska Akademia Umiejętności. Rozprawy Wydziału Historyczno-Filozoficznego, lxx (= Ser. 2, xlv)] (Cracow, 1939), pp. 51–75.

[2] This letter is mentioned by J. Domański, *Początki humanizmu* (Wrocław, 1982), p. 114. The text is printed in *Der Briefwechsel des Eneas Silvius Piccolomini*, ed. R. Wolkan, 3 vols [Fontes Rerum Austriacarum, 2. Abt, lxii, lxvii & lxviii] (Vienna, 1909–18), iii, pp. 245–53.

academic culture, as well as its location on the commercial crossroads of east central Europe, Cracow at this time led the rest of Poland in accepting new, foreign intellectual and artistic movements. But while a fierce determination to keep up with international trends may well have propelled the Cracow court to adopt humanist cultural currents coming from Italy, the city's university did not experience the same impulse, and its acceptance of Italian humanism was delayed. In fact, fifteenth-century humanism at Cracow can be characterized by these two currents: court and *collegium*. The court milieu, as demonstrated by Cardinal Oleśnicki's example, was eager for contact with Italy and eager to be able to write and speak in an elegant, humanist-inspired Latin. The literature that the court élite engendered, either through the writings of its own circle or through patronage, would, by the end of the century, exhibit clear Italianate, paganizing tendencies. In contrast, the university community would settle on a transalpine form of humanism, which would crystallize in the early sixteenth century into a pious, Christian literature, influenced by German scholarly trends and the writings of Erasmus. The court current would prove the stronger of the two and would nurture the Italianate style not only in literature, but also in the other arts, especially architecture and music. It was the culture of the court that initiated the Renaissance in Poland and presided over its flowering in the mid-sixteenth century.

The split of Polish humanism into two camps in the fifteenth century was largely the result of a difference in their political motivations. The royal court actively sought to keep up with the cultural and intellectual trends coming from Italy because it aspired to function in an early modern Europe as a power of the highest rank.[3] For the college scholars, interest in the new Italian learning stemmed from their trips to Italy to study law (and, to a certain extent, medicine) and through

---

[3] N. Nowakowska, *Church, State and Dynasty in Renaissance Poland: the career of Cardinal Fryderyk Jagiellon (1468–1503)* (Aldershot, 2007), pp. 12–15.

their involvement in the conciliar movement. But this stimulus was lost with the failure of the Council of Basel; the University of Cracow, increasingly dominated by a rich but lacklustre Faculty of Theology, felt no incentive to integrate humanist educational methods into its curriculum.[4] These two factors tempt one to conclude that Renaissance humanism grew in Poland hand-in-hand first with the emergence of the country on the pan-European political and ecclesiastical scene and, then, more intensively, with the development of the imperial pretensions of the ruling Jagiellonian dynasty. This dynasty, with its foreign (that is, Lithuanian) and pagan origins, had ascended to power after the extinction of the old ruling family, the native Piasts, toward the end of the fourteenth century.[5] The Jagiellons needed to legitimize their rule in Poland and wrest control of the government from the nobles and bishops of the magnate, oligarchical faction (as represented by Oleśnicki), before they could set out to establish their influence throughout east central Europe.

This distinct split in Polish humanism and the reasons why the court current became stronger than the university current can be illustrated by examining two points in the fifteenth century – one at mid-century and the other at the end of the century – at which the court took advantage of an opportunity to acquire the benefits of humanist learning and the university either ignored or rejected such an opportunity: the first was afforded by the Council of Basel (1431–1449) and the second was the presence in Cracow of the wandering humanists FILIPPO BUONACCORSI (1472–1496) and Conrad Celtis (1489–1491). The conciliar movement brought court and college together because university scholars, with their legal and theological

---

[4] The University of Cracow is commonly known in Poland as the Jagiellonian University because it was refounded during the reign of Władysław Jagiełło, in 1400. At the time of its original founding in the 1360s, it was referred to as the *studium generale*; in the early sixteenth century, *Academia Cracoviensis* or *Gymnasium Cracoviense*.

[5] On Piast Poland, see P. Knoll, *The Rise of the Polish Monarchy: Piast Poland in East Central Europe, 1320–1370* (Chicago, 1972).

expertise, were needed to provide representation and argumentation at the Councils. Buonaccorsi and Celtis brought court and college together through their personal interaction. Buonaccorsi served many years as a royal advisor and diplomat, while the German scholar Celtis based himself for two years at the university, lecturing and writing. Their time in Cracow overlapped and they became friends; Buonaccorsi was active in Celtis' literary society, the Sodalitas Litteraria Vistulana.

At the time of the opening of the Council of Basel in 1431, the royal court was controlled by the extremely influential bishop of Cracow, Zbigniew Oleśnicki (1389–1455), who took on the role of regent during the reign of the teenage King Ladislaus III (Władysław Warneńczyk; 1434–1444); after 1440, Ladislaus was mostly absent from Cracow, as he was simultaneously holding the throne of Hungary and fighting off the Turks. In the wake of Ladislaus' death at the Battle of Varna, Oleśnicki retained control of the government, though this was to cause friction with Ladislaus' brother, the new king, Casimir IV (Kazimierz Jagiellończyk; 1447–1492).[6] Oleśnicki, as demonstrated by his correspondence with Piccolomini, knew that to carry out diplomacy on a level commensurate with a major European power required the Cracow court to adapt to the prevalent trend in communication, that is, to speak and write in a humanist Latin style.

Moreover, Oleśnicki evidently thought it essential to have a literature to promote the image of Poland as such a power, both in its secular and its ecclesiastic aspects and to both an international and a domestic audience. To this end, he encouraged his secretary and chancellor, John (Jan) Długosz (Johannes Dlugossius; 1415–1480), in the task of chronicling the history of the Polish nation; Długosz worked on his *Annales seu Cronicae incliti Regni Poloniae* from 1455 until the year of his death. He also wrote Church history – including the lives of the Polish bishops, a life of St Stanislaus (the patron of Poland), and a list of the benefices of the diocese of Cracow –

---

[6] Nowakowska, *Church, State and Dynasty*, p. 22.

and he composed books of heraldry.⁷

Długosz spent twenty-four years in the service of Oleśnicki; he entered the bishop's court at the age of seventeen, not having completed his studies at the University of Cracow. He became Oleśnicki's spokesperson and was sent on diplomatic missions to Italy. In spite of spending time in the birthplace of humanism, Długosz's Latin is generally not considered to be humanist in style, even though his writing shows that he knew the works of Petrarch, Boccacio, and Æneas Silvius Piccolomini. Długosz, moreover, did set Livy as his model and imitated that author's vocabulary, phraseology, and syntax; at the same time, he was also influenced by the Vulgate. However, his connexion to medieval literary convention was overwhelming – at the University of Cracow, he had been educated in the old, scholastic grammar and rhetoric. In sum, his writing, an amalgamation of heterogeneous elements, is uneven in its application of classical standards and is characteristic of this era of transition. Still, Długosz's historiographical methods can be considered modern: his research was meticulous.⁸

Having been trained in Oleśnicki's school of thought and formed according to the notions that steered Oleśnicki's politics, Długosz tried to show in his writings the kind of relationship of the Church to the state that Oleśnicki favoured, one based on a theocratic view, that the country, ruled by a strong oligarchic monarchy, should be subservient to the authority of the Church. Długosz, like Oleśnicki, would have preferred to see the native Piasts on the Polish throne rather than the Jagiellons, yet, like Oleśnicki, who pushed for the Jagiellons

---

[7] Ulewicz, 'Polish Humanism and its Italian Sources,' pp. 221–22; *Polski Słownik Biograficzny*, ed. W. Koropczyński et al. (Cracow, 1935–), v, pp. 176–80. The *Annales* are available in the edition of J. Dąbrowski et al., 12 vols (Warsaw, 1964–2005), while an abridged English translation has been produced as *The Annals of Jan Długosz: a history of Eastern Europe from A.D. 965 to A.D. 1480*, trans. M. Michael, with commentary by P. Smith (Chichester, 1997).

[8] D. Turkowska, *Études sur la langue et sur le style de Jean Długosz* (Wrocław, 1973), pp. 89–91.

to obtain dynastic rights to the Czech and Hungarian thrones, Długosz was extremely patriotic, rejoicing over the successes of his country and expressing pain over its losses.[9] He expressed his patriotism most precisely in his *Annales* through his use of the terms *genus* (origin), *gens* (people), *natio* (nation) (all three rooted in the ideas of 'race', 'tribe', or 'breed') to formulate his idea of the nation as one of a political collectivity united by a common racial origin and occupying a territory defined as the boundaries of the state, and speaking the same language (Polish). Długosz's idea of nationality and his aspirations for his country were not unusual — such expressions could be found in other humanist writers of the times.[10]

Although Oleśnicki's and Długosz's outlook on domestic government was anachronistic for the time — the Polish nobility was gaining more economic power, diminishing that of the old-style theocrats, while the Jagiellonian family, under the leadership of Casimir IV, was succeeding in legitimizing its rule and securing its leadership of the country — the bishop's prompting of his secretary's writing paid off (if only posthumously for both patron and author): in the *Annales*, Długosz left a literary monument to the Polish nation. If his work did not find an immediate readership, it did circulate in manuscript and served as ground-work for the historians of the sixteenth century: Bernard Wapowski (*c.* 1450–1535), Matthias of Miechów (Maciej z Miechowa; 1453/57–1523) and Martin (Marcin) Kromer (*c.* 1512–1589), all writing in Latin, and Martin (Marcin) Bielski (*c.* 1495–1575), writing in

---

[9] *Polski Słownik Biograficzny*, xxiii, p. 779; J. Dąbrowski, *Dawne dziejopisarstwo Polskie (do roku 1480)* (Wrocław, 1964), pp. 236–38; H. Barycz, *Szlakami dziejopisarstwa staropolskiego. Studia nad historiografią w. XVI–XVIII* (Wrocław, 1981), pp. 76–77; M. Koczerska, 'Długosz jako sekretarz Zbigniewa Oleśnickiego' in F. Kiryk ed., *Jan Długosz w pięćsetną rocznicę śmierci* (Olsztyn, 1983), pp. 53–64 at pp. 53, 63.

[10] T. Michałowska, *Średniowiecze* (Warsaw, 1995), p. 776. See also S. Gawlas, 'Świadomość narodowa Jana Długosza', *Studia źródłoznawcze. Commentationes*, xxvii (1980–81[1983]), pp. 3–66, esp. pp. 17–37.

Polish.[11] The *Annales* continued to attract national attention into the seventeenth century because of the heroic image of the ideal citizen as a landowner and knight that Długosz had created. A group of the gentry who had formed an opposition party to King Sigismund (Zygmunt) III prepared an *editio princeps* of the *Annales* in 1614. The following year the king ordered the confiscation of what had been printed (the first six books, in one volume). With this incident, the *Annales* gained international attention. Conscious that the political context would make the distribution of the book difficult in Poland, the chief editor, Jan Szczęsny Herburt, had sought a powerful authority to lend moral support to the publication of the *Annales* and had dedicated the aborted edition to the Senate of Venice, so bridging the aspirations of the Polish gentry to models of government and politics found in Italy. According to Venetian records, the book was taken there and presented.[12]

Długosz viewed his literary work, in a broad sense, as didactic in purpose. In his personal life, in addition, he became a patron of education, supporting various monasteries and student residences. His sponsorship had an impact on the development of architecture in Poland as the buildings that resulted from his patronage were constructed in a hybrid Gothic-Renaissance style, and sported a characteristic stonework, which came to be known as the Długosz style.[13] To be sure,

---

[11] Michałowska, *Średniowiecze*, p. 776, reports that eighty-two manuscripts of the *Annales*, either complete or fragments, have been found. She does not give details as to their dating.

[12] Barycz, *Szlakami dziejopisarstwa staropolskiego*, pp. 125–27; S Cynarski, 'Uwagi nad problemem recepcji 'Historii' Jana Długosza w Polsce XVI I XVII wieku' (with English summary) in Stanisław Gawęda ed., *Długossiana. Studia historyczne w pięćsetlecie śmierci Jana Długosza* (Cracow, 1980), pp. 281–92.

[13] A. Buczek, 'Mecenat artystyczny Jana Długosza w dziedzinie architektury' (with a summary in English) in Gawęda ed., *Długossiana*, pp. 108–40 at p. 108. Examples of the Długosz style include churches at Chotel Czerwony, Szczepanów, and Raciborowice; houses for clergy at Wiślica, Sandomierz, and on Wawel Hill in Cracow; and the several

Długosz's activities served as a cultural bridge from his own times to the flowering of the Renaissance in Poland in the sixteenth century. After Oleśnicki's death, King Casimir IV, besides sending Długosz on ambassadorial missions to the Czech lands and Hungary, made him a tutor to his sons: in this way, Długosz had some sway over the cultural outlook of the future Jagiellonian kings.[14]

Although Oleśnicki did not attend the Council of Basel in person – he was prevented by the death of Ladislaus III – he zealously kept in touch with council events through his correspondence. He sent two personal representatives to the Council, both members of the university: Nicholas (Mikołaj) Kozłowski, a professor of theology, and John (Jan) Elgot, who taught canon law.[15] Oleśnicki's overriding political concerns – to make Poland a real force in a Christian world threatened by the Turks and to protect his own control over the Polish church – made him, by the end of 1441, an ardent conciliar-

---

residences for students at Cracow that Długosz funded (Buczek, pp. 110–18, 139).

[14] Dąbrowski, *Dawne dziejopisarstwo*, pp. 235–36; Barycz, *Szlakami dziejopisarstwa staropolskiego*, pp. 75–78.

[15] P. Knoll, 'The University of Cracow and the Conciliar Movement' in J. M. Kittelson and P. J. Transue ed., *Rebirth, Reform and Resilience: universities in transition, 1300–1700* (Columbus, OH, 1984), pp. 190–212 at p. 199; K. Niemczycka, 'Jan Elgot–życie i twórczość', *Przegląd Tomistyczny*, v (1992), pp. 9–42; T. Wünsch, *Konziliarismus und Polen* (Paderborn, 1998), pp. 74, 87–90. Elgot's opinions were essential in the formulation of the official university position on the Council and led to his being chosen by Oleśnicki as his representative to the Council. Elgot, a doctor of decretals, spent four months in Basel, from the end of October 1441 to the end of February 1442. While there, he had a private audience with Felix V and also delivered a public oration (Niemczycka, 'Elgot', pp. 13–16). Kozłowski was named Oleśnicki's representative to the Basel council in July 1433 and took up his duties there in October of that year. He stayed in Basel until April 1436, when, having been named the Polish general commissioner for the preaching of indulgence by the Council, he returned to his homeland (Wünsch, *Konziliarismus*, p. 74).

ist, although, in the middle of 1447, he would come to recognize Pope Eugenius IV's legitimate successor, Nicholas V.[16]

The Council of Basel upheld the principle of a general council, as a representative assembly of the Church, being the highest authority in the Church, superior even to the Pope.[17] This council, as compared to previous ones, was innovative in the formation of its membership and in its procedures for decision-making. These were based not only on theology and canon law but on communal notions of society and government as reflected in the structure of the universities, religious orders, and republican cities of the time. Almost any cleric could enter the council with full speaking and voting rights, and all members were given freedom of speech and were exempted from any authority but the council's own.[18] It was at the Council of Basel that university doctors were admitted to a council for the first time with voting rights, and university clerics were prominent in official posts at the Council and on conciliar embassies. But, while university men never formed a majority at the Council in numerical terms or even a cohesive voting bloc, their role was decisive in the formulation and propagation of the Council's doctrines, and they can be identified as the intellectual leaders of the Council.[19]

In this respect, the University of Cracow, which sent some half-dozen of its members in various representative tasks,

[16] *Polski Słownik Biograficzny*, xxiii, pp. 780–81; M. Koczerska, *Zbigniew Oleśnicki i Kościół krakowski w czasach jego pontyfikatu 1423–1455* (Warsaw, 2004), pp. 135, 185.

[17] For a summary of the tenets of the Council of Basel, see *New Catholic Encyclopedia*, 2nd ed., 15 vols (Detroit, 2003), ii, pp. 133–35.

[18] A. Black, *Council and Commune: the Conciliar Movement and the fifteenth-century heritage* (London, 1979), p. 28.

[19] A. Black, 'The Universities and the Council of Basle: ecclesiology and tactics', *Annuarium Historiae Conciliorum*, vi (1974), pp. 341–51 at pp. 344–46, and id., 'The Universities and the Council of Basle: Collegium and Concilium' in J. IJsewijn and J. Paquet ed., *The Universities in the Late Middle Ages* (Leuven, 1978), pp. 511–23 at p. 515 [both articles are reprinted in A. Black, *Church, State and Community: historical and comparative perspectives* (Aldershot, 2003)].

played a significant role in forming the nucleus of the pro-conciliar party at Basel.[20] The university committed itself wholeheartedly to the cause, developing theological arguments in support of council beliefs and – often in advance of, or in opposition to, royal policy – composing treatises, letters, and orations in connexion with council events, even continuing to support the council-elected pope, Felix, when the king and the bishop of Cracow switched their allegiance to the Roman-elected Nicholas V in 1447.[21] Granted, the university had participated in the Council of Constance some twenty years earlier, but there the university, sending only two of its members, had served as a spokesperson for state interests, as that Council had revolved, for the Poles, around the resolution of their conflict with the Teutonic Knights, who had been attacking Polish territory.[22] The Council of Constance had drawn on the Cracow faculty's expertise in law, while during the Council of Basel the stress was on its knowledge of theology.[23] The shift in emphasis from law to theology is important, as we shall see.

[20] Black, 'The Universities and the Council of Basle: Collegium and Concilium', p. 515. Black notes (p. 516) that university support for the conciliar programme 'was motivated not only by attachment to the ideal of conciliar government but also by the hope of reforms which would improve the status of doctors in the church'. Thus, the university clerics may have had the increase of their own benefices in mind as well as improvement of ecclesiastical governance.

[21] See *Polski Słownik Biograficzny*, xxxix, pp. 537–40; Zarębski, *Stosunki Eneasza Sylwiusza z Polską*, p. 2; J. Fijałek, *Mistrz Jakub z Paradyża*, 2 vols (Cracow, 1900), i, pp. 154–70, 196–249, 331–80, and Knoll, 'The University of Cracow and the Conciliar Movement', pp. 198–99.

[22] Knoll, 'The University of Cracow and the Conciliar Movement', pp. 191–92, 198, 204–5. The thirteenth-century background to Poland's conflict with the Teutonic Knights is given in Knoll, *The Rise of the Polish Monarchy*.

[23] P. Knoll, 'The University Context of Kochanowski's Era: Humanism and the Academic Culture of the Early Renaissance in Poland' in S. Fiszman ed., *The Polish Renaissance in its European Context* (Bloomington, IN, 1988), pp. 189–212 at pp. 190–91. The representatives to

If the Council of Basel gave Oleśnicki and the royal court an increased opportunity to develop means of communication and propaganda along Italian-inspired lines, it also gave the university the possibility of increased contact with Italian humanist scholarship. But, unlike the interests in humanist Latin fostered by Oleśnicki, university interests in the *studia humanitatis* arising at the time of the Council were narrow and short-lived. While it is true that university participation at the Council of Basel did result in a growing number of humanist manuscripts being brought to Cracow and eventually being deposited in the university library, this influx produced no changes in the outlook of the professoriat at Cracow as a whole and, thus, no changes in the official curriculum. Even the tastes of such an active collector of classical and humanist writings as John (Jan) Dąbrówka (d. 1472) had no bearing on his involvement in the reforms of the Arts Faculty in 1449, which resulted in the repertoire of lectures being expanded only gradually to include more classical authors. The effect of these reforms, which were in no way suggestive of a humanist incentive, would not be felt until the end of the fifteenth or beginning of the sixteenth century. For example, although Quintilian's *Institutio oratoria* was referred to in the documents of 1449 – and this was probably the full text as recovered by POGGIO BRACCIOLINI early in the fifteenth century – it is not known for sure that this text was lectured on before 1526 (by Leonard Cox).[24]

Likewise, although individual scholars from Cracow were already going to study in Italy before or at the outbreak of the Council of Basel, the international platform of the Council did

Constance, Piotr Wolfram and Paweł Włodkowic (Paulus Vladimiri), had both studied law in Italy. Both were influenced by Italian humanism. Wolfram, for example, sent back a report to Cracow, insisting on the study of the classics and praising Petrarch, and brought back several manuscripts of classical and humanist works.

[24] Knoll, 'The University Context of Kochanowski's Era', pp. 195–200. Dąbrówka served as university rector nine times after 1449 and university vice-chancellor from 1458 to 1465.

not inspire the transfer of their interest in humanist study to the rest of the university; rather, the interest of these scholars in humanist learning and writing remained a personal matter. For example, John of Ludzisko (Jan z Ludziska) (*c.* 1400–*c.* 1460), who, as the university's orator, welcomed the 1440 visiting mission from the Basel council, had gone to Padua to study medicine and had become absorbed in the study of rhetoric there, carrying out extensive research on contemporary rhetorical norms and collecting examples into a notebook. Although he composed his orations in the quattrocento style, relying on such authors as GUARINO DA VERONA, GASPARINO BARZIZZA, and Poggio Bracciolini for models, his originality was limited, for in many instances his compositions ended up as a pastiche of the Italians. In spite of his lack of originality, Ludzisko's writing reflected new, humanist cultural currents and was linked to contemporary events in Poland.[25] Still, Ludzisko's texts consisted mainly of welcoming speeches that were connected to occasions at the Polish royal and ecclesiastical courts, and – in spite of including an oration in praise of the art of eloquence (*De laudibus et dignitate eloquentiae*, delivered in 1440) – had no real effect on the university community but, rather, could be said to have supported the development of court culture and political propaganda, and the advancement of the Jagiellonian dynasty.

This lack of transfer of a personal interest in the *studia humanitatis* to curricular reform at the University of Cracow in the 1440s can be explained by the role that theology had come to play at the university by this time. The Cracow *studium generale* had been founded in the fourteenth century as an institution to train lawyers. After a period of disintegration, it was renewed at the beginning of the fifteenth century with a theology faculty. What had originally been established

---

[25] Fijałek, *Mistrz Jakub*, i, pp. 237–39; Knoll, 'The University Context of Kochanowski's Era', pp. 193–5; Ulewicz, 'Polish Humanism and its Italian Sources', pp. 220–21. John of Ludzisko received his doctorate in Italy in 1433. His orations have been edited as *Ioannis de Ludzisko Orationes*, ed. H. S. Bojarski (Wrocław, 1971).

as a university of the state became progressively more dependent on the Church for its administration and finance. The bishop of Cracow was made the chancellor of the university, and the remuneration of the teachers, who were clerics, was grounded in ecclesiastical benefices.[26] The Faculty of Theology, which was the most powerful (because its professors carried out the most important functions in the university), was also the wealthiest (because of the benefices it received). But, during the time of the Council of Basel, the Cracow theologians became overly focused on the immediate issues of Church reform so that when the Council collapsed at the end of the 1440s, the Faculty of Theology, now not oriented towards wider or more long-term speculative and theoretical issues, found it had no significant contribution to make to the cultural life of the capital or to the political life of the state.[27] Its interests in humanism had been both stimulated and retarded by its participation in the Council. In defence of the University of Cracow and its theologians, however, one may note that few universities anywhere in Europe significantly revised their curricula at this time. At least the benign indifference of the theologians at Cracow allowed scholars such as Ludzisko to develop their own interests.

[26] Z. Kozlowska-Budkowa, 'La fondation de l'Université de Cracovie, en 1364, et son rôle dans le développement de la civilisation en Pologne' in S. Stelling-Michaud ed., *Les Universités européennes du XIVe au XVIIIe siècle* (Geneva, 1967), pp. 13–25 at pp. 15, 24; J. Wyrozumski, 'L'Université de Cracovie à l'époque conciliaire' in id. ed., *The Jagiellonian University in the Evolution of European Culture* (Cracow, 1992), pp. 7–24 at pp. 8–9.

[27] H. Barycz, *Historja Uniwersytetu Jagiellońskiego w epoce humanizmu* (Cracow, 1935), pp. 166–68; I. Zarębski, 'Okres wczesnego humanizmu' in K. Lepszy ed., *Dzieje Uniwersytetu Jagiellońskiego w latach 1364–1764* (Cracow, 1964), pp. 151–88 at pp 181–84; J. Garbacik, 'Ognisko nauki i kultury renesansowej (1470–1520)' in Lepszy ed., *Dzieje Uniwersytetu Jagiellońskiego*, pp. 189–220 at pp. 193–94; Kozlowska-Budkowa, 'La fondation de l'Université de Cracovie', p. 24; Knoll, 'The University of Cracow and the Conciliar Movement', pp. 206–7.

Meanwhile, the subjects of mathematics and astronomy, which were being developed at the university through private foundations, began to attract international attention.[28] These subjects would be linked with poetry with the arrival of Conrad Celtis from Nuremberg and Italy in 1489. Celtis had apparently been attracted to Cracow by the possibility of studying astrology under Albert Blar (Brudzewski; *c.* 1445 – *c.* 1497), who was also the teacher of Copernicus. In the 1510s and 1520s, humanist scholars such as Paul of Krosno, Rudolf Agricola Junior, and Leonard Cox would befriend the teachers of mathematics and astronomy and write commendatory verses for their publications. But these friendships would have no effect on the official curriculum of the university. In the mid-fifteenth century, as at the end of the century, there was simply no incentive to introduce the new methods of humanistic study into the curriculum or administration.

Similarly, the lectures of the young Gregory of Sanok (Gregorius Sanocensis; d. 1477) on Virgil in 1439 are traditionally cited as marking the coming of humanism to the university, but Gregory made his career in the Church, as archbishop of Lwów, and his real contribution to the establishing of a humanist movement at Cracow – and this would be at the royal court – was his sheltering and promoting of the Italian refugee Filippo Buonaccorsi.[29] Buonaccorsi, whose Latin pseudonym was Callimachus, had fled Rome following Pope Paul II's suppression of POMPONIUS LAETUS' Academy and

---

[28] P. Knoll, 'The Arts Faculty at the University of Cracow at the End of the Fifteenth Century' in R. S. Westman ed., *The Copernican Achievement* (Berkeley, CA, 1975), pp. 137–56 at pp. 144–49; C. Morawski, *Histoire de l'Université de Cracovie. Moyen Age et Renaissance*, trans. P. Rongier, 3 vols (Paris, 1900–1905), iii, pp. 173–203.

[29] On Gregory of Sanok, see H. B. Segel, *Renaissance Culture in Poland: the rise of humanism, 1470–1543* (Ithaca, NY, 1989). Knowledge of Gregory's lectures comes from a mention in Buonaccorsi's biography; there is no text extant, and the year of their delivery is not certain – if Gregory even delivered them at all: *Philippi Callimachi Vita et mores Gregorii Sanocei*, ed. I. Lichońska (Warsaw, 1963), p. 18 (n. 6).

had been granted refuge by Gregory in 1470.[30] Buonaccorsi remained at Gregory's court only until the autumn of 1472, when he matriculated at the university, but this official contact with the university was brief.[31] In the same year, through the authority of Gregory and through that of the nephew of the deceased Cardinal Oleśnicki – the younger Zbigniew (1430–1493), who was taking over the vice-chancellorship of the kingdom – Buonaccorsi was appointed a tutor to the royal sons. By the spring of 1473 he would enter international diplomacy, becoming an advisor on foreign policy to the kings Casimir IV and Jan Olbracht (John Albert, 1492–1501). It was in Cracow that Buonaccorsi died on 1st November 1496.

Buonaccorsi's contribution to Polish diplomacy and cultural affairs was immense. In him, the Jagiellonian dynasty had a champion for their cause who spoke and wrote Latin in a contemporary Renaissance style. Buonaccorsi's role as a political advisor and diplomat centred upon helping the Polish court to resist pressures from Rome and Venice to enter into a 'holy alliance' and confront the Turks, which would have resulted in

[30] For a summary of Callimachus' activities in Poland, see Segel, *Renaissance Culture in Poland*, pp. 36–82; J. Kotarska, 'Poeta i historyk–Filip Kallimach' in S. Grzeszczuk ed., *Pisarze staropolscy. Sylwetki*, 3 vols (Warsaw, 1991), i, pp. 174–207; K. Baczkowski, 'Kallimachs Stelle in der Kulturgeschichte Polens' in S. Füssel and J. Pirożyński ed., *Der polnische Humanismus und die europäischen Sodalitäten. Akten des polnisch-deutschen Symposions vom 15.–19. Mai 1996 im Collegium Maius der Universität Krakau* (Wiesbaden, 1997), pp. 73–90. Fuller biographies are J. Olkiewicz, *Kallimach doświadczony* (Warsaw, 1981), a popular treatment of the subject, and G. Paparelli, *Callimaco Esperiente* (Salerno, 1971). J. Garbacik, *Kallimach jako dyplomata i polityk* (Cracow, 1948), covers Buonaccorsi's diplomatic career in detail. A conference on Callimachus and his work was held in Italy in October 1985; the papers were published as G. C. Garfagnini ed., *Callimaco Esperiente poeta e politico del '400* (Florence, 1987).

[31] It is supposed that Buonaccorsi was fruitlessly seeking a post at the university. Although he had no official influence over the university, he had close friendships with many of the professors. He left a bequest to the university upon his death. See Knoll, 'The University Context', p. 201, and Baczkowski, 'Kallimachs Stelle', p. 77.

a military campaign that could only weaken Poland. Buonaccorsi worked towards strengthening the Polish presence in east central Europe both by seeking the succession to the throne of Bohemia for Casimir IV's eldest son, Ladislaus (in order to neutralize the Hungarians, who, under the leadership of King Matthias Corvinus, maintained an aggressive stance towards the Turks) and by attempting to maintain peaceful relations between the Poles and the Turks.[32]

In connexion with the first effort, to avert the pressure of the Venetians and the Pope to engage in a war with the Turks, Buonaccorsi participated in a Polish embassy to Constantinople in the spring of 1476, which was successful in ending the tension between the Turks and Moldavia, whose voivode was nominally a vassal of the Polish crown. At the end of the same year, Buonaccorsi was put in charge of a mission to Italy. This time, the goal of the journey was to obtain the recognition of the Pope for Ladislaus as king of Bohemia, but Buonaccorsi stopped in Venice first, where, in January 1477, he presented his case against the Pope's plan to employ Persian and Tartar troops against the Turks (a plan which would have necessitated armed Tartars passing through Polish lands), against Venetian financing of the Hungarian king, Matthias Corvinus (who was agitating against Polish interests in Bohemia), and for the formation of a coalition of Venice and Hungary together with Bohemia and Poland to face the Turks. Buonaccorsi then travelled to Rome, where he argued for the claim of the Polish king to the Bohemian throne. The Pope favoured the Hungarians under Matthias Corvinus because he believed they would be more effective in combatting the Hussite heresy then rampant in Bohemia and which had earlier found some support in Poland. On his return in June to Cracow, he again passed through Venice, and with the issue of the Bohemian succession still on his agenda, pleaded with the Venetians to intercede and put pressure on Matthias Corvinus

---

[32] Segel, *Renaissance Culture in Poland*, pp. 55–8; Morawski, *Histoire de l'Université de Cracovie*, iii, p. 11.

to accept an agreement with the Habsburg emperor, Frederick III, and with the kings of Poland and Bohemia.[33]

Buonaccorsi's diplomatic efforts of 1476 and 1477 were reflected in his writing.[34] He had already composed his *Consilium non ineundae societatis cum Italis in bello contra Turcos suscipiendo* in 1474, in which he had expressed resistance to the idea of joining the Venetians in a crusade against the Turks.[35] In his treatise *De his quae a Venetis tentata sunt Persis ac Tartaris contra Turcos movendis*, written most likely between 1487 and 1492, he took up the themes of that first mission to Italy, ten years earlier, and highlighted his own role in the negotiations with the Venetians.[36] In his final piece dealing with the Italian push for war with the Turks, *Ad Innocentium VIII de bello Turcis inferendo oratio*, Buonaccorsi, now a mature diplomat, echoed his earlier view that a pan-European league (or crusade) was impractical and proposed, rather, that in dealing with the Turks all the Christian powers should accept the authority of the Polish king, whose bearing, valour, skills and merits he praised.[37] In any case, Buonaccorsi's experi-

---

[33] Paparelli, *Callimaco Esperiente*, pp. 135–46; Segel, *Renaissance Culture in Poland*, pp. 54–60.

[34] Future ambassadorial journeys would include Vienna and Buda, as well as repeat visits to Venice, Constantinople, and Rome.

[35] The text is printed in A. Działyński, A.Tytus, W. Kętrzyński, Z. Celichowski and W. Pociecha, ed., *Epistole. Legationes. Responsa. Actiones. Res gestae ... Sigismundi ... Regis Poloniae .... Per S. Górski collecte et in tomos XXVII digeste [Acta Tomiciana]* (Poznań, 1852–), Appendix to vol. i (1852), pp. 15–18.

[36] The work is in A. Kempfi & T. Kowalewski, ed. (Warsaw, 1962).

[37] Buonaccorsi may or may not have delivered this as an oration at the congress summoned by the Pope in 1490 in an attempt to instigate a league against the Turks. See Philippus Callimachus, *Ad Innocentium VIII de bello Turcis inferendo oratio*, ed. and trans. I. Lichońska, with commentary by T. Kowalewski (Warsaw, 1964), pp. 7–8, 13; and Garbacik, *Kallimach jako dyplomata*, p. 115. Like most of Buonaccorsi's writing, this oration was not published until after his death. Kowalewski mentions a first edition of 1519 (Callimachus, *Ad Innocentium*, p.9).

ences as an emissary had led him to believe that the Christian nations had overrated Turkish military power, a power that according to him resided not in the number of its soldiers nor in its armaments, but in the erroneous views of the Christians.[38]

Buonaccorsi, then, served the Polish kings not only as an energetic diplomat, but as an effective propagandist, who not only transmitted Polish political views to the international arena, but who helped solidify the reputation of the Jagiellonian dynasty and glorify its rule, while casting an image of Poland as a power to be negotiated with in east central Europe. In his biographical writing, Buonaccorsi, influenced most likely by Neapolitan court historiography and the work of the Venetian MARCANTONIO SABELLICO, cast aside the old-fashioned chronicle format in favour of modern historiography, and so initiated a 'historiography of the state' in Poland, in which he combined history and politics, subordinating historiography to the requirements of publicist persuasion, while maintaining a certain aesthetic quality that would attract and entertain his readers.[39] In his biography of Casimir's brother, Ladislaus III, who had been killed fighting the Turks at Varna in 1444, *Historia de rege Vladislao* (1487), Buonaccorsi praised the Jagiellonian line, but rather than

---

[38] Paparelli, *Callimaco Esperiente*, pp. 161–63; Kotarska, 'Poeta i historyk–Filip Kallimach', p 203. A later political text, the *Consilia*, long attributed to Buonaccorsi (cf. Garbacik, *Kallimach jako dyplomata*, pp. 145–49, and Segel, *Renaissance Culture in Poland*, pp. 66–67), survives in manuscripts from the sixteenth and seventeenth centuries. The text is printed in G. Agosti, *Un politico italiano alla corte polacca nel secolo XV* (Turin, 1930).

[39] H. Barycz, *Szlakami dziejopisarstwa staropolskiego*, p. 17; J. Ślaski, 'La fortuna dell'opera letteraria di Callimaco in Polonia' in Garfagnini ed., *Callimaco Esperiente*, pp. 73–90 at pp. 85–86. On Sabellico, see R. Chavasse, 'The *studia humanitatis* and the Making of a Humanist Career: Marcantonio Sabellico's exploitation of humanist literary genres', *Renaissance Studies*, xvii (2003), pp. 27–38 and, on his international reputation, ead., 'The Reception of Humanist Historiography in Northern Europe: M. A. Sabellico and John Jewel', *Renaissance Studies*, ii (1988), pp. 327–38.

concentrating on the character of Ladislaus himself, he gave more attention to historical events, narrating the circumstances leading to the election of Ladislaus to the Hungarian throne, outlining the political situation in southern and south-eastern Europe at the time, sketching the deeds of the outstanding men who supported the king in maintaining his rule, and presenting the position of the Christian nations, especially Poland, in the preparation for war with the Turks, and, finally, detailing the Battle of Varna.[40] In his lives of Cardinal Zbigniew Oleśnicki (*Vita et mores Sbignei Cardinalis*, 1480) and of the Hungarian leader Attila (to be read as an allegory for a biography of King Matthias Corvinus) (*Attila*, 1486–88), Buonaccorsi devoted more attention to the characters of his protagonists, but he nevertheless put his historical narrative at the fore; in the former work, he provided much background on the history of Poland and the origins of the Polish and Lithuanian peoples, and on the Oleśnicki family; in the second, he related the history of the Huns and their country and described their customs.[41]

Buonaccorsi's influence on Polish culture extended further than the field of politics. As a result of his correspondence with MARSILIO FICINO he was responsible for introducing neo-Platonism into Poland.[42] And, besides his political treatises and propagandistic biographies, he composed a humanist biography of his patron, Archbishop Gregory of Sanok (*Vita et mores Gregorii Sanocei*, 1476) and was most likely the author

[40] Kotarska, 'Poeta i historyk–Filip Kallimach', p. 198. The work is available in T. Kowalewski and I. Lichońska, ed. (Warsaw, 1961).

[41] Paparelli, *Callimaco Esperiente*, p. 161; Kotarska, 'Poeta i historyk–Filip Kallimach', pp. 198–99. *Vita et mores Sbignei Cardinalis* is available in I. Lichońska, ed. (Warsaw, 1962), and *Attila* in T. Kowaleski, ed. (Warsaw, 1962).

[42] For details, see J. Domański, 'La Fortuna di Marsilio Ficino in Polonia nei secoli XV e XVI' in G. C. Garfagnini ed., *Marsilio Ficino e il ritorno di Platone. Studi e documenti*, 2 vols (Florence, 1986), ii, pp. 565–86 and J. Domański, 'Filippo Buonaccorsi e la cultura filosofica del '400 in Polonia' in Garfagnini ed., *Callimaco*, pp. 25–44.

of a life of John Długosz.[43] Inspired by Długosz's prose life of the patron saint of Poland, St Stanislaus, he composed a poem, *Carmen sapphicum in vitam gloriosissimi martyris sancti Stanislai episcopi Cracoviensis Polonorum gentis patroni*.[44] Buonaccorsi penned copious lines of verse – occasional, satirical, erotic – in the form of epigrams and elegies in imitation of the classics.[45] He also wrote a handbook on rhetoric.[46] Such was his impact that humanist writing would continue to flourish at the Cracow court after his death, supported by the patronage not only of members of the Jagiellonian family, especially King Sigismund (Zygmunt) I (1506–1548), but also of the Polish bishops who had had direct contact with him, such as Matthias (Maciej) Drzewicki and Erasmus (Erazm) Ciołek.[47] Two humanist poets connec-

[43] *Vita Ioannis Dlugosch senioris canonici Cracoviensis*, ed. M. Brożek (Warsaw, 1961), with a discussion of Buonaccorsi's authorship at pp. 9–11. *Vita et mores Gregorii Sanocei* is available in the edition of I. Lichońska (Warsaw, 1963).

[44] Długosz's work was entitled *Vita beatissimi Stanislai Episcopi Cracoviensis* and was composed about 1460–65. It was printed at Cracow by the Haller press in 1511 in a volume along with Długosz's lives of other Polish saints. It is available in the edition of A. Przezdziecki in *Joannis Dlugossii senioris Canonici Cracoviensis Opera*, ed. I. Polkowski and I. Żegota Pauli (Cracow, 1863–78, 1887), i (1887), pp. 1–182. The date of the composition of Buonaccorsi's poem is uncertain. It was printed at Cracow in an undated edition, c. 1521, by the Haller press. Helena Kapełuś locates a copy at the Ossoliński Library in Wrocław; see *Polonia typographica saeculi sedecimi*, ed. A. Kawecka-Gryczowa (Wrocław, 1959–), iv: *Jan Haller*, ed. H. Kapełuś, p. 61.

[45] See Kotarska, 'Poeta i historyk–Filip Kallimach' for an overview of Buonaccorsi's poetic output.

[46] The *Rhetorica*, composed most likely between 1472 and 1476, has been edited by C. Kumaniecki as *Philippi Callimachi Rhetorica* (Warsaw, 1950), with the suggestion at p. viii that the book may have been intended for the royal sons, as Buonaccorsi would have been involved in their education at this time.

[47] Drzewicki was a pupil of Buonaccorsi: Morawski, *Histoire de l'Université de Cracovie*, iii, p. 80; Baczkowski, 'Kallimachs Stelle', p.

ted to the royal court in the 1520s, Andrzej Krzycki (Andreas Cricius) and Stanislaus (Stanisław) Hosius, would praise Buonaccorsi in their own works. Buonaccorsi's writing would continue to be admired later in the sixteenth century, most notably by the historian Martin Kromer.[48]

It was the study of astronomy that finally brought to the university a humanist scholar whose reputation would equal that of Buonaccorsi. Conrad Celtis (1459–1508) arrived at Cracow in the spring of 1489, on his way back north from Italy.[49] He was to stay in the city only two years, until 1491. If he taught at all at Cracow, it was on an informal and extramural basis and most likely at the *Bursa Hungarorum*, where most of the German students lived. It was there that he announced a lecture on epistolography in the summer of 1489. Celtis' immediate influence led a teacher in the Collegium Minus, Johannes Æsticampianus (Sommerfeld) the Elder, to introduce university-sanctioned courses that made use of humanist handbooks on letter-writing.[50] While at

90; on Buonaccorsi's relationship with him, see Garbacik, *Kallimach jako dyplomata*, pp. 142–43. Ciołek studied at Cracow from 1485 to 1491, then lectured there as *extraneus* from 1491 to 1493. He entered the service of the Jagiellonian family in 1494 and began a diplomatic career in 1501, when he was sent to Rome by Grand Duke Alexander (later king) that would last until his death in 1522. Ciołek was made bishop of Płock in 1504: *Polski Słownik Biograficzny*, iv, pp. 78–80.

[48] Ślaski, 'La fortuna dell'opera letteraria di Callimaco in Polonia', pp. 83, 85.

[49] On Celtis in Poland, see A. Jelicz, *Konrad Celtis na tle wczesnego Renesansu w Polsce* (Warsaw, 1956); Segel, *Renaissance Culture in Poland*, pp. 83–106; G. Koziełek, 'Konrad Celtis in Krakau' in P. Thiergen and L. Udolph ed., *Res slavica. Festschrift für Hans Rothe zum 65. Geburtstag* (Paderborn, 1994), pp. 557–70. On Celtis more generally, see pp. 89–115 above.

[50] A. Gorzkowski, *Paweł z Krosna. Humanistyczne peregrynacje krakowskiego profesora* (Cracow, 2000), pp. 61–62, remarks that Celtis' pedagogical innovations actually took effect only after he left Cracow, and indeed, only after he had settled in Vienna. Johannes Æsticampianus the Elder, a dialectician who dabbled in rhetoric and the new poetics, was the first to lecture on AGOSTINO DATI's and

Cracow, Celtis cultivated a whole group of disciples and formed one of his literary academies, the *Sodalitas Vistulana*.[51] Buonaccorsi became a member, indicating that he was friendly with Celtis; in this way some exchange between humanism at court and humanism at the university took place.

The most active of Celtis' associates in promoting humanist pedagogy was the Silesian Laurentius Corvinus (1462–1527).[52] Corvinus studied at Cracow from 1484 to 1489, when he received the degree of Master of Arts, and continued to lecture there as *extraneus*, giving classes on Petrus Hispanus,

---

Francesco Negro's treatises on letter writing (in 1492 and 1493, respectively). On Aesticampianus, see *Liber diligentiarum Facultatis Artisticae Universitatis Cracoviensis. Pars I (1487–1563)*, ed. W. Wisłocki (Cracow, 1886), p. 496; Morawski, *Histoire de l'Université de Cracovie*, iii, pp. 81–84; L. Winniczuk, 'The Latin Manuals of Epistolography in Poland in the Fifteenth and Sixteenth Centuries' in I. D. McFarlane ed., *Acta Conventus Neo-Latini Sanctandreani. Proceedings of the Fifth International Congress of Neo-Latin Studies* (Binghamton, NY, 1986), pp 549–59 at p. 550, and J. Glomski, 'The Italian Grammarians and Early Humanism at Cracow', *Studi Umanistici Piceni*, xix (1999), pp. 47–53 at pp. 48–49.

[51] Jelicz, *Konrad Celtis*, pp. 41–2. There is no document extant that testifies to the founding of this society, but Celtis did mention it in his poems. The membership of the society has been reconstructed by J. Fijałek, 'Z dziejów humanizmu w Polsce. Niemcy w uniwersytecie Krakowskim w w. XV i XVI', *Pamiętnik literacki*, i (1902), pp. 257–64 at 261–62.

[52] On Corvinus, see G. Bauch, 'Laurentinus Corvinus, der Breslauer Stadschreiber und Humanist', *Zeitschrift des Vereins für Geschichte Schlesiens*, xvii (1883), pp. 230–302; J. Krókowski, 'Laurentius Corvinus und seine Beziehungen zu Polen' in J. Irmscher ed., *Renaissance und Humanismus in Mittel- und Osteuropa*, 2 vols, (Berlin, 1962), ii, pp. 153–72; Segel, *Renaissance Culture in Poland*, pp. 107–9; J. Glomski, 'Poetry to Teach the Writing of Poetry: Laurentius Corvinus' *Carminum structura* (1496)' in Y. Haskell & P. Hardie ed., *Poets and Teachers. Fifth Annual Symposium of the Cambridge Society for Neo-Latin Studies, September 1996* (Bari, 1999), pp. 155–66; G. McDonald, 'Laurentius Corvinus and the Flowering of Central European Humanism', *Terminus*, ix (2007), pp. 49–74.

Virgil, Boethius, and Aristotle.[53] He wrote lyric and didactic poetry and was the author of a series of handbooks on Latin composition that became widely used and were constantly reprinted, well into the first quarter of the sixteenth century. But none of Corvinus' educational works was published before 1494, the year he left Cracow, and none was printed in Poland. Corvinus returned to Silesia, evidently because of financial necessity, and took up employment as a schoolmaster in the town of Świdnica (Schweidnitz). There he completed, first of all, his handbook on the writing of poetry, *Carminum structura*, which he had printed at Leipzig in 1496. The *Carminum structura* was addressed to the students at the University of Cracow, and it is clear that Corvinus had started work on it while still working in Cracow since not only is the work based on Celtis' theories of poetry, but in it Corvinus inserted samples of his own poetry depicting the daily events of academic life, with one of the poems specifically naming another member of Celtis' literary circle, Sigismund Fusilius (Gossinger), who, like Corvinus, was an *extraneus non de facultate* lecturer at Cracow.[54]

Corvinus is a prime example of how, after Celtis left Cracow, academic interests in humanism lingered on the margins of the university: neither Corvinus nor any other of Celtis' disciples would be granted an official university post. Not until 1508, when Paul of Krosno (Paweł z Krosna, Paulus Crosnensis) (*c.* 1470–1517) was accepted into the Collegium Minus, would a university lecturer actively work towards the reform of the arts curriculum.[55] Paul, who had completed an

---

[53] *Liber diligentiarum*, ed. Wisłocki, p. 395.

[54] For details, see Glomski, 'Poetry to Teach the Writing of Poetry', pp. 160–65.

[55] *Polski słownik biograficzny*, xxv, pp. 384–68; M. Cytowska, 'Twórczość Pawła z Krosna na tle ówczesnej literatury humanistycznej', *Meander*, xvi (1961), pp. 502–15 at pp. 512–13, and Segel, *Renaissance Culture in Poland*, pp. 109–19. See also the editor's introduction to *Pauli Crosnensis Ioannisque Vislicensis carmina*, ed. B. Kruczkiewicz (Cracow, 1887). The most recent work on Paul, a much-needed

MA at Cracow in 1506, taught such authors as Terence, Seneca, Cicero, Ovid, and Virgil and based his lectures on the work of the Italian commentators, such as FILIPPO BEROALDO, POLITIAN, and ANTONIO URCEO (known as Codrus). He also composed religious and panegyric poetry, and edited the work of the Hungarian poet Janus Pannonius, whom he admired.[56] But by 1517, Paul had fled Cracow for fear of the plague and perished before he could accomplish much as far as pedagogical renewal.[57]

Two of Paul's students, Rudolf Agricola Junior and Valentin Eck, together with a later arrival, Leonard Cox, carried on the struggle to integrate the humanist curriculum into university and school education by publishing texts, handbooks, and treatises for teachers and students of classical Latin. Although Agricola Junior, Eck, and Cox emulated the works of the Italians not only as a means of achieving the imitation of the classics, but as examples of beautiful and pure Latinity themselves, and although they filled their poems with classical, pagan colouring, this was never erotic or lascivious, as in Italian neo-Latin poetry, or even as in the works of Celtis and Corvinus. Rather, the writing of these three scholars shows the influence of the Italians as communicated through a pious, German medium and through the works of Erasmus. Indeed, they favoured the Erasmian subjects of Christian piety, marriage, and the family, and they took up Erasmus' interest in patristics and the education of youth. For these three men, the purpose of writing literature was to change their readers' lives for the better, whether it be ridding their Latin of barbarisms or leading them onto the path of virtue.[58]

---

monograph, is A. Gorzkowski, *Paweł z Krosna. Humanistyczne peregrynacje krakowskiego profesora* (Cracow, 2000).

[56] On Pannonius' reputation more generally, see pp. 161–3 below.

[57] Gorzkowski, *Paweł z Krosna*, p. 96.

[58] J. Glomski, *Patronage and Humanist Literature in the Age of the Jagiellons: court and career in the writings of Rudolf Agricola Junior, Valentin Eck, and Leonard Cox* (Toronto, 2007), pp. 31–33.

None of these three scholars, however, achieved real success at Cracow. Valentin Eck left the city in 1517, four years after completing his bachelor's degree, and established himself at Bardejov (Bártfa – then in the kingdom of Hungary, now in the eastern region of Slovakia), where he was made headmaster of the town school, but then assumed jobs of increasing responsibility in the town government and rose to become the town's mayor. Cox had matriculated at Cracow in September 1518, but in 1520, without stable work, he, like Eck, travelled south, becoming headmaster of the school in Levoča (Lőcse), then, at the end of 1521, of the school in Košice (Kassa). Cox did return to Cracow in 1525 and took up lecturing at the university again that autumn, but by 1529 he was back in England, where he secured employment as the master of the grammar school at Reading. Finally, the poor Rudolf Agricola Junior left Cracow around Easter 1514, having finished his bachelor's degree just over two years earlier. Passing through Buda, he spent the next few months at Esztergom (Gran) in charge of the cathedral school. He then resided for two and a half years in Vienna, but not obtaining stable employment there, he returned to Poland at the end of 1517. Back in Cracow, Agricola Junior was finally offered an official post at the university through the financial backing of a consortium of Polish bishops. Yet, he complained in his correspondence that he was not being paid for his teaching and stated that he intended to return to his home region of Lake Constance to enter a low-level Church career there. But before he could do so, he died at Cracow, exhausted and penniless, in March 1521.[59]

Following the death of Rudolf Agricola Junior, the number and frequency of humanist-inspired topics continued to grow on the official university lecture list, but these were mainly

---

[59] E. Arbenz & H. Wartmann, 'Die Vadianische Briefsammlung der Stadtbibliothek St. Gallen [part II]', *Mitteilungen zur Vaterländischen Geschichte*, xxv (1894), pp. 191–482 at pp. 284–85, 308–10, 319–21, 338–39 (letters 196, 216, 225, 240). For further discussion of the reasons for the lack of support of these early humanists, see Glomski, *Patronage and Humanist Literature*, pp. 33–45.

concerned with the classics, with Cicero, Sallust, Florus, Virgil, Ovid, and Horace being the most frequent. Of the Italian authors, the most influential was FRANCESCO NEGRO, whose *Epistolae sive de conscribendis epistolis* was lectured on nearly without a break during the 1520s. FRANCESCO FILELFO's *Epistolae* was also in use to teach epistolography while NICCOLÒ PEROTTI's *Rudimenta grammatica* and LORENZO VALLA's *Elegantiae linguae latinae* were employed for instruction in Latin grammar. At the same time, the work of the Italians was mediated through Polish and German scholarship, as the epistolographical handbooks of Johannes Sacranus (Jan z Oświęcimia) and Johannes Ursinus (Ber) and the grammar book of Jacob Heinrichmann were also being taught, although less frequently.[60] What remained missing on the lecture lists in the 1520s was a manual of Latin versification written by an Italian. The *ars versificandi*, the staple of humanist teaching, would stay confined to unofficial classes conducted in the university residences.

[60] Even though such lectures were being conducted with university sanction, they were only optional; the old curriculum, based on Aristotle and the dialectic, remained the obligatory course of study on which the students were examined. The strength of humanist teaching at Cracow would remain in unofficial classes conducted in the university residences. So, in the 1520s, this offering of a sprinkle of humanist content was too little, too late. The institution was losing its European reputation and, from 1524, the number of matriculations, especially of foreigners, started to slip. Then, when, from 1525, the Polish nobility began to send their sons *en masse* to Italy for higher education, the University of Cracow quickly slid into decline. See Morawski, *Histoire de l'Université de Cracovie*, iii, pp. 93–105, 121–37, 165–70; Barycz, *Historja Uniwersytetu Jagiellońskiego*, pp. 16–24, 67–84, 127–30; A. Wyczański, 'Uniwersytet Krakowski w czasach złotego wieku' in Lepszy ed., *Dzieje Uniwersytetu Jagiellońskiego w latach 1364–1764*, pp. 221–52 at pp. 229–31; Glomski, 'The Italian Grammarians', pp. 48–49. Wyczański argues against the decline in the numbers of matriculations at the university at this time ('Uniwersytet Krakowski', pp. 244–45). His conclusions may have been politically motivated, but he has to admit that the new, humanist trends were attractive to students and were not being taught as part of the obligatory university programme at Cracow (ibid., pp. 246, 250).

Meanwhile, at the courts of the king and the magnates (both lay and ecclesiastic), the taste for the Italian style had taken firm hold. King Sigismund I, already before his ascent to the Polish throne, had summoned to Cracow from Hungary the Italian artist Francesco Fiorentino and commissioned him to sculpt an architectural surround for the niche tomb of his deceased brother, King Jan Olbracht; this arch was the first piece of art in the Italian Renaissance style to be completed at Cracow.[61] In their literary endeavours, the early sixteenth-century royal secretaries Justus Ludovicus Decius, Johannes Dantiscus, and Andrzej Krzycki[62] followed in the footsteps of

[61] The arch was completed in 1505. J. Białostocki, *The Art of the Renaissance in Eastern Europe: Hungary, Bohemia, Poland* (Ithaca, NY, 1976), p. 10; T. DaCosta Kaufmann, *Court, Cloister and City: the art and culture of Central Europe, 1450–1800* (London, 1995) p. 54, and A. Miłobędzki, 'Architecture under the Last Jagiellons in its Political and Social Context' in Fiszman ed., *Polish Renaissance in its European Context*, pp. 291–300 at p. 292. On King Sigismund's patronage of the arts, see K. Lewalski, 'Sigismund I of Poland: Renaissance king and patron', *Studies in the Renaissance*, xiv (1967), pp. 49–72, and M. Fabiański, 'Art and Architecture of the Renaissance in Kraków 1500–1550: an introduction' in F. Ames-Lewis, ed., *Polish and English Responses to French Art and Architecture: contrasts and similarities* (London, 1995), pp. 141–52. Jan Ślaski signals the link between Poland and Hungary in the formation of a 'golden triangle' with Italy during this period, in his 'L'Umanesimo nella Polonia del XV secolo e l'Italia' in T. Klaniczay and J. Jankovics, ed., *Matthias Corvinus and the Humanism in Central Europe* (Budapest, 1994), pp. 211–222.

[62] On Decius (Decjusz), see *CE*, i, pp. 380–82; *Polski słownik biograficzny*, v, pp. 42–45; C. Bonorand, *Vadians Humanisten Korrespondenz mit Schülern und Freunden aus seiner Wienerzeit: Personenkommentar IV zum Vadianischen Briefwerk* (St. Gallen, 1988), pp. 45–49; and W. Budka, 'Biblioteka Decjuszów', *Silva rerum*, iv (1928), pp. 110–26. On Dantiscus (Dantyszek), see *CE*, i, p. 377; *Polski słownik biograficzny*, iv, pp. 424–30; Segel, *Renaissance Culture in Poland*, pp. 161–90; H. de Vocht, *John Dantiscus and his Netherlandish Friends* (Louvain, 1961); Z. Nowak, *Jan Dantyszek. Portret renesansowego humanisty* (Wrocław, 1982), and id., 'Polityk, poeta i duchowny' in Grzeszczuk ed., *Pisarze staropolscy*, pp. 344–76. On Krzycki (Cricius), see *Polski słownik biograficzny*, xv, pp. 544–49, and *CE*, ii, pp. 275–78; A. Jelicz, 'Die Dichtung des Andreas Cricius' in Irmscher ed.,

Buonaccorsi: they all glorified, in humanist Latin style, the deeds of the Jagiellonian kings. The court, furthermore, extended patronage to a whole range of poets, including the aforementioned Rudolf Agricola Junior and Leonard Cox, as well as John of Wiślica (Jan z Wyślicy, Johannes Visliciensis)[63] and Nicholas of Hussów (Mikołaj Hussowczyk, Nicolaus Hussovianus).[64] Through the sponsorship of such writers, along with that of architects, artists, and musicians, King Sigismund I and his magnates escorted Poland into its Golden Age of Renaissance art and culture.

Renaissance und Humanismus in Mittel- und Osteuropa, ii, pp. 131–38; J. S. Gruchała, 'Zmarnowany talent–Andrzej Krzycki' in Grzeszczuk ed., *Pisarze staropolscy*, pp. 256–305, and Segel, *Renaissance Culture in Poland*, pp. 191–226.

[63] On Visliciensis and his military epic, *Bellum Prutenum*, see Segel, *Renaissance Culture in Poland*, pp. 119–26.

[64] On Hussovianus and his poem on hunting the bison, see Segel, *Renaissance Culture in Poland*, pp. 138–60.

THE POWER OF THE BOOK AND THE KINGDOM OF HUNGARY DURING THE FIFTEENTH CENTURY

CRISTINA NEAGU

In 1477 MARSILIO FICINO (1433–1499) dispatched a telling letter to his humanist friend and follower, FRANCESCO BANDINI, who had recently arrived in Buda.[1] The letter accompanied a copy of Ficino's biography of Plato sent as a gift to Bandini. In it, Ficino told the recipient, in no uncertain terms, that he did not send his Plato to Athens, but rather to the kingdom of Hungary, because 'there flourishes the great King Matthias who, sustained at once by a wonderful power and wisdom in these years of manifest decline, will provide once more a sanctuary to the wise and powerful Pallas'.[2]

---

[1] On Bandini and his role at the Hungarian court, see P. O. Kristeller, 'An Unpublished Description of Naples by Francesco Bandini' and id., 'Francesco Bandini and his Consolatory Dialogue upon the Death of Simone Gondi' in id., *Studies in Renaissance Thought and Letters* [Storia e Letteratura, liv] (Rome, 1956), pp. 395–410 & 411–35; R. Feuer-Tóth, *Art and Humanism in Hungary in the Age of Matthias Corvinus* (Budapest, 1990), esp. pp. 56–66 and 105–113; V. Rees, 'Pre-Reformation changes in Hungary at the end of the fifteenth century' in K. Maag ed., *The Reformation in Eastern and Central Europe* (Aldershot, 1997), pp. 19–35, and ead., 'Ad Vitam Felicitatemque: Marsilio Ficino to his Friends in Hungary', *Budapest Review of Books*, viii (1998), pp. 57–63.

[2] 'Ibi enim floret magnus rex ille Mathias, qui mira quadam potentia simul et sapientia fretus certis relabentibus annis aedem potenti sapientique Palladi, hoc est Graecorum gymnasia, reparabit.' Quoted in *Analecta nova ad historiam Reneascentium in Hungaria litterarum spectantia*, ed. E. Abel & S. Hegedüs (Budapest, 1903), p. 274. This letter was originally included in the fifth book of Ficino's *Epistolae*. English translation in *The Letters of Marsilio Ficino*, 8 vols to date

This was an exceptional period in the history of the kingdom of Hungary. Despite major tensions caused by, on the one hand, external bids for supremacy and, on the other, internal frictions between political parties, the time was one of significant intellectual achievements.[3]

An increasing number of Hungarians were educated abroad, in most cases at Ferrara and Padua.[4] The best known of these, Janus Pannonius (1434–1472), is probably Hungary's most accomplished neo-Latin poet.[5] At GUARINO DA VERONA's school in Ferrara and later at the University of Padua, Pannonius' poetic gifts rapidly developed and he became widely acknowledged and respected for the originality of his style. Guarino's impact on the Hungarian poet is obvious in the repeated praises he addresses to his former teacher. Thus, in one epigram he compares Guarino to Phoebus, Faunus, Hammon and Serapis, while in another he recalls the image of 'Nestor Homericus linguae dulciloquo nectare'.[6]

(London, 1975–2009), iii (1981), pp. 77–78. The letter is also quoted in the volume dedicated to the history of the now lost Corvinian Library by C. Csapodi, *The Corvinian Library: history and stock* (Budapest, 1973), p. 47. For discussion, see S. Gentile, 'Marsilio Ficino e l'Ungheria di Mattia Corvino' in S. Graciotti & C. Vasoli ed., *Italia e Ungheria all'epoca dell'umanesimo corviniano* (Florence, 1994), pp. 89–110.

[3] The Ottomans and the Venetians threatened the kingdom from the south, Emperor Frederick III from the west, and Casimir IV of Poland from the north, with both Frederick and Casimir claiming the throne.

[4] See *Matricula et acta Hungarorum in universitate Patavina studentium, 1264–1864*, ed A. Veress (Budapest, 1915).

[5] On Pannonius, see M. Birnbaum, *Janus Pannonius: poet and politician* (Zagreb, 1984); ead., *The Orb and the Pen: Janus Pannonius, Matthias Corvinus and the Buda Court* (Budapest, 1996), and I. Thomson, *Humanist Pietas: the Panegyric of Ianus Pannonius on Guarinus Veronensis* (Bloomington, 1988).

[6] Good examples of the kind are Pannonius' acclaimed panegyric for his master and epigrams 15, 37, 185 and 188. See *Iani Pannonii Quinque Ecclesiensis Episcopi, Antiquis vatibus comparandi, ad Guarinum Veronensem panegyricus.* [...] (Venice: Gualtherus Scottus, 1553); I. Thomson, *Humanist Pietas* (and id., 'The Scholar as Hero in Ianus Pannonius' Panegyric on Guarinus Veronensis', *Renaissance Quarterly*, xliv (1991), pp.

Of the geographical variants of Italian humanism, it was the Ferrarese that during the fifteenth-century had the most significant influence on the Hungarian Renaissance. The model of Guarino is important to take into account, as he had been especially associated with a school that attempted a union of philosophy and rhetoric in education. As a consequence, his method would ultimately result in influencing fields far beyond letters and would develop 'una filosofia non servile' able to question the very principles of authority.[7] Pannonius is a classic case to illustrate this. On his return to Hungary, he became one of the chief advisers on King Matthias' foreign policy. Their ever more frequent differences of opinion were visible both in historical context, with Pannonius finally joining the enemies of the King in a well-known conspiracy, but also in the poetry he wrote, uncompromising and intensely personal in tone.

In contrast, the foreigners invited by Matthias to Hungary appear more content with the *status quo*. The most compelling figures of the period present at the court of Buda were Francesco Bandini and ANTONIO BONFINI. The latter's unfinished work constitutes one of the main sources of information regarding early Hungarian and east European history, in which King Matthias Corvinus (1440–1490) played an essential role.[8] The second son of Johannes Hunyadi, a suc-

197–212), and Janus Pannonius, *Epigrams*, ed. and trans. A. A. Barrett (Budapest, 1985). For a different interpretation, see pp. 317–18 below.

[7] See E. Garin, *Ritratti di umanisti* (Florence, 1967), p. 95. For further details on Guarino, see J. Ward, 'The Lectures of Guarino da Verona on the *Rhetorica ad Herenium*: a preliminary discussion' in W. B. Horner and M. Leff ed., *Rhetoric and Pedagogy: its history, philosophy, and practice* (Mahwah, NJ, 1995), pp. 97–128. For a discussion on Guarino's originality of rhetorical teaching, see A. Grafton and L. Jardine, *From Humanism to the Humanities: education and the liberal arts in fifteenth- and sixteenth-century Europe* (Cambridge, MA, 1986), pp. 1–28.

[8] *Antonii Bonfinii Rerum Vngaricarum decades quatuor cum dimidia. His accessere I Sambuci appendices; vna cum priscorum regum Vngariae decretis*, ed. Joannes Sambucus (Basel: Officina Opporiniana, 1568); a second edition was published at Frankfurt by Andreas Wechelus in 1581. The work is also available in the edition of I. Fógel et al., 4 vols

cessful general of Romanian origin in service of the Kingdom of Hungary, and of Erzsébet Szilágyi, from a Hungarian noble family, Matthias was elected king at the age of fifteen, in a complex and convoluted context, involving the former king, Ladislaus Posthumus, Hungary's various quarrelling barons and Matthias' own elder brother.[9] This was the first time in Hungarian history when a member of the nobility, without royal ancestry, mounted the throne. The result was a major upset to the course of royal succession, which, while inevitably creating underground political unrest, also cleared the way for renewal. In this sense, Matthias proved to be providential, as he managed to shake the establishment to its very foundations. After decades of feudal anarchy, Matthias consciously attempted to reconstruct the Hungarian state by means of an array of financial, military, judiciary, administrative and cultural reforms.

It is not difficult to see why humanists such as GALEOTTO MARZIO or Antonio Bonfini considered Matthias' court as the first outpost of Italian art north of the Alps.[10] At that time, however, this was something more obvious to foreign eyes, Ficino being one of the most articulate and unconditional in his praise. So much so that in effect he turned the king into something ap-

---

(Leipzig & Budapest, 1936–76). On Bonfini see G. Amadio, *La vita e l'opera di Antonio Bonfini primo storico della nazione ungherese e di Mattia Corvino in particolare* (Monalto Marche, 1930).

[9] For a recent detailed overview of the king, his reign and his patronage, see [Budapest History Museum exhibition catalogue], *Matthias Corvinus, the King. Tradition and renewal in the Hungarian royal court 1458–1490* (Budapest, 2008).

[10] On Marzio, see C. Vasoli, 'Note su Galeotto Marzio', *Acta literaria Academiae Scientiarum Hungaricae*, xix (1977), pp. 51–69, reprinted at id., *La cultura delle corti* (Bologna, 1980), pp. 38–63. He wrote a collection of anecdotes about Matthias, *De egregie, sapienter, iocose dictis ac factis regis Mathiae* (1485). The work, which survives in two manuscripts, was first printed by Sigismundus Torda (see note 54 below) and was most recently edited by L. Juhász (Leipzig, 1934): for full bibliographical details, see P. Kulcsár, *Inventarium de operibus litterariis ad res Hungaricas pertinentibus ab initiis usque ad annum 1700* (Budapest, 2003), available on-line at http://www.tankonyvtar.hu/konyvek/inventarium-deoperibus/inventarium-de-operibus-081028-4 .

proaching an archetype. Panegyric formulae were commonplace at the time, but the role Ficino casts Matthias in is somewhat unusual. Memorably, his references to Matthias Corvinus built on the concept of the Platonic ideal of the philosopher-king.[11]

Ficino might have been the most extravagant in his praise, but he was building on an existing humanist tradition of interest in the Hungarian Quattrocento. ÆNEAS SILVIUS PICCOLOMINI was among the first to put Hungary on the intellectual map for cultivated Italians. He was simultaneously an immensely respected humanist and a very able politician who, when elevated as Pope Pius II, tried to persuade Europe to unite against the Turks. His plea was at its most articulate in *De Europa* (1458), a comprehensive and very popular chorography at the time.[12] Significantly, Piccolomini began his study by focusing on the kingdom of Hungary the survival of which he viewed as essential to avoid direct conflict with the Ottoman empire in Western Europe.[13]

Even before Piccolomini's voice could be heard however, Italian humanists were present and personally involved in the Hungarian scene. Among those who had a strong impact was PIER PAOLO VERGERIO whose acquaintance with Hungary was to prove a lasting one, as he settled there in 1418 and it remained his home until his death.[14] One of the leading scholars

---

[11] Such commonplaces were, of course, not original to Ficino – to give just one humanist example, PIER CANDIDO DECEMBRIO emphasised the same topos when translating Plato's *Republic* for Humfrey, duke of Gloucester: [Bodleian Library exhibition catalogue], *Duke Humfrey and English Humanism* (Oxford, 1970), no. 9.

[12] Æneas Sylvius Piccolomini, *De Europa*, ed. A. van Heck [Studi e Testi, cccxcviii] (Vatican City, 2001).

[13] J. Hankins, 'Renaissance Crusaders: Humanist Crusading Literature in the Age of Mehmed II', *Dumbarton Oaks Papers*, xlix (1995), pp. 111–207. For Piccolomini's comments on Matthias Corvinus, see I. Boronkai, 'Matthias im Bilde des Memorien des Pius II' in T. Klaniczay & J. Jankovics ed., *Matthias Corvinus and the Humanism in Central Europe* (Budapest, 1994), pp. 59–69.

[14] For detailed studies on Vergerio, see D. Robey, 'P.P. Vergerio the Elder: Republicanism and Civic Values in the Work of an Early

of his generation, he is perhaps best remembered for writing *Paulus* (c. 1390), the earliest known comedy of the Italian Renaissance, and for having produced the first humanist pedagogical treatise, *De ingenuis moribus et liberalibus studiis adulescentiae* (c. 1402).[15] Vergerio had both the ability and the enthusiasm to embrace a wide range of challenges. His acceptance therefore of King Sigismund's invitation to Buda should not surprise us. Vergerio's brief was to reorganize the chancellery according to humanistic principles. But he did much more than this. Under his influence Hungarian scholars gained a chance to achieve and maintain close contacts with humanist circles in Italy.[16]

An associate of Vergerio who was to be influential in the direction of fifteenth-century humanism in the kingdom of Hungary was Johannes Vitéz (1408?-1472), the future archbishop of Esztergom.[17] As a prominent prelate and chancellor,

---

Humanist', *Past & Present*, lviii (1973), pp. 3–37; J. M. McManamon, 'Pier Paolo Vergerio (The Elder) and the Beginnings of the Humanist Cult of Jerome', *The Catholic Historical Review*, lxxi (1985), pp. 353–371, and id., *Pierpaolo Vergerio the Elder: the humanist as orator* (Tempe, AZ, 1996). See also pp. 309–10 below.

[15] Both works have recently appeared in parallel text, *Paulus* in *Humanist Comedies*, ed. and trans. G. R. Grund [ITRL, xix] (Cambridge, MA, 2005) and *De Ingenuis* in *Humanist Educational Treatises*, ed. and trans. C. W. Kallendorf [ITRL, v] (Cambridge, MA, 2002).

[16] Very few of Vergerio's letters from his time in Sigismund's service survive but see *Epistolario di Pier Paolo Vergerio*, ed. L. Smith (Rome, 1934), pp. 388–98; see also J. W. Sedlar, *East Central Europe in the Middle Ages, 1000–1500* (Seattle WA, 1994), p. 452.

[17] On Vitéz and his library, see K. Csapodiné Gárdonyi, *Die Bibliothek des Johannes Vitéz* [Studia Humanitatis, vi] (Budapest, 1984), and [National Széchényi Library exhibition catalogue], *A Star in the Raven's Shadow, János Vitéz and the Beginnings of Humanism in Hungary* (Budapest, 2008). For his relations with Vergerio, see Csapodiné Gárdonyi, *Bibliothek des Johannes Vitéz*, pp. 20–28 and McManamon, *Vergerio*, pp. 158–59; for his patronage of one Byzantine humanist, see J. Monfasani, *George of Trebizond. A biography and a study of his rhetoric and logic* (Leiden, 1976), pp. 194–200, and, more generally, P. Ekler, '*Propugnacula christianitatis–studia humanitatis*. Relations between Byz-

he was at the centre of state affairs at the courts of both Sigismund and Matthias. Vitéz was also intrinsically linked with the foundation of the capitulary school, library and astronomical observatory, at Oradea in Transylvania and with the short-lived Universitas Histropolensis he established in 1465 at Bratislava. It has been said that Vitéz's 'great triumph' was to convince Johannes Müller of Königsberg, better known as Regiomontanus, to join him; the latter was one of the most celebrated young astronomers of the time.[18] Another significant innovation that Vitéz is credited with is a volume containing his correspondence.[19] This is considered to be the first philological text produced in Hungary. It contains several exchanges on the inadequacy of medieval Latin and stresses the all important task of producing error-free texts. However, as Marianna Birnbaum notes, humanist correspondence was not an end to Johannes Vitéz's aspirations, but a means by which his political and episcopal functions could attain a high level of success. The archbishop became famous for his tact and style, for being capable of couching the most devastating message in an artistically formulated phrase, mellowing its sting by his charm and wit, and often by a disarming personal tone.[20]

What makes Vitéz a hugely influential figure is his striking talent for inter-personal relations. This together with geography

antium and Byzantine humanists active in Italy and Hungary in the middle of the 15th century' in *A Star in the Raven's Shadow*, pp. 105–16.

[18] M. Tanner, *The Raven King. Matthias Corvinus and the fate of his lost library* (New Haven, CT, 2008), p. 52. See also Z. Nagy, 'Ricerche cosmologiche nella corte umanistica di Giovanni Vitéz' in T. Klaniczay ed., *Rapporti veneto-ungheresi all'epoca del Rinascimento* (Budapest, 1975), pp. 65–93. On Regiomontanus, see pp. 104–5 above.

[19] Johannes Vitéz's *Epistolae* were first collected and edited by Paulus Ivanich, canon of Várad (in or about 1451). For details, see Johannes Vitéz, *Opera quae supersunt*, ed. I. Boronkai (Budapest, 1980), and, for discussion, E. Zsupán, 'János Vitéz' Book of Letters. Prologue' in *A Star in the Raven's Shadow*, pp. 117–39.

[20] See M. Birnbaum, review of Vitéz, *Opera quae supersunt*, ed. Boronkai, in *Renaissance Quarterly*, xxxv (1982), p. 272.

pure and simple had a direct impact on the very essence of humanism in that part of the world. Essentially cosmopolitan in nature, the Hungarian Renaissance fostered the idea of asserting itself as the prime custodian of European Christian values against the Turkish threat. This was achieved, among other things, through a remarkable openness to everything Italian. To cite just one instance, the Bolognese architect Aristotile Fioravanti (who would later spend his years in Muscovy) was called to Hungary for brief periods in 1466 and 1467 for his skill, it was said, was needed in building works required for war against the Infidel.[21] At its most accomplished, what looked like an unconditional accommodation occurred between Italy and Hungary during the reign of King Matthias. Once again, a great deal is owed to Vitéz, who played a key role in securing both Matthias' education (he was the King's tutor through childhood) and his throne, as a firm supporter of the Transylvanian Hunyadis.

The impact of this cultivated king was enormous. Matthias managed to stay in the limelight both in domestic politics and on the wider European scene for the duration of a long rule. He understood the significance of opinion-makers and was skilled at making a good impression on others. Humanists, moved by this impossible-to-ignore, charismatic character, felt compelled to write about him, acknowledging his support of art and scholarship, his taste for speculative discussion and his language skills.[22]

As a king, Matthias was determined and confident enough to attempt major reforms. He chose to look back into history for inspiration and put much of his knowledge and love of the classics to practical effect in the everyday running of the kingdom. Among the books Matthias claimed to be his favourites were Quintus Curtius' *Life of Alexander*, Silius Italicus' recently

---

[21] J. Balogh, 'Aristotele Fioravanti in Ungheria', *Arte Lombarda*, xliv / xlv (1976), pp. 225–27.

[22] For details regarding Matthias' language skills, see chapter iv of Galeotto Marzio's *De dictis ac factis regis Mathiae* (see footnote 10), with a short English quotation provided by Tanner, *The Raven King*, p. 28.

refound epic of the Punic wars and Caesar's *Gallic Wars*.[23] Books and the example of history were powerful sources of inspiration in the way the king managed his state affairs. With the advantage of hindsight, what he did looks very much like a bold experiment, masterminded via a series of concerted changes, implemented simultaneously in the army (Matthias aimed to reintroduce Roman practices), in administration (essentially by designing a new centralized tax system eroding the power of both the church and the landed aristocracy), but most visibly and long lastingly in the arts and learning.[24]

Unsurprisingly, Matthias' spectacular but tightly controlled system of governance did not survive him. Resentment ran deep both among the old baronial families and the prelates, who, after his death, seized upon the opportunity to elect a weak king. In normal circumstances, this might not have mattered much. However, at that particular moment in history, the choice ended in disaster.

The disintegration of the kingdom was inevitable. After a relatively slow process of stagnation under weak leadership, the situation came to a dramatic end on 29th August 1526, when the Hungarian army was annihilated by the Turks and King Louis II (1506–1626) was killed in battle at Mohács. Under Ottoman pressure, Hungary was shattered beyond recognition, with one part ruled directly by the Turks, another under the Habsburgs and a third, the principality of Transylvania, semi-independent as usual, but under Turkish suzerainty.

In terms of geography as well, the kingdom had spread too large over a multi-ethnic territory to be able to hold together

---

[23] V. Rees, 'Hungary's Philosopher-King and his Queen Consort: Renaissance Theory in Practice', *The European Legacy*, i (1996), pp. 227–232 at p. 228. The letter of thanks sent in the king's name to POMPONIUS LAETUS for the printed copy of Silius the humanist had sent him is now available on-line at http://www.repertoriumpomponianum.it/textus/corvinus_leto.htm [accessed 18th December 2011].

[24] J. Bak, 'The Kingship of Matthias Corvinus: a Renaissance State?' in Klaniczay & Jankovics ed., *Matthias Corvinus and Humanism in Central Europe*, pp. 37–47.

naturally. This territory included a great diversity of people: Hungarians, Croats, Slovenes, Bosnians, Serbs, Dalmatians, Bohemians, Moravians, Romanians and Germans among others, each with their own history and culture. It may appear paradoxical, but it seems that at a time of total meltdown, it is precisely the strength of the component parts that kept the values of the old kingdom alive. In other words, where there was a choice, that is where direct Turkish rule was kept at bay, humanists, both those in exile and those who remained in what was left of Hungary, finally started to look with undivided attention at the rich Renaissance culture they were now so close to losing.

The story of the beginning of printing in Hungary convincingly illustrates this phenomenon. Printing began in Buda relatively early, with the first book issued from Andreas Hess' press in 1473. This may seem surprising. The export of a press and relevant craftsmen must have been a significant financial gamble. However, the taste for books was already manifest (*inter alia*) in the founding of exquisite private libraries, such as those of Johannes Vitéz and Janus Pannonius, and the great *Bibliotheca Corvina*.

The first two are now somewhat less famous. In the eyes of their contemporaries however, they were deeply significant. Vitéz's library is thought to have numbered around 500 volumes. Scholars such as Galeotto Marzio, George Peuerbach, Regiomontanus and FILIPPO BUONACCORSI referred to it in their writings.[25] We know far less about Pannonius' collection, but the famous Florentine bookseller, Vespasiano da Bisticci (1421–1498) mentions Pannonius' library in his writings.[26]

In contrast, the *Bibliotheca Corvina* has always been much talked of and remains the achievement for which King Matthias

---

[25] See Csapodiné Gárdonyi, *Die Bibliothek des Johannes Vitéz* and *A Star in the Raven's Shadow* (see footnote 17).

[26] Vespasiano da Bisticci, *Le vite*, ed. A. Greco, 2 vols (Florence, 1970–76), i, p. 333.

is now perhaps most likely to be remembered.[27] He put enormous effort into its development, appointing the right people to organize it and source important holdings, inviting contributions from the best and most qualified to transform the small collections he inherited into the celebrated repository it became during his reign.

To start with, it seems likely that large sections of the Johannes Vitéz's and Janus Pannonius' libraries were incorporated into the royal collection in 1472 after their owners' deaths. Several works now associated with the Corvinian library contain brief comments, especially by Vitéz. In comparison with the luxurious volumes commissioned by the king in the 1480s, these earlier books are sparsely decorated.

The *Corvina*'s development is connected with four key names: the two aforementioned Hungarian scholars, Vitéz and Pannonius, and two Italian humanists, Galeotto Marzio and TADDEO UGOLETO. However, even though in the *De doctrina promiscua*, a work he dedicated to Lorenzo de' Medici, Marzio describes himself as 'Bibliothecae Budensis Praefectus', the sudden change in the speed and character of upgrading the king's library is due to Ugoleto. Born in Parma in the mid-1440s, he grew up in a milieu of book-producers, and he would eventually return to it after King Matthias' death, collaborating with his brother, Angelo, one of their hometown's first printers, by editing classical texts.[28]

The upgrading of the library entailed the commissioning and purchase of a large number of manuscripts (mainly from Italy).

---

[27] See, in particular, C. Csapodi, *The Corvinian Library*, O. Mazal, *Königliche Bücherliebe. Die Bibliothek des Matthias Corvinus* (Graz, 1990) and J.-F. Maillard, I. Monok & D. Nebbiai ed., *Matthias Corvin, Les bibliothèques princières et la genèse de l'état moderne* (Budapest, 2009). Note also the on-line 'Bibliotheca Corviniana Digitalis': http://www.corvina.oszk.hu/ [accessed 18th December 2011].

[28] The main biography of Ugoleto remains I. Affò, *Memorie di Taddeo Ugoleto Parmigiano, bibliotecario di Mattia Corvino, re di Ungheria* (Parma, 1781). On his work with his brother Angelo, see L. Balsamo, 'Editoria e umanesimo a Parma fra quattro e cinquecento' in P. Medioli Masotti ed., *Parma e l'umanesimo italiano* (Padua, 1986), pp. 77–95.

Excavations in Buda Castle have brought to light tantalising fragments from the Matthias period, among which are paints and paint pots, possibly signalling the existence of the celebrated *scriptorium* mentioned in contemporary sources among which is for instance Antonio Bonfini's *Rerum Ungaricarum*.[29] Speaking of it in *Hungaria-Athila*, a chorography composed during the period 1536–37, Nicolaus Olahus[30] (1493–1568) who spent many years at the court of Buda said: 'I have heard from my predecessors that King Matthias [...] engaged around thirty illuminators in his service.'[31] This would have been a significant workshop therefore, founded to play an important role in the development of one of the largest and most refined libraries of the Renaissance.[32] All this was wiped off the face of the earth,

---

[29] *Antonii Bonfinii Rerum Vngaricarum decades*, iv, p. 137. More generally on the palace, see Tanner, *The Raven King*, pp. 167, 180–88.

[30] On Nicolaus Olahus, Counsellor to Queen Mary of Hungary in the Low Countries, then Archbishop of Esztergom, and Primate of Hungary, who, through his paternal grandmother, Johannes Hunyadi's sister, was related to King Matthias, see C. Neagu, *Servant of the Renaissance: the poetry and prose of Nicolaus Olahus* (Bern, 2003).

[31] See Nicolaus Olahus, *Hungaria-Athila*, ed. C. Eperjessy and L. Juhász (Budapest, 1938), I, 5, 2. The *Athila* survives in one incomplete manuscript (*Athila seu Hungaria*) of c.1537, now ÖNB, MS. 8739, fols. 1–31. The *Hungaria* survives in another incomplete codex dated to 1631, now Cologne, Erzbischöflichen Diözesan und Dombibliothek, MS. 293. First edition of *Athila* (*Atila, sive de rebus bello paceque ab suo gestis*) in *Antonii Bonfini Rerum Vngaricarum decades quatuor*, ed. Joannes Sambucus (Basel: Officina Opporiniana, 1568), pp. 107–136. First edition of *Nicolai Oláhi Archi-Episcopi Strigoniensis Hungaria, Sive De Originibus Gentis, Regionis Situ, Diuisione, Habitu atque Opportunitatibus, Liber Singularis, Nunc primum in lucem editus. Decadis I, Monvmentum I, Accessit, Eiusdem, Compendiarium Aetatis Suae Chronicon*, in: *Adparatvs ad Historiam Hvngariae*, ed. Matthias Bel (Bratislava, 1735), pp. 1–41.

[32] For recent sceptical comment, see J. J. G. Alexander, 'Francesco da Castello in Lombardy and Hungary' in P. Farbaky & L. A. Waldman ed., *Italy and Hungary. Humanism and art in the Early Renaissance* ([Florence], 2011), pp. 267–91.

destroyed with overwhelming force by the Ottomans after the battle of Mohács in 1526. It is now impossible to guess the size of Matthias' collection. However, the 216 volumes, containing more than 600 works, identified in various libraries around the world show the king's predilection for richly decorated manuscripts. The introduction of the press did not seem to have much effect on him.[33]

The arrival, therefore, of the printing press in Hungary only two decades after the publication of Gutenberg's 42-line Bible is no little achievement. Even though it was sadly a short-lived enterprise, its quick introduction tells a story that once again has the royal Chancellor Johannes Vitéz at the centre.

Through his Vice-Chancellor, László Karai, in 1471, an invitation was offered to Andreas Hess, then based in Rome in the workshop of Georg Lauer, to move his printing press to Buda.[34] Hess agreed and started preparing the first publication of the *Chronica Hungarorum*, also known as the *Buda Chronicle*, which appeared in 1473. The choice of the first title is self-evident. This is a Latin history of the Hungarians compiled from several medieval manuscript chronicles. The volume, a rather plain, small folio of 133 pages printed using matrices Hess imported from the Lauer press, probably had a print-run of about 240 copies.[35] Just a few years later the book was already out of print and the text began to spread in

---

[33] I. Monok, 'La *Bibliotheca Corviniana* et les imprimés' in Maillard et al. ed., *Matthias Corvin*, pp. 161–75.

[34] See C. W. Maas, 'German Printers and the German Community in Renaissance Rome', *The Library*, 5th ser., xxxi (1976), pp. 118–126 at p. 121.

[35] *Chronica Hungarorum* (Buda: Andreas Hess, 5 June 1473) [ISTC, no. ic00484900]. Only eleven extant copies are presently known. Of these two are in Hungary, both in Budapest: one in the National Széchényi Library (shelfmark: 279.172) and the other in the University Library (shelfmark: Inc 10). Of the extant copies, just two have original bindings, products of the Buda binding workshop that made bindings also for the famous Corvina Library.

manuscript.[36] Despite its rather unexciting looks, the popularity of this little volume against its more richly decorated rivals seems undisputed.

Shortly after the publication of the *Chronicle*, Hess issued another volume, containing two works: *De libiris legendis* by Saint Basil and Xenophon's *Apologia Socratis*, both in LEONARDO BRUNI's translation. The usual companion piece to the Basil is Bruni's translation of Xenophon's *Hieron*, so introducing the *Apologia Socratis* instead is an interesting choice, signalling this particular edition as rather special.[37] Like most incunables of the age, both volumes were issued without a title page (the place and date of publication, together with the printer's name are given in the closing lines of the volume). Also, both volumes were printed in Roman type, most likely imported from Lauer's printing shop in Rome. Compared to the *Chronica*, the volume containing Basil's *De legendis* and Xenophon's *Apologia* is of smaller format and contains only 20 leaves.

There is no further documentary evidence regarding Hess' printing press in Buda after this. However in 1474 he was back in Rome working with Georg Lauer again. To make matters more difficult, there was not one, but two printing presses flourishing in Hungary during the incunable period which disappeared soon after being established. Like Hess, the second Hungarian typographer – known as the *Confessionale* printer after the work of the same title by the saintly Florentine Archbishop Antoninus, published in 1477 – also worked with

---

[36] Heidelberg: Universitätsbibliothek, MS. Pal. Germ. 156 (Bayern, c.1490), available on-line at: http://digi.ub.uni-heidelberg.de/diglit/cpg 156/0018?sid=577e4209f52bfea3ad07875f9339af6d [accessed 18th December 2011]; Cambridge (MA): Houghton Library, Harvard University, MS. Ger. 43 (c.1500).

[37] Basilius Magnus, *De legendis antiquorum libris, sive De liberalibus studiis*; Xenophon, *Apologia Socratis* (Buda: A[ndreas] H[ess], c.1473) [ISTC, no. ib00271500]. Copies in Eichstätt: Universitätsbibliothek der Katholischen Universität and the ÖNB; a third copy is listed in the on-line catalogue of the National Széchényi Library (shelfmark: Inc 269).

Italian types.³⁸ Unlike Hess' printing shop which had only one Roman type, the *Confessionale* office was equipped with at least four black-letter Fraktur types of different scales. Based on the choice of printing types, three publications have been identified, the one mentioned above, an edition of Laudivius Zacchia's *De vita beati Hyeronimi* and a single-leaf printed formula of indulgence with a hand-written note 'Posonium on 11 May 1480', signed 'Johannes Han'.³⁹

The situation of printing in Hungary is rather symptomatic of the general state of atrophy that followed Matthias' death. Boasting an early start, shortly after the first presses in Germany, Italy and France, (simultaneously with the developments in the Netherlands and before Spain and England) Hungary seems to have fallen by the wayside somewhat abruptly.

Everything had started so well. Along with humanists and artists, printers seemed fascinated by Hungary. Given the popularity of the *Chronicle*, their (or at least Hess's) intuition appears to have been right. Although not consisting in exclusively humanist texts, there was a market sufficiently large, mature and open for the acquisition of printed books.

So, what happened? Why this sudden collapse at the turn of the sixteenth-century? One might be tempted to assume that the gravity of political crises, especially the Turkish threat, was the main cause for the many cultural meltdowns of which the loss of the printing presses in Hungary was just one. To mention but a few others, the Universitas Histropolensis that Johannes Vitéz founded in 1465 at Bratislava ceased to exist. After his and Janus Pannonius' deaths in 1472 foreign teachers

---

[38] Antoninus Florentinus, *Confessionale: defecerunt scrutantes scrutinio.* ([Buda?, Printer of the 'Confessionale'], 1477) [ISTC, no. ia00804500]. There are two copies at Egyetemi Könyvtár, Budapest (shelfmarks: Inc 45 and Inc 46).

[39] The two printings are ISTC, no. il00085700 and ih00004550. See E. Soltész, *A Picture Book of Printing in Hungary: 1473–1979* (Budapest, 1973), p. 7 and 'The Hand-Press Period', on the website of the National Széchényi Library: http://typographia.oszk.hu/html/uk/nyomdak/confessionale_uk.htm [accessed 18ᵗʰ December 2011].

returned home and the university began to decline. It was closed in 1474. As for the *Corvina*, even before its total destruction by the Ottomans following the battle of Mohács in 1526, the library had suffered depredations. A significant number of manuscripts were carried off to the sultan's Seraglio in Contantinople, but in the days between the battle and Suleiman's entry into Buda, pilfering had occurred. But even earlier, the library had fallen into a neglected state soon after Matthias' death. Given the sheer number of Corvinian codices identified in libraries in Munich, Paris, Venice, Modena, Florence, and even Oxford and Cambridge, contemporary accounts of exposure to spoliations and irresponsible management seem plausible. For these no foreign agents or unkind external context can be blamed.[40]

A clue to a possible answer as to what might explain the failure of so many fifteenth-century Hungarian achievements may lie in one of its extraordinary success stories, that of Janus Pannonius. His talent, as well as the controversies of a career steeped in politics, had always kept him in the limelight. It is the reception of his work by his contemporaries, the manner in which other writers related to Pannonius' *opus*, which may provide some useful insight into the rapid rise and fall of the cultural phenomenon that was the kingdom of Hungary in the Quattrocento.

Like Vitéz, Pannonius was initially one of the staunchest allies of the King. He discharged numerous difficult diplomatic missions abroad, where his was a voice profoundly respected. Yet, ultimately at odds with the martial atmosphere at the court and discontented with Matthias' policy, Pannonius became involved in a plot against the King which also included Johannes Vitéz. When discovered, Pannonius promptly went

---

[40] [National Széchényi Library exhibition catalogue], *Bibliotheca Corviniana, 1490–1990*, ed. C. Csapodi & K. Csapodiné Gárdonyi (Budapest, 1990), esp. pp. 57–61; M. Rady, 'The Corvina Library and the Lost Royal Hungarian Archive' in J. Raven ed., *Lost Libraries: the destruction of great book collections since Antiquity* (London, 2004), pp. 91–105.

into exile, but died in less than a fortnight, on 27 March 1472. He was thirty-eight years old.

In contrast to his life, Pannonius' work was not only outstanding, it was also universally embraced.[41] Far from being a private pastime, the texts Pannonius composed gave readers an unprecedented view of the rich and multi-faceted world in which he, as a writer and a statesman, had been deeply immersed. While studying in Italy, his name was usually associated with panegyrics and a lively, often irreverent, series of epigrams. The latter in particular are outstanding mainly on account of their ingenuity and formal brilliance. After his return to Hungary in 1458, Pannonius tended to embrace the elegiac mode with more and more pathos.[42] Increasingly, he wrote as a rhetorician, not just in the sense that he composed in an elegant style, but also as a means to persuade and encourage others to action. His writings thus established a symbiotic relationship with society, acting as a channel of creative energy for the humanist as a *vir civilis* engaged in the exercise of duty.

Everything Pannonius aimed at in his literary works was accomplished. Humanists abroad applauded him without reserve, but in his own land, as a poet, Pannonius was greeted

---

[41] There are several sixteenth-century editions of Pannonius' works but few extant manuscripts bearing substantial witness to his œuvre. Those that have survived include two copies of his *Panegyricus in Renatum Andegavensem* (1453) – in Naples: Biblioteca nazionale Vittorio Emanuele III, MS X B 63, and BAV, MS. Vat. lat. 2847 (with thanks to Oren Margolis for drawing attention to Géza Szentmártoni Szabó's discovery of the first) – and the following copies of *Silva panegyrica ad Guarinum Veronensem* (1460): Brussels: Bibliothèque royale, MS. 14876; Budapest: Országos Széchényi Könyvtár, MS. Lat. 357; Seville: Biblioteca Capitular y Colombina, MSS. 7-1-15 & 82-4-8; Stuttgart: Württembergische Landesbibliothek, MS. Poet. 4° 21; Venice: Biblioteca Marciana, MS. 12.135 (4100); BAV, MS. Vat. lat. 2847; ÖNB, MS. 3274.

[42] See for instance poems such as *Blasio militanti Janus febricitans; Threnos de morte Barbarae matris; Ad animan suam; De inundatione* and *Mathias rex Hungarorum* in *Iani Pannonii [...] Poemata* (Utrecht: Bartholomeus Wild, 1784), pp. 279, 286–296, 296–302, 332–333 and 304–312.

with silence during his lifetime. What happened almost immediately after his death is a very different story.

Towards the end of the 1470s already King Matthias entrusted the collecting of the epigrams of his once-favourite poet to Peter of Warda (Péter Váradi; c. 1450–1501), who himself had studied at Bologna and who was to become the king's Chancellor and archbishop of Kalocsa-Bács.[43] Soon afterwards a veritable cult of Pannonius developed and during the early sixteenth-century his was probably the name most mentioned by the new wave of Hungarian humanists, centred around the Sodalitas Literaria Danubiana (which had orginally been founded in 1491 by Conrad Celtis). Between 1512 and 1527 editions of Pannonius' poetry came out with bewildering frequency, each carrying small crops of previously unknown verse.[44] Given the silence of just a few years before, it may seem surprising that most of those involved in bringing Pannonius to light with such tremendous enthusiasm were no longer foreign scholars, but Hungarian humanists.

The context for all this could not have been more difficult: a once rich and powerful kingdom was now unrecognizable. At Mohács the cream of Hungarian nobility perished within a few hours. The whole establishment had collapsed, never to recover. What was once a place in which a wide variety of people thrived in relative harmony had suddenly disintegrated into hopelessness. The effect this had on cultural matters was bound to be dramatic. Hungarian humanists ended up in exile, strewn all over Europe.

Before this occurred, however, allegiances and influences had already started to take a different turn. Although Italian contacts still had a very strong impact upon the Hungarian Renaissance

---

[43] On him, see *Petri de Warda ... epistolae*, ed. K. Wagner (Bratislava, 1776). For further details about Peter of Warda, see K. Csapodiné Gárdonyi, 'Die Reste der Bibliothek eines ungarischen Humanisten, Péter Váradi', *Gutenberg-Jahrbuch* [lii] (1977), pp. 363–368.

[44] See M. Birnbaum, *Humanists in a Shattered World: Croatian and Hungarian Latinity in the sixteenth century* (Columbus, OH, 1986), pp. 56–64. For one example, see p. 146 above.

at the turn of the fifteenth to the sixteenth century, cultural life in the kingdom was gradually shifting towards northern humanist influences.[45]

The major figure blending the fifteenth-century Italian Renaissance tradition with the model of northern humanism was Conrad Celtis (1459–1508).[46] His philosophy, based on the assimilation of neo-platonism, had a strong and long-lasting impact upon such scholars as the Silesian Caspar Ursinus Velius (1493–1539), historian to King Ferdinand I, and Johannes Alexander Brassicanus (c. 1500–1539), who, like Velius, taught Greek at the University of Vienna.[47] While still lured by Italy, it was increasingly Vienna that attracted this new generation of scholars. Among them were the aforementioned Nicolaus Olahus, his successor as archbishop of Esztergom, Antonius Verantius (1504–1573), who was educated at the University of Padua, and another alumnus of that University, Stephanus Brodericus (c. 1471–1539), bishop of Szerém and author of an eye-witness history of the battle of Mohács; to this list should be added, as we shall see, a scholar a few years their junior, Johannes Sambucus (1531–1584).[48] They all lived through a period of political shockwaves and religious turbulence and also at a time when the European intellectual climate was profoundly influenced by Erasmian ideas.

For this new generation of Hungarian humanists the context was one which, for the most part, denied them the safety of a

---

[45] As well as Bonfini's continuing presence, note, for instance, BATTISTA GUARINI's contacts with Hungary and, in particular, with Miklós Báthory, bishop of Vać: D. E. Rhodes, 'Battista Guarini and a Book at Oxford', *Journal of the Warburg and Courtauld Institutes*, xxxvii (1974), pp. 349–53.

[46] On Celtis, see pp. 89–115 and p. 138 above.

[47] On both of these, see the brief biographies in *CE*, i, pp. 191–192 and ii, pp. 356–57.

[48] On Olahus, see footnote 30 above. On Brodericus, whose account of Mohács was printed as *De Conflictu Hungarorum cum Turcis ad Mohatz verissima descriptio* (Cracow: H. Wietor, 1527), see *CE*, i, pp. 203–204 (sub István Brodarics).

homeland. Most were in self-imposed exile for long periods. Trying to find a home outside the borders of what was once their country, they ended up recovering the idea of *patria* in both their writings and their acts. If the idea of a ruling élite imbued with culture was characteristic of fifteenth-century humanism in Hungary, the beginning of the sixteenth-century favoured a more acutely aware political generation.

Exile and hardship created a nostalgia for what was increasingly perceived as a realm of security, a golden age, which, though no longer attainable, was not forgotten.

What this realm of security required was reflection and clarity, manifest, among other things, in a noticeable change of focus from the lyrical to the narrative in the literature produced following the disaster of Mohács.[49]

It is during this period of displacement and turbulence that manuscripts on the history of Hungary, produced by authors at the court of Matthias, started to appear in print. To take just a few examples, the first three decades of Antonio Bonfini's manuscripts on the history of Hungary were only published in 1543 through the editorial efforts of the Transylvanian Martin Brenner.[50] Until then, despite the fact that it never ceased to be at the centre of interest, the *Rerum Vngaricarum decades* spread only in manuscript form.[51] Interestingly, the last part of Bonfini's work, describing the times of Matthias Corvinus, was missing in the first edition. By 1561, however, there was a real urgency about editing the complete Bonfini. As Gábor Almási notes in his in-depth study of sixteenth-century Hungarian humanism, the project had become highly politicised, with patrons such as Tamás Nádasdy (the Hungarian Palatine), Ferenc Révai (the Deputy Palatine), Ferenc Forgách (bishop of

---

[49] Birnbaum, *Humanists in a Shattered World*, pp. 60–1.

[50] Antonius Bonfinius, *Rervm Vngaricarvm decades tres* [...] (Basel: Per Robertus Winterus, 1543).

[51] There are five extant manuscripts: see Kulcsár, *Inventarium*, available on-line (as at footnote 10).

Várad) and the already-mentioned Antonius Verantius.[52] We know about these efforts from the correspondence of the Hungarian humanist Sigismundus Torda with the Basel publisher Johannes Opporinus. Torda was very keen to bring the whole of Bonfini's work to light, but, in the end, it was Johannes Sambucus who finally published it in 1568. This, as Gábor Almási remarks, was a 'great nod of current Hungarian humanism towards the Corvinian golden age'.[53] The same thing happened with Galeotto Marzio's collection of anecdotes on a selection of notable words and deeds of King Matthias. This work, giving a very complimentary account of the excellence and greatness of king and court, written in the previous century, was published by Torda in 1563.[54] Similarly, the *Epithoma rerum Hungaricarum*, written for presentation to Matthias Corvinus by the Sicilian episcopal diplomat PIETRO RANZANO, found its way out of obscurity, being published in quick sucession by both Sambucus and Lukács Pécsi.[55] In his preface dedicated to the future Emperor Maximilian II, Sambucus

---

[52] G. Almási, *The Uses of Humanism: Johannes Sambucus (1531–1584), Andreas Dudith (1533–1589), and the Republic of Letters in East Central Europe* (Leiden, 2009). Of those listed, note that Ferenc (Franciscus) Forgách (1530–1577) was the author of *De statu reipublicae Hungaricae Ferdinando, Johanne, Maximiliano regibus ac Johanne Secundo principe Transylvaniae commentarii* (Bratislava, 1788), in which he treated of the events of the fifty years following the Battle of Mohács.

[53] Almási, *The Uses of Humanism*, p. 172.

[54] *De egregie, sapienter, iocose dictis ac factis regis Mathiae* (Vienna, 1563). See note 10 above.

[55] *Epitome rerum Ungaricarum auctore P. Ranzano, nunc primum edita una cum appendice quadam*, ed. Johannes Sambucus (Vienna, 1558); *Epitome rerum Hungaricarum velut per indices descripta, auctore Petro Ransano, eliminatione et relectione* (Trnava: Luca Peechius Pannonius, 1579). The original manuscript of the work is Budapest: Országos Széchényi Könyvtár, MS. Lat. 249, which is now fully digitized and on-line at the Bibliotheca Corviniana Digitalis project: www.corvina.oszk.hu/corvinas-html/hub1codlat249.htm [accessed 18th December 2011]. The latest edition of the work is that by P. Kulcsár (Budapest, 1977).

asserted the importance and lessons of history for men in positions of power.

In parallel to works such as these written during Matthias' reign, there was also a trend for producing new historical accounts centred on the accomplishments of the fifteenth century. One of the first to set the tone was Nicolaus Olahus. In his chorography *Hungaria-Athila* the author lingers on the beauty, wealth and glory of Matthias' age for no less than nineteen chapters. The pieces were composed during 1536–7, when the humanist was becoming an ever more influential figure at Queen Mary's court in Brussels. We know from Olahus' correspondence that the manuscripts were circulated among the author's scholarly friends.[56] Despite their popularity in intellectual circles, no edition of *Hungaria* appeared until 1735, when Matthias Bel published it in his *Adparatus ad historiam Hungariae*.[57] The delay in the case of *Athila* was less striking. This was due, once again, to Joannes Sambucus including it in his celebrated edition of Antonio Bonfini's *Rerum Vngaricarum decades* published in 1568.[58] His was a monumental edition comprising not only the first thirty books by Bonfini previously published by Brenner plus volumes 31 to 40 issued by the Transylvanian printer Gáspár Heltai (d.1574) in 1565; it also printed texts from manuscripts owned by Révai and Forgách, as well as Sambucus' own work continuing Bonfini's treatise with details on the Jagiellonian period (1496–1526), and Stephanus Brodericus' account of the battle of

---

[56] *Nicolai Oláh Ludouico II Regi Hungariae et Mariae Reginae a Secretis, Ferdinandi I Cancellarii, dein Archiepiscopi Strigoniensis Primatis Regni Hungariae et Locumtenentis Regii Codex Epistolaris MDXXVI–MDXXXVIII*, ed. I. Arnold (Budapest, 1876), p. 600. For further details, see C. Neagu, *Servant of the Renaissance*.

[57] *Hungaria* in *Adparatus ad Historiam Hungariae*, ed. M. Bel (Bratislava, 1735), pp 1–41.

[58] *Atila, sive de rebus bello paceque ab suo gestis* in *Antonii Bonfini Rerum Vngaricarum decades quatuor*, ed. Sambucus, pp. 107–136.

Mohács.[59] To round things off, Sambucus also translated into Latin the work of the poet and historian, Sebestyén Tinódi (c. 1510–1556), on the city of Eger, and added his own contribution on the battle of Sziget (1566).[60]

It is not by accident that Sambucus and a large number of his contemporaries felt the need to cast a close and attentive eye on their past.[61] Taken for granted by most while the Hungarian kingdom was still basking in days of glory and political stability, the cultural achievements of the fifteenth century began to be treasured, almost obsessively, when they became part of Hungary's past. Filtered through the eyes of the new generation, these achievements acquired a meaning capable not only of helping to restore self-confidence, but also of building up something resembling a resistance movement. By looking deep into a world that was disappearing before their eyes, sixteenth-century scholars instinctively assumed the role of new image-builders.

Again, it is no accident that the emblem, as a genre, was one of their preferred media. Interestingly, the first emblem books associated with Hungary came complete with theoretical glosses.[62] This contributed to making emblematic works more accessible and ensured direct communication of knowledge and ideas. This bi-medial form of expression, blending text and

[59] On Révai's manuscripts (known to Antonius Verantius in 1550), see Birnbaum, *Humanists in a Shattered World*, p. 234; on Brodericus and Mohács, see note 48 above.

[60] The *Historia az Eger várnak a törökektöl való megmenekedéséröl* originally appeared in Tinódi's *Cronica* (Cluj, 1554).

[61] For detailed accounts on sixteenth-century views of Matthias Corvinus, see S. Csernus, 'Les Hunyadi, vus par les historiens français du quinzième siècle', A. di Francesco, 'Il mito di Mattia Corvino nei canti storici ungherezi del XVI secolo', and G. Gömöri, 'The Image of János Hunyadi and Matthias Corvinus in the 15th–17th Century England', all in Klaniczay & Jankovics ed., *Matthias Corvinus and Humanism in Central Europe*, pp. 75–93, 95–108 & 109–118.

[62] É. Knapp and G. Tüskés, *Emblematics in Hungary: a study of the history of symbolic representation in Renaissance and Baroque literature* (Tübingen, 2003), p. 20.

image, had the capability to juggle the well-established poetical principle of *imitatio*, making it work in conjunction with often intriguing uses of symbolic imagery. It proved to be a potent and inspired combination.

Sambucus, for one, is not remembered as much for his grand historiographic *opus*, as he is for *Emblemata*, his book of emblems.[63] This is the volume into which readers like us, generations after, are perhaps most likely to delve. At first sight it is just another display of exuberant penmanship, revealing, as one would expect, a wide and thorough knowledge of classical authors and of ideas that circulated among humanists such as Andrea Alciati, Paolo Giovio and Petrus Ramus. Beneath the surface however, many of Sambucus' emblems are permeated with subtle meditations on past greatness and the author's deep concern for the tragic state of affairs in a kingdom torn apart by Turkish conquests and internal dissension.

A good illustration of Sambucus' approach to emblem writing is 'Virtus unita valet' (Virtue is powerful when united).[64] The poem focuses on the current situation in Hungary, addressing its kings fighting for power. After the death of Louis II (1506–1526) on the in battle-field of Mohács, very unusually, two candidates stepped in for the Hungarian crown: one was János Zápolya (1487–1540), Transylvania's voivode and Hungary's most prominent aristocrat. The other was Ferdinand I (1503–1564), then archduke of Austria, the late king's brother-in-law and the brother of the Holy Roman Emperor, Charles V. Their unremitting contest for power would determine the course of Hungary's history. Ferdinand was elected King of Hungary by a rump diet in Bratislava in December 1526. After defeat by Ferdinand at the Battle of Tarcal in September 1527 and again in the Battle of Szina in March 1528, Zápolya gained the support of Sultan Suleiman the Magnificent. Following the unsuccessful attacks by the

---

[63] Joannes Sambucus, *Emblemata, cum aliquot nummis antiqui operis* (Antwerp, 1564).

[64] Joannes Sambucus, *Emblemata* (Antwerp, 1564), p. 70, emblem 62.

Ottoman armies on Vienna in 1529 and 1533, Ferdinand signed a peace treaty with the Sultan, splitting Hungary into a Habsburg sector in the west and Zápolya's domain in the east (the latter was effectively a vassal state of the Ottoman Empire). After Zápolya death, János II suceeded his father as an infant in 1540, but ultimately the former king's widow, Isabella Jagiełło, ceded Royal Hungary and Transylvania to Ferdinand in the Treaty of Weissenburg of 1551. In September 1563 Ferdinand was crowned king of Hungary by the archbishop of Esztergom, Nicolaus Olahus.

By directly addressing the two kings in their incessant squabble for the crown, Sambucus' emblem places readers in a contemplative frame of mind, pleading to his contemporaries to look back to the past, to a period which, in the eyes of many, had already become a golden age of Hungary, namely the reign of King Matthias Corvinus, when the court at Buda was an important centre of Renaissance culture and effective administration. Building its argument on the power of *exemplum*, the text concludes with an emphatic plea for unity:

> Fluctibus in mediis patriae tot cladibus actae
> Concordi proceres subveniatis ope.
> Nec vos exosae mentes, propriaeque salutis
> Oblitae exagitent, et nota turpis alat.
> Huniadis memores, ac Regis quaeso Mathiae
> Estote, ad quorum nomina Thurca tremit.
> Diversum ne vos studium disiungat inique,
> Colligat in patriae vos amor unus opem.[65]

In the middle of the waves, you leaders, with united effort, come to the aid of your country, driven along by so many disasters. May no hateful minds, forgetting personal safety, stir you up, no ugly slur feed you. I beg you, remember Hunyadi and King Matthias, whose names have the Turks trembling. May no divisive partisanship unjustly disunite you, but may one single love strengthen you to the aid of your country.

---

[65] The text of the entire 1564 edition of Sambucus' *Emblemata* is available on-line at *French Emblems at Glasgow*: http://www.emblems.arts.gla.ac.uk/french/books.php?id=FSAb&o= [accessed 18th December 2011].

Fig. 1: Virtus unita valet, emblem 62 of Johannes Sambucus, *Emblemata* (Antwerp, 1556), p. 70. Oxford: Christ Church, shelfmark f.8.4. Reproduced with kind permission of the Governing Body, Christ Church, Oxford.

As expected, the moralistic vein is clearly discernable in the underlying structure of the emblem. However, the way Sambucus handles the relationship between text and representation creates an enigmatic as well as playful effect. Without the woodcut, the poem is dry, pedantic and lacking in coherence:

> Nil mare corrumpit, salsum a putredine tutum est,
> Multaque perpetuis motibus acta, vigent.
> Si tamen in fossas derives, atque paludes,
> Vim patitur, dotes nec tenet inde suas.
> Dulcibus amittit vires, nitrique vapores
> Exhalant, quoties mutat origo novi.
> Plus unita potest virtus, dispersa labascit,
> Atque suo durant quaelibet apta loco.
> Pignore commutat suavi translata veneno
> Persicus, et tutis carpitur illa gulis.

The sea corrupts nothing, safe in its saltiness from putrifying, and many things flourish when driven by perpetual motion. However, if you were to divert it into ditches and marshes, it suffers violence and no longer keeps its qualities. It loses its powers to sweet waters, and new nitrous vapours exhale whenever the source changes. When united virtue can do more, separated it dissolves and everything appropriate in its place endures. The peach, when it is transplanted, exchanges its poison for a sweet quality and is enjoyed safely.

At first sight, the illustration seems simply to mirror the words in what might be perceived as a plain and unimaginative manner. The artist appears to play safe, following the 'letter' of the text. In many cases, authors had no say in the visual dimension of emblem books. Sambucus, however, is documented to have played a role in the design of the woodcuts. In the summer of 1563 he commissioned Lucas d'Heere to provide the images. At that time the writer was in Ghent which strongly suggests that he may have met d'Heere and possibly advised on the design.[66]

If we look carefully, we notice that the image emphasises the idea of separation, fragmentation and inaccessibility. The space is divided on a diagonal, with two very different landscapes emerging above and beneath it. On the one side, there is the plane of the sea, firm, majestic and holding afloat a variety of ships. Beneath the diagonal the image is breathtakingly busy. There is a man with a spade. Next to him, a bundle of what appear to be arrows is lying on the ground, presumably a reference to the story of the Scythian King Scylurus who pleaded for unity by showing that a bundle of arrows was strong, whereas individually each could be easily broken. There is also a multitude of animals and vegetation in the image. Interestingly, this plane of reference is further separated into another two sections by the short diagonal of a man-made canal. The first impression is that fresh waters plus land equals fertility. If we focus on what the woodcut actually depicts however, we see the man as isolated from all around him. Surrounded by waters in perpetual

---

[66] See A. S. Q. Visser in *Joannes Sambucus and the Learned Image: the use of the emblem in Late-Renaissance humanism*, (Leiden, 2005), p. xxvi.

motion like quicksand, his is the smallest of islands. A space totally arid of everything but symbolic weapons and an ox or a cow (representing Europa), reminding us of how precarious man's present position is and urging him to reconsider where power truly lies. Thus image and words are intertwined both pointing in the direction of an exemplary *illo tempore*, an unspoilt golden age lost to the present, but still attainable in the future, provided man learns from the past.[67] Remembering this past is essential. Through memory, one is able to distill something of importance in an act of repetition, thus projecting reality into a quasi-mythical time, a time with redeeming qualities over the present, desperate and desolate such as it is. As a consequence, Sambucus' intensely contrived and puzzling poem may be read as an open invitation to recollection as an act of faith.

This, together with the rest the 167 emblems of the first edition, is just a glimpse to illustrate a trend.[68] Wherever we turn, the sixteenth century becomes an unavoidable point of reference in any attempt to talk about Hungarian literary culture in the fifteenth century. It is mainly through sixteenth-century sensibility that we meet what we now call the golden age of the Hungarian Renaissance. It might be even fair to say that the next generation of humanists not only recovered the values of that lost century, they turned them into a lifeline, the equivalent of the North Star to a world which had lost its compass. In the end, this now widely recognized and admired period became a priceless refuge, the true *patria* of those who for a long time no longer had a country. Within what appeared to be the lost kingdom of Hungary all notion of belonging had been shattered. The *respublica litteraria* was the only safe haven left.

---

[67] For a detailed analysis of the concept, see M. Eliade, *The Myth of the Eternal Return: cosmos and history*, 2nd edn (Princeton, NJ, 2005).

[68] The first edition was followed by an extended Latin edition in 1566, with 56 new emblems. The same year Christopher Plantin published a Dutch version, with translations by Marcus Antonius Gillis van Diest. A French edition followed in 1567, translated by Jacques Grévin. After this, the Latin edition was reprinted four more times in Plantin's workshop in Antwerp and later Leiden, in 1569, 1576, 1584 and 1599.

HUMANISM AND THE COURT IN FIFTEENTH-CENTURY CASTILE

JEREMY LAWRANCE

On 15 January 1444 the lord of Hita wrote to the bishop of Burgos in the following terms:

> I was reading the other day, reverend lord and my dear and special friend, a little work by Leonardo of Arezzo in which he set out to show the source, origins and beginning of the office of knighthood – which indeed, brief as it is, I think he explains clearly enough, supporting his view with the Stoic philosopher Plato, Phileas of Carthage, Archidamus of Miletus (who is said to have been the first to write on the best state of the commonwealth), and in certain places with Romulus; and it is likewise shown by him how great is the dignity of the knight's duty [*ofiçio*], its prerogatives and privileges, and what his duty should be in the city when he returns from war, and why knights have more right than others to wear this gold they have on their collars, belts, and swords.[1]

The lord, Íñigo López de Mendoza (1398–1458), was a gifted poet, an avid bibliophile, and, after King Juan II (1406–54), the chief patron of letters in Castile; he was also a powerful baron, soon to be showered with royal grants of lands, castles, and vassals culminating in the noble titles of count of Real de Manzanares and marquis of Santillana (8 August 1445).[2] The

---

[1] *Qüestión fecha al obispo de Burgos*, in Íñigo López de Mendoza, marqués de Santillana, *Obras completas*, ed. Á. Gómez Moreno & M. P. A. M. Kerkhof (Barcelona, 1988), pp. 414–17 (p. 414). Throughout this article, all translations and emphases are mine.

[2] On Mendoza's military and political career see R. Pérez Bustamante & J. M. Calderón Ortega, *El marqués de Santillana: Biografía y*

bishop, Alfonso de Cartagena (1385–1454), was a *letrado* ('lettered' official), a canon lawyer and scholastic theologian with posts in the royal chancery and ecclesiastical hierarchy who served on occasion as the king's ambassador to foreign courts and, from 1434 until 1439, as his orator at the Council of Basel; he was also the author of numerous ethical, historical, and devotional works addressed to royal and noble patrons in Latin and Spanish, including translations of Cicero and Seneca.[3] Finally, the treatise on the classical origins of chivalry about which Mendoza was asking, and on which Cartagena wrote a lengthy reply, was the *De militia* of LEONARDO BRUNI,

    documentación, intro. R. Lapesa (Santillana del Mar, 1983); on the literary side, R. Lapesa, *La obra literaria del marqués de Santillana* (Madrid, 1957) and the introductions to Marqués de Santillana, *Poesías completas*, ed. M. Á. Pérez Priego, 2 vols (Madrid, 1983–91); *Obras completas*, ed. Gómez Moreno & Kerkhof, and *Comedieta de Ponza, sonetos, serranillas y otras obras*, ed. R. Rohland de Langbehn, intro. V. Beltrán (Barcelona, 1997).

[3] L. Fernández Gallardo, *Alonso de Cartagena (1385–1456): una biografía política en la Castilla del siglo XV* ([Valladolid], 2002); on the literary side, among much recent work, for the matter in hand see O. Di Camillo, *El humanismo castellano del siglo XV* (Valencia, 1976), pp. 128–33, 135–75, 203–26; J. Lawrance ed., *Un tratado de Alonso de Cartagena sobre la educación y los estudios literarios* (Bellaterra, 1979); S. González-Quevedo Alonso ed., *El 'Oracional' de Alonso de Cartagena* (Valencia, 1983); G. Breslin, 'The *Duodenarium* of Alfonso de Cartagena: A brief report on the manuscripts and contents', *La Corónica*, xviii (1989), pp. 90–102; N. Fallows, *The Chivalric Vision of Alfonso de Cartagena: study and edition of the 'Doctrinal de los caualleros'* (Newark, 1995); M. Morrás, '*Sic et non*: en torno a Alfonso de Cartagena y los *studia humanitatis*', *Euphrosyne*, xxiii (1995), pp. 333–46, and her edition of A. de Cartagena, *Libros de Tulio: De senetute, De los ofiçios* (Alcalá de Henares, 1996); N. G. Round, '"Perdóneme Séneca": the translational practices of Alonso de Cartagena', *Bulletin of Hispanic Studies*, lxxv (1998), pp. 17–29; T. González Rolán, A. Moreno Hernández, & P. Saquero Suárez-Somonte ed., *Humanismo y teoría de la traducción en España e Italia en la primera mitad del siglo XV: edición y estudio de la 'Controversia Alphonsiana': Alfonso de Cartagena vs. L. Bruni y P. Candido Decembrio* (Madrid, 2000); M. Campos Souto ed., *El 'Memorial de virtudes': la traducción castellana del 'Memoriale virtutum' de Alfonso de Cartagena* (Burgos, 2004).

chancellor of the Republic of Florence, and renowned in his day as Italy's foremost humanist.[4] Mendoza's letter thus signalled a conjuncture of three major strands in fifteenth-century culture: aristocratic chivalry, scholastic learning, and the humanist revival of Antiquity.

To suggest how this moment was significant requires attending above all to the motives of the first of our three protagonists, the knight – a figure often ignored or side-lined in histories of humanism.[5] In his own day panegyrists singled out Mendoza's combination of arms and letters as an attribute no less novel than noteworthy; he was, according to his nephew Gómez Manrique, *'the first man in our time* of such noble ancestry and great estate to combine science with knighthood, hauberk with toga [*la loriga con la toga*]'.[6] His secretary Diego

---

[4] C. C. Bayley, *War and Society in Renaissance Florence: the 'De Militia' of Leonardo Bruni* (Toronto, 1961), pp. 360–97 (text). For Cartagena's reply see n. 23 below.

[5] In the wake of J. Huizinga, *Herfsttij der middeleeuwen* (Haarlem, 1919) [*The Autumn of the Middle Ages*, trans. R. J. Payton & U. Mammitzsch (Chicago, 1996)] the chivalric culture of fifteenth-century courts has often been portrayed as a late harvest of medieval mentalities opposed to new currents from Italy; see N. G. Round, 'Renaissance culture and its opponents in fifteenth-century Castile', *Modern Language Review*, lvii (1962), pp. 204–15; P. E. Russell, 'Las armas contra las letras: para una definición del humanismo español del siglo XV" in his *Temas de 'La Celestina' y otros estudios: del 'Cid' al 'Quijote'*, trans. A. Pérez (Barcelona, 1978), pp. 207–39 (rev. and enlarged from 'Arms versus Letters: towards a definition of Spanish humanism' in A. R. Lewis ed., *Aspects of the Renaissance: a symposium* (Austin, 1967), pp. 45–58). However, see now S. Anglo, ed., *Chivalry in the Renaissance* (Woodbridge, 1990); F. Tateo, 'Le armi e le lettere: per la storia di un *tópos* umanistico' in A. Dalzell et al. ed., *Acta Conventus Neo-Latini Torontonensis: proceedings of the Seventh International Congress of Neo-Latin Studies, Toronto 8 August to 13 August 1988* (Binghamton, 1991), pp. 63–81.

[6] Dedication 'Al reverendo señor don Pero Gonçalez de Mendoça, obispo de Calahorra', *Planto de las Virtudes e Poesía por el magnífico señor don Íñigo López de Mendoça, marqués de Santillana* [1458] in Gómez Manrique, *Cancionero*, ed. F. Vidal González [Letras Hispánicas, dxli] (Madrid, 2003), §CXXXII, pp. 362–418 at p. 363. See also the selection

de Burgos was even more emphatic, and more specific about the link with humanism, noting that nothing like the marquis's learning had been seen since Antiquity and asserting that the role of Italian scholarship in this revival was not so much a source as a target of (successful) emulation:

> Seeing his motherland [*patria*] robbed and laid waste of all her treasure from the olden days of Lucan, Seneca, Quintilian, and other ancient sages, this paladin of exalted intellect [*varón de alto ingenio*] took pity on her; he strove, through his own studies and skill in arms and with many illustrious works of his own composition, to make her equal to the glory of the famous men of Athens or Academe and of the Romans, importing great store of previously unknown books in every branch of philosophy [...]. If Apollonius lamented that eloquence was taken from the Greeks to the Romans through Cicero's industry, how much more must Italians today lament and complain that it has been stolen from them and brought to our Castile through the fame and intellect of this lord! [...] Even this was not enough for the glorious marquis, for he has given even greater cause for complaint and regret to those who have acquired renown in the science and exercise of war, and won great rewards and titles by force of arms.[7]

---

of testimonia in Santillana, *Obras completas*, pp. xxix–xxxii, including the Latin epitaph by the Milanese humanist Pier Candido Decembrio. The number of these panegyrics, from Juan de Mena's *Calamicleos* or *Coronación del marqués* (c. 1442) onwards, is unparalleled, and itself constitutes significant evidence for the argument below about Mendoza's court milieu.

[7] Diego de Burgos, *Triunfo del Marqués* in *Retórica y humanismo: el 'Triunfo del Marqués de Santillana' (1458)*, ed. C. Moreno Hernández (Valencia, 2008), pp. 131–214 (p. 136–7), available on-line at: http://parnaseo.uv.es/Lemir/Textos/Carlos_Moreno/Carlos_Moreno.pdf [accessed 4th October 2011]. Apollonius Rhodius' chagrin at the *translatio studii* from Greece to Rome (Plutarch 862f–863a, in *Plutarchi Opera*, ed. T. Doehner & F. Dübner, 5 vols (Paris, 1839–55), II: *Vitae II*, p. 1029 = Κικέρων, iv.3) is lifted – apart from its sequel, Italy to Spain – from Leonardo Bruni's *Cicero novus*, which was turned into both Tuscan and Castilian for Mendoza's circle (*Vita di Cicerone scritta da messer Lionardo Bruni*, [ed. L. Lamberti] (Parma, 1804), pp. 12–13; J. Lawrance, 'Nuño de Guzmán and early Spanish humanism: some

Modern scholars tend to scoff at these claims, seeing the 'arms and letters' trope as a simple reworking of the ancient *fortitudo et sapientia* commonplace, the classical name-dropping as naïve exhibitionism, and the claim to have outstripped Italy as boastful envy. I argue, on the contrary, that Mendoza's contemporaries were exactly right; the marquis's patronage and practice of letters represented the first signs of a new configuration of society, one in which the court was starting to assume the central cultural and political role it was to play in the early-modern absolutist state, replacing the diffuse late-medieval *Ständestaat*.[8]

In this light, the ubiquity of the 'arms and letters' theme (and, even more, of a conservative or romantic opposition to it) may be seen not as literary commonplace, but as a key indication of social change. By entering the ambit of the court – that is, the characteristic Renaissance formation of society and state – the knight in effect relinquished, on literally bended knee, the nexus of land, vassals, castle, and the right to wage private war that was the mainstay of his rank, power, and self-esteem. Thenceforth rank would be determined by a new nexus: wealth, distinction, and the courtier's geometric proximity to the person of the king through the grant of household offices such as *copero* (royal cup-bearer), which was Mendoza's own

---

reconsiderations', *Medium Ævum*, li (1982), pp. 55–84 at pp. 66–7). Moreno explains this and *Triunfo*'s general significance for our debate.

[8] The terms of my account are from N. Elias, *Die höfische Gesellschaft* (Neuwied, 1969) [*The Court Society*, trans. E. Jephcott, rev. edn (Dublin, 2006)]; 'social configuration' implies not just the political subjugation and uprooting from their rural castles of the feudal nobility, but also the new court style of life with its elaborate hierarchy and rigid etiquette for binding courtiers within the constellation of the king. The term 'absolutist' is debatable (Elias, *op. cit.*, p. 11 [trans. p. 5] 'the power of the ruler was by no means so unrestricted [...]; the omnipotent absolute monarch proves on closer scrutiny to be an individual who was enmeshed through his position as king in a specific network of interdependences'), but I use it here as shorthand for the ideological aspect of the *ancien régime* that concerns us.

first step up from relative obscurity, at the court of Juan II's kinsman and rival, Alfonso V of Aragon (1416–58).

We may freely admit that fifteenth-century Castile had not yet reached this stage of court 'civilization', as Norbert Elias called it. The aristocracy had by no means relinquished their castles and feudal wars – Mendoza being no exception – and, more strikingly, there was no fixed royal abode, no physical centre, no palace to house a court.[9] However, these facts make the precocious signs of a new court mentality among the men of letters around Juan II all the more notable. The monarch and his *privado* or minister Álvaro de Luna – *privanza* or favouritism being a characteristic institution of the future Baroque state – were not successful in their political plan to curb the independence and factions of the nobility, but they were strikingly prescient in their exploitation of certain cultural means – chief among them, the recourse to humanist-style literary publicity – to create the illusion, before the fact, of a distinctive court style, a show capable of representing the omnipotent majesty of monarchy.[10]

[9] In Spain this remained the case until the late sixteenth century; Madrid did not become the permanent court until the seventeenth. To the question, 'What is the court?', Juan del Encina still replied in the 1480s: 'It is where the king and queen happen to be [*Allí es corte real | donde el rey y reyna fueren*]' ('Porque algunos le preguntavan qué cosa era la corte y la vida della' in *Cancionero de las obras de Juan del Enzina* (Salamanca, 1496), fol. 60). For a useful parallel, see J. Watts, 'Was there a Lancastrian court?' in J. Stratford ed., *The Lancastrian Court* (Donington, 2003), pp. 253–71.

[10] I use 'represent' in its performative sense for the kingly 'representative publicity' (*monarchische Repräsentation, repräsentative Öffentlichkeit*) of J. Habermas, *Strukturwandel der Öffentlichkeit* (Neuwied, 1962) [*The Structural Transformation of the Public Sphere*, trans. T. Burger [Cambridge, MA, 1989)]. On this 'style' in the reign of Juan II's daughter Isabel the Catholic see J. Lawrance, '*Fabulosa illa aurea secula*: The idea of the Golden Age at the court of Isabel' in D. Hook ed., *The Spain of the Catholic Monarchs: papers from the Quincentenary Conference (Bristol, 2004)* (Bristol, 2008), pp. 1–43; with her we can talk without reserve of the advent of a court configuration, as Machiavelli recognized when he took Isabel's consort Ferdinand of Aragon as the model of a

In this style, besides the traditional features of any performing or representative kingship (formal shows of rank, etiquette, and dress, honorific decorations and titles, festivals and ceremonies), there were two that may surprise anyone familiar with the modern apparatus of state publicity: namely, the decorative but indispensable role of women, and the ostentatious display of literary erudition as a primary form of access to prestige and power.[11] Strange as it may seem, women and erudition were in fact closely connected, through poetry. In ways that are well known but have been little analysed from a sociological point of view, poetry assumed a place in the life of the court (or rather, given the absence of an actual palace, in the process of 'courtization', *Verhöflichung*) that proved decisive for the fate of humanism in Spain. In the prologue (c. 1430) to his anthology of poets at the court of Juan II, Juan Alfonso de Baena undertook a eulogy of the dignity and necessity in any

'new prince' while discussing 'Quod principem deceat ut egregius habeatur' – the very point that concerns us (*Il Principe*, XXI 'si può chiamare quasi *principe nuovo*; [...] è diventato *per fama e per gloria* el primo re de' Cristiani', in N. Machiavelli, *'Il Principe' e 'Discorsi sopra la prima deca di Tito Livio'*, ed. S. Bertelli (Milan, 1960), pp. 89–90). The overall title given to the essays in J. M. Nieto Soria ed., *Orígenes de la Monarquía Hispánica: propaganda y legitimación (ca. 1400–1520)* (Madrid, 1999) shows that historians are now accustomed to thinking of our period as the origin of the early-modern state; see further Nieto Soria's *Ceremonias de la realeza: propaganda y legitimación en la Castilla trastámara* ([Madrid], 1993), and, for a parallel case, R. Costa Gomes, *The Making of a Court Society: kings and nobles in late medieval Portugal* (Cambridge, 2003) [rev. & enlarged trans. of *A Corte dos Reis de Portugal no Final da Idade Média* (Linda-A-Velha, 1995)].

[11] With the exception of the last, these features also typified the cultural politics of medieval courts; see, for example, M. Vale, *The Princely Court: medieval courts and culture in north-west Europe, 1270–1380* (Oxford, 2001), pp. 165–246 and 247–94. Yet, though cultural forms tend to preserve obsolete features from earlier stages, the new social configuration transforms their meaning; hence, for example, Elias, *Die höfische Gesellschaft*, pp. 363–447 [*The Court Society*, pp. 230–85] cites the sixteenth-century taste for chivalric romances of knight errantry as a case of *Romantisierung*, romantic discontent with courtization expressed as a nostalgic desire for a simpler, uncorrupted past.

noble circle, but especially at the courts of princes, of poetic erudition. Quaintly, he calls the *arte de la poetría e gaya ciencia* a 'science, teaching, and doctrine [...] gained by innate grace from God', but he ends with a more down-to-earth social comment that incidentally explains why in cultural terms – not by God's grace – beautiful women were a requirement of court society:

> [Poetry] is an art of such exalted understanding and subtle intellect that it cannot be learnt or mastered except by a man of high and subtle imagination, exalted and pure discrimination, [...] and such as has seen, heard and *read many different books* and writings, *knows all languages*, has spent his career *in royal and seigneurial courts*, has practical experience of many *worldly affairs*, is an *hidalgo of noble blood*, courteous, gentle, and well-mannered, gracious, polished, witty and with honey and sugar, salt and breeze and humour in his speech, and is also *a lover who takes pride in love and always pretends to be enamoured*.[12]

In this sentence, which patently describes not the unkempt and impecunious beast we call a poet, but a perfect courtier, the vital words are such overtly social terms as 'exalted' (*elevado*), 'high' (*alto*), 'seigneurial' (*grandes señores*, grandees), 'noble' (*noble fidalgo*), 'courteous' (*cortés*, which we could also render 'courtly'), 'gentle' (*gentil*, 'of gentle birth'), and 'polished' (*polido*, which we could also render 'polite'). Literary erudition and eloquence are presented as necessary and sufficient forms of distinction; like courtly love, they confer *noblesse*, distinction, a passport to court society and style.

The number of 'poets' active at Juan II's court – that is, not minstrels but men of quality, noblemen and *letrados* like Mendoza and Cartagena – is arresting; almost 200 are known by name. No less noteworthy is the milieu in which they wrote; poetry's overtly public face was exemplified, on one hand, by a discrete atmosphere of rivalry and attention-seeking (for example, in *preguntas y respuestas*, a sport consisting in wittily

---

[12] BnF, MS. esp. 37, fol. 1ᵛ–3ᵛ, 'Prologus Baenenssis': *Cancionero de Juan Alfonso de Baena*, ed. B. Dutton & J. González Cuenca (Madrid, 1993), pp. 3–8 (emphases mine). Strictly speaking not 'ends', since there was a lacuna in the archetype after this point (*Cancionero*, p. 8, n. 67), but nevertheless an apt peroration for our purpose.

matching the metre and rhymes of the 'answers' to often abstruse 'questions' about love, morality, or religion; or *jeux d'esprit* such as *glosas*, or *contrafacta*), and, on the other, by the large proportion of circumstantial pieces, from birthday greetings for the monarch to the obligatory courtly-love poetry and – for the first time in Castilian – overtly political verse.[13] Juan II himself presided over the proceedings, leading the way by composing verses and conversing on literary matters.[14] In this light it becomes easier to see the significance of the panegyrics which, besides the 'arms and letters' topic, praised Mendoza for combining his prowess as knight with a role as courtier, which modern biographers sometimes deny. The royal secretary and chronicler Fernando de Pulgar, for example, after a customary reference to the marquis's 'two notable occupations in life, one as soldier [*la disciplina militar*] and the other as scholar [*el estudio de la sciencia*]', added a eulogy that explicitly identifies the setting for the latter as the court:

[13] On the first point see A. Chas Aguión, 'Querellas burlescas e ingeniería retórica en el *Cancionero de Baena*', *La Corónica*, xxxviii (2009), pp. 191–210; on the last, with specific reference to poetic erudition and humanism, J. Lawrance, 'Santillana's political poetry' in A. Deyermond, *Santillana: A Symposium* [Papers of the Medieval Hispanic Research Seminar, xxviii] (London, 2000), pp. 7–37; and in general, from broader viewpoints and to greater effect, Di Camillo, *El humanismo castellano*, pp. 67–109; J. Weiss, *The Poet's Art: literary theory in Castile, c. 1400–60* [Medium Ævum Monographs, new ser., xiv] (Oxford, 1990).

[14] Fernán Pérez de Guzmán, *Generaciones y semblanzas*, ed. R. B. Tate (London, 1965), p. 39 'He liked listening to well-informed and witty men [*avisados e graçiosos*], and took much note of what he heard; spoke and understood Latin, read very well, was very fond of books and histories, delighted to listen to poems and could criticize them; took great pleasure in listening to merry, well-aimed quips, and could even make them himself.' For Guzmán – Mendoza's uncle, shut away in his country castle at Batres – these 'graces' were part of the king's 'odd, strange character [*condiçión estraña e maravillosa*]'; he had limited empathy with the new court style, and was therefore rusticated, rendered marginal, despite his literary talents.

The king [Juan II] *entrusted him with his person, and sometimes with the governance of his kingdoms*, which he governed with such prudence that poets said of him that *at court he was great Phoebus* through his illustrious governance, and *in the field Hannibal* through his great valour.[15]

Gómez Manrique, too, saw the court as the proper locus of Mendoza's intellectual distinction, the theatre of his fame, the litmus of culture and style:

> Lloren los ombres valientes
> por tan valiente guerrero;
> e plangan los eloquentes
> e los varones prudentes
> lloren por tal compañero,
> e los lindos cortesanos
> lloren más que los tebanos
> por su pueblo destroýdo,
> pues han el mejor perdido
> de todos los palançianos.[16]

---

[15] Fernando de Pulgar, *Claros varones de Castilla* [1486], ed. M. Á. Pérez Priego (Madrid, 2007), pp. 102–14 (pp. 104–5, 110); the reference to the king's 'person' points to the link between royal favour and offices in the king's household; the *annominatio* on 'govern' is in the original. Pulgar modelled his compilation of *semblanzas* (biographical sketches) on Plutarch and Valerius Maximus with the express aim, as he told Isabel the Catholic in his prologue, of providing a portrait of the monarchy's élite, 'with their lineages, characters, and notable deeds [...] in both science and arms', worthy to vie with 'those Greeks, Romans, and Frenchmen who are so praised in *their* histories' (p. 73). The telltale omission of Italians is instructive, as is the comparison of Mendoza's generalship to that of Rome's arch-enemy, Hannibal.

[16] *Planto de las Virtudes e Poesía por el marqués de Santillana*, stanza LXXXIX, lines 881–90 (Manrique, *Cancionero*, p. 401). The lexis matches Baena's in social precision: *lindo* 'elegant, stylish', a synonym of *gentil, polido* (Alfonso de Ulloa, *Introdutione nella quale s'insegna pronunciare la lingua Spagnuola, con una Espositione nella Italiana di parecchi vocaboli Spagnuoli difficili* [1553], 2nd edn (Milan, 1621), p. 30: '*Lindos* o *gentiles*, per eleganti & gentili'; J. Minsheu, *A Dictionarie in Spanish and English* (London, 1599), p. 159a: '*Líndo*, cleane, neate, fine, handsome'; C. Oudin, *Tesoro de las dos lenguas francesa y española* (Paris, 1607), fol. [T4]'b: '*Lindo*, beau, gentil, joly, élégant, mignon,

Weep, valiant men, for so valiant a warrior; lament, eloquent men and wise paladins, weep for such a companion; and let polite courtiers [*lindos cortesanos*] weep more than the Thebans for their ruined city, for they have lost the cynosure of courtliness.

The long survival of courtly love and chivalry in the new context of court society shows not that either was still relevant in practice, but the romantic tenacity of nostalgia, habit, and tradition in cultural formations. Renaissance courtiers would continue to dream of both, but in ever more distanced or romantic ways, the former in the guise of Petrarchism, the latter through the etiolated surrogate of chivalric romance. Sydney Anglo argues that, in this respect, there was no essential difference between the late-medieval Burgundian or Castilian knight and Castiglione's Renaissance *cortigiano*.[17] The Spanish critic Marcelino Menéndez Pelayo took a different view: for him, Mendoza's was 'an age of courtly aristocratic vulgarization and *dilettantism* rather than grammatical learning', whereas 'the definitive achievement of the Renaissance' lay in the future importation by Antonio de Nebrija (1444–1522) of professional Latin philology, half a century behind Italy. Using a phrase of Mendoza's own, Menéndez Pelayo summed up with a paradox: the first period sought the content (surface), the

---

poly'); *palanciano* 'courtly' (Alfonso de Palencia, *Universal vocabulario en latin y en romance*, 2 vols (Seville, 1490), ii, fol. 335ʳ *s.v.* palatium: '*palatinos* se llaman los que acostumbran morar en el palaçio principal, conversando ende de continuo', and i, fol. 151ᵛ *s.v.* facetus: '*faceta* [i.e. of a woman] cortés, palantiana, gratiosa, plazible, bien acostumbrada'; Ulloa, *Introdutione*, p. 34: '*Palanciano*, per cortigiano & accorto'; Minsheu, *Dictionarie*, p. 182b: '*Palanciáno*, a courtier'; Oudin, *Tesoro*, fol. Cc2ᵛ: '*Palanciano*, courtisan, homme de palais & de court').

[17] S. Anglo, 'The Courtier: The Renaissance and changing ideals' in A. G. Dickens ed., *The Courts of Europe: politics, patronage and royalty 1400–1800* (London, 1977), pp. 32–53. The topic is discussed with reference to Spain in J. Lawrance, 'On fifteenth-century Spanish vernacular humanism' in I. Michael and R. A. Cardwell ed., *Medieval and Renaissance Studies in Honour of R. B. Tate* (Oxford, 1986), pp. 63–79.

second the forms (substance) of classical literature.[18] From the perspective of this essay, both views are insufficient: the advent of the new requirement for the courtier to be cultivated in *belles lettres* – the cultural component destined to replace knightly prowess in the court's formula of distinction – radically changed the social basis of aristocratic life (*pace* Anglo); but Latin humanism and the revival of classical forms were a consequence, not a cause, of that change (*pace* Menéndez Pelayo).

[18] M. Menéndez Pelayo, *Antología de poetas líricos castellanos: desde la formación del lenguaje hasta nuestros días* [1890–1908], 3rd edn, ed. E. Sánchez Reyes [Edición Nacional de las Obras Completas, xvii–xxvi], 10 vols (Santander, 1944–5), ii, 15, quoting Mendoza's 'A su hijo D. Pero Gonçález, quando estava estudiando en Salamanca' (Santillana, *Obras completas*, pp. 455–57): 'Since we cannot have what we want, let us want what we can; if we lack the forms [*formas*], let us be content with the content [*materias*]' (p. 456). The paradox is compounded by the fact that Mendoza was asking for a translation of Homer's *Iliad* (via the Latin of Leonardo Bruni and Pier Candido Decembrio) because, despite having 'plenary and extensive notice' of its subject from Guido Delle Colonne's *Trojan History*, 'it would be pleasurable to see for myself the work of so great a man, the sovereign prince of poets as it were, especially on what is thought to have been the greatest and most ancient military dispute or war in the world' (P. M. Cátedra, 'Sobre la biblioteca del Marqués de Santillana: la *Ilíada* y Pier Candido Decembrio', *Hispanic Review*, li (1983), pp. 23–28; G. Serés, *La traducción en Italia y España durante el siglo XV: la 'Ilíada en romance' y su contexto cultural* (Salamanca, 1997)); so: was Mendoza interested in content – or form? Menéndez Pelayo lifted his hypothesis from J. Amador de los Ríos, *Historia crítica de la literatura española*, 7 vols (Madrid, 1861–5), vi, pp. 9–54 at pp. 29–30 & n. 1, 53–4, yet Amador shows that Juan II's writers went to great lengths to imitate the syntax and lexis of their classical sources, illustrating Castilian by the most astounding project of Latinization in its history, so capturing the 'spirit' (pp. 47–52 at p. 47; see also 'La poesía erudita en la corte de Juan II' at pp. 55–189). For recent overviews of the debate on this 'vernacular' stage of humanism see Á. Gómez Moreno, *España y la Italia de los humanistas: primeros ecos* (Madrid, 1994) and id., 'La *militia* clásica y la caballería medieval: las lecturas *de re militari* entre Medievo y Renacimiento', *Euphrosyne*, xxiii (1995), pp. 83–97; O. Di Camillo, 'Fifteenth-century Spanish humanism, thirty-five years later', *La Corónica*, xxxix (2010), pp. 19–66.

Returning to Mendoza's *Qüestión fecha al obispo de Burgos*, we are now in a better position to appreciate the significance of his exaggerated admiration for Bruni and reverent name-dropping of classical authorities, both typical of the enthusiastic Iberian reception of humanism at that date.[19] Fifteenth-century court writers crammed their texts with litanies of such names, usually known to them only in the most vague and distant way, culled at second hand from translations and compendia.[20] Yet their peers did not curl the lip; instead, they reverently hailed these weird displays of pedantry, which neither author nor audience could understand without a gloss (which was often provided by engaging a *letrado* to write a commentary), as the most magnificent attainments of humane learning since Antiquity. We may conjecture that the names functioned aesthetically as what Ezra Pound called *melopoeia* (word-music, magic charm, patter, glamourous noise), not *logopoeia* (conceptual meaning); and this in itself reveals, as few other things do, the nature and function of the prestige of humanist erudition within the embryonic court style of that time.

Nevertheless, it would be a gross error to conclude from the foregoing that the effect and impact of the erudite music was merely decorative. Prestige – its creation, acquisition, sharing,

[19] Mendoza's references to Archidamus [*sic*] (for the town-planner Hippodamus; Aristotle, *Politics* 1267b22–3, Bk II.8) and Phileas of Carthage [*sic*] (for Phaleas of Chalcedon, ibid. 1266a39–1267b21) are taken or miscopied from Bruni's *De militia* (Bayley, *War and Society*, p. 372), but the description of Plato as a Stoic *avant la lettre* and the notion that Romulus might have been some kind of authority appear to be muddles of the marquis's own devising.

[20] For instance, 'Phoebus', 'Thebans', or the confused mention of 'Academe' as if it were a place like Athens in the quotations above from Pulgar, Manrique and Diego de Burgos. The derivative character of fifteenth-century erudition is remarked in all literary studies, e.g. the editions listed in n. 2 above, and most fully in M. R. Lida de Malkiel, *Juan de Mena, poeta del Prerrenacimiento español* [1950], 2nd edn (México, 1984); for an illustration, J. Lawrance, 'Juan Alfonso de Baena's versified reading-list: A note on the aspirations and the reality of fifteenth-century Castilian culture', *Journal of Hispanic Philology*, v (1981), pp. 101–22.

guarding – is the core of culture, and especially of court culture. The question posed by Mendoza may look academic, but it went to the heart of the matter: could the study of ancient history illuminate the ideology of chivalry, and hence be used to reform society by showing a way out of the lawless violence of rule (not 'government') by a feudal aristocracy? His specific enquiry concerned the oath taken by Roman armies; in broader terms, the nature of allegiance, the 'duty' of the *miles* (soldier/knight) to the republic or commonwealth – a concept of duty for which Mendoza borrowed the Latinism *ofiçio* from Cartagena's translation of Cicero's *De officiis* (*On Duties*) – and not just in war but, more tellingly, 'in the *civitas* when he returns from war'.[21] The nub of the letter, however, is Mendoza's description of Castile's 'scandals, quarrels, and revolts', which he calls 'a second labyrinth or house of Daedalus' in tribute to his client Juan de Mena's epic political allegory *Laberinto de Fortuna*, which was to be presented to the king only a month later, on 22 February 1444. The passage's typically spiky melopoetic classical name-dropping is expressed in rhetorically chiselled periods that seem neither dilettante nor naïve, and which incidentally imply that the *Qüestión* was no private letter, but intended as a potentially public oratorical display:

> And what can anyone now think of, my lord, to repair these great damages (for here we see all the pride of Agamemnon and Achilles, here the treachery of Theban Eteocles, here Cytherea's thefts, here the greed and avarice of Midas, here the cruelty and ferocity of Thracian Diomedes and the corrupt shamelessness of Nero)? Nothing, surely, but that these very vices and sins have aroused, admonished, and provoked the men of this unhappy hemisphere and call them every day, like the trumpet of Misenus, to martial arms. We no longer remember the words of our Lord and Redeemer, 'Every kingdom divided against itself is brought to desolation', nor Rome's 'worse than civil wars' described so loftily and elegantly by Lucan, nor the Catilinarian conspiracy and Cethegus' mad impetuosity, nor the cruel recent Gallic wars,

---

[21] See my opening quotation, and cf. Cartagena, *Libros de Tulio* (*De los ofiçios*), ed. Morrás.

so close to us in time and place that they should always be before our eyes but are in fact already forgotten, because we are estranged from every virtue, every desire for peace, and all love of living well; so we should be denied whatever rewards were promised or granted to those virtuous champions and seekers of the good of their native country [*patria*], the vanquishers and conquerors of her enemies and defenders of the commonwealth [*república*].[22]

By using the pronoun 'we' Mendoza reveals that pride, greed, lust, and treachery are, *par excellence*, the vices of his own estate, the nobility. Hence it is easy to see that his learnèd question was of burning contemporary relevance and, in its foreshadowing of the social transformation I spoke of above (since, *de facto*, any public oath to the monarch and commonwealth challenged the knight's right to wage private war), prophetic. What is most indicative is that the future marquis represents not his peers' viewpoint but that of the monarch's court, or what in the next century would come to be thought of as the state. Cartagena

---

[22] Santillana, *Obras completas*, pp. 416–7. Rhetoric (anaphora: five *aquís*, five *no/nis*; tricola, e.g. the last two sentences, with further anaphora of *todo* 'every ~ every ~ all') is embossed by alliteration, rhythm, rhyme (e.g. in the last period, *denegados nos deven ser ~ otorgados, pugnadores e deseadores ~ propulsadores e debelladores ~ defensores*) and elaborate Latinate lexis, but above all—boldly sacrificing intelligibility (*robos çitareos*, for example, could never be understood without a gloss; see below)—by the melopeia of names. 'Their *patria*' at the end means Rome; the preceding sentences touch on Homer's *Iliad*, Statius' *Thebais* (Eteocles), and Sallust's *De coniuratione Catilinae*, with allusions to Ovid, *Metamorphoses* iv.174–90 ('*furta ~ Cythereia*', of Venus' adultery with Mars, illicit sex as 'theft'; cf. *P. Ovidii Metamorphosis, cum integris ac emendatissimis enarrationibus*, ed. R. Regio (Venice, 1493), fol. F1ʳ *ad loc.* '*Furta*, stupra & adulteria, quod furtim fiant'); Virgil, *Aeneid* VI. 164–5 (Misenus *quo non praestantior alter | aere ciere viros Martemque accendere cantu*, 'renown'd | The warrior trumpet in the field to sound, | With breathing brass to kindle fierce alarms', trans. Dryden); Matthew 12.25; and Lucan, *Pharsalia* i.1 ('Bella per Emathios *plus quam civilia* campos'). The passage paraphrases Mendoza's contemporaneous *Soneto* XVIII *Quexándose de los daños deste regno* ('¿Oy qué diré de ti, triste emisperio?' in Santillana, *Obras completas*, pp. 63–4); see Lawrance, 'Santillana's political poetry', pp. 25–29.

duly answered (as required of a king's man, but also as inclined by conviction) that yes, a more civilized – to wit, more governable – social order might come from a revival of the civic spirit of Roman 'republicanism', despite noting carefully the semantic difference between Latin *miles*/Spanish *caballero* and the historical distinction between professional Roman legions and medieval chivalry, a dignity of explicitly Christian origin unknown to the ancients:

> It would not be unreasonable, among the many new customs that came in during these [Christian] times, to revive this one ancient and forgotten one [i.e. the Roman military oath], [...] for if we cared to ponder the matter, [knights and vassals] appear to represent in this kingdom the same as what those *milites* or knights chosen by Romulus did in Rome, since they are obliged to be ready to wage war for the commonwealth [*república*] with their persons, horses, and arms whenever the prince orders it [...]. What I mean is, since [men-at-arms] live at the public expense, they should make public oaths.[23]

However, the key passage comes when, after a eulogy of Mendoza's public spirit in dedicating himself to letters, Cartagena delivers this analysis of the drawback, for what he directly calls a court polity, of an uncivil knighthood:

[23] *Respuesta del obispo de Burgos* in Santillana, *Obras completas*, pp. 417–34 (pp. 433–4). *Miles*, 'which in our common parlance we have been using quite improperly for a long while' (p. 423), meant 'combatant, soldier', *eques* was 'man at arms', i.e. combatant on horseback (pp. 425–6), the most apt equivalent to knights being *Quirites*, 'citizens' (p. 424), though 'I would not venture to affirm that a dignity like our knighthood existed then, [...] for these things [ceremonies of dubbing, etc.] gradually came in later, when the Christian commonwealth [*república*] began to flourish' (p. 431–2). Given Bruni's different audience and ideology, it is no wonder that the term *res publica* caused crossed wires; for Mendoza, Cartagena, and the Spanish monarchy the model commonwealth was Caesar's dictatorship, or *imperium* – no Spanish writer praised the Republic's constitution other than in a romantic, antiquarian way (e.g. Cato's suicide). Cartagena clearly understood that any dream of an actual revival of Antiquity was doomed to be unrealizable, a point made in more wide-ranging terms by F. Rico, *El sueño del humanismo: De Petrarca a Erasmo* [1993], 2nd edn (Barcelona, 2002).

So great is the spirited belligerence [*animosidat e brío*] of the nobility of Spain that, if it does not exercise its forces in just war [i.e. against Islam], it immediately channels them into those conflicts which the Romans called 'civil' [*çibdadanas*, cf. Lucan's phrase in n. 22 above] because they were waged about the government of their city [*çibdat*] [...], and which we may properly call 'courtly' [*cortesanas*] because they are waged about favour at court [*el valer de la corte*] (p. 420).

The last, pivotal phrase reflects the immediate political circumstances of this correspondence: the tense struggle for power (Mendoza was in the act of changing sides) between Juan II's *valido* or favourite Luna, Constable of Castile, and the league of nobles led by his rivals, the Admiral of Castile and the king of Navarre, in the run up to the resounding defeat of the latter at the battle of Olmedo on 19 May 1445.[24] By portraying this *contienda cortesana* (struggle for ascendancy at court) as equivalent to the Roman Civil War (struggle for power between the conservative Republican nobility and the new imperial autocracy of the Caesars), Cartagena not only contrived to gild the politics of Juan II's court with the sheen of antique prestige, but also revealed, perhaps unwittingly, a parallel capable of illuminating the underlying sense of his society's shift towards royal absolutism. The exchange between Mendoza, Cartagena, and (by proxy) Bruni is thus one of the earliest documents of the practical impact of humanism in Spain, perhaps the first in which we glimpse the revival of Antiquity being called upon to shape mentalities. In the new context of 'court wars', publicity and culture would eventually replace horse-borne combat as the

---

[24] *Crónica de Juan II*, Año 38º (1444) in *Crónicas de los reyes de Castilla*, ed. C. Rosell [Biblioteca de Autores Españoles, lxvi, lxviii, lxx], 3 vols (Madrid, 1875–8), ii, 614–25, in particular §XI, p. 620 on Mendoza's change of sides. In view of the thesis of this paper, and since biographers often assert that Mendoza stayed aloof from court politics, holding no major court office, it is worth underlining that at the time of writing the *Qüestión* he was a key player in Luna's victory (and its principal beneficiary in terms of royal *mercedes*, along with Luna's eventual successor, Juan Pacheco), as he would be again in Luna's downfall in 1453.

gateway to power, and Mendoza's aspiration to make the pen mightier than the sword would come to be a political reality.[25]

A notable aspect of all this is the resolution of all parties (king, noble courtiers, professional bureaucrats and men of letters) to conduct the new court culture in the vernacular. The *translatio imperii* from Italy to Spain – and by the next century, who would doubt that this boast of fifteenth-century Castilian publicity had been vindicated? – could have little meaning without such a substitution of Latin by Castilian as a new imperial language.[26] Although, like other churchmen, Cartagena continued to write his more important works in Latin, he was no exception to the trend, lending his advocacy to the cause of an aristocracy lettered in the vulgar language by his translations from classical works. Thus it was quite logical for Juan de Lucena's Platonic dialogue *De vita beata* –composed in Rome, where its author served in the household of Pius II and corresponded with LORENZO VALLA before returning c. 1464 to posts in the Castilian court under Enrique IV (1454–74) and Isabel the Catholic (1474–1504) –to make its first collocutor, Mendoza, praise its second, Cartagena, for having brought philosophy from Italy to Castile precisely through his vernacular works and 'new lessons in Castilian style [*nueva doctrina del fablar castellano*]':

> Reverend father, I see that for my sake you are struggling to translate [*romançar*] what can scarcely be expressed even in Latin. Philosophy was born in Greece, Socrates called it down from the sky; after Socrates, in the days when Brutus liberated Rome,

---

[25] Aspects of this later development are studied, through the prism of Santillana's own family, by H. Nader, *The Mendoza Family in the Spanish Renaissance, 1350–1550* (New Brunswick, 1979), now available on-line at http://libro.uca.edu/mendoza/mendoza.htm [accessed 4th October 2011].

[26] That the use of Castilian was a 'resolution' is made likely by the fact that Juan II knew Latin (n. 14 above) but did not use it; clear, by the literary output of his court; and explicit, in his successor's reign, by Nebrija's composition of a Castilian grammar on the grounds that 'language is the companion of empire' (Lawrance, '*Fabulosa illa aurea secula*', pp. 4–7).

Pythagoras planted it in Italy; now you transplant it to Spain. Blessèd she, happy Castile! [...] You have written in *volgare* of chivalry, the commonwealth, the Christian faith, and given us the famous works of our moral Seneca in the vernacular. Were you to talk alone with Juan de Mena [the third collocutor], you would reason *Latino sermone*, I know it, woe on me![27]

In turn Cartagena is made to brush aside the marquis's modest self-denigration with the remark: 'You praise my words; I praise your deeds. It is more glorious to do well than to speak well.' It is, then, wholly appropriate that this re-imagined dialogue (for it is imitated from a neo-Latin text by BARTOLOMEO FACIO) should be set, not like its model in a scholar's house, but 'in the royal salon', at a gathering – urbane, erudite, and conversing in pure and elegant Spanish – of 'the leading members of the court'.[28]

With the hindsight of history this preference of Juan II's court for turning the humanist intellectual property it acquired from Italy into cultural capital as vernacular erudition seems unremarkable; but scholars lay too little emphasis on the message it sent out in the 1430s and 1440s, when there was as yet no evidence to substantiate the claim – explicit in Mena's *Laberinto* – that Castile's monarchy, and hence language, would replicate the glory of Rome.[29] Its audacity proved too

[27] J. de Lucena, *De vita felici*, ed. O. Perotti (Pavia, 2004), pp. 72–3, quoting, as noted in a marginal gloss (Lucena, p. 141 *ad* 126), Cicero, *Tusculan Disputations*, iv.1–2 (Pythagoras and Brutus – the reference is to the murder of Julius Caesar), v.10 (Socrates). Lucena's dialogue counters Menéndez Pelayo's dictum about content versus form (n. 18 above); cf., for example, A. Vian Herrero, 'El *Libro de vita beata* de Juan de Lucena como diálogo literario', *Bulletin Hispanique*, xciii (1991), pp. 61–105; J. M. Martínez Torrejón, 'Neither/nor: dialogue in Juan de Lucena's *Libro de vida beata*', *Modern Language Notes*, cxiv (1999), pp. 211–22; A. Medina Bermúdez, 'Los inagotables misterios de Juan de Lucena', *Dicenda*, xvii (1999), pp. 295–311.

[28] 'Convinieron un día *en la sala real* todos los *primarios de la corte*', p. 70.

[29] Juan de Mena, *Laberinto de Fortuna*, stanzas 1, lines 1–4 'al gran rey de España, al Çésar novelo' (Juan II a 'new Caesar', with dominions on earth coterminous with Jupiter's in heaven), 142, lines 1–4 '[rey] de España no sola, mas de todo el mundo' (king of the world): *Obras*

bold for the times, and for a while Spanish monarchs fell back, for international publicity, on Latin (in Juan II's case, commissioned from Cartagena, Bruni and PIER CANDIDO DECEMBRIO; in Isabel's, from Nebrija and Italians resident in the Spanish kingdoms, such as ANTONIO and ALESSANDRO GERALDINI, PIETRO MARTIRE D'ANGHIERA and LUCA MARINEO).[30] Nevertheless, Mendoza, Cartagena, and their compeers at Juan II's court were to prove more forward-looking, with their championship of an easy vernacular erudition, than the advocates of a neo-Latin revival. In the next two centuries every court in Europe would be inhabited by its crowd of noble courtiers, all with their smattering of small Latin and less Greek, all furiously penning sonnets to court ladies and courtesans, and

completas, ed. M. Á. Pérez Priego (Barcelona, 1989), pp. 209–303 at pp. 209, 254.

[30] For Bruni, see his *Epistolarum libri VIII*, ed. L. Mehus, 2 vols (Florence, 1741), ii, pp. 158–60, *Ep*. IX.11 to Cartagena (4 September 1442): 'Misi vero iampridem ad dominum regem Hispaniae, qui hoc per suas litteras postulaverat, libellos quosdam meos, in quibus fuit opusculum cuius titulus est *Isagogicon moralis philosophiae*'. Apart from the *Isagogicon*, we know of only two *libelli* addressed to the king: *Ep*. VII.2 (21 March [1435?], ed. Mehus, ii, 77–79) in praise of Spain's Roman emperors, and *Ep*. VII.6 (7 December [1436?], ed. Mehus, ii, 93–4) in praise of Juan's literary studies. Both were translated into Castilian for Santillana, along with other works including *De militia*, which suggests that Juan II's connexion with Bruni was well publicized (Madrid: Biblioteca Nacional de España, MS. 10212, fol. 17^v–20^r; M. Schiff, *La Bibliothèque du marquis de Santillane* (Paris, 1905), Notice LIII.D, pp. 361–3). For P. C. Decembrio's dedication to the king, again through the good offices of Cartagena, of his Latin prose version of *Iliad*, I–IV and X (1442) – also subsequently translated into Castilian for Santillana – see the documents in A. Morel-Fatio, 'Les deux *Omero* castillans', *Romania*, xxv (1896), pp. 111–29 at pp. 123–26, and studies cited in n. 18 above. We know also of a commission from Cardinal Bessarion (Madrid: Biblioteca Nacional de España, MS. 10445, fols 69^r–74^v; dedication to Juan II edited from the Castilian translation in Schiff, *La Bibliothèque*, p. 81). For a recent overview of humanists at Isabel's court, see D. Paolini, 'Los Reyes Católicos e Italia: los humanistas italianos y su relación con España' in N. Salvador Miguel & C. Moya García ed., *La literatura en la época de los Reyes Católicos* (Madrid, 2008), pp. 189–205.

all queuing in the antechambers of the king and his ministers hoping to catch the eye of favour with their elegant wit and cultured mien.

These facts raise a final question in relation to our *Qüestión fecha al obispo de Burgos*. It is generally agreed that Latin was essential to humanism, and though all great humanists before Erasmus wrote in the vernacular as well, the general point is borne out by contemporary usage: *studia humanitatis* meant the study of classical letters, while *umanista* was a condescending term for a professional grammarian.[31] To what extent, then, is it licit to talk of humanism having influenced or changed fifteenth-century Spanish court culture, as opposed to merely being used as an ingredient in the rather peculiar and distinct form of erudition that it evolved for itself? Where was the chicken, where the egg? Which was the horse, and which the cart?

The humanists did two things, seemingly insignificant, but fundamental to Renaissance culture: first, they argued that the study of Latin letters, instead of serving as an elementary prerequisite for entry to the senior faculties of theology and law, should be an end in itself; and second, they introduced a new empirical and historical rigour into that study by basing it upon reading of a careful canon of ancient literary texts. Humanism, in other words, was not a philosophy but a pedagogical reform; its primary aim was to teach correct Latinity and rhetoric. In these respects what was going forward at the court of Juan II bore little affinity to the humanist endeavour, and we cannot talk of a Spanish humanism before the succeeding generation of

---

[31] This now general view stems from P. O. Kristeller's famous description of the *studia humanitatis* as 'a characteristic phase in [...] the rhetorical tradition in Western culture' ('The Humanist Movement', in id., *Renaissance Thought: the classic, scholastic, and humanist strains* [1956], 2nd edn (New York, 1961), pp. 3–23 at p. 11; for the semantics of the term, see pp. 9–10). The point is further expounded, in less reverent tone but to similar effect, by A. Grafton & L. Jardine, *From Humanism to the Humanities: education and the liberal arts in fifteenth- and sixteenth-century Europe* (London, 1986). See also p. 6 above.

Palencia, Nebrija, and the Hellenist Hernán Núñez.[32] A potent indication is that Juan de Mena, who spent time in Florence and was the most erudite of Juan II's court poets, was appointed royal secretary of Latin letters c. 1441, and yet left not a single line written in Latin.[33] If we attend, however, to the social context of the new learning, matters appear less clear-cut. Humanist scholarship was produced, as scholarship always is, by humble drudges, but for the most part it was consumed by nobles. Yet the old theory that the ruling elite acquired a training in humanist Latin because it needed skills for an increasingly bureaucratic administration is beside the mark, since the entire point of the classical education was its practical and vocational uselessness. The explicit idea of humanist pedagogues was to educate men in overtly non-technical, liberal forms of civilization. PIER PAOLO VERGERIO declared in his *De ingenuis moribus* :

> Aristotle, bearing in mind the demands of men's civil and business life [*civilem hominum vitam negotiosamque*], desired us not to indulge or linger to excess on the liberal sciences in pursuit of perfection, since anyone who dedicates himself wholly to speculation and the allurement of letters may please himself, but certainly does little service to the city [*urbi*], be he prince or private citizen.[34]

---

[32] Gómez Moreno, *España y la Italia de los humanistas*, documents the earlier chain of Italo-Iberian contacts, but his sub-title cunningly opts to call them 'echoes', not 'influence'.

[33] Mena's key role is extensively explored in the forthcoming papers of the conference *Juan de Mena: entre la corte y la ciudad*, directed by Cristina Moya (Córdoba, 2011). We see a notable contrast with his direct successor in the post, who wrote numerous Latin works; see Alfonso de Palencia, *Gesta Hispaniensia ex annalibus suorum dierum collecta: libri I–X*, ed. & trans. B. Tate & J. Lawrance, 2 vols (Madrid, 1998–99), i, pp. xxxv–lxix (in particular xlvii–lv 'Obras literarias y humanísticas'), but no poetry. Only with Nebrija do we get the full humanist package of Latin, vernacular and (neo-Latin) poetic texts.

[34] *Humanist Educational Treatises*, ed. & trans. C. Kallendorf [ITRL, v] (Cambridge, MA, 2002), pp. 2–91 (§48, p. 58). Vergerio refers to Aristotle, *Politics* 1337b15–17 (VIII.2); Kallendorf also adduces Seneca,

The passage comes in Vergerio's longest chapter, 'Excellens studium tractat, armorum scilicet et litterarum' ('The Finest Studies: Arms and Letters'); a good half of his treatise is devoted to *armorum studium* and other pursuits of the nobility. What he seeks constantly to do is not to advocate a rigorous training in Latin philology, but to emphasise the connexion between social class, distinction and the need to shun anything that might reek of vulgar training for some kind of job:

> For liberal ['truly noble', trans. Kallendorf] minds and those who must become involved in public affairs and society, the more fitting subjects are history and moral philosophy. The other arts are called 'liberal' because they are becoming to free men, philosophy is liberal because its study makes men free. [...] To these, if I am not mistaken, should be added a third, eloquence, which is a part of civil education [*civilis scientiae pars*].[35]

The line leading from this to Castiglione's notions of courtierly *virtù* and *sprezzatura* is short; but Vergerio's attitude is also not so very far from that of Cartagena, who in a Latin letter of c.1440 written to accompany the gift of two of the *libri minores*, *Disticha Catonis* and *Contemptus mundi*, to the king's chamberlain Pedro Fernández de Velasco, count of Haro, argues that, since each of the three estates has its own designated *officium* (*laboratores, oratores, defensores*), the kind of learning appropriate to the nobility, engaged in ruling the commonwealth, should consist of *studia honesta* – in effect, history, moral philosophy, and eloquence, *belles lettres* – leaving the sublimities of theology or the technicalities of law and the sciences to professionals; 'my purpose in this treatise', he says,

---

Ep. 88.36–37 (translated by Cartagena *c.* 1431 for Juan II's greatest self-aggrandizing cultural project, a complete cycle of versions of the Corduban philosopher, as 'Libro segundo, de las artes liberales', *Cinco libros de Seneca* (Seville, 1491), fol. 32–42; see K.-A. Blüher, *Séneca en España* (Madrid, 1983), pp. 132–55); and, for the last sentence, (ps.-)Plutarch 7c–d (*Plutarchi Opera*, III: *Moralia I*, p. 8 = Περὶ παίδων ἀγωγῆς, 10), popular in GUARINO DA VERONA's version, *De liberis educandis* (1411).

[35] *Humanist Educational Treatises*, p. 48, §40.

'has been not to show what knights should read, but rather to list the books they should not read'.³⁶

A training in classical letters explicitly did not *fit* a man for an office at court, therefore; but this was not to say that it did not *get* him one. Noble interest in the humanist curriculum had nothing to do with leisure or conspicuous expenditure, everything to do with the fierce demands of court society and competition for preferment and favour. At Juan II's court we see only the first, balbucient signs of courtization, the tentative growth of a new mentality; by the end of the century the movement was in full swing. Queen Isabel ostentatiously took up the study of Latin at the age of thirty-one, instituted a grammar school (under the charge of an Italian humanist, Pietro Martire d'Anghiera) for young noblemen in her court, and lent her support to the founding new colleges and chairs of humanist studies in the universities. By these means the Crown demonstrated that a curriculum in classical letters was considered a fitting training for any gentleman who aspired to high office and favour in the royal court. The count of Haro's request to Cartagena for some elementary Latin primers can thus be seen in retrospect as the vanguard of a movement which, in the next seventy years, would transform the cultural and social life of his class. His biographer Fernando de Pulgar remarked in

---

[36] *Epistula ad Petrum Fernandi de Velasco*, §11 'nobis ad presens non tantum quid legere militares uiri, sed a quibus abstinere debeant aliquantulum aperire in proposito fuit', in Lawrance, *Un tratado de Alonso de Cartagena*, p. 58. On Cartagena's prescription and its relation to humanist pedagogy see Lawrance, *Un tratado*, pp. 12–25. It offers striking parallels to cultural attitudes at the court of Ferrara under Leonello d'Este in the 1440s, as described by ANGELO DECEMBRIO, another Italian humanist pedagogue well known in Spain. In Bk I, Partes i–ix of his *De politia litteraria* of *c.* 1450, revised in 1463 (ed. N. Witten [Beiträge zur Altertumskunde, clxix] (Munich, 2002), pp. 146–72), Decembrio speaks of the 'modus ordoque servandus in curanda poliendaque bibliotheca, [...] scilicet qui libri in ea ex Latinis et Graecis opportuni' (p. 148). In pride of place come poetry, rhetoric, history ('ad profusiorem eloquentiam compescendam', p. 161), then 'libri vernaculi sermonis', ethics, and Greek authors; divinity and 'nostrae tempestatis auctores' form a brief appendix.

the 1480s, as a matter of note, that the count 'learnt Latin letters, and gave himself to the study of chronicles and history'.[37] It was because noblemen such as Haro wanted access to Latin, previously the preserve of the clergy, that humanist educators provided a new curriculum of *litterae humaniores*, not the other way around. Mendoza ruefully confessed to his cleric son, the future Grand Cardinal of Spain, that he had never found time to master Latin.[38] By contrast, his great-nephew Garcilaso de la Vega, Spain's first outstanding Renaissance poet and a member of the so-called Pontanian Academy at Naples, was praised by Pietro Bembo for the elegance of his Latin verses.[39] The difference between the two men's training and accomplishments was wide; their motives and attitude to the role of literature in court life were recognizably the same.

It is clear, in fact, that in Spain the opposition to the *studia humanitatis*, or *studia vanitatis* as the papal castellan and bishop Rodrigo Sánchez de Arévalo called them, came from the clergy, who rightly surmised that the nobility's access to Latin, and the humanists' way of giving it to them, constituted a direct attack on a monopoly that formed the firmest bastion of ecclesiastical

---

[37] Pulgar, *Claros varones de Castilla*, p. 100.

[38] 'A su hijo D. Pero Gonçález' in Santillana, *Obras completas*, p. 456: 'It would be difficult now, after so many years and no less trouble, for me to decide to set myself to wrestle with the Latin language'; see also Lucena's testimony at n. 27 above.

[39] In a letter of 26 August 1535 Bembo thanked Garcilaso for a gift of his *carmina*: 'nihil enim legi fere hac aetate confectum aut elegantius aut omnino probius et purius, aut certe maiori cum dignitate' (*Epistolae omnes quotquot extant* (Basel, 1567), pp. 690–93 = *Epp. fam.*, VI, 'Garsilasso Hispano'). Paolo Giovio rolled out the old 'arms and letters' topos (cf. n. 6 above), admiring Garcilaso's death in battle aged 35, and praising his 'Horatian' skill in Latin verse: *Elogia veris clarorum virorum imaginibus apposita, quae in Musaeo Ioviano comi spectantur* (Venice, 1546), fol. 79[v:] 'quum vigente adhuc seniorum opinione ipsi etiam totius Hispaniae proceres haec studia tanquam importuna militiae penitus abdicarent, [...] agnovere tamen nonnulli maiorum incuriam, Nebrissa monitore, ingeniaque sua ad hanc laudem feliciter extulerunt; in queis nuper emicuit Garcias Lassus, Horatiana suavitate odas scribere solitus.'

power.⁴⁰ In my hypothesis, however, the humanist project in Iberia had little to do with Burckhardtian notions of progress and individualism, with civic virtue, with an attack on scholasticism, or even with nostalgia for antiquity. Certainly it would eventually involve redrawing the map of the *episteme*, not so much to exclude scholastic theology as to include new fields and forms of secular knowledge, particularly those embraced in the encyclopaedia of ancient urban or urbane culture. But such things were ideological representations of the true cause, which was the social revolution that Elias described as courtization. One of the most interesting projects for students of humanism and the early Renaissance in Spain to undertake would be to compile an anthology of key texts, in Latin and Spanish, somewhat along the lines of those produced for Italy by Eugenio Garin in the 1950s.⁴¹ Such a collection would undoubtedly contain the texts I have discussed here, whether or not they be defined as 'humanist' by current criteria. And the first remarkable thing to emerge from such a compilation, I contend, would be to reveal the astonishing

---

[40] Rodericus ep. Zamorensis, *Speculum vitae humanae* (Rome, 1468), fol. 64, Lib. I.36: 'recte oratorum exercitia studia humanitatis sunt, quippe et vanitatis, dum vanitati sermonis incumbunt'; he also spoke of 'libros humanitatis [...] libros crudelitatis' (*De remediis afflictae ecclesiae* [1469], §22, in Venice: Biblioteca Nazionale Marciana, MS. Lat. Z.90 (=1515), fol. 66, cited by K. Kohut, 'Sánchez de Arévalo (1404–1470) frente al humanismo italiano' in A. M. Gordon & E. Rugg ed., *Actas del Sexto Congreso Internacional de Hispanistas, celebrado en Toronto del 22 al 26 agosto de 1977* (Toronto, 1980), pp. 431–4 (p. 433)), though in his youth Arévalo wrote Ciceronian dialogues and the first Spanish pedagogical treatise based on humanist sources: R. Sánchez de Arévalo, *Tratado sobre técnica, método y manera de criar a los hijos, niños y jóvenes (1453)*, ed. L. Velázquez Campo, trans. P. Arias Fernández (Pamplona, 1999), available on-line at http://hdl.handle.net/10171/9760 [accessed 4ᵗʰ October 2011]. For further discussion of the clerical quarrel with humanism see Di Camillo, *El humanismo castellano*, pp. 195–226; J. Lawrance, 'La autoridad de la letra: Un aspecto de la lucha entre humanistas y escolásticos en la Castilla del siglo XV', *Atalaya*, ii (1991), pp. 85–107.

[41] *Prosatori latini del Quattrocento*, ed. and trans. E. Garin (Milan, 1952).

precision with which we can date both the first impact of humanism and the beginnings of courtization, each of them much earlier than would seem on the surface to be likely or even, strictly speaking, possible. They happened at the same time, and in the extraordinarily brief space of the decade around 1440, at the height of the *contiendas cortesanas* of the Castilian court mentioned above – and in many ways, perhaps, as a direct result of them.[42]

---

[42] I thank David Rundle and Anthony Lappin for their saintly patience in getting me to present this paper, and the former for many valuable comments and suggestions; and Ángel Gómez Moreno, Luis Fernández Gallardo, Noel Fallows, María Morrás, Nick Round, Antonio Doñas Beleño, Mar Campos Souto, Pedro Cátedra, Guillermo Serés, Julian Weiss, Ottavio Di Camillo, Miguel Ángel Pérez Priego, Rita Costa Gomes, and Francisco Rico for, among many other things, generous gifts of books and articles mentioned in my notes.

THE AMBIVALENT INFLUENCE OF ITALIAN LETTERS AND THE REDISCOVERY OF THE CLASSICS IN LATE MEDIEVAL FRANCE

CRAIG TAYLOR

Humanist rhetoric traditionally presented the Renaissance as a profound break from the medieval past not just in Italy but also across Europe.[1] Modern historians have therefore searched for the moment at which this new dawn arrived, and in the case of France, this is usually associated with the introduction of printing in the 1470s and the French invasion of Italy in 1494.[2] The great enterprise that King Charles VIII launched following the death of Ferdinand ('Ferrante') of Naples in 1494 was ultimately unsuccessful, but it did serve to strengthen cultural ties between France and Italy, and was certainly a pivotal moment in the impact of the Renaissance in

---

[1] For introductions to fifteenth-century French humanism, see D. Cecchetti, *Il primo umanesimo francese* (Turin, 1987); E. Beltran, 'L'humanisme français au temps de Charles VII et Louis XI' in C. Bozzolo and E. Ornato ed., *Préludes à la Renaissance: aspects de la vie intellectuelle en France au XVe siècle* (Paris, 1992), pp. 123–62; P. Gilli, 'L'humanisme français au temps du Concile de Constance' in D. Marcotte ed., *Humanisme et culture géographique a l'époque du Concile de Constance autour de Guillaume Fillastre. Actes du Colloque de l'Université de Reims, 18–19 novembre 1999* (Turnhout, 2002), pp. 41–62; S. Lefèvre, 'Humanisme, pré-humanisme et humanistes: un singulier pluriel', *Perspectives médiévales*, xxx (2005), pp. 303–18.

[2] H. Hornik, 'Three Interpretations of the French Renaissance' in W. L. Gundersheimer ed., *French humanism, 1470–1600* (New York, 1969), pp. 19–47.

France.³ It is also true that humanist scholarship in France was given tremendous momentum by the introduction of printing twenty-five years earlier. The first printers to set up shop in Paris in late 1469 were Ulrich Gering, Michael Friburger and Martin Crantz. Under the direction of two masters in theology at the Sorbonne, Johann Heynlin (c. 1425–1496) and Guillaume Fichet (1433–1480), the press quickly published works of classical history, models of letter-writing and oratory, and manuals of advice on eloquence: the works of Sallust, Cardinal Bessarion's *Epistolae et orationes* on a crusade against the Turks, LORENZO VALLA's *Elegantiae linguae latinae*, AGOSTINO DATI's *Praecepta eloquentiae*, GASPARINO BARZIZZA's *Epistolae*, and his *Orthographia*, as well as GUARINO DA VERONA's *Ratio diphthongis* and Fichet's own *Compendiosus dialogus de arte punctandi* and *Rhetorica*.⁴

Yet before either of these liminal moments, humanism had already established tentative roots in France. Without doubt, the impact of humanism in France from the middle of the fourteenth century through to the arrival of printing was inferior both in quantity and quality to that of Italy, as was true of most European countries. Moreover, like their international counterparts, there were many kinds of French humanists as individuals engaged with the new movement in

---

[3] F. Simone, *The French Renaissance: Medieval tradition and Italian influence in shaping the Renaissance in France*, trans. H. G. Hall (London, 1969), pp. 37–42; Donald R. Kelley, 'France' in R. Porter and M. Teich ed., *The Renaissance in National Context* (Cambridge, 1992), pp. 123–45 at pp. 127–28.

[4] ISTC, no.s is00053000, ib00519000, iv00052000, id00053300, ib00260500, ib00269000, if00147000. The printers continued to publish both classical and more commercial works after Heynlin and Fichet left Paris in 1472: R. Hirsch, 'Printing in France and Humanism, 1470–1480' in W. Gundersheimer ed., *French humanism, 1470–1600* (London, 1969), pp. 113–30 at pp. 116–18; P. Burke, 'The Spread of Italian Humanism' in A. Goodman and A. MacKay ed., *The Impact of Humanism on Western Europe* (London, 1990), pp. 1–22 at p. 12.

very different manners, from simply copying works by classical and neo-Latin authors to attempting to emulate them.[5]

During the late middle ages, cultural contacts between France and Italy were driven by two particular contexts. The first was a series of crises affecting the international church. In 1309, Pope Clement V (1305–1314) moved the papal curia from Rome to Avignon, establishing a rich centre for scholarly activity just outside the southern borders of the French kingdom. Avignon famously became home to Petrarch (1304–1374) for almost forty years, both as a child but also as an adult when he returned in 1326 and finally left in 1353.[6] One of Petrarch's greatest admirers and champions was the Neapolitan Giovanni Moccia (fl. 1370s–1400s) who declared that the great writer had earned a place alongside Horace, Cicero and Seneca.[7] Before becoming secretary to the Avignonese Popes Clement VII (1378–1394) and Benedict XIII (1394–1417), Moccia had served in the same capacity under Cardinal Amedeo di Saluzzo (1362–1419), alongside the Frenchman Laurent de Premierfait (c. 1380–1418), who left Avignon by 1398 and returned to Paris where he enjoyed a successful career as a translator of works by Cicero and Boccaccio.[8] Moccia was also in correspondence with Italian scholars like Coluccio Salutati (1331–1406), as well a network of French scholars who either served at or visited the papal curia at Avignon during this time including Gontier Col (d.1418), Jean de Montreuil (d.1418), Jean Muret (d.1419–

---

[5] Beltran, 'L'humanisme français au temps de Charles VII et Louis XI', pp. 150–51.

[6] M. Skafte Jensen, 'Petrarch's Farewell to Avignon: *Bucolicum Carmen* VIII' in M. Pade et al. ed., *Avignon & Naples. Italy in France – France in Italy in the fourteenth century* (Rome, 1997), pp. 69–82.

[7] Simone, *The French Renaissance*, pp. 60–61. While at Avignon, Petrarch had played a central role in the reconstitution of the Decades of Livy's *Ab urbe condita* from which the chief contemporary Italian translations derived.

[8] C. Bozzolo ed., *Un traducteur et un humaniste de l'époque de Charles VI, Laurent de Premierfait* (Paris, 2004), and see pp. 231–33 below.

20), Pierre d'Ailly (1351–1420) and Jean Gerson (1363–1429) and Nicolas de Clamanges (c. 1360/63–1437).[9] Collectively, these individuals represent the crest of the first wave of humanism in France.

By the end of the fourteenth century, the cultural influence of the papal curia at Avignon was on the wane. In 1377, Pope Gregory XI decided to return the papal curia to Rome, but after his death the following year, the French cardinals refused to endorse the election of Pope Urban VI (1378–1389) and returned to Avignon which became the home of an anti-pope. In an effort to put an end to the Schism, both King Charles VI (1380–1422) and the University of Paris (led by Gerson and d'Ailly), called upon the rival popes to resign, and to force this to happen, introduced the idea of 'subtraction of obedience' in order to limit papal authority and revenues. The first withdrawal of French obedience between 1398 and 1403 forced many of the papal secretaries like Muret and Clamanges to return temporarily to Paris or to their benefices. New opportunities for contact with Italian scholars and acquisition of manuscripts emerged thanks to the series of international church councils that were held to end the Schism (achieved by deposing the rival popes and by electing, in 1417, a new one, Martin V), and subsequently to attempt to reform the church. Members of the French delegation to the Council of Constance (1414–1418) included Gerson, Clamanges and Guillaume Fillastre (1348–1428). Similarly, leading French scholars of the second wave of humanism in France like Jean Jouffroy (c. 1412–1473), the younger Guillaume Fillastre (d.1473) and Guillaume Fichet attended the great council of

---

[9] A. Coville, *Gontier et Pierre Col et l'humanisme en France au temps de Charles VI* (Paris, 1934), pp. 148–84 and 235–42, and E. Ornato, *Jean Muret et ses amis Nicolas de Clamanges et Jean de Montreuil: contribution à l'étude des rapports entre les humanistes de Paris et ceux d'Avignon (1394–1420)* (Paris, 1969).

Mantua in 1459, keen to support Pope Pius II and Cardinal Bessarion against the Turkish threat.[10]

The second great influence on cultural contact between Italy and France was the tantalizing promise of the Angevin claims to Naples and Sicily which dated back to 1266 and which were ultimately to inspire King Charles VIII's invasion of Italy in 1494. Louis I duke of Anjou's expedition to seize the throne of Naples ended with his sudden death on 20 September 1384. At that moment, a French army of reinforcements led by Enguerrand de Coucy had just captured the Tuscan town of Arezzo. Recognising that the mission had failed, Coucy decided to return home to France, but before leaving began to negotiate for the sale of Arezzo to Florence. Jean de Montreuil, a young secretary accompanying the army, was ordered to initiate the negotiations. He wrote to the chancellor of Florence, the celebrated humanist Coluccio Salutati, nervously expressing his anxiety at the limitations of his own Latin. This was the start of a letter exchange between the two humanists, during which Salutati provided Montreuil with works of Petrarch, including his Latin translation of Boccaccio's tale of Griselda and various of the letters from the *Rerum senilium libri*, as well as copies of Salutati's own public and private letters, and works of his own such as his *Declamatio Lucretiae* and the first part of his *De fato et fortuna*.[11]

[10] As noted above at p. 204, Bessarion's *Epistolae et orationes* on a crusade against the Turks (ISTC No. ib00519000) was one of the first books printed in Paris. See M. Meserve, 'Patronage and Propaganda at the First Paris Press: Guillaume Fichet and the First Edition of Bessarion's *Orations against the Turks*', *Papers of the Bibliographical Society of America*, xcvii (2003), pp. 521–88.

[11] Coluccio Salutati, *Epistolario*, ed. F. Novati, 4 vols in 5 (Rome, 1891–1911), and G. Ouy, 'La première correspondance échangée entre Jean de Montreuil et Coluccio Salutati', *IMU*, vii (1964), pp. 337–74 and Jean de Montreuil, *Opera*, 2 vols to date (Turin, 1963–), i, *Epistolario*, ed. E. Ornato, p. 160 (letter 107). Pierre d'Ailly subsequently made a copy of these materials, including the *Declamatio*, that survives in Cambrai: Bibliothèque municipale, MS. 940, discussed in G. Ouy, *Le*

Over fifty years later, the claim to Naples inspired René of Anjou, duke of Lorraine and Anjou, count of Provence and grandson of Louis I of Anjou.[12] In 1438 René arrived in Italy to take charge of the war against the rival claimant, King Alfonso V of Aragon. On 28 February 1441, while confined to the Castelnuovo in Naples by the forces of Alfonso, René attended a dramatic spectacle based upon GIOVANNI AURISPA's translation of a dialogue of the dead by Lucian.[13] Scipio Africanus, Hannibal and Alexander debated which of them deserved the palm as the greatest warrior. At the end, a Genoese naval captain named Cipriano de' Mari presented a Latin oration explaining the allegory and applying a moral to the spectacle: Hannibal came from Spain and was initially successful, but the wise and virtuous wait for fortune to turn in their favour; like Scipio, René was young, prudent and just, and would be favoured by fortune.[14] This prediction turned out to be far too optimistic, but even after his Neapolitan expedition came to an inglorious end in 1442, René and his son Jean duke of Calabria continued to be heavily engaged in both Italian affairs and culture.[15] René commissioned the Hun-

---

recueil épistolaire autographe de Pierre d'Ailly et les notes d'Italie de Jean de Montreuil (Amsterdam, 1966).

[12] J.-M. Matz and E. Verry ed., *Le roi René dans tous ses états* (Paris, 2009). I am extremely grateful to Oren Margolis for his expert advice on this paragraph.

[13] B. Croce, *Teatri di Napoli: secolo XV–XVIII* (Napoli, 1891), pp. 4–6; N. F. Faraglia, *Storia della lotta tra Alfonso V d'Aragona e Renato d'Angiò* (Lanciano, 1908), pp. 264–65; D. Cast, 'Aurispa, Petrarch and Lucian: An Aspect of Renaissance Translation', *Renaissance Quarterly*, xxvii (1974), pp. 157–73 at pp. 158–60.

[14] St-Dié-des-Vosges: Bibliothèque municipale, MS. 37, fol. 14ᵛ–15ʳ. See also O. Margolis, 'Le roi René, Janus Pannonius, et la politique de la transmission culturelle en Italie à la Renaissance' in F. Bouchet ed., *René d'Anjou, écrivain et mécène (1409–1480)* (Turnhout, 2010), pp. 271–305.

[15] In 1460/1, while in Naples pursuing the war that broke out for the succession following the death of Alfonso V's son Ferdinand, Jean of Calabria was unsuccessful in persuading PANORMITA (Antonio

garian humanist Janus Pannonius to write the *Carmen pro pacanda Italia* which he presented to the visiting emperor, Frederick III, at Ferrara in January 1452.[16] The same year, Pannonius was commissioned to write a panegyric of René by Jacopo Antonio Marcello, a Venetian who had joined René's chivalric Order of the Croissant in 1449.[17] Marcello gave further gifts to René including a *mappamondo* with a manuscript of Ptolemy's *Cosmographia* in the Latin version of Jacopo Angeli da Scarperia, Guarino da Verona's translation of Strabo's *De situ orbis*, and Quintilian's *Institutio oratoria*.[18] Meanwhile, the Neapolitan Giovanni Cossa left Italy with René in 1442 and remained in his service until his death in 1476; he joined the Order of the Croissant and also commissioned a French translation of the Florentine humanist MATTEO PALMIERI's *Liber de temporibus* for René's second wife Jeanne de Laval.[19] Finally, the first French translations of Boccaccio's Italian works, the *Filostrato* and *Teseida*, were produced during the 1450s by Louis de Beauvau, René's

---

Beccadelli) to provide him with a copy of his life of Alfonso V of Aragon, *De dictis et factis Alphonsi* (1455): N. Patrone, *Príncipe y mecenas: Alfonso V en los "dichos y hechos" de Antonio Beccadelli* (New York, 1995) and *Splendeurs de la cour de Bourgogne. Récits et chroniques*, ed. and trans. D. Régnier-Bohelle (Paris, 1995), pp. 629–736.

[16] On Pannonius, see pp. 146–47 above.

[17] Naples: Biblioteca nazionale Vittorio Emanuele III, MS. X. B. 63, fol. 17ʳ–37ᵛ, and M. L. King, *The Death of the Child Valerio Marcello* (Chicago, 1994), pp. 125–26.

[18] The first two are BnF, MS. lat. 17542 and Albi: Bibliothèque Municipale, MS. 77, discussed in King, *The Death of the Child*, pp. 315–36 and M.-E. Gautier ed., *Splendeur de l'enluminure: le roi René et les livres* (Arles, 2009), pp. 224–29. For the Quintilian, see M. Meiss, *Andrea Mantegna as Illuminator. An episode in Renaissance art, humanism and diplomacy* (New York, 1957), pp. 32 and 89n.

[19] Gautier ed., *Splendeur de l'enluminure*, pp. 370–71.

seneschal of Anjou and of Provence, and by a second, anonymous author.[20]

Even without these grand matters, French and Italian scholars were regularly engaged in diplomatic missions that fostered cultural contact. The most famous example was Petrarch himself. In 1360, he travelled to Paris as the ambassador of Galeazzo II Visconti of Milan, sent to congratulate King Jean II on his release from English captivity. The dauphin Charles heard his oration on 13 January 1361 and is said to have been greatly impressed by it.[21] In 1389, Charles V's second son, Louis, duke of Orléans married the Italian duchess, Valentina Visconti of Milan; two years earlier, a number of Milanese agents had visited Paris to arrange the matter, including Ambrogio Migli, who remained in France to become secretary and counsellor to the duke.[22] ÆNEAS SYLVIUS PICCOLOMINI served Cardinal Niccolò Albergati during his diplomatic mission to Arras in 1435 to negotiate between the French, Burgundians and the English, and offered an account of the complex diplomatic work of this period in his *Commentaries*.[23] As a member of the Florentine

---

[20] G. Biancotto, 'La cour de René d'Anjou et les premières traductions d'œuvres Italiennes en France' in C. Brucker ed., *Traduction et adaptation en France à la fin du Moyen Age et à la Renaissance: actes du colloque organisé par l'Université de Nancy II, 23–25 mars 1995* (Paris, 1997), pp. 187–203.

[21] R. Delachenal, *Histoire de Charles V*, 5 vols (Paris, 1909–31), ii, pp. 270–72 and Simone, *The French Renaissance*, pp. 88–90. See also Petrarch's letter to Pierre Bersuire: *Le Familiari*, ed. V. Rossi, 4 vols (Florence, 1933–1942), iv, ed. U. Bosco, pp. 136–38 [XXII. 13], available in English in Francesco Petrarca, *Letters on Familiar Matters. Rerum familiarum libri XVII–XXIV*, trans. A. S. Bernardo (Baltimore, 1985), pp. 240–41.

[22] G. Ouy, 'Humanisme et propagande politique en France au début du XVe siècle: Ambrogio Migli et les ambitions impériales de Louis d'Orléans' in F. Simone ed., *Culture et politique en France à l'époque de l'humanisme et de la Renaissance* (Turin, 1974), pp. 13–42.

[23] Æneas Sylvius Piccolomini, *Commentarii rerum memorabilium que temporibus suis contingerunt*, ed. A. von Heck, 2 vols (Vatican City,

embassy, DONATO ACCIAIUOLI presented King Louis XI on 2 January 1462 with a elegant, illuminated manuscript containing the *Vita Caroli Magni* that he had written.²⁴ At the same time, Cardinal Jean Jouffroy, presented Louis XI with humanist translations of Strabo and Thucydides, the first by Guarino and the latter by LORENZO VALLA, Jouffroy's former tutor at Pavia.²⁵ Shortly afterwards the Milanese established a resident ambassador at the court of Louis XI.²⁶ Jean Jouffroy, who was bishop first of Arras and later of Albi, was one of the most prominent French diplomats to put his skills with oratory and rhetoric to practical effect, during missions representing both the duke of Burgundy and the king of France to the papacy, the kings of Portugal and Castile.²⁷ Robert Gaguin (1433–1501), author of *De arte metrificandi* (1473) and the great *Compendium de Francorum origine et gestis* (1495),

---

1984) and Pius II, *Commentaries*, ed. and trans. M. Meserve and M. Simonetta, 2 vols to date [ITRL, xii & xxix] (Cambridge, MA, 2004–07). During Arras, Piccolomini presented the Burgundian duke Philip the Good with a (now lost) poem.

[24] D. Gatti, *La Vita Caroli di Donato Acciaiuoli. La Leggenda di Carlo Magno in funzione di una* historia di gesta (Bologna, 1981), with the text at pp. 99–123. The presentation copy is now Cambridge: Fitzwilliam Museum, MS 180, on which see P. Binski and Stella Panayotova ed., *The Cambridge Illuminations: Ten Centuries of Book Production in the Medieval West* (Cambridge, 2005), pp. 338–339.

[25] BnF, MSS Latin 4797 and 5713. On the latter, see M. Pade, 'Thucydides' in *CTC*, viii, pp. 120–26.

[26] V. Ilardi, 'France and Milan: the Uneasy Alliance, 1452–1466' in *Gli Sforza a Milano e in Lombardia e i loro rapporti con gli Stati italiani ed europei (1450–1535)* (Milan, 1982), pp. 415–47 and also see P. Savy, 'Les ambassadeurs milanais à la cour de Charles le Téméraire', *Annales de Bourgogne*, lxviii (1996), pp. 35–56; R. J. Walsh, 'Relations Between Milan and Burgundy in the Period 1450–1476' in *Gli Sforza a Milano e in Lombardia*, pp. 369–96 [reprinted in id., *Charles the Bold and Italy, 1467–1477: politics and personnel* (Liverpool, 2005) as chapter 5].

[27] Beltran, 'L'humanisme français au temps de Charles VII et Louis XI', pp. 142–47; C. Märtl, *Kardinal Jean Jouffroy (†1473): Leben und Werk* (Sigmaringen, 1996).

frequently served as a diplomat on behalf of Kings Louis XI and Charles VIII, travelling not only to Italy but also to Germany and England where he also came into contact with Italian humanists.[28] A generation earlier, the French royal secretary Alain Chartier (d.c.1430) took part in an embassy to the Emperor Sigismund in 1424 and gave three orations that survive, two before the emperor, and a third intended to persuade the Hussites to abandon their heresy.[29]

Other Italian humanists travelled to France, and northern Europe in general, in search of manuscripts and employment. For example, in 1415 POGGIO BRACCIOLINI claimed to have discovered an old manuscript in the abbey of Cluny that contained previously unknown orations by Cicero and which he sent to Florence. In fact, Jean de Montreuil had discovered the Cluny Cicero in 1413, from which Clamanges copied variants and the 'new' orations *Pro Roscio Amerino* and *Pro Murena* into a collection of his own.[30] Montreuil complained about the mediocrity of his library, but he and his colleagues had access to much better resources than he implied.[31] There

---

[28] F. Collard, *Un historien au travail à la fin du XVe siècle: Robert Gaguin* (Geneva, 1996), and 'Robert Gaguin (1433–1501)', *Histoire littéraire de la France*, xliii (2005), pp. 173–213. For his English connexions, see further pp. 301–02 below.

[29] Chartier subsequently took part in embassies to Venice, Rome and Milan. G. di Stefano, 'Alain Chartier ambassadeur à Venise' in F. Simone ed., *Culture et politique en France à l'époque de l'humanisme et de la Renaissance. Atti del convegno internazionale promosso dall'Accademia delle Scienze di Torino in Collaborazione con la Fondazione Giorgio Cini di Venezia, 29 marzo–2 aprile 1971* (Turin, 1974), pp. 155–68.

[30] BnF, MS. lat. 14749, discussed by G. Ouy, 'Humanism and Nationalism in France at the Turn of the Fifteenth Century' in B. P. McGuire ed., *The Birth of Identities: Denmark and Europe in the Middle Ages* (Copenhagen, 1996), pp. 107–125 at pp. 117–18; cf. *T&T*, pp. 82, 88–89 and 95.

[31] See, for instance, Jean de Montreuil, *Opera*, ed. E. Ornato et al., 4 vols (Turin, 1963–86), i, pp. 162 (letter 108) and 217 (letter 150), and R. Sabbadini, *La scoperte dei codici latini e greci ne'secoli XIV e XV*, 2 vols (Florence, 1905– 14), ii, p. 87, together with E. Ornato, 'La

were rich libraries in Paris, particularly those of the College of Navarre and the Sorbonne.[32] Individual scholars also developed personal libraries. For example, Jean Lebègue, greffier of the Chambre des comptes from 1407 to his death in 1457, owned thirty manuscripts, including LEONARDO BRUNI's *Cicero novus*.[33] There were also treasure-troves in church libraries across France, including not only Cluny but also the cathedral of Reims, replete with classical and Italian humanist texts thanks in part to the work of Cardinal Guillaume Fillastre.[34]

Despite the strength of these contacts, French humanists did not readily accept the superiority of Italian culture and scholarship.[35] The conception of a Renaissance of antiquity and of Latin was in key senses a challenge to the language,

redécouverte des classiques, révélateur de ruptures et de continuités dans le mouvement humaniste en France au XVe siècle' in D. Cecchetti et al. ed, *L'aube de la Renaissance* (Geneva, 1991), pp. 83–101, and id., 'Les humanistes français et la redécouverte des classiques' in Ornato ed., *Préludes à la Renaissance*, pp. 1–45.

[32] *Le Registre de prêt de la bibliothèque du collège de Sorbonne, 1402–1536: Diarium Bibliothecae Sorbonae, Paris, Bibliothèque Mazarine, ms 3323*, ed. J. Vielliard (Paris, 2000).

[33] N. Pons, 'Érudition et politique. La personnalité de Jean Lebègue d'après les notes marginales de ses manuscrits' in *Les serviteurs de l'État au Moyen Âge. Actes du XXIXe Congrès de la SHMESP (Pau, 1998)* (Paris, 1999), pp. 281–297 and ead., 'Leonardo Bruni, Jean Lebègue et la cour. Échec d'une tentative d'humanisme à l'Italienne?' in Marcotte ed., *Humanisme et culture géographique*, p. 97. See further p. 235 below.

[34] C. Jeudy, 'La bibliothèque cathédrale de Reims, témoin de l'humanisme en France au XVe siècle' in M. Ornato and N. Pons ed., *Pratiques de la culture écrite en France au XVe siècle: actes du Colloque Internationale de CNRS, Paris 16–18 mai 1992, organisé en l'honneur de Gilbert Ouy par l'unité de recherche* (Louvain, 1995), pp. 75–92 and ead., 'La bibliothèque de Guillaume Fillastre' in Marcotte ed., *Humanisme et culture géographique*, pp. 245–91.

[35] For Italian views of France, see P. Gilli, *Au miroir de l'humanisme: les représentations de la France dans la culture savante italienne à la fin du moyen âge, c. 1360–c. 1490* (Rome, 1997).

cultural past and history of countries outside of Italy. Indeed, Petrarch's influence in France was complicated by his involvement in the debate over the return of the papal curia to Rome. In 1368 Petrarch had famously declared in a letter addressed to Pope Urban V that one would search in vain for orators and poets outside of Italy.[36] The letter was written shortly after Petrarch had taken part in a debate over whether the papal curia should return to Rome after its temporary residence in Avignon. The leader of the French embassy, Anseau Choquart, had argued that France was a more worthy home than Rome.[37] Choquart cited the presence of so many important relics in France, longstanding prophecies and also the notion of *translatio studii*, the claim that Charlemagne had instructed Alcuin to transfer the *studium*, the main centre of learning, from Rome to Paris. This was a longstanding claim by French scholars, most famously raised around 1176 by Chrétien de Troyes in the prologue to *Cligès*, when he had announced that Greece's fame for 'chevalerie' had passed to Rome while the light of learning that had marked its pre-eminence in 'science' had come to France.[38] In response,

---

[36] 'Oratores et poetae extra Italiam non quaerantur, de Latinis loquor vel hinc orti omnes vel hic docti': Francesco Petrarca, *Le "Senili" secondo l'edizione Basilea 1581*, ed. M. Guglielminetti (Savigliano, 2006), p. 175 (IX.1, spring 1368) and cf. pp. 139–55 (VII.1, June 1366). See E. Casamassima, *L'autografo Riccardiano della seconda lettera del Petrarca a Urbano (Senile, IX, 1)* (Rome, 1986), and N. Margolis, 'Culture vantée, culture inventée: Christine, Clamanges et le défi de Pétrarque' in E. Hicks ed., *Au champ des escriptures. IIIe colloque international sur Christine de Pizan* (Paris, 2000), pp. 271–74, together with the wider discussion of Petrarch's letters to Pope Urban V in U. Dotti, *Vita di Petrarca* (Bari, 1987), pp. 366–67, 381–84 and 395–98.

[37] Choquart's speech appears in C. Égasse du Boulay, *Historia universitatis Parisiensis*, 6 vols (Paris, 1665–1673), iv, pp. 396–412, where it is incorrectly attributed to Nicole Oresme.

[38] S. Lusignan, *Vérité garde le roy. La construction d'une identité universitaire en France (XIIIe – XVe siècle)* (Paris, 1999), p. 233, and in general pp. 226–91. See also S. Lusignan, 'La logique de la *translatio studii* et les traductions françaises de textes savants au XIVe siècle' in

Petrarch argued that the Holy See of Rome represented both the centre of Christendom and its principal seat of culture. He also belittled Choquart for his clumsy and archaic style which served to demonstrate his contention that it was useless to look for orators and poets outside of Italy.[39]

In short, Petrarch can be seen as the father of French humanism not only because of influence of his desire to discover, imitate and revive Antiquity, but also because of the way that he provoked French scholars to defend their cultural heritage.[40] Petrarch's remarks became a source of annoyance for French humanists, rhetorically at least, because of the notions that French culture was inherently inferior to Italian, that Italians had an exclusive right to Latin culture, and that their Ciceronian style was pre-eminent. This inevitably pushed French scholars to assert a greater mastery of classical Latin than their Italian peers but also made it difficult for them to acknowledge their own debt to Petrarch's eloquence, preferring instead to claim inspiration directly from Cicero or other

G. Contamine ed., *Traduction et traducteurs au Moyen Âge: actes du colloque international du CNRS organisé à Paris, Institut de recherche et d'histoire des textes, les 26–28 mai 1986* (Paris, 1989), pp. 303–15, and G. Ouy, 'La dialectique des rapports intellectuels franco-italiens et l'humanisme en France aux XIVe et XVe siècles' in *Rapporti culturali ed economici fra Italia e Francia nel secoli dal XIV al XVI, Atti del 'Colloqui Italo-Francese'* (Rome, 1978), pp. 137–57. For a contrasting reading of the passage, see L. C. Reis, 'The Paratext to Chrétien de Troyes' *Cligès*', *French Studies*, lxv (2011), pp. 1–16.

[39] In response to Petrarch, Jean de Hesdin immediately wrote an *epistola* before 1370 which drove Petrarch to compose in 1373 his *Invectiva contra eum qui maledixit Italie*, now available in both Francesco Petrarca, *In difesa dell'Italia*, ed. G. Crevatin (Venice, 1995), and id., *Invectives*, ed. and trans. David Marsh [ITRL, xi] (Cambridge, MA, 2004), pp. 364–474. On this, see E. Cocchia, 'La polemica del Petrarca col maestro Giovanni da Hesdin per il transferimento della sede pontificia da Avignone e Roma', *Atti della Reale Accademia di archeologia, lettere e belli arti di Napoli*, vii (1920), pp. 112–39, and Dotti, *Vita di Petrarca*, pp. 418–20.

[40] Beltran, 'L'humanisme français au temps de Charles VII et Louis XI', p. 125.

classical authors. In 1389, Jean Gerson carefully redirected Petrarch's claims in his treatise against the teachings of the Spanish Dominican, Juan de Monzón, on the doctrine of the Immaculate Conception. Gerson accepted that France had lacked skilled orators and poets in the past, but argued that the situation had changed now that France finally enjoyed the calibre of writers capable of praising those brave warriors who, alongside its wise men, had contributed to its glory.[41] As a result the French were now better off than the Italians because they had heroes to outshine those of Rome or Greece.[42] Yet despite the rhetoric Gerson was certainly influenced by Petrarch. Indeed, Gerson was perhaps the first author in northern Europe to be inspired by Petrarch when he composed his *Pastorium carmen* shortly before October 1382, a work that was very similar to the Italian's *Bucolicum carmen*.[43] The treatise that Gerson wrote in response to Juan de Monzón is now regarded as 'one of the first samples, perhaps even the very first, of the revival of classical Latin in fourteenth-century France, and certainly the best piece of Latin prose of the period'.[44] Later in his life, Gerson regretted the use of the 'mannered brand of Latin' employed by arts students at Paris

---

[41] G. Ouy, 'La plus ancienne œuvre retrouvée de Jean Gerson: le brouillon inachevé d'un traité de Gerson contre Jean de Monzon', *Romania*, lxxxiii (1962), pp. 433–492 at p. 472, and also see id., 'Humanism and nationalism in France', pp. 112–13.

[42] Ouy, 'Le brouillon inachevé', p. 472. In letters to Gontier Col, Clamanges also claimed the honour of having revived eloquence, long buried in France: Cecchetti, *Il primo umanesimo francese*, p. 53.

[43] G. Ouy, 'Gerson, émule de Pétrarque. Le *Pastorium carmen*, poème de jeunesse de Gerson, et la Renaissance de l'églogue en France à la fin du XIVe siècle', *Romania*, lxxxviii (1967), pp. 175–231; G. Ouy, 'Discovering Gerson the Humanist: Fifty Years of Serendipity' in B. P. McGuire ed., *A Companion to Jean Gerson* (Leiden, 2006), pp. 79–132 at pp. 90–96 and 127–28.

[44] This was the judgement of Heinrich Denifle, as reported in Ouy, 'Discovering Gerson the Humanist', p. 99 (and in general see 96–104). Also see Ouy, 'Le brouillon inachevé', 433–92.

before he fell under the influence of Petrarch.⁴⁵ In 1417, while attending the Council of Constance, Gerson wrote the poem *Josephina*, inspired at least in part by the desire to present a Christian response to Petrarch's *Africa*, celebrating the chaste husband of Mary rather than the pagan Scipio.⁴⁶ Shortly afterwards, he wrote *Deploratio super civitatem*, inspired perhaps by works like Coluccio Salutati's *Declamatio Lucretiae* that Montreuil had brought back from Italy in 1384.⁴⁷

Nicolas de Clamanges claimed that the French style was more clear, efficient and refined than that of the Italians and frequently denounced the loquacious style of Petrarch.⁴⁸ Clamanges wrote an eclogue inspired by Virgil's *Georgics* and by Ovid, in which he rejected Petrarch's claims in *Bucolicum carmen* for the superiority of Italian culture; Clamanges presented the University of Paris as the heir to that pure fountain that had been worshipped by the Greeks and the Romans, and hence the embodiment of the *translatio studii*.⁴⁹ In a letter *Ut tibi* written in 1394, Clamanges famously denounced the corrections made by well-intentioned friends at Avignon to

---

⁴⁵ Ouy, 'Discovering Gerson the Humanist', p. 89, citing *Contra curiositatem studentium*, III, 247: 'non eloquentia est, sed inanis et verbosa loquacitas'.

⁴⁶ Jean Gerson, *Josephina: introduction, texte critique, scansion, index des termes avec indication des quantités prosodiques, tables des formes métriques*, ed. G. M. Roccati (Paris, 2001) and Ouy, 'Discovering Gerson the Humanist', pp. 113–15.

⁴⁷ G. Ouy, 'Gerson et la guerre civile à Paris: la *Deploratio super civitatem*', *Archives d'histoire doctrinale et littéraire du Moyen Âge*, lxxi (2004), pp. 255–86 and Ouy, 'Discovering Gerson the Humanist', pp. 115–20.

⁴⁸ D. Cecchetti, 'Sulla fortuna del Petrarca in Francia: un testo dimenticato di Nicolas de Clamanges', *Studi francesi*, xxxii (1967), pp. 201–22 at p. 211 and Margolis, 'Culture vantée, culture inventée', p. 280.

⁴⁹ D. Cecchetti, 'Un'egloga inedita di Nicolas de Clamanges' in F. Simone ed., *Miscellanea di studi e richerche sul Quattrocento francese* (Turin, 1967), pp. 25–57 and Ouy, 'Humanism and nationalism in France', 115–16.

one of his previous letters concerning the Schism, written on behalf of the University of Paris to Benedict XIII. Cardinal Galeotto da Pietramala had praised Clamanges for the merits of his Latin style which he described as exceptional for a Frenchman. This condescending attitude was clear proof for Clamanges that Petrarch's prejudices were alive and well both in Pietramala's Avignon but also across the Alps.[50] In response, Clamanges asserted his rhetorical superiority to these men and hence his freedom to speak – they might correct the substance but not the form.[51] Clamanges completely redrafted the original letter *Ut tibi* between 1420 and 1430 as *Perpulchras pater*, and added a second letter, *Quod in superiori*, fictionally addressed to the Cardinal who had died in 1398, echoing Petrarch's letter to Cicero and Vergerio's to Petrarch. *Quod in superiori* cited classical texts by Quintilian and Ælius Donatus which had only recently been rediscovered, and thereby 'proving' that the French had access to such works before the Italians![52] In the same vein, Clamanges developed his own script, drawing upon a mixture of French book-Gothic and Italian pre-Humanistic scripts. In his early work, he had offered imitations of scripts by Salutati and other Italians, but quickly dropped this in favour of a 'purely French Humanistic script',

---

[50] Cecchetti, 'Sulla fortuna del Petrarca in Francia', p. 222 and E. Ornato, 'La prima fortuna del Petrarca in Francia. I, Le letture petrarchesche di Jean de Montreuil', *Studi francesi*, xiv (1961), pp. 201–207 at p. 204 and Margolis, 'Culture vantée, culture inventée', p. 277.

[51] Ornato, *Jean Muret et ses amis*, pp. 22–30; D. Cecchetti, '"Sic me Cicero laudare docuerat": la retorica nel primo umanesimo francese' in Ornato ed., *Préludes à la Renaissance*, p. 57 and Gilli, 'L'humanisme français au temps du Concile de Constance', p. 50.

[52] This may have been, in part, a response to Poggio Bracciolini stealing his thunder for discovering lost orations of Cicero: D. Cecchetti, *Petrarca, Pietramala e Clamanges: storia di una 'querelle' inventata* (Paris, 1982) and Ouy, 'Humanism and nationalism in France', p. 119. On the rediscovery of these texts, see *T&T*, pp. 153–56 and 332–334.

borrowed from local manuscripts copied in the twelfth century.⁵³

Later in the fifteenth century, French scholars were more engaged with Italian scholars such as Guarino da Verona and above all Lorenzo Valla, whose work was welcomed both because of its value in teaching proper Latin but also because of the underpinning notion that Latin represented the single language that united all who studied it, manifested in the correspondence between international scholars.⁵⁴ Nevertheless, the controversy that Petrarch had raised continued to occupy the mind of French humanists. Robert Gaguin declared in the *Compendium de Francorum gestis* that his authorship of such a work in elegant Latin prose disproved Petrarch's comment. Around 1514, Symphorien Champier (1472–c.1539) and Girolomo da Pavia engaged in a *Duellum epistolare* in which the Frenchman declared that they had seized the glory of learning and the honour of teaching from the Romans and were the true heirs to the Athenians.⁵⁵ Guillaume Budé (1467 - 1540) argued in *De asse* that anyone could emulate ancient and modern authors (even if the Italians had been the first to do so), that France had a glorious literary tradition stemming back to the Greek colony at Marseilles and the early inhabitants of Gaul as reported by Strabo, and that the most

---

⁵³ G. Ouy, 'Nicolas de Clamanges (ca. 1360–1437) philologue et calligraphe: imitation de l'Italie et réaction anti-italienne dans l'écriture d'un humaniste français au début du XVe siècle' in J. Autenrieth ed., *Renaissance- und Humanistenhandschriften* (Munich, 1988), pp. 31–50 and id., 'Manuscrits autographes d'humanistes en latin et en français' in P. Chiesa and L. Pinelli ed., *Gli autografi medievali: problemi paleografici e filologici* (Spoleto, 1994), pp. 269–306. It is important to note, though, that Clamanges' 'French national script' was an experiment not taken up by other French scholars.

⁵⁴ Simone, *The French Renaissance*, pp. 97–98 and Beltran, 'L'humanisme français au temps de Charles VII et Louis XI', p. 125.

⁵⁵ Simone, *The French Renaissance*, p. 84.

important obstacle to literary development in France was an exaggerated servility and respect to Italian culture.[56]

Paris was the pre-eminent centre of humanism in late medieval France. In 1384, while Montreuil was corresponding with Salutati, the Frenchman was also eloquently expressing his desire to return to Paris in letters sent to his friends there, describing it as the home of all virtues and sciences.[57] Yet how strong were the root of humanism in Paris? The University remained largely indifferent to the *studia humanitatis*. In the rough draft of his treatise against Juan de Monzón, Gerson reported that there was talent in the university, but the fear of not finding work and becoming destitute prevented university men from exploring new paths, so in forgetting the glories of the past, the university neglected the present.[58] The sole institutional home for early French humanism was the College of Navarre, *alma mater* to almost all of the first generation of Parisian humanists, such as Montreuil, Gerson, d'Ailly and Clamanges, and hence described by modern commentators as the 'cradle of French humanism'.[59] The College had the privilege of offering courses outside the university schools and independent of all other 'cursus universitaire'. From 1360, when such courses were first offered, there was a permanent certification of masters of theology and masters or sub-masters of grammar, but less is known about rhetoric. During the reign of Charles VI, a sub-master of the arts was introduced in 1404 and may have included rhetoric and eloquence, rather than grammar, but with only a first-year foundation course in the

---

[56] Simone, *The French Renaissance*, pp. 85–86.
[57] Ouy, 'Humanism and nationalism in France', p. 121.
[58] Ouy, 'Le brouillon inachevé', p. 472, along with Ornato, *Jean Muret et ses amis Nicolas de Clamanges et Jean de Montreuil*, p. 37.
[59] G. Ouy, 'Le Collège de Navarre, berceau de l'humanisme français' in *Enseignement et vie intellectuelle (IXe–XVIe siècles), Actes du 95e Congrès National des Sociétés Savantes: philologie et histoire jusqu'à 1610. Reims, 1970*, 2 vols (Paris, 1975), i, pp. 276–300.

study of ancient writings.⁶⁰ Moreover, the fact that the masters of the College could give courses outside at the rue de Fouarre and were bound to use students from outside the institution to assist with their *lectiones*, reminds us of the danger of ignoring the non-Navarrists (*foranei*) who remain in the shadows. Finally, the library of the College of Navarre may not have been wonderfully endowed, despite its great status as a centre for Parisian humanism.⁶¹ There was no trace of writings by Petrarch, the letters of Cicero, Pliny the Younger or Seneca, all of which had to be located by the young humanists in monastic libraries. It was only in 1421 that Nicolas de Clamanges offered to the University of Paris his collection of speeches by Cicero.⁶² Thus the importance of the College of Navarre perhaps lay more in its role as a welcoming spot for new scholars rather than an institution pushing them to study new things, and as the main location where other influences came together, such as the reading of Petrarch. Certainly of the first generation of humanists who attended the College of Navarre, most seem to have taken up humanist interests later.⁶³ The one exception is Gerson who wrote an eclogue, a letter and a draft of his treatise against Juan de Monzón in the 1380s, when he was becoming a master of the arts.⁶⁴ Yet the

---

[60] Gilli, 'L'humanisme français au temps du Concile de Constance', p. 44, who notes the primarily institutional focus of the study by Natalie Gorochov, *Le collège de Navarre et sa fondation (1305) au début du XVe siècle (1418). Histoire de l'institution, de sa vie intellectuelle et de son recrutement* (Paris, 1997).

[61] Gilli, 'L'humanisme français au temps du Concile de Constance', pp. 44–45.

[62] Ouy, 'La dialectique des rapports intellectuels franco-italiens', p. 149.

[63] G. M. Roccati, 'La formation des humanistes dans le dernier quart du XIVe siècle' in Ornato and Pons ed., *Pratiques de la culture écrite en France*, pp. 55–73, especially pp. 59–61.

[64] G. Ouy, 'L'humanisme du jeune Gerson' in *Genèse et débuts du grand schisme d'Occident. Avignon, 25–28 septembre 1978* (Paris, 1980), pp. 253–68, and G. M. Roccati, 'La formazione intellettuale di Jean Gerson (1363–1429): un esempio di rinnovamento umanistico degli

shared background of the college of Navarre may have given the early humanists a common knowledge of antiquity, acquired piece by piece, which created a sentiment or even *sodalitas* capable of rivalling that of the Italian masters.[65]

They probably learned more by personal imitation than a fixed curriculum, copying letters of their friends and fellow students, as Pierre d'Ailly did with the letters of Jean de Montreuil.[66] The possibility that there was an informal apprenticeship amongst the private literary set is suggested by Clamanges in his letter *Quod in superiori* (1430).[67] Responding to Petrarch's claim that only in Italy could one learn the arts, Clamanges replied that he himself learned them both while studying in Paris where he followed courses on Ciceronian rhetoric, but also in private.[68] At the end of the letter, he admitted that only in Italy could one be taught true eloquence and literary style but this did not mean that only Italy could produce poets and orators. He argued that it is by the fruit that one judges the tree and not the inverse; in other words, the fact that he and his colleagues had acquired such eloquence was more important than the structures of humanist teaching.[69] In another letter that was supposedly rewritten by Clamanges and again fictionally addressed to Pietramala, he claimed only to have been taught by study, constant training

studi' in L. Rotondi Secchi-Taruggi ed., *L'educazione e la formazione intellettuale nell' età dell'umanesimo* (Milan, 1992), pp. 229–44.

[65] Gilli, 'L'humanisme français au temps du Concile de Constance', p. 44.

[66] Ouy, 'La dialectique des rapports intellectuels franco-italiens', p. 141.

[67] Gilli, 'L'humanisme français au temps du Concile de Constance', p. 46. This was originally thought to have been written to Cardinal Galeotto da Pietramala (d. 1398) but was in fact drawn up at the moment that the old Clamanges re-collected his letters: Cecchetti, *Petrarca, Pietramala e Clamanges*.

[68] Cecchetti, *Petrarca, Pietramala e Clamanges*, p. 172.

[69] Cecchetti, *Petrarca, Pietramala e Clamanges*, pp. 172–4.

and exercise, and the reading of good authors, those recommended by Augustine.[70]

The informal and personal nature of these humanist circles has perhaps led modern scholars to overestimate the impact of the Armagnac-Burgundian civil war and in particular the massacres in Paris in July 1418 on early French humanism. Many scholars, including Gontier Col and Jean de Montreuil, died in that brutal conflict, and others were forced into exile. As a result, this has traditionally been viewed as a critical rupture in French humanism between the generation of Montreuil, Clamanges and Gerson and that of Fichet, Guillaume Tardif (c. 1440 – c. 1500) and Gaguin after 1450.[71] Dario Cecchetti, for example, has argued that the concentration of humanism in Paris, the massacre of so many influential scholars and the dispersal of the survivors, along with the difficult economic, social and political conditions during the continued wars both with the English and between Frenchmen, all combined to mark a devastating blow to the nascent shoots of humanism in France.[72]

The first point to make is that humanism in France was not solely confined to the capital. In general, support outside Paris depended upon the patronage of princes like René of Anjou and the dukes of Burgundy, as well as great prelates. For example, during the period of the English occupation of Normandy (1417–1450), a small number of Italian scholars from the diocese of Milan were drawn to Caen following the

---

[70] Cecchetti, *Petrarca, Pietramala e Clamanges*, p. 143.

[71] 'The history of the French Renaissance might have been different had not most of the French humanists been killed in the Burgundian massacre of 1417 [sic]', according to L. Walters, 'Chivalry and the (En)gendered Poetic Self. Petrarchan Models in the *Cent Balades*' in M. Zimmermann and D. De Rentiis ed., *The City of Scholars: new approaches to Christine de Pizan* (Berlin, 1994), pp. 43–66 at p. 66n. Also see Coville, *Gontier et Pierre Col*, and the comments of Gilli, 'L'humanisme français au temps du Concile de Constance', p. 41n.

[72] Cecchetti, *Il primo umanesimo francese*, and in particular the chapter 'La crisi'.

foundation of the university in 1432. They gathered around Zanone da Castiglioni (d. 1459), who was both chancellor of the new university and bishop of Bayeux, and who was aided by his humanist secretary ROLANDO TALENTI.[73] Avignon was slowly declining as an intellectual centre because of the Great Schism, but between 1430 and 1432, the Lombard humanist COSMA RAIMONDI taught rhetoric there.[74] The *studia humanitatis* made little impact upon the universities of the Midi, but there was a brief flourish when the Spaniard Juan Serra (d. c. 1470) taught rhetoric at the university of Montpellier around 1447 and then at Toulouse between approximately 1455 and 1458, following in the footsteps of Pierre Flamenc.[75]

Secondly, in the aftermath of massacres in Paris, Jean Gerson wrote his *Carmen lugubre pro desolacione Universitatis Parisiensis*, expressing his dismay at the murder and exile of so many Parisian scholars, including himself, but also seeing hope in the survival of men like Pierre d'Ailly, Nicolas de Clamanges and Gérard Machet.[76] In 1420, Clamanges rejected the opportunity to serve as a secretary to the new Pope Martin V and instead chose to return to Paris to take charge of the College of Navarre, thanks to the intervention of the

[73] T. Foffano, 'Umanisti italiani in Normandia nel secolo XV', *Rinascimento*, xv (1964), pp. 3–34, id. 'Charles d'Orléans e un gruppo di umanisti lombardi in Normandia', *Aevum*, xli (1967), pp. 452–73, and S. Saygin, *Humphrey, Duke of Gloucester (1390–1447) and the Italian Humanists* (Leiden, 2002), pp. 144–71. For the significance of Castiglioni and Talenti for humanist contacts with England, see Weiss[4], pp. 85–109 & Appendix, Texts A.

[74] S. Floro Di Zenzo, *Un umanista epicureo del secolo XV e il ritrovamento del suo epistolario* (Naples, 1978).

[75] J. Verger, 'Le livre dans les universités di Midi de la France à la fin du moyen âge' in Ornato and Pons ed., *Pratiques de la culture écrite en France*, pp. 403–20 and Beltran, 'L'humanisme français au temps de Charles VII et Louis XI', pp. 147–49.

[76] Jean Gerson, *Œuvres complètes*, ed. P. Glorieux, 10 vols (Paris–Tournai, 1960–73), iv, pp. 5–7, and Ouy, 'Gerson et la guerre civile à Paris', pp. 255–86.

Burgundian Guillaume Érard.[77] They were assisted by Machet who served as head of the College of Navarre and Dean of the Faculty of Theology of the University of Paris. In 1442, Machet reported that his reintroduction of his course of lectures recalled to mind the glory of former days when scholarship flourished.[78] Ten years later, Cardinal Guillaume d'Estouteville's reforms of the university statutes required a knowledge of the metres of Latin verse as part of the requirement for a baccalaureate. Yet humanists like Guillaume Tardif complained that too much emphasis continued to be placed upon imitating Christian Latin rather than reading and emulating ancient authors.[79] Change was slow: in 1453, Guillaume Fichet began to teach rhetoric at the college Saint-Bernard in Paris, in the face of some opposition, parallelling the work of Juan Serra at Montpellier and Toulouse. Fichet's *Rhetorica*, published in 1471 was the fruit of the courses that he taught.[80] In 1457 Fichet's most famous student, Robert Gaguin, came to Paris, and the following year GREGORIO TIFERNATE was appointed as the first teacher of Greek at the

[77] Ouy, *Le recueil épistolaire autographe de Pierre d'Ailly*, pp. 120–21. For the continued importance of the networks of pupils of the College of Navarre, see Ouy, 'Le Collège de Navarre, berceau de l'humanisme français', pp. 289–95. Érard is better known for his role in the trial of Jeanne d'Arc in 1431: C. Robillard de Beaurepaire, *Notes sur les juges et les assesseurs du procès de condamnation de Jeanne d'Arc* (Rouen, 1890), pp. 32–38.

[78] Machet's correspondence appears in BnF, MS. lat. 8577, and also see P. Santoni, 'Les lettres de Gérard Machet', *Positions de thèses de l'École Nationale des Chartes*, année 1968, pp. 175–82.

[79] Beltran, 'L'humanisme français au temps de Charles VII et Louis XI', pp. 152–53, and also see the concerns of Francesco Florio when he presented a discourse on rhetoric at the university in 1466, in E. Beltran, 'Un discours inconnu de Francesco Florio sur la Rhétorique', *Bibliothèque d'Humanisme et Renaissance*, xlvii (1985), pp. 101–109 at p. 108.

[80] See *Humanistes français du milieu du XVe siècle. Textes inédits de P. de la Hazardière, J. Serra, G. Fichet*, ed. E. Beltran (Geneva, 1989), p. 157 and Beltran, 'L'humanisme français au temps de Charles VII et Louis XI', pp. 133–35.

Sorbonne.[81] Such pioneers paved the way for significant changes at the University of Paris and across France.

In the late fourteenth and early fifteenth century, financial necessity and the powerful political crises affecting France meant that most writers put their talents to practical services. Humanists were no exception, and hence were dependent upon the practical value of their skills in the service of lay patrons. Most of the early scholars earnt a living as notaries and secretaries in the service of either the papal curia or of king and princes, just as so many of their Italian counterparts were employed in the administrations of the city-states. The victories of Petrarch over French orators in the 1360s had vividly illustrated to the Valois monarchy the value of skilful oratory and rhetoric.[82] It is not surprising, then, that the early French humanists laid great emphasis upon their eloquence. Montreuil declared that the great authors of antiquity, both in Latin and in Greek, profane and patristic, were all strongly versed in the art of oratory and hence that there was a connexion between knowledge and eloquence.[83] In a letter to Clamanges dated the end of 1397, Montreuil defended Virgil against the attacks of Ambrogio Migli, secretary to the duke of Orléans, claiming that Virgil possessed all of the qualities of the great orators, as if eloquence was what made the poet superior.[84] In the letter *Gratulor plurimum*, addressed to Martin Talayerus between 1413 and 1416, Clamanges argued that eloquence without wisdom is meaningless. He criticized the late Antique writer Martianus Capella for making eloquence a god, Mercury, married to Philology in *De nuptiis*

---

[81] M. C. Cosenza, *A Biographical and Bibliographical Dictionary of the Italian Humanists...1300–1800*, 5 vols (New York, 1962), iv, pp. 3412–14.

[82] Ouy, 'La dialectique des rapports intellectuels franco-italiens ', pp. 137–57.

[83] Montreuil, *Opera*, i, p. 260 (letter 170).

[84] Montreuil, *Opera*, i, p. 189 (letter 129).

Philologiae et Mercurii, a work that was extremely influential throughout the Middle Ages and particularly in scholastic culture. Yet though Clamanges argued that eloquence is merely a servant, he did emphasis that it was the closest to its mistress wisdom, and the most intimate and the most elegant of the auxiliaries.[85] In the revised version of his letter *Perpulchras pater* addressed to cardinal Pietramala, Clamanges called upon his correspondent to respect eloquence which prepared all the civic, social and moral virtues.[86]

More directly, classical wisdom and learning was itself presented as morally and practically useful.[87] The French scholars were keen to emphasise that classical wisdom was not incompatible with Christian theology. Defending poetry against claims that it was harmful, Montreuil stressed the importance of eloquence and cited Coluccio Salutati in defence of the notion that there was no contradiction between poetry and the respect due to the teachings of the Church Fathers, who themselves were not as hostile to secular learning as some might claim.[88] In a sermon on the Archangel Michael, Gerson recounted the dream that St Jerome had in which the angels punished him for preferring to read Cicero over the Scriptures. Gerson argued that this did not mean that one should renounce such pagan books which had been used to great effect by countless philosophers, jurists and artists, and

---

[85] Nicolas de Clamanges, *Opera omnia*, ed. I. M. Lydius (Leiden, 1613), p. 188 and Gilli, 'L'humanisme français au temps du Concile de Constance', pp. 50–51.

[86] Cecchetti, *Petrarca, Pietramala e Clamanges*, pp. 147–49.

[87] Simone, *The French Renaissance*, pp. 67–68; Roccati, 'La formation des humanistes', pp. 68–69, and also see N. Mann, 'La fortune de Pétrarque en France: recherches sur le *De remediis*', *Studi francesi*, xxxvii (1969), pp. 1–15, and id., 'Petrarch's Role as Moralist in Fifteenth Century France' in A. H. T. Levi ed., *Humanism in France at the End of the Middle Ages and in the Early Renaissance* (Manchester, 1970), pp. 6–28.

[88] Montreuil, *Opera*, i, p. 143 (letter 102) and also see *Opera*, iv, pp. 178–79.

emphasised the value of reading the works of authors like Plato, Augustine and Cicero, before concluding that 'poetry, rhetoric and philosophy can very well get on with theology and the holy books'.[89]

This first generation of French humanistic scholars like Montrueil, Gerson and Clamanges were influenced by not just the philological lessons offered by Petrarch, but also his moral wisdom. Montreuil praised Petrarch as both a famous writer but also a devout and Catholic moral philosopher, reporting that after two months of reading the Italian's *De remediis utriusque fortunae*, he could recommend it as a work of civil, moral and humane doctrine that would instruct the reader on how to live well and happily and which used classical erudition to support Christian values.[90] When Jean Daudin (d. 1382) translated the *De remediis* in 1378, he presented it as a source of moral doctrine and praised Petrarch as a master of both Latin eloquence and ethics.[91]

By far the largest opportunity for scholars was offered by the remarkable Valois patronage of learning, especially for writings in the vernacular. Building upon the example set by his predecessors, King Charles V (1364–1380) had amassed a great library of around 1200 manuscripts, including over thirty works translated from Latin into French.[92] Christine de Pizan suggested that Charles V could read Latin but wanted the French translations in order to provide the knowledge

---

[89] Gerson, *Œuvres complètes*, v, p. 321, discussed in Ouy, 'Discovering Gerson the Humanist', p. 127.

[90] Montreuil, *Opera*, i, pp. 315–17 (letter 208).

[91] L. Delisle, 'Anciennes traductions françaises du traité de Pétrarque sur *Les remèdes de l'une ou l'autre fortune*', *Notices et extraits des manuscrits de la Bibliothèque Nationale*, xxxiv (1891), pp. 273–304 at pp. 291–92.

[92] M.-H. Tesniere, 'La librairie modèle' in F. Pleybert ed., *Paris et Charles V* (Paris, 2001), pp. 225–33, and ead., 'Les livre de Charles V' in J. Chapelot and E. Lalou ed., *Vincennes aux origines de l'Etat moderne. Actes du colloque scientifique sur 'Les Capétiens et Vincennes au Moyen Age'*, *Vincennes, 8, 9 et 10 juin 1994* (Paris, 1996), pp. 96–103.

necessary to be virtuous to those who could only read the vernacular.[93] Buonaccorso Pitti, the Florentine ambassador to France during the reign of Charles VI, claimed that Louis of Orléans was the only Valois duke able to read Latin.[94] Certainly the limits of the Latin of Jean d'Angoulême, brother of Charles d'Orléans, was revealed when he copied a draft text of Gerson's *Pastorium carmen* around 1430 and made errors 'so serious that they render parts of the text unintelligible'.[95]

Christine de Pizan listed the ten most noteworthy examples of Charles' translations in her biography of the king, including works by Augustine and Aristotle, Vegetius and Livy.[96] One work she does not mention is Petrarch's *De remediis*, translated by Jean Daudin in 1374. In this version, the canon of the Sainte-Chapelle in Paris claimed that King Charles V should be guided by Petrarch's advice, and transform the knightly prowess normally expected of a monarch into 'armes de raison'.[97] Petrarch had also encouraged the application of lessons from Roman military history in the face of the crisis raised by the war with the English. Writing in 1361 to Pierre Bersuire, prior of the abbey of Saint-Eloi in Paris, Petrarch had argued that French success in the wars with the English could only be built upon the inculcation of Roman virtues, inclu-

---

[93] Christine de Pizan, *Le livre des fais et bonnes meurs du sage roy Charles V*, ed. S. Solente, 2 vols (Paris, 1936–40), ii, p. 42, though this claim about Charles V's Latinity may have been a rhetorical commonplace: S. Lusignan, *Parler vulgairement: les intellectuels et la langue française aux XIIIe et XIVe siècles* (Montreal, 1986), pp. 133 and 149.

[94] L. Mirot, 'Bonaccorso Pitti, aventurier, joueur, diplomate et mémorialiste', *Annuaire-bulletin de la Société de l'histoire de France*, année 1930, pp. 183–252 at p. 209.

[95] Ouy, 'Discovering Gerson the Humanist', p. 91.

[96] Christine de Pisan, *Le livre des fais et bonnes meurs*, pp. 43–44 (III.12).

[97] 'Mais votre magnificence, considerant comment très puissant elle demoureroit forte et victorieuse contre tout assaut de fortune, s'est voulue garnir de la doctrine de ce livre aussi comme d'armes de raison inexpugnables': Delisle, 'Anciennes traductions françaises du traité de Pétrarque', p. 293.

ding military ones.[98] Bersuire had already written the *Livre de Tytus Livius de hystoire roumaine* (1354–6), a translation of the first and third decades of Livy, as well as nine books of the fourth decade, to which Bersuire added notes and commentary as well as a glossary of 80 terms, using manuscripts and information supplied by Petrarch and the humanists at Avignon where there were five copies in the library by 1375.[99] Between 1375 and 1379, and probably at Avignon, Simon de Hesdin translated the first four books of Valerius Maximus as *Faits et dits dignes de mémoire*, heavily influenced by the Latin commentaries written between 1327 and 1342 by Dionigi di Borgo San Sepolcro, friend of Petrarch and teacher of Boccaccio. Petrarch often used Valerius Maximus and there was a manuscript of his work in the Avignon library by 1369, and by 1379 the commentary.[100] Charles V also owned a copy of the French translation of the letter of Seneca to Lucilius, commissioned by the Great Chamberlain of Naples between 1308 and 1310.[101] It is not surprising that information on Roman military history featured so heavily in the list of twenty-two books that Jean Gerson recommended for the Dauphin, such as Vegetius' *Epitoma rei militaris* and Giles of

---

[98] Petrarca, *Letters on Familiar Matters*, trans Bernardo, p. 2401 (XXII.13), and C. Samaran and J. Monfrin, 'Pierre Bersuire, Prieur de Saint-Eloi de Paris (1290?–1362)', *Histoire litteraire de la France*, xxxix (1962), pp. 259–450 at pp. 297–99.

[99] J. Monfrin, 'La traduction française de Tite-Live', *Histoire littéraire de la France*, xxxix (1962), pp. 358–414 and G. Billanovich, 'Petrarch and the Textual Tradition of Livy', *Journal of the Warburg and Courtauld Institutes*, xiv (1951), pp. 137–208.

[100] Simone, *The French Renaissance*, p. 56.

[101] Brussels: Bibliothèque Royale, MS. 9091. See L. Delisle, *Recherches sur la librairie de Charles V, roi de France, 1337–1380*, 2 vols (Paris, 1907), i, pp. 257–58, and C. R. Sherman, 'Les thèories humanistes dans le programme de traduction de Charles V: compilation des textes et illustration' in Ornato and Pons ed., *Pratiques de la culture écrits en France*, pp. 527–37 at p. 530.

Rome's *De regimine principum*, as well as Valerius Maximus, Livy, Suetonius and Frontinus.[102]

To the early French humanists, the Latin works of Boccaccio that provided specialist information and anecdotes concerning the classical world may have appeared indistinguishable from those of Petrarch. Boccaccio's *De casibus virorum illustrium* and *De claris mulieribus* must originally have been the most widely known works that they considered useful for classical learning. They were translated into French as early as the start of the fifteenth century by Laurent de Premierfait, who also translated the *Decameron*,[103] as well as Cicero's *De senectute* and *De amicitia*.[104] Yet the case of Laurent de Premierfait illustrates an important tension at the heart of French humanism. Premierfait was well-known in humanist circles for his mastery of Latin verse, the work that had brought him to the attention of first Jean Muret and then Giovanni Moccia, who secured Premierfait a position as a secretary to Cardinal Amedeo Di Saluzzo.[105] Premierfait was also highly

---

[102] A. Thomas, *Jean Gerson et l'éducation des dauphins de France. Étude critique suivie du texte de deux de ses opuscules et de documents inédits sur Jean Majoris précepteur de Louis XI* (Paris, 1930), pp. 48–51 and J. Verger, 'Ad prefulgidum sapiencie culmen prolem regis inclitam provehere. L'initation des dauphins de France à la sagesse politique selon Jean Gerson' in D. Boutet and J. Verger ed., *Penser le pouvoir au moyen âge (VIIIe–XVe siècle)* (Paris, 2000), pp. 427–40.

[103] A. D. Hedeman, *Translating the Past. Laurent de Premierfait and Boccaccio's De casibus* (Los Angeles, 2008), and *Decameron, traduction de Laurent de Premierfait (1411–1414)*, ed. G. di Stefano (Montreal, 1999). *Filostrato* was not translated until around 1453–55 by Louis de Beauvau as *Troyle et Criseida*, and *Teseida* anonymously a few years later: Louis de Beauvau, *Le roman de Troyle*, ed. G. Bianciotti, 2 vols (Rouen, 1994).

[104] Laurent de Premierfait, *Le livre de vieillesse*, ed. S. Marzano (Turnhout, 2009).

[105] C. Bozzolo, 'Le dossier Laurent de Premierfait', *IMU*, xxii (1979), pp. 439–47 at p. 444 and ead. 'Introduction à la vie et à l'œuvre d'un humaniste' in Bozzolo ed., *Un traducteur et un humaniste*, pp. 18–20. Antonio Loschi, secretary of the duke of Milan, praised Premierfait: 'Primus enim Gallorum Latiis es factus in oris': see F. Picco, 'Une

regarded by Gontier Col, who in 1398, sent Premierfait's poem on the death of the Cardinal Galeotto of Pietramala to Clamanges, and shortly afterwards, Jean de Montreuil wrote to Col, gently criticizing him for praising Premierfait and Ambrogio Migli as poets and prophets.[106] Premierfait also prepared a Latin abridgement of Statius' *Thebais* and *Achilleis*, used by both Jean de Montreuil and the canon and lawyer Nicolas de Baye (d.1419), as well as a *Commentum* on certain pieces by Terence.[107] Yet, Premierfait never secured patronage for his Latin writing and instead made a living as a notary and secretary, while preparing translations for patrons, most prominent of whom were the dukes of Bourbon and Berry. Indeed, his enduring fame is as a translator. His translation of Boccaccio's *De casibus virorum et mulierum illustrium*, drafted in 1400 and completed in 1409, was extremely successful, surviving in sixty-nine fifteenth-century manuscripts, most of which were produced after his death.[108] The irony of the situation was not lost on Premierfait, who had shared Petrarch's extremely low opinion of French poetry, much to the dismay of many of his fellow French humanists such as Jean de Montreuil.[109] Moreover, Premierfait repeatedly stressed his anxiety about translating into the vernacular, famously complaining in his rendering of Cicero's *De amicitia* that the

---

épitre inédite d'Antonio Loschi à Laurent Premierfait', *Études italiennes*, iii (1933), pp. 241–53.

[106] Bozzolo, 'Introduction à la vie et à l'œuvre d'un humaniste', p. 28.

[107] C. Jeudy, 'L'abrégé de la *Thébaïde* de Laurent de Premierfait', *IMU*, xxii (1979), pp. 422–38 and Bozzolo ed., *Un traducteur et un humaniste*, pp. 117–80. For Montreuil and Baye, see Bozzolo, 'Le dossier Laurent de Premierfait', p. 477n and ead., 'La lecture des classiques par un humaniste français: Laurent de Permierfait' in Bozzolo ed., *Un traducteur et un humaniste*, pp. 69–82 at p. 72.

[108] C. Bozzolo, *Manuscrits des traductions françaises d'œuvres de Boccace. XVe siècle* (Padua, 1973), pp. 1–3.

[109] Ornato, *Jean Muret et ses amis*, pp.15–33 and Bozzolo, 'Introduction à la vie et à l'œuvre d'un humaniste', pp. 25–28.

Latin was being humilated and lessened when expressed in the vulgar tongue.[110]

Of course, other scholars were more positive, or at least pragmatic. When translating Aristotle for King Charles V, Nicole Oresme (d. 1382) had argued in the *Excusacion et commendacion de ceste œuvre*, that French was the richest and more precise language, capable of rendering even the most complex thoughts, and able to play a role equivalent to that of Latin in Antiquity.[111] Indeed, Oresme even argued that Latin had been a living vernacular for the Romans, learned by imitation more than by rule, and as such it was not necessary to contrast new vernaculars with a Latin that was supposedly learned by rule.[112] In translating Petrarch's *De remediis* into French, Jean Daudin had acknowledged the difficulties he faced in rendering the Latin into a vernacular that was neither eloquent not able to offer equivalent words, a problem that he solved like Oresme by the use of neologisms supported by a glossary.[113] Lori Walters has suggested that Christine de Pizan sought to be a 'Pétrarque français' in her early lyric poetry, the *Cent balades*, perhaps influenced by the lyric eloquence and reconfiguration of Ovid offered in Petrarch's vernacular poems, the *Rerum vulgarium fragmenta* or *Rime sparse*.[114] Certainly

[110] J. Monfrin, 'Humanisme et traductions au Moyen Âge' in A. Fournier ed., *L'humanisme médiéval dans les littératures romanes du XIIe au XIVe siècle* (Paris, 1964), p. 236.

[111] Lusignan, 'La topique de la *translatio studii*', p. 312. Sherman argues that Oresme's effort to explore etymologies, identify geographical locations and people, and explain events and customs represented humanist tendencies: Sherman, 'Les thèories humanistes dans le programme de traduction de Charles V', pp. 530–31.

[112] Lusignan, *Parler vulgairement*, pp. 154–66.

[113] The complete glossary does not survive in any of the manuscripts. Delisle, 'Anciennes traductions françaises du traité de Pétrarque', p. 294 and Lusignan, *Parler vulgairement*, p. 148.

[114] Walters, 'Chivalry and the (En)gendered Poetic Self', pp. 43–66. See also L. Walters, '"Translating" Petrarch: *Cité des dames*, II.7.1, Jean Daudin and Vernacular Authority' in J.Campbell and N. Margolis ed., *Christine de Pizan 2000. Studies on Christine de Pizan in Honour*

Christine avoided writing in Latin, whether during the debate over the *Roman de La Rose* or in her subsequent books, perhaps fearing that she might have 'locked herself into a masculine world of *litterati* [sic] where the idea of writing as a form of moral, public activism was of little interest'.[115]

Yet while so many late medieval scholars did write in French, the legitimacy of doing so remained a hotly contested issue given the inadequacies of the vernacular to meet the increasing standards of eloquence and rhetoric.[116] There was a clear tension between Latinate scholarship and vernacular classicism, and it is difficult to describe writing or translation into French as humanism. For Nicolas de Clamanges, the vernacular was not capable of offering the clarity, elegance and verbal economy of Latin.[117] Yet even he did touch upon French in his translations into Latin of Philippe de Vitri's *Dit de Franc Gontier* as *Descriptio vite rustice* and of Pierre d'Ailly's *Contredit* as *Descriptio vite tirannice*.[118] Indeed, Premierfait was

---

of Angus J. Kennedy (Amsterdam, 2000), pp. 283–97. It is important to note that Petrarch's vernacular work was largely unknown in France until the sixteenth century, though the *Trionfi* was a source for Jean and François Robertet and Jean Molinet.

[115] T. S. Fenster, 'Perdre son latin: Christine de Pizan and Vernacular Humanism' in M. Desmond ed., *Christine de Pizan and the Categories of Difference* (Minneapolis, MN, 1998), p. 102 (and cf. p. 91). For the debate over Pizan's humanist credentials, see, for example, S. Lusignan and E. Ornato, 'Conclusions du colloque' in Ornato and Pons ed., *Pratiques de la culture écrite en France*, p. 557 and Margolis, 'Culture vantée, culture inventée', pp. 269–308.

[116] These debates continued into the sixteenth century, as seen for example in Joachim DuBellay's *La défense et illustration de la langue française*, written in 1549, that made the case for the capability of French to handle literature, history and philosophy: Kelley, 'France', pp. 131–34.

[117] Cecchetti, *Il primo umanesimo francese*, p. 52 and Margolis, 'Culture vantée, culture inventée', p. 284.

[118] J.-C. Mühlethaler, 'Le tyran à table: intertextualité et référence dans l'invective politique à l'époque de Charles VI' in J. Blanchard ed., *Représentation, pouvoir et royauté à la fin du moyen âge* (Paris, 1995),

not the only French humanist to write in both Latin and French. Jean de Montreuil employed the vernacular when writing about historical and political matters, and 'wrote several political tracts in a sturdy French which contrasts sharply with his intricate and sometimes awkward Latin'.[119] Jean Gerson not only wrote well in the vernacular but also used it as a medium to address themes such as the contemplative life.[120] He wrote French 'with the utmost purity and clarity, treating it with philological respect and carefully avoiding ... latinisms and neologisms.'[121] In 1455, Jean Lebègue translated into French Leonardo Bruni's commentary on the first Punic war, and he also translated Sallust's *De coniuratione Catiliniae* and *Bellum Iurgurthinum*.[122] Yet ironically, his French version was subsequently absorbed into a thoroughly medieval tradition, when it was used by Jean Mansel in his *Fleurs des histoires*. It was a mounting awareness of the inability of French to stand alongside Latin that led Robert Gaguin to redraft the text in Latin of his *Compendium de origine et gestis francorum*, a work that strongly supported French identity but did so without resorting to the vernacular.[123]

Indeed, the second wave of French humanistic scholars that came to the fore in the mid-fifteenth century such as Fichet, Tardif and Gaguin were influenced by Italian scholars like Guarino da Verona and, above all, Lorenzo Valla, and recognised a deeper division between Antiquity and their age,

pp. 49–62 and Lefèvre, 'Humanisme, pré-humanisme et humanistes: un singulier pluriel', p. 314.

[119] Ouy, 'Humanism and nationalism in France', p. 114.

[120] Ouy, 'Discovering Gerson the Humanist', pp. 109–11 and 128–29.

[121] Ouy, 'Humanism and nationalism in France at the turn of the fifteenth century', p. 114.

[122] Pons, 'Leonardo Bruni, Jean Lebègue et la cour', pp. 95–125; A. D. Hedeman, 'Making the Past Present: Visual Translation in Jean Lebègue's 'Twin' Manuscripts of Sallust' in G. Croenen and P. Ainsworth ed., *Patrons, Authors and Workshops. Books and book production in Paris around 1400* (Leuven, 2006), pp. 173–97.

[123] Pons, 'Leonardo Bruni, Jean Lebègue et la cour', pp. 113–14.

the Middle Ages. Where their predecessors had been willing to accommodate itself to the remains of Antiquity, these new scholars echoed the desire of their Italian counterparts to revive its soul and began to turn it into an idealized and abstract image. They placed much greater emphasis on the importance of eloquence, as they were focused on the teaching of rhetoric and classical metre in schools by means of manuals, but also the spreading of classical texts, above all through printing.[124] In the early 1470s, the first printed edition of Lorenzo Valla's *Elegantiae* included a letter to Johann Heynlin from a royal secretary named Pierre Paul Vieillot, highlighting the value of the work for students at a time when the quality of both Latin and copying were so poor, and when the princely courts were having such a malign effect on learned men because of the value placed upon martial rather than intellectual skills.[125] This was powerful advertising to support the opportunities presented by printing to deepen and entrench the value of Latinity and classical culture in France.

---

[124] Beltran, 'L'humanisme français au temps de Charles VII et Louis XI', p. 125.

[125] Hirsch, 'Printing in France and humanism, 1470–1480', pp. 129–30.

THE DEVELOPMENT OF HUMANISM IN LATE-FIFTEENTH-CENTURY SCOTLAND

THOMAS RUTLEDGE

In 1953, in his seminal essay on 'The Beginnings of Humanism in Scotland,' John Durkan, with beguiling modesty, proposed for his work that it might 'at least' serve 'to remove two prevalent misconceptions: that the Renaissance was only felt in Scotland for a very brief period at the court of James IV' (1488–1513) and that its full force was only experienced after 1560, once 'the Reformation had swept the clerical opposition out of control.'[1] Subsequent scholarship, no small part of it Durkan's own (for he surely stands at least as authoritatively and influentially in relation to the study of early humanism in Scotland as Roberto Weiss does to the study of fifteenth-century humanism in England), has ensured that such misconceptions no longer prevail.[2] The exaggerations of

[1] J. Durkan, 'The Beginnings of Humanism in Scotland', *Innes Review*, iv (1953), pp. 5–34 at p. 5.

[2] Especially important are Durkan, 'Beginnings of Humanism' and id., 'The Cultural Background in Sixteenth-Century Scotland', *Innes Review*, x (1959), pp. 382–439, reprinted in D. McRoberts ed., *The Scottish Reformation* (Glasgow, 1962), pp. 274–331. All of Durkan's work, though, richly rewards revisiting and must be the starting-point for every subsequent engagement; a bibliography of his writings is given in P. Asplin, 'Writings of John Durkan 1931–1994' in A. A. MacDonald et al. ed., *The Renaissance in Scotland: studies in literature, religion, history and culture offered to John Durkan* (Leiden, 1994), pp. 417–28. Important, too, are John MacQueen's 'Some Aspects of the Early Renaissance in Scotland', *Forum for Modern Language Studies*, iii (1967), pp. 201–22 and id., 'Aspects of Humanism in Sixteenth- and

Pinturicchio's fresco in the Duomo in Siena, portraying ÆNEAS SILVIUS PICCOLOMINI's visit to Scotland in 1435, may be suggestively balanced against Piccolomini's own words: 'nam terra Scotia et Angliae pars vicina Scotis nihil simile nostrae habitationis habet – horrida, inculta atque hiemali sole inaccessa' (for Scotland and the parts of England nearest to it are utterly unlike the land we inhabit, being rude, uncultivated and untouched by the winter sun)'.[3] Similarly, John MacQueen offers in confident rejoinder to Walter Scott's vision of a learned Gavin Douglas (c. 1475–1522), translator of Virgil, isolated in 'rude Scotland [...] in a barbarous age' that '[a]lmost the contrary is the truth; Douglas' *Aeneid* is in a very real sense the natural outcome of a century of university life and more than half a century of humanism in Scotland'.[4] Certainly, the range of works in circulation within Scotland in the final quarter of the fifteenth century, many of them from Italian presses, is a sure marker of the spread of humanism.[5] So

    Seventeenth-Century Literature' in id. ed., *Humanism in Renaissance Scotland* (Edinburgh, 1990), pp. 10–31, P. Bawcutt, *Gavin Douglas: a critical study* (Edinburgh, 1976), pp. 23–35, R. Mason, *Kingship and the Commonweal: political thought in Renaissance and Reformation Scotland* (East Linton, 1998), pp. 104–38, and N. Macdougall, *James III* (Edinburgh, 2009), pp. 245–82.

[3] Pius II, *Commentaries*, ed. M. Meserve and M. Simonetta, 2 vols to date [ITRL, xii & xxix] (Cambridge, MA, 2003– 2007), i, p. 26.

[4] MacQueen, 'Some Aspects of the Early Renaissance in Scotland', p. 215; MacQueen quotes from Walter Scott, *Marmion: a tale of Flodden Field* (Edinburgh, 1855), p. 336 (Canto 6, Stanza 11, ll. 17–25). See also Bawcutt, *Gavin Douglas*, pp. 23ff. Douglas tells us that he completed his *Aeneid* in July, 1513: G. Douglas, *Virgil's Aeneid Translated into Scottish Verse by Gavin Douglas, Bishop of Dunkeld*, ed. F. C. Coldwell, 4 vols [Scottish Text Society, 3rd series, xxx, xxv, xxvii, xxviii] (Edinburgh, 1957–64), 'Heir followys the tyme, space and dait of the translatioun of this buke', ll. 1–4. For the details of Douglas's life, see Bawcutt, *Gavin Douglas*, pp. 1–22. On Douglas, see further at pp. 258–60 below.

[5] For early Scottish book-ownership, see especially J. Durkan and A. Ross, *Early Scottish Libraries* (Glasgow, 1961), and the succession of supplements to that work: A. Ross, 'Libraries of the Scottish

too is the quality of the Latin of a document such as the celebrated address to Richard III at Nottingham in 1484 by Archibald Whitelaw (1415/16–1498), royal secretary and archdeacon of Lothian.[6]

And yet it is true that the evidence of humanist interest and practice within Scotland in the fifteenth century is relatively sparse and comes quite late – particularly in comparison with

---

Blackfriars, 1481–1560', *Innes Review*, xx (1969), pp. 3–36; J. Durkan and R. V. Pringle, 'St Andrews Additions to Durkan & Ross: Some Unrecorded Scottish pre-Reformation Ownership Inscriptions in St Andrews University Library', *The Bibliothek*, ix (1978–79), pp. 13–20; J. Durkan, 'Further Additions to Durkan and Ross: Some Newly Discovered Scottish Pre-Reformation Provenances', *The Bibliothek*, x (1980–81), pp. 87–98; J. Durkan and J. Russell, 'Additions to J. Durkan and A. Ross, *Early Scottish Libraries*, at the National Library of Scotland', *The Bibliothek*, xi (1982–83), pp. 29–37; J. Durkan, 'Addenda to "Further Additions to Durkan and Ross"', *The Bibliothek*, xi (1982–83), pp. 57–58; and J. Durkan and J. Russell, 'Further Additions (Including Manuscripts) to J. Durkan and A. Ross, *Early Scottish Libraries*, at the National Library of Scotland', *The Bibliothek*, xii (1984–85), pp. 85–90. See also J. Durkan, 'Scheves and Kinloss Libraries: Additions and a Correction', *Innes Review*, iv (1953), pp. 119–20; L. Macfarlane, 'William Elphinstone's Library', *Aberdeen University Review*, xxxvii (1957–58), pp. 253–71; R. Lyall, 'Books and Book Owners in Fifteenth-Century Scotland' in J. Griffiths and D. Pearsall ed., *Book Production and Publishing in Britain, c. 1375–1475* (Cambridge, 1989), pp. 239–56; J. Higgitt, *Scottish Libraries* [Corpus of British Medieval Library Catalogues, xii] (London, 2006), and N. R. Ker ed., *Medieval Libraries of Great Britain: a list of surviving books*, 2nd ed. (London, 1964), with the *Medieval Libraries of Great Britain [...]: supplement to the second edition*, ed. A. G. Watson (London, 1987).

[6] The address is printed as A. Whitelaw, 'Minutes of the Proceedings of the Commissioners at Nottingham, in September, MCCCC.L. XXXIV' in *The Bannatyne Miscellany; Containing Original Papers and Tracts, Chiefly Related to the History and Literature of Scotland*, 3 vols (Edinburgh, 1827–55), i, pp. 37–48 [hereafter Whitelaw]. It has been translated by D. Shotter in A. J. Pollard ed., *The North of England in the Age of Richard III* (Stroud, 1996), pp. 193–200 [hereafter Shotter], with the discussion of the quality of Whitelaw's Latinity at pp. 199–200; the oration is more fully discussed by A. Grant, 'Richard III and Scotland' in Pollard ed., *North of England*, pp. 115–48 at pp. 137–40.

that from England. It is worth attending to this for a moment. It may simply reflect the amount of material that has been lost: the ravages of time and of the Reformation have not been kind to Scottish materials, as may at once be suggested by comparison of the early booklists recorded in John Higgitt's *Scottish Libraries* with the paucity of surviving volumes. Equally, though, there is almost no sign of humanistic influence in the curricula and booklists associated with the Scottish universities before the foundation of the University of Aberdeen by Bishop William Elphinstone in 1495 and Alexander Inglis's remarkable donation of books to the Faculty of Arts and the Pedagogy of St John the Evangelist at St Andrew's in 1496.[7] What emerges strongly from accounts of the teaching at St Andrews and Glasgow in the fifteenth century is their essentially conservative and scholastic nature.[8] This is not altogether surprising; one probably should not expect the medieval universities to lead the way in the adoption and promulgation of the new learning. Certainly, though, there is nothing here to compare with the impetus given to humanist studies in England by the donations of Humfrey, duke of Gloucester, to Oxford in the 1430s and 1440s.[9] And this is all the more notable given the evident

---

[7] For the foundation and early development of the University of Aberdeen, see L. J. Macfarlane, *William Elphinstone and the Kingdom of Scotland, 1431–1514: the struggle for order* (Aberdeen, 1985), pp. 290–402; for the details of Inglis's donation, see Higgitt, *Scottish Libraries*, pp. 382–85.

[8] See, for instance, Macfarlane, *William Elphinstone and the Kingdom of Scotland*, pp. 23–27 and, more generally, pp. 16–52, and, most recently, I. Woodman, 'Education and Episcopacy: The Universities of Scotland in the Fifteenth Century' (unpublished PhD. Thesis, University of St Andrews, 2011), pp. 12–86, available on-line at http://hdl.handle. net/10023/1882 [accessed 16th December 2011]. For the books associated with the universities, see esp. Higgitt, *Scottish Libraries*, pp. 155–66 and 375–82.

[9] Weiss[4], pp. 96–106. See also the forthcoming volume of the Corpus of British Medieval Library Catalogues, edited by R. M. Thomson, *The University and College Libraries of Oxford*.

sensitivity of the Scottish universities to other academic developments on the Continent. It seems clear, for instance, that the foundation of St Salvator's College in St Andrews in 1450 and of the University of Glasgow the following year in part reflected directly the renewed influence of Albertist Realism at Paris, Cologne, and Louvain.[10] If, then, humanism emerges relatively slowly within Scotland, this is to be explained not by recourse to the careless and outdated cliché of a country geographically and culturally isolated but, rather, the opposite: as a measure of Scotland's cultural proximity to the countries of northern Europe. Unsurprisingly, many of the developments of Italian humanism were mediated to Scotland via the experience of Scottish students in Paris, in particular; their arrival in Scotland, then, necessarily awaited their emergence in Paris.[11] The fuller development of Scottish humanism from the beginning of the sixteenth century follows closely the opportunity of men such as Hector Boece, John Mair, and Patrick Paniter to experience the growing influence of FILIPPO BEROALDO, GIROLAMO BALBI, FAUSTO ANDRELINI, Robert Gaguin, Jacques Lefèvre, and Erasmus during their time as students at the College of Montaigu in the 1490s.[12]

I have emphasised this point, in part, because it relates closely to another. There is a tendency in accounts of the development of Renaissance humanism (so often written, of course, by keen appreciators of classical and humanist

[10] Woodman, 'Education and Episcopacy', pp. 53–63; Macfarlane, *William Elphinstone and the Kingdom of Scotland*, pp. 23–26. The founding statutes of the University of Glasgow record that its constitution was expressly modelled on that of the University of Bologna (Macfarlane, *William Elphinstone and the Kingdom of Scotland*, p. 21).

[11] Compare Durkan, 'Cultural Background', pp. 278–79; Bawcutt, *Gavin Douglas*, pp. 25–26: 'It would be difficult to over-emphasise the importance of Paris to educated Scotsmen during the fifteenth and early sixteenth centuries.'

[12] Bawcutt, *Gavin Douglas*, p. 26; Mason, *Kingship and Commonweal*, p. 119; Macfarlane, *William Elphinstone and the Kingdom of Scotland*, p. 323.

achievement – among whom I should certainly wish to include myself) to suggest that it radically revivified a moribund late-medieval culture, dominated by the sterile distinctions and pedantic controversies of an obsolescent scholasticism and constrained by a cripplingly narrow privileging of the authority of Aristotle. In the Scottish context, this has naturally led, at times, to the desire to find evidence of Italian and humanist influence as early as possible, as signs of the progressive nature of fifteenth-century Scotland. In fact, however, I am inclined to think that the relatively belated arrival of humanism serves, rather, as a marker of the confidence and continuing vitality of late-medieval Scottish culture which was open to enrichment but hardly in pressing need of renewal. I shall wish to return to this point when we consider the humanist quality of Robert Henryson's vernacular poetry at the close of this essay.

We may perhaps use Whitelaw's 1484 address itself as evidence of this relative belatedness. Its style is assuredly Ciceronian. To express Richard III's manifold virtues, Whitelaw invokes Cicero himself: 'uix Cicero, si superesset, sufficeret (Were Cicero still alive, his skills would scarcely suffice to describe your virtues fully or sing your praises to the skies).'[13] He quotes from Statius, Seneca, Sallust, and Livy, and from Virgil's *Eclogae* as well as from the *Aeneid*:

> In freta dum fluuii current, dum montibus umbre
> Lustrabunt conuexa, polus dum sidera pascet,
> Dum iuga montis aper, fluuios dum piscis amabit,
> Dumque thimo pascentur apes, dum rore cicade,
> Semper honos, nomenque tuum, laudesque manebunt.[14]

> So long as rivers flow into the sea, so long as shadows move on the mountain-slopes; so long as the pole feeds the stars; so long as the wild boar delights in the mountains and the fish in the

---

[13] Whitelaw, p. 43 (Shotter, p. 193).

[14] Whitelaw, p. 43 (Shotter, p. 193); cf. Virgil, *P. Vergili Maronis Opera*, ed. R. A. B. Mynors (Oxford, 1969), *Aeneid*, Book 1, ll. 608–09; Virgil, *Ecloga* 5, ll. 76–78.

rivers; so long as bees feed on thyme and grasshoppers on dew – your honour, your name and your glory will survive for ever.

The horror of war, which the oration elaborates most fully, is developed through further reference to Book 6 of the *Aeneid* ('Ne, pueri, ne tanta animis assuescite bella: / Neu patrie ualidas in uiscera uertite uires (Do not, my children, let yourselves become used in your thoughts to such great warfare; nor turn your stout strength upon your own country's heart)'), and through skilful manipulation of the traditional tropes of classical bucolic poetry: 'bello horrescunt omnia inculti; et curue rigidos falces conflantur in enses; siluescunt uineta; hominum cruore campi, gramina, et herbe madescunt. (In time of war, all the land is left uncultivated and overgrown; curved sickles are forged into straight swords; vineyards are turned into thickets; and fields, grass and vegetation grow moist with the blood of men).'[15]

It is an important document: it seems to be 'the earliest extant piece of extended humanist prose to be composed by a Scot,' and it clearly illustrates the confidence with which the Scots could assume the Ciceronian manner to represent themselves on the public stage of international diplomacy (Whitelaw spoke as a member of the Scottish embassy negotiating a peace treaty with Richard III).[16] Delivered in September 1484, though, the oration falls, of course, only just within the limits Weiss set for his account of *Humanism in England during the Fifteenth Century* (however irrelevant those

---

[15] Virgil: Whitelaw, p. 44 (Shotter, p. 196); cf. Virgil, *Aeneid*, Book 6, ll. 832–33. Bucolic: Whitelaw, p. 44 (Shotter, p. 197); the trope is, of course, Biblical (Isaiah, 2. 4) as well as bucolic. J. MacQueen, 'The Literature of Fifteenth-Century Scotland' in J. Brown ed., *Scottish Society in the Fifteenth Century* (London, 1977), pp. 184–208 at p. 194: 'The Latinity is that of a Christian humanist, modelled on Cicero.'

[16] MacQueen, 'Some Aspects of the Early Renaissance in Scotland', p. 207 (see, however, the discussion of Elphinstone's oration below). For the diplomatic context of the oration, see Grant, 'Richard III and Scotland', pp. 135–45.

particular limits may be to a specifically Scottish context). Moreover, Whitelaw's address is notable in part for its very singularity, for the manner in which it seems to stand out from other fifteenth-century Scottish material. The degree to which it might represent wider cultural developments, then, is not unproblematic.

This may be to overplay the document's singularity.[17] We have to look later in time, though, to find its like: to, for instance, another oration to an English king, this time to Henry VII, composed by Walter Ogilvie at the beginning of 1502.[18] The address, and particularly the continuity it evinces with Whitelaw's, may perhaps suggest further something of the quality of Scottish humanism in the final two decades of the fifteenth century.[19]

[17] I may also have overplayed its belatedness: David Rundle observes that the earliest equivalents of Ciceronian diplomatic oratory of English production are the orations of John Gunthorpe of the late 1460s and 1470s (see Weiss[4], pp. 188–91 and cf. pp. xl – xli). There is certainly, though, little evidence of a Scottish tradition of humanist scholarship and practice that precedes Whitelaw's address.

[18] The address, probably in the author's own hand, is preserved as Edinburgh: National Library of Scotland [hereafter NLS], MS. Adv. 33.2.24. Reference to the manuscript is by folio; translation is my own. The address is noted in Durkan and Ross, *Early Scottish Libraries*, pp. 13, 134 and discussed briefly by MacQueen, 'Some Aspects of the Early Renaissance in Scotland', pp. 208–09.

[19] If attending in some detail to a piece from the very beginning of the sixteenth century in an account of fifteenth-century humanism requires further justification, I should point to the strange neglect Ogilvie's oration has suffered (all the more conspicuous in comparison with the attention afforded Whitelaw's). John MacQueen, 'Some Aspects of the Early Renaissance in Scotland', p. 208, observed in 1967 that the address had been 'curiously neglected' and the neglect has continued. Publication (and translation) of Ogilvie's manuscript would be a valuable contribution to the study of early-Renaissance Scotland. Hector Boece enthusiastically celebrates Ogilvie's eloquence: 'Walter Ogilvie, possessed of such a flood of oratorical power, that one would have said that he not only delighted, but (so to speak) even revelled and luxuriated in copiousness of diction, elegance of speech and wealth of wisdom' (H. Boece, *Hectoris Boetii Murthlacensium et*

John MacQueen characterised Ogilvie's address as 'floridly Ciceronian,' although Cicero might have been slightly surprised by Ogilvie's rhetorical exuberance.[20] Henry is 'traiano iustissimo iustior, clementissimo Julio clementior, Metello fortunatissimo fortunatior (more just than most just Trajan, more merciful than most merciful Julius, more fortunate than most fortunate Metellus).' Elizabeth, his wife, is the 'reginarum gemma ... Cui nulla Lucretia nulla penelope castitate conferri queat (jewel of queens with whom in purity neither Lucretia nor Penelope can be compared).'[21] Suetonius is adduced to testify to Caesar's famed clemency, and the authority of Cicero, Sallust, and Valerius Maximus is similarly rallied.[22] Ogilvie quotes from the famous prophecy of Jupiter from the opening book of the *Aeneid* which Patrick Paniter would redeploy in celebration of Julius II five years later: 'Claudentur belli porte, furor impius intus / seua sedens super arma & centum vinctus ahenis (The gates of war will be shut up, impious Fury within, sitting atop his savage arms and bound by a hundred bronze chains)'.[23] Ogilvie owned a copy of Livy's *Ab urbe condita* printed in Venice in 1498 and in the oration he closely paraphrases one of the central formulations of Livy's preface: 'Et profecto in hystoricorum voluminibus omnium rerum exempla atque documenta uelut in illustri monumento posita intueri & que imitanda sunt imitari & que fugienda sunt fugere possimus (And certainly we can see in the volumes of histories examples and instances of all things, set forth as on a conspicuous monument, and we can imitate what must be

---

Aberdonensium Episcoporum Vitae, ed. J. Moir (Aberdeen, 1894), p. 88); cf. Durkan and Ross, *Early Scottish Libraries*, p. 13.

[20] MacQueen, 'Some Aspects of the Early Renaissance in Scotland', p. 209.

[21] Ogilvie, fol. 3^r, 3^v–4^r.

[22] Ogilvie, fol. 3^r, 5^r, 8^v, 9^r, 12^v, 13^r and *passim*.

[23] Ogilvie, fol. 7^r; cf. Virgil, *Aeneid*, Book 1, ll. 294–95. For Paniter's letter to Julius II, see James IV, *The Letters of James IV, 1503–1513*, ed. R. K. Hannay (Edinburgh, 1953), p. 85; cf. Bawcutt, *Gavin Douglas*, p. 71.

imitated and avoid what must be avoided)'.[24] He also repeats the bucolic trope employed by Whitelaw in praise of freshly realised peace: 'gladii et rusticorum lacertosa inuentus non iam amplius ad bellum sicut ad agriculture opus'.[25]

We may also adduce the 'elegant Renaissance Latin address' Hector Boece ascribes to William Elphinstone in the *Murthlacensium et Aberdonensium episcoporum vitae*, delivered on the occasion of a Scottish embassy to Louis XI of France, probably in 1482.[26] There must be some doubt as to whether the oration, as it is preserved, accurately represents Elphinstone's original words, as Boece claims.[27] Boece, whose historiographical practice was so richly informed by Livy's, was hardly incapable of composing elegant, humanist speeches to put in the mouths of his historical figures; nonetheless, the close relationship of the two men at the University of Aberdeen (Elphinstone invited Boece to return from Paris to be one of the first teachers at the new institution in 1497 and Boece was its first Principal) suggests that Boece's claim to be recording

---

[24] Ogilvie owned T. Livius, *Historiae Romanae decades* (Venice: Bartholomaeus de Zanis, 1498) [ISTC No. il00248000]; cf. Durkan and Ross, *Early Scottish Libraries*, p. 134. The quotation is from Ogilvie, fol. 13ʳ; cf. Livy, *Titi Liui Ab urbe condita, Libri I–V*, ed. R. M. Ogilvie (Oxford, 1974), *Praefatio*, 10: 'Hoc illud est praecipue in cognitione rerum salubre ac frugiferum, omnis te exempli documenta in inlustri posita monumento intueri; inde tibi tuaeque rei publicae quod imitere capias, inde foedum inceptu foedum exitu quod uites.'

[25] Ogilvie, fol. 3ʳ.

[26] The address is recorded in Boece, *Murthlacensium et Aberdonensium Episcoporum Vitae*, pp. 66–73; the assessment of its quality is from Macfarlane, *William Elphinstone and the Kingdom of Scotland*, p. 123; for the dating of the embassy, see Macdougall, *James III*, p. 274.

[27] Boece, *Murthlacensium et Aberdonensium Episcoporum Vitae*, p. 66: 'orationis non sententiam solum sed et verba, ne quid varietur, visum est referre, ut quantum prudentia pollebat, quantumque valebat eloquentia, dignoscant qui eam legerint (I have thought it right to give not only the substance, but the actual words of his speech in order that there may be no difference of opinion, but that all who read it may recognise how great was the bishop's sagacity and how powerful his eloquence)'.

Elphinstone's actual words may be more than a rhetorical topos.[28] The oration quotes confidently from Aristotle's *Nicomachean Ethics* and from Cicero's *De amicitia* and Sallust's *Bellum Iugurthinum*.[29] The *Nicomachean Ethics* are quoted in the translation of John Argyropoulos. Boece owned a copy of this translation printed at Paris in 1488 and this, together with the prevailing popularity of LEONARDO BRUNI's translation in the late fifteenth century, may give cause to doubt that Boece records Elphinstone's very words as he delivered them in 1482 and suggest that the extant oration records a mix of late-fifteenth- and early-sixteenth-century humanist interests.[30] If we may, then, take for granted the influence of humanism in Scotland by the close of the fifteenth century, it is also worth emphasising that almost all of the extant evidence of this quickening influence comes from the final quarter of the century.

The development of humanism within Scotland may be further observed in the volumes demonstrably in the hands of fifteenth-century Scottish readers. R. J. Lyall has demonstrated that there was a marked increase in the production of

[28] For Boece and Elphinstone at Aberdeen, see Macfarlane, *William Elphinstone and the Kingdom of Scotland*, pp. 290–402, and especially pp. 323–24, 358–59. Boece's claim that he provides Elphinstone's original oration is cautiously accepted by both Macfarlane, *William Elphinstone and the Kingdom of Scotland*, p. 123, and Macdougall, *James III*, p. 275. On Boece's life and work, the fullest treatment is N. Royan, 'The *Scotorum Historia* of Hector Boece: A Study' (unpublished D.Phil. thesis, University of Oxford, 1996); see also, for instance, ead., 'The Uses of Speech in Hector Boece's *Scotorum historia*' in L. A. J. R. Houwen, A. A. Macdonald, and S. L. Mapstone ed., *A Palace in the Wild: essays on vernacular culture and humanism in Late-Medieval and Renaissance Scotland* (Leuven, 2000), pp. 75–93.

[29] Boece, *Murthlacensium et Aberdonensium episcoporum vitae*, pp. 66, 152.

[30] Aristoteles, *Ethica ad Nicomachum*, trans. J. Argyropoulos (Paris: Johannes Higman, 1488–89) [ISTC no. ia00982000], bound with Leonardo Bruni's translations of Aristotle's *Politica* and the pseudo-Aristotelian *Oeconomica* (Paris: Georg Wolf, 1490) [ISTC No. ia01023000]; Durkan and Ross, *Early Scottish Libraries*, p. 77.

manuscripts within Scotland from about 1470, suggestive both of the influence of an important group of bibliophilic collectors and of a new array of appropriately skilled native scribes able to stimulate and to respond to new demand.[31] At the same time, many new volumes were imported from the Continent, many of these from the new Italian printing presses.[32] A 'striking number' of these incunabula had reached Scotland before 1500.[33] At the centre of the story of fifteenth-century Scottish humanist book-ownership are, again, Whitelaw and Elphinstone, and also William Scheves.[34]

Scheves, archbishop of St Andrews, was an important figure in the administration – and the factional machinations – of the reign of James III.[35] He visited Italy twice, first for three

---

[31] Lyall, 'Books and Book Owners in Fifteenth-Century Scotland', pp. 240–41.

[32] The importation of books has been quantitatively described in M. L. Ford, 'Importation of Printed Books into England and Scotland' in L. Hellinga and J. B. Trapp ed., *The Cambridge History of the Book in Britain, Volume III, 1440–1557* (Cambridge, 1999), pp. 179–201 at pp. 193–96; see also D. Ditchburn, *Scotland and Europe: the Medieval kingdom and its contacts with Christendom, 1214–1560*, I: *Religion, Culture and Commerce* (East Linton, 2000), pp. 120–30.

[33] Durkan and Ross, *Early Scottish Libraries*, p. 15.

[34] The importance of the three men as 'precursors' of Scottish humanism was emphasised by Durkan, 'Beginnings of Humanism', p. 5 and discussions of fifteenth-century Scottish humanism invariably return to them. See, for instance, the surveys of Gray, *Robert Henryson*, pp. 22–23 and I. S. Ross, *William Dunbar* (Leiden, 1981), pp. 33–36. Especially useful is Macdougall, *James III*, pp. 262–76. See also Lyall, 'Books and Book Owners in Fifteenth-Century Scotland'; R. J. Lyall, 'Scottish Students and Masters at the Universities of Cologne and Louvain in the Fifteenth Century', *Innes Review*, xxxvi (1985), pp. 55–73; and, for Whitelaw, Mason, *Kingship and Commonweal*, pp. 117–18.

[35] Scheves is a central figure in Macdougall's accounts of the reign of James III and of the early years of the reign of James IV (Scheves died in 1497): Macdougall, *James III*, *passim*; N. Macdougall, *James IV* (East Linton, 2006), *passim*. Macdougall's account of Scheves' reading, in *James III*, pp. 263–70, is especially valuable.

months from December 1486 to February 1487, and then again at the beginning of 1493.[36] His library was commended in his own day and seems to have had a reputation particularly for its scientific and medical books.[37] He owned a Venetian edition of Johannes Mesue's *Opera medicinalia* and a Pavian edition of Nicholas Falcutius' *Sermones medicinales*, which may at least serve to illustrate Scottish access to books printed in Italy.[38] Similarly, he owned a copy of the first volume of Nicholas de Lyra's *Biblia Latina* printed in Venice.[39] Much more striking – since it is hardly surprising that the Italian presses were also a source of non-humanist material – is his possession of Venetian editions of Martial's *Epigrams* with the commentary of DOMENICO CALDERINI, Lucan's *Pharsalia*, and Horace's *Opera*.[40] He also owned a copy of Juvenal's and Persius' *Satires*, printed at Louvain, and evidently had a particular interest in Scottish historiography for his library included manuscript copies of at least three important Scottish historical works: Walter Bower's *Scotichronicon*, the chronicles of John of Fordun, and the anonymous *Liber Pluscardensis*.[41]

[36] Macdougall, *James III*, pp. 226–32; Macfarlane, *William Elphinstone and the Kingdom of Scotland*, p. 292.

[37] Lyall, 'Books and Book Owners', p. 246; cf. Lyall, 'Scottish Students and Masters', pp. 65–66 and Macdougall, *James III*, pp. 264–65.

[38] These are, respectively, ISTC nos im00515000 and if00045000; see Durkan, 'Further Additions', p. 90; Durkan and Ross, *Early Scottish Libraries*, p. 49.

[39] ISTC, no. ib00611000; Durkan and Ross, *Early Scottish Libraries*, p. 47.

[40] These are, respectively, ISTC, nos im00306000, il00296000 and ih00443000; see Durkan and Ross, *Early Scottish Libraries*, p. 48; Durkan, 'Further Additions', p. 90. The Martial is lightly annotated and a number of the epigrams have been underlined; if these annotations are Scheves' own, they might suggest his favourites among the collection. The *Biblia Latina* and *Sermones Medicinales* are also lightly annotated.

[41] The printed book is ISTC, no. ij00636300; Durkan, 'Further Additions', p. 90. The manuscripts are, respectively, BL, MSS Harley 712 and Cotton Vitellius E. xi, and Glasgow: University Library, MS.

Whitelaw's extant books and manuscripts record interests suggestively different from Scheves': 'in Roman history rather than that of Scotland, and in canon law rather than in medicine and astronomy.'[42] He also owned a copy of Lucan's *Pharsalia*, printed at Louvain circa 1475–76, Venetian editions of Horace's works, Sallust's works, Asconius' *Commentarii in orationes Ciceronis*, and PIER CANDIDO DECEMBRIO's translation of Appianus' *Historia Romana*.[43] Whitelaw's most significant manuscript was a transcription of Sweynheym and Pannartz's 1471 *editio princeps* of Cicero's philosophical writings, which opens with the *De officiis*, 'a work which was to become one of the key texts in the lay humanist canon'.[44] Whitelaw seems to have owned the manuscript before 1482, and it is steadily annotated in his hand, primarily with descriptions which articulate the *ordinatio* of the work, presumably to facilitate referencing and re-reading.[45] He also

Gen. 333; cf. Lyall, 'Books and Book Owners', pp. 245–48; Lyall, 'Scottish Students and Masters', p. 69. See also Macdougall, *James III*, p. 268, and S. Mapstone, 'The *Scotichronicon*'s First Readers' in B. E. Crawford ed., *Church, Chronicle and Learning in Medieval and Early Renaissance Scotland, Essays Presented to Donald Watt on the Occasion of the Completion of the Publication of Bower's Scotichronicon* (Edinburgh, 1999), pp. 31–55 at pp. 39–40.

[42] Lyall, 'Books and Book Owners', p. 248. Rich interest in historiography is a striking a feature of medieval and humanist Scottish culture.

[43] These are, respectively, ISTC, nos il00294000, ih00443000, is00068000, ia01154000, ia00928000; Durkan and Ross, *Early Scottish Libraries*, p. 159.

[44] St Andrews: University Library, MS. PA6295.A2A00; N. R. Ker et al., *Medieval Manuscripts in British Libraries*, 5 vols (Oxford, 1969–2002), iv (1992), pp. 250–22. It is transcribed from a copy of ISTC, no. ic00558000, on which, see M. Flodr, *Incunabula Classicorum: Wiegendrucke der griechischen und römischen Literatur* (Amsterdam, 1973), p. 111. The quotation is from Mason, *Kingship and the Commonweal*, p. 118.

[45] Lyall, 'Books and Book Owners', pp. 248–49. Whitelaw seems also to have added *sophian* and *phronesin* to complete the Latin text on fol. 14^r.

owned copies of Suetonius' *Lives of the Caesars*,[46] Raimondo Marliani's index to the *Commentaries* of Julius Caesar,[47] an *Ilias Latina*,[48] and the histories of Orosius, Florus and Cornelius Nepos.[49] The copy of Marliani was probably written by a Scottish scribe, in 1481.[50] All four manuscripts contain marginalia in Whitelaw's hand, and the Suetonius and the collection of histories are richly annotated. The consistent interlinear and marginal annotation suggests Whitelaw was an attentive reader of the books he owned.

Lyall has further observed that Whitelaw's manuscripts are also characterised by the consistent introduction of 'features

[46] NLS, MS. Adv. 18.3.11; Durkan and Russell, 'Further Additions (Including Manuscripts)', p. 89; Lyall, 'Books and Book Owners', pp. 248–49; see also I. C. Cunningham, 'Latin Classical Manuscripts in the National Library of Scotland', *Scriptorium,* xxvii (1973), pp. 64–90 at p. 72.

[47] NLS, MS. Adv. 18.3.10; Durkan and Russell, 'Further Additions (Including Manuscripts)', p. 89. The manuscript also contains a copy of Paulus Diaconus' *Historia Romana*, though it is uncertain whether the two sections were already associated in Whitelaw's time and only the Marliani *Index* is accompanied by annotation in his hand. See Cunningham, 'Latin Classical Manuscripts', pp. 71–72, and Lyall, 'Books and Book Owners', pp. 248–49.

[48] NLS, MS. Adv. 18.4.8; Durkan and Russell, 'Further Additions (Including Manuscripts)', p. 89. The manuscript contains a collection of disparate material, including ANTONIO BECCARIA's translation of Dionysius Periegetes. The material, in four different hands, has been bound together since at least the sixteenth century, but only the *Ilias Latina* bears Whitelaw's marginal annotation. See Cunningham, 'Latin Classical Manuscripts', pp. 75–76, and Lyall, 'Books and Book Owners', pp. 248–49. The annotation of the *Ilias Latina* is discussed by S. Mapstone, 'The Origins of Criseyde' in J. Wogan-Browne et al. ed., *Medieval Women: texts and contexts in Late Medieval Britain. Essays for Felicity Riddy* (Turnhout, 2000), pp. 131–47, esp. pp. 131–32, 147.

[49] Aberdeen: University Library, MS. 214; M. R. James, *A Catalogue of the Medieval Manuscripts in the University of Aberdeen Library* (Cambridge, 1932), p. 60, suggests that the three histories were '[v]ery likely all copied from printed texts.'

[50] Lyall, 'Scottish Students and Masters', p. 69.

apparently intended to give a humanist appearance to the text'.[51] The Cicero manuscript, for instance, has been written by two scribal hands, one of which, Lyall's Scribe II, responsible for the bulk of the manuscript, evinces a highly suggestive mingling of distinctively humanist and native, 'Bastard Scoticana,' letter formations.[52] The humanist forms predominate in the first folios for which the scribe is responsible but are gradually displaced by the older Scottish forms. At folio 153^r, where the copy of the *De fato* begins, following the conclusion of the *Somnium Scipionis*, the humanist letters return but again quickly recede. The evidence suggests a scribe struggling to adopt an unfamiliar script, prompted, perhaps by his patron, perhaps in part by the form of the printed material in front of him, to attempt to achieve a manuscript of both humanist content and appearance. The Suetonius, Marliani, and *Ilias Latina* manuscripts evince similar scribal struggles to impose apparently unfamiliar quasi-humanist forms upon a differently trained native hand, and the presentation of the historical works in his manuscript of Orosius and others combines a native Scots 'Academica' script in which the texts themselves are written with titles 'and a short poem [...] in a more calligraphically formed quasi-humanist style, apparently adopted here as a display script.'[53] The manuscripts stage a suggestive collision of humanist aspiration and more traditional local habit.

Elphinstone, who also visited Italy – he travelled to Rome in 1494–95 to obtain a papal Bull of foundation for the university in Aberdeen – seems largely to have owned books of a less obviously humanistic stamp, pertaining rather to his

---

[51] Lyall, 'Books and Book Owners', pp. 248–49 at p. 249. See also below, pp. 319–22.

[52] Lyall, 'Books and Book Owners', p. 249. This scribe writes fol. 81^r–263^v of the manuscript.

[53] Lyall, 'Books and Book Owners', pp. 248–49 at p. 249.

interest in canon law.⁵⁴ He did, however, own a fifteenth-century copy of LORENZO VALLA's *Elegantiae Latinae linguae*, which Lyall suggests may have been made in Scotland or France as early as circa 1470.⁵⁵ And there is further evidence of developing Scottish interest in the traditions of rhetoric. Gilbert Haldane, rector of Dalry and a student at St Andrews in 1478, owned editions, all from the press of Ulrich Zel at Cologne, of Ps-Ciceronian *Liber de proprietatibus terminorum*, the *De uariis loquendi regulis* and *De uariis loquendi figuris* of AGOSTINO DATI, and the *Praecepta de studendi origine* of GUARINO DA VERONA.⁵⁶ William Wawan, official of St Andrews in Lothian, who seems to have been active around 1500, possessed a Venetian copy of Quintilian's *Institutes of Oratory*.⁵⁷ The volumes look forward to the intriguing Scots translation of Donatus' Latin grammar, the *Rudimenta puerorum artem grammaticam*, which was among the works printed by Walter Chepman and Andrew Myllar in 1508.⁵⁸ It has been suggested that the translation was completed by John Vaus, who later compiled several Latin grammars of his own

---

⁵⁴ For Elphinstone's travels in Italy, see Macfarlane, *William Elphinstone and the Kingdom of Scotland*, pp. 290–308. Elphinstone had initially intended to accompany Scheves to Italy at the beginning of 1493. For his library, see Macfarlane, 'William Elphinstone's Library', and Lyall, 'Books and Book Owners', p. 250.

⁵⁵ Aberdeen: University Library, MS. 222, on which see James, *Catalogue*, p. 66; Durkan and Ross, *Early Scottish Libraries*, p. 32; Lyall, 'Books and Book Owners', p. 250. See also pp. 333–34 below.

⁵⁶ These are respectively, ISTC, nos ic00668000 and id00087500; see Durkan and Ross, *Early Scottish Libraries*, p. 110.

⁵⁷ ISTC, no. iq00026000; Durkan and Ross, *Early Scottish Libraries*, p. 158. The book is richly annotated in the hand, most probably Wawan's, which has inscribed 'Liber Willelmi Wawan presbiteri.'

⁵⁸ Only a fragment of the edition now remains in the Aberdeen University Library; see S. Mapstone, 'Introduction: William Dunbar and the book culture of sixteenth-century Scotland' in ead. ed., *William Dunbar, 'The Nobil Poyet': essays in honour of Priscilla Bawcutt* (East Linton, 2001), pp. 1–23 at p. 8.

and was a student at Aberdeen at the very beginning of the sixteenth century.[59]

Hector Boece, who, as we have seen, was teaching at Aberdeen from 1497, inherited Whitelaw's Suetonius and *Ilias Latina* manuscripts and owned a number of other important fifteenth-century Italian humanist volumes: a copy of Pliny's *Historia naturalis* printed at Parma, a Parisian edition of MARSILIO FICINO's *De triplici vita*, and a Venetian copy of MARCANTONIO SABELLICO's *Enneades*.[60] The Sabellico edition passed from Boece to Vaus; it also bears the inscription of another of Boece's colleagues at Aberdeen, David Guthrie, canon of Aberdeen, Provost of Guthrie, and doctor of both Civil and Canon Law.[61] Guthrie had been teaching at the

---

[59] Macfarlane, *William Elphinstone and the Kingdom of Scotland*, pp. 367–69; Mapstone, 'Book Culture of Sixteenth-Century Scotland', p. 8. Vaus's grammars are most fully treated in K. Jensen, 'Text-Books in the Universities: the evidence from the books' in Hellinga and Trapp ed., *Cambridge History of the Book in Britain*, III, pp. 354–79. Vaus is an interesting figure. A number of the books he owned mark him as a product of the humanist culture at Aberdeen led by Elphinstone and Boece: Durkan and Ross, *Early Scottish Libraries*, pp. 155–57, 187; MacQueen, 'Some Aspects of the Early Renaissance in Scotland', p. 209; Bawcutt, *Gavin Douglas*, p. 32. On the other hand, as the translation of the Donatus may suggest and as Jensen illustrates, the influences his grammars evince are not exclusively or unambiguously humanist.

[60] These are, respectively, ISTC, nos ip00792000, if00159000 and is00007000; see Durkan and Ross, *Early Scottish Libraries*, pp. 77–78, and Royan, 'The *Scotorum Historia* of Hector Boece', pp. 319–22. There is a marginal note in the *Enneades* edition not recorded by Durkan and Ross; it is in faded red ink and reads either 'Hector Boetius. 1500' or 'Hector Boetius. 1506' (Edinburgh: University Library, Inc.138, fol. a^r). That Boece's reading of Ficino's *De triplici vita* may have influenced the arrangement and use of the rooms at King's College, Aberdeen, has recently been proposed in J. Stevenson and P. Davidson, 'Ficino in Aberdeen: The Continuing Problem of the Scottish Renaissance', *Journal of the Northern Renaissance*, i (2009), pp. 64–87.

[61] Macfarlane, *William Elphinstone and the Kingdom of Scotland*, pp. 319–21, 377–78; Durkan and Ross, *Early Scottish Libraries*, p. 110.

University from its foundation, before Boece's arrival, and also owned a copy of Suetonius' *Lives of the Caesars*, printed at Treviso in 1480, and Ovid's *Heroides*, printed at Venice in 1481, and a manuscript of the *Metamorphoses*.[62]

To these we may add that Thomas Cranston, canon of St Andrews who became Abbot of Jedburgh in 1484, owned a fifteenth-century edition of Virgil's *Æneid* bound with the satires of Persius and Juvenal.[63] And, in addition to his copy of Livy's *History*, Walter Ogilvie owned a copy of Lorenzo Valla's *Ilias Latina*.[64] We should also note the fine manuscript of Virgil's works, including Maffeo Vegio's 'Thirteenth Book', which was probably owned by James III.[65]

Moreover, the work of Durkan and Ross records a number of later sixteenth-century Scottish owners of important fifteenth-century volumes. Some – most, even – of these may not have been brought to Scotland until after 1500; their

---

Guthrie seems to have owned the manuscript before Boece did, since a marginal note records 'Liber M. Joannis Waus ex dono M. Hecthori Boethii.'

[62] The printed books are, respectively, ISTC, nos is00820000 and io00151500; see Durkan and Ross, *Early Scottish Libraries*, p. 178. The manuscript is now Aberdeen: University Library, MS. 165, on which see James, *Catalogue*, p. 56.

[63] ISTC, nos iv00196700 and ij00636300; Durkan and Ross, *Early Scottish Libraries*, p. 84.

[64] Durkan and Ross, *Early Scottish Libraries*, p. 13; Flodr, *Incunabula classicorum*, p. 204.

[65] Edinburgh: University Library, MS. D.b.VI.8. See C. R. Borland, *A Descriptive Catalogue of the Western Mediaeval Manuscripts in Edinburgh University Library* (Edinburgh, 1916), pp. 281–83 (no. 195), and MacQueen, 'Some Aspects of the Early Renaissance in Scotland', p. 206. For the place of Vegius' book in editions of Virgil, see A. Cox Brinton, *Maphaeus Vegius and his Thirteenth Book of the Aeneid: A Chapter on Virgil in the Renaissance* (Stanford, 1930), pp. 29–30, C. Kallendorf, *In Praise of Aeneas* (Hanover, 1989), pp. 100–28, and Bawcutt, *Gavin Douglas*, pp. 104–05; for the medieval Virgilian tradition more generally, see C. Baswell, *Virgil in Medieval England: Figuring the Aeneid from the Twelfth Century to the Chaucer* (Cambridge, 1995).

earlier provenances, though, are uncertain and the displacement of many of these incunabula by later editions more readily available and more fashionably up-to-date in the sixteenth century might suggest that they had arrived in Scotland while they were still relatively new. Thus, for instance, James Bachelor, vicar, St Andrews diocese, who in 1531 inscribed some verses in his edition of one of Vaus's grammars and who died in 1548, owned a 1494 Venetian edition of Caesar's *Gallic War*.[66] Further fifteenth-century editions of the following works were in the hands of Scottish owners in the middle of the following century: Cicero's *Tusculan Disputations*,[67] and *De officiis*;[68] Quintilian's *Institutes of Oratory*, with the commentaries of Lorenzo Valla and POMPONIUS LAETUS and Giovanni Sulpizio;[69] Sallust's works with the commentaries of Laetus and Josse Bade;[70] the *Liber illustrium uirorum* of Aurelius Victor, though here still attributed to Pliny the Younger;[71] Apuleius' works, edited by

---

[66] ISTC, no. ic00024000; Durkan and Ross, *Early Scottish Libraries*, p. 73.

[67] ISTC, no. ic00663000; Durkan and Ross, *Early Scottish Libraries*, p. 164. This was owned by King's College, Aberdeen.

[68] ISTC, no. ic00610000; Durkan and Ross, *Early Scottish Libraries*, p. 98. This was owned by John Forman, Vicar of Anstruther c. 1550, perhaps born c. 1513.

[69] ISTC, no. iq00030000; Durkan and Ross, *Early Scottish Libraries*, p. 98, and Flodr, *Incunabula classicorum*, pp. 264–65. This was owned by Robert Forman, incorporated as precentor in Glasgow University in 1503 and dean at the University until c. 1529. John Hamilton, regent of the Pedagogy in Glasgow in 1548, owned another copy of this edition; Durkan and Ross, *Early Scottish Libraries*, p. 111. The Edinburgh Dominicans possessed a further copy of the *Institutiones* (Venice?, c. 1470); Ross, 'Libraries of the Scottish Blackfriars', p. 16.

[70] Lyons, 1500, owned by David Abercromby, Principal of Glasgow University in 1517; Durkan and Ross, *Early Scottish Libraries*, p. 66.

[71] ISTC, no. ia01386000; Durkan and Ross, *Early Scottish Libraries*, pp. 103–04. This was owned by Henry Gibson, notary in Glasgow University in 1549 and at St Andrews in 1553.

GIOVANNI ANDREA BUSSI;[72] Vitruvius' *On Architecture*;[73] Frontinus' *De aquaeductibus*, edited by Laetus;[74] LEON BATTISTA ALBERTI's *De re aedificatoria*;[75] the *Cosmographia* of Pomponius Mela;[76] and PICO DELLA MIRANDOLA's *Opera*.[77]

This may seem too speculative. Let us turn again, then, to a work from the very beginning of the sixteenth century to suggest the spread of humanist influence in the final decades of the fifteenth. Gavin Douglas' *Palis of Honoure* was written in 1501; it is an extravagantly learned and allusive poem.[78] Priscilla Bawcutt wryly observes that in its 'bravura' it seems to her 'very much a young man's poem.'[79] Homer, Virgil, Ovid, Lucan, Plautus, Persius, Terence, Donatus, Servius, Valerius

---

[72] ISTC, no. ia00936000; Durkan and Ross, *Early Scottish Libraries*, pp. 140, 184. This was owned by John Rutherford, Provost of St Salvator's College in 1560 and previously lecturer at the College and at the universities of Bordeaux, Coimbra, and Paris.

[73] ISTC, no. iv00306000; Durkan and Ross, *Early Scottish Libraries*, pp. 128–29; see also Ditchburn, p. 132. This and the two following volumes were owned by John Marjoribanks, mid-sixteenth-century lawyer, recipient of a royal gift in 1555.

[74] ISTC, no. if00324000.

[75] ISTC, no. ia00215000.

[76] Printed c.1478; this was also owned by Henry Gibson; Durkan and Ross, *Early Scottish Libraries*, pp. 103–04, and Flodr, *Incunabula classicorum*, p. 215.

[77] ISTC, no. ip00634000; Durkan, 'Further Additions', p. 98. This was owned by the Stirling Franciscans.

[78] At the end of the *Eneados* Douglas tells us not only that that work was completed in 1513 but that also that the earlier one was written 'weil twelf ȝheris tofor' (Douglas, *Virgil's Aeneid*, 'Tyme, space and dait', ll.1–4). Douglas's reading has been meticulously reconstructed by Bawcutt, not only in her book-length study, *Gavin Douglas*, but also in P. Bawcutt, 'The 'Library' of Gavin Douglas' in A. J. Aitken, M. P. McDiarmid, and D. S. Thomson ed., *Bards and Makars: Scottish Language and Literature, Medieval and Renaissance* (Glasgow, 1977), pp. 107–26, in ead., 'New Light on Gavin Douglas' in MacDonald et al. ed., *The Renaissance in Scotland*, pp. 95–106, and in the notes to her editions of *The Shorter Poems of Gavin Douglas*: see below, n. 84.

[79] Bawcutt, *Gavin Douglas*, p. 67.

Flaccus, Cato, Quintilian, Juvenal, Martial, Statius, Horace, Cato, Cicero, Petrarch and Boccaccio, as well as POGGIO BRACCIOLINI, Lorenzo Valla, Fausto Andrelini and Pomponius Laetus all appear in the poem as figures in attendance at the court of Calliope.[80] Quite how well – and in what form – Douglas knew the works of *all* of these writers must remain open to question. If he had read Homer, for instance, it was almost certainly in the form of an *Ilias Latina*, since there is no evidence that Douglas could read Greek, and the allusions to the *Thebaid* within the poem suggest familiarity with the mediations of Chaucer, in *Troilus and Criseyde*, as much as with the work of Statius itself.[81] His familiarity with many of the other classical writers, though, is confirmed by more substantial reference and allusion elsewhere in his work. His knowledge of Poggio and Valla is corroborated by references in the *Eneados* and in John Mair's *Dialogus*.[82] There is little reason to doubt his acquaintance with the work of Andrelini. It is possible that if Douglas did not know Petrarch's Italian *Trionfi*, as R. D. S. Jack has proposed, that he was at least familiar with the pictorial tradition that surrounded

---

[80] G. Douglas, *The Shorter Poems of Gavin Douglas*, ed. P. Bawcutt [Scottish Text Society, 5th ser., ii (revised edition)] (Edinburgh, 2003), pp. 60–63 (ll. 895–915).

[81] Douglas' claim in the opening prologue of the *Eneados* that he had been requested by Lord Henry Sinclair to 'translait Virgill or Homeir' should almost certainly be understood in these terms too: as imagining a translation from Latin into the vernacular (Douglas, *Virgil's Aeneid*, 1.Pro.86–88). On his knowledge of Statius, see Bawcutt, 'The 'Library' of Gavin Douglas', p. 112.

[82] Douglas, *Virgil's Aeneid*, 1.Pro.108 and 1.Pro.127–30; the *Dialogus* is printed in J. Mair, *A History of Greater Britain by John Major, As Well England as Scotland Compiled from the Ancient Authorities by John Major, by Name Indeed a Scot, but by Profession a Theologian, 1521*, trans. A. Constable, ed. A. J. G. Mackay [Scottish Historical Society, x] (Edinburgh, 1892), pp. 425–28; see Bawcutt, *Gavin Douglas*, pp. 28–29.

the work.[83] And the *Palis of Honoure* itself almost certainly reflects the influence of Boccaccio's *De montibus*, and, perhaps most impressively of all, of Raffaele Regio's recent humanist commentary on Ovid's *Metamorphoses*.[84] In 1515, on trial before the Lords of Council, Douglas would declare that he had 'passit his tyme in Scotland, Ingland, France and Rome,' but the evidence suggests that Douglas was in Paris only after 1505 and in Rome later still, in which case the *Palis of Honoure* surely compellingly suggests the rich array of material already available within Scotland itself.[85]

This has remained, by and large, slightly inert work, recording the range of humanist material available within late-fifteenth-century Scotland rather than exploring the more imaginative uses to which humanist influence was put. This is, in large part, a reflection of the extant evidence: the creative achievement of the *Palis of Honoure*, *per se*, for example, remains outside our remit and the highpoints of Scottish humanism – the Latin poetry of James Foullis and the Livian

---

[83] R. D. S. Jack, *The Italian Influence on Scottish Literature* (Edinburgh, 1972), pp. 23–27; Bawcutt, *Gavin Douglas*, pp. 50–51. On the pictorial tradition, see K. Eisenbichler and A. A. Iannucci ed., *Petrarch's Triumphs: allegory and spectacle* (Ottawa, 1990).

[84] For Boccaccio's *De montibus*, see Douglas, *Shorter Poems*, pp. 194–96, 305–06, 318–21; Jack, *Italian Influence*, p. 22, and S. Cairns, '*The Palice of Honour* of Gavin Douglas, Ovid, and Raffaello Regio's Commentary on Ovid's *Metamorphoses*', *Res Publica Litterarum*, vii (1984), pp. 17–38 at pp.19–23. On Regio, see Cairns, '*The Palice of Honour* of Gavin Douglas', pp. 17–38, and Douglas, *Shorter Poems*, pp. 302–06. Bawcutt, in Douglas, *Shorter Poems*, pp. 302–04, discusses the early publication history of the commentary: the first authorised edition was published in 1493 in Venice by Bernardinus Benalius (ISTC, no. io00189000), though illegal editions had been printed in 1492 and 1493. It was repeatedly printed in the following ten years; Bawcutt observes '[i]t is difficult (and probably impossible) to ascertain which of these editions Douglas consulted' (Douglas, *Shorter Poems*, p. 303).

[85] R. K. Hannay ed., *Acts of the Lords of Council in Public Affairs, 1501–1554* (Edinburgh, 1932), p. 41; Bawcutt, *Gavin Douglas*, pp. 27–28.

historiography of Hector Boece, or Douglas's and John Bellenden's translations of Virgil and Livy – belong to the sixteenth century.[86] That the annotation of the humanist volumes is predominantly of the '*ordinatio*'-type, or otherwise cursory, also limits the possibilities for more ambitious interpretation of late-fifteenth-century Scottish reading of the kind exemplified in Daniel Wakelin's *Humanism, Reading, and English Literature 1430–1530*.[87] I should like to turn, though, in conclusion, briefly to two further aspects of early Scottish humanism which may suggest avenues for further enquiry.

The first of these is the vernacular poetry of Robert Henryson, though here again, on the face of it, the evidence might be deemed to be negative. Repeated claims have been made for humanist influence on Henryson's work: parallels have been posited with Boccaccio,[88] Marsilio Ficino,[89] POLITIAN,[90] and Pico della Mirandola.[91] The suggestions are

[86] For Foullis's poetry, see J. Ijsewijn and D. F. S. Thomson, 'The Latin Poems of Jacobus Follisius or James Foullis of Edinburgh', *Humanistica Lovaniensia*, xxiv (1975), pp. 102–52; for Boece's history, see H. Boece, *Scotorum Historiae* (Paris, 1527); for Bellenden's Livy, see J. Bellenden, *Livy's History of Rome, The First Five Books Translated into Scots by John Bellenden, 1533*, ed. W. A. Craigie, 2 vols [Scottish Text Society, xlvii, li] (Edinburgh, 1900–03).

[87] D. Wakelin, *Humanism, Reading, and English Literature, 1430–1530* (Oxford, 2007).

[88] J. MacQueen, *Robert Henryson: a study of the major narrative poems* (Oxford, 1967), pp. 18, 28, 47–50, 95–98; id., 'Some Aspects of the Early Renaissance in Scotland', p. 209; id., 'Neoplatonism and Orphism in Fifteenth-Century Scotland', *Scottish Studies*, xx (1976), pp. 69–89 at p. 86; id., 'Literature of Fifteenth-Century Scotland,' p. 204.

[89] MacQueen, 'Neoplatonism and Orphism.'

[90] Jack, *Italian Influence*, pp. 9–14.

[91] S. R. McKenna, 'Robert Henryson, Pico della Mirandola, and Late Fifteenth-Century Heroic Humanism' in G. Caie, R. J. Lyall, S. Mapstone, and K. Simpson ed., *The European Sun: Proceedings of the Seventh International Conference on Medieval and Renaissance Scottish Language and Literature* (East Linton, 2001), pp. 232–41.

important, not only for the possibility they propose of more imaginative engagement with the developments of humanism but also for the way they look forward to the 'vernacular humanism' which is such a striking feature of sixteenth-century Scottish culture.[92] Unfortunately, however, none of the suggestions seems quite to withstand sustained scrutiny.[93] What emerges most strongly, though, is a sense of the convergence between important humanist achievements and Henryson's art. This may be especially true of McKenna's account of the 'heroic humanism' of Henryson's poetry. McKenna argues that Henryson articulates 'the human capacity for self-determination' in a manner which invites comparison with Pico della Mirandola's *De hominis dignitate*.[94]

[92] I have taken the term from Bawcutt, *Gavin Douglas*, p. 36; the importance of Scottish vernacular humanism may be seen at once in the achievements of Douglas and Bellenden.

[93] The suggestion that the catalogue of the Muses in Henryson's *Orpheus and Eurydice* reflects the influence of Boccaccio's *De genealogia deorum* must be rejected now: D. Allen Wright, 'Henryson's *Orpheus and Eurydice* and the Tradition of the Muses', *Medium Ævum*, xl (1971), pp. 41–47 has demonstrated Henryson's reliance on the *Graecismus* of Eberhard of Béthune and his school, and all of the other parallels MacQueen notes between the works of Henryson and Boccaccio have been persuasively challenged by R. J. Lyall, 'Henryson and Boccaccio: a problem in the study of sources', *Anglia*, xcix (1981), pp. 38–59. Jack's suggestion of Politian's influence has been strongly challenged by R. J. Lyall, 'Did Poliziano influence Henryson's *Orpheus and Eurydices?*' *Forum for Modern Language Studies*, xv (1979), pp. 207–21. See also A. Petrina, "Aristeus Pastor Adamans': The Human Setting in Henryson's *Orpheus and Eurydice* and its Kinship with Poliziano's *Fabula di Orpheo*', *Forum for Modern Language Studies*, xxxviii (2002), pp. 382–95 and T. Rutledge, 'Robert Henryson's *Orpheus and Eurydice*: A Northern Humanism?' *Forum for Modern Language Studies*, xxxviii (2002), pp. 396–412. I argue there, as here, that the novelty of Henryson's poem – attested to in Douglas's reference to it as Henryson's 'New Orpheus' (Douglas, *Virgil's Aeneid*, *ad*.1.1.13) – may merit more attention. There are suggestive similarities between Poliziano's and Henryson's works which may reflect not influence but convergence of approach.

[94] McKenna, 'Henryson, Pico', p. 232.

In fact, however, in Henryson's poetry that articulation is most forcibly realised through manipulation of very traditional, medieval material: by opposing a morally accountable will or intellect to a recalcitrant affection or appetite. The strain of Augustinian pessimism which runs through Henryson's poetry must also seriously undermine any celebration of an 'heroic humanism.' What McKenna points to here, I think, is the extraordinarily subtle way in which Henryson balances a sense of essential human weakness with the moral imperative of self-determination. Henryson's vision is *tragicomic* (in the most serious sense of that term), rather than humanist, and in pursuing the possibility of new humanist influences on his poetry we run the risk of failing to attend sufficiently carefully to the arrestingly powerful manner in which it exploits the far-from-exhausted potential of older medieval and scholastic resources.[95] The availability of new humanist materials in late-fifteenth-century Scotland accompanied rather than displaced the continuing vitality of older traditions; it is in this heterogeneity that its greatest and distinctive richness lies.

The second aspect emerges directly from Mason's extremely suggestive account of '*Regnum et Imperium*: Humanism and the Political Culture of Early Renaissance Scotland.'[96] Mason provocatively associates the development of Scottish humanism not simply with the laicisation of Scottish culture (he apologises for the ugliness of the phrase himself), but also with the growing imperialism of Stewart royal rule, an imperialism which 'crystallis[ed] around the Roman law maxim *rex in regno suo est imperator*.'[97] The association is a challenge, of course, to

---

[95] The slipperiness which the term 'humanism' assumes in such a context suggests I may simply be repeating the arguments of Douglas Gray in, for instance, 'Humanism and Humanisms in the Literature of Late Medieval England' in S. Rossi and D. Savoia ed., *Italy and the English Renaissance* (Milan, 1989), pp. 25–44.

[96] Mason, *Kingship and Commonweal*, pp. 104–38.

[97] Mason, *Kingship and Commonweal*, pp. 106, 108.

the assumptions of a republican 'civic humanism.'[98] In the context of Scottish humanism, it is especially interesting for the manner in which it looks forward to Bellenden's translation of Livy, for that translation evinces a complex balance, articulating a republican historiography in which the deposition and displacement of a king is centrally presented, while also dressing that historical narrative in the much more traditional and reassuring terms of Scottish 'advice to princes' literature. It would be extremely interesting were the reticent and resistant annotations of Whitelaw's Cicero – or of Forman's *De Officiis* or of Ogilvie's Livy or of any of these other works – to be found to offer an incisive intervention on this territory. That late-fifteenth-century Scots were reading pertinent and provocative material is sure; how they were reading it remains to be explored further.

---

[98] For brief discussion of civic humanism, see pp. 23–24 above and the secondary works cited there.

ENGLAND: HUMANISM BEYOND WEISS

DANIEL WAKELIN

An important moment in the story of humanism in sixteenth-century England is the foundation in 1517 by Richard Fox, bishop of Winchester, of Corpus Christi College, Oxford, designed to foster the *studia humanitatis*, and extremely successful in doing so.[1] It is intriguing, then, to find Fox making another gift, this time to a collegiate church, in the fifteenth century. In 1499, while bishop of Durham, Fox gave to the church at Bishop Auckland a donation of fifty-three books.[2] Yet something seems different: for in 1499 the books he gave, and so presumably the thinking he hoped to foster, were largely in theology and canon law, subjects useful to the church but seemingly devoid of humanist influence. What causes the difference between the two gifts? Is it geographical: the difference between cultural centre and periphery? Is it institutional and practical: the differing needs of a university college and a collegiate church? Or is it that the turn of the fifteenth century into the sixteenth effected a transformation in Fox's concerns? Is this the shift from 'medieval' to 'Renaissance' in English culture? This donation could be an iconic moment for the story of humanism in the fifteenth century, for England in that century is still often seen as resistant to the influence of

---

[1] J. K. McConica, *English Humanists and Reformation Politics under Henry VIII and Edward VI* (Oxford, 1965), pp. 80–83.

[2] M. P. Howden ed., *The Register of Richard Fox, Lord Bishop of Durham 1494–1501* [Surtees Society, cxlvii] (Durham, 1932), pp. 93–96, reedited by James Willoughby, ed., *The Libraries of Collegiate Churches, Corpus of British Medieval Library Catalogues*, 15 (London: British Library, 2013), SC212.

humanism, unlike the England of the age of Corpus Christi College.

In fact the difference is not so all-or-nothing: in the foundation of Corpus Christi College and other secular colleges we might find some influence of monastic practice,[3] and in Fox's donation to Bishop Auckland there is some slight humanist influence, if we look carefully. At least two books would let the clergy pursue the *studia humanitatis*: Cicero's *De officiis* with the commentary of PIETRO MARSO, and another volume containing both Cicero's letters with a printed commentary and Silius Italicus' *Punica*.[4] To espy such tiny signs of humanist learning in fifteenth-century England, we need to look, if not through rose-tinted spectacles, then at least through ones which allow us to see the subtle humanist colouring in the records of the period – rather than blanching out any signs of humanism because they are not as bold or bright as some later shining examples, such as Corpus Christi College.

For when we look at a record such as Fox's donation, we might see this as *two intriguing volumes, at least* or we might see it as *only two books, after all*. On the one hand, this donation might be evidence that, even in a church in the north of England far from the richer cultural centres of certain universities and cathedrals, there were some tools for humanist study. This donation, then, could show the widespread dispersal of humanist study. Though there seem to be only two humanist volumes, one is declaredly a *Sammelband* (a book which binds together several printed editions) and the second is an edition of *De officiis* which circulated in England with other Ciceronian works which seem to be printed to travel together: so we might wonder whether there were even more classical and

---

[3] J. G. Clark, 'Monasteries and Secular Education in Late Medieval England' in J. Burton and K. Stöber ed., *Monasteries and Society in the British Isles in the Later Middle Ages* (Woodbridge, 2008), pp. 145–67 at p. 165.

[4] Howden ed., *Register of Richard Fox*, p. 94. The donation also included Boethius' *De Consolatione Philosophiae*, which might reflect an interest in antiquity.

humanist texts hidden in *Sammelbände* in Fox's gift.[5] That is the positive interpretation. But on the other hand, these classical texts and humanist commentaries comprise only two volumes out of fifty-three more proper to the business of the church. And because Cicero's *De officiis* and *Epistolae ad familiares* tended to serve rudimentary grammatical and rhetorical study,[6] then humanism might only be contributing something superficial – polishing the clergy's Latin, with comments on Cicero's style and his exemplary correspondence. Whether or not we think that this or other records reveal the spread of humanism in fifteenth-century England depends in part on the perspective from which we read them.

[5] The *secundo folio* of Fox's copy of Cicero's *De Officiis* is given as 'Sed eciam' which probably identifies it as Cicero, *De Officiis*, with commentary by Pietro Marso (Louvain: Johannes de Westfalia, 2nd press, [c. 1483]), of which the second printed folio begins 'sed etia*m*' (sig. a3r). As the Incunabula Short Title Catalogue suggests (ISTC, no. ic00599000), this edition is often bound with *Paradoxa* and with *De Amicitia* and *De Senectute* similarly presented with commentaries, from the same press and presumed date: see for example Cambridge: University Library, printed book Inc. 3.F.2.2 [3184], [3183] and [3182]. Incidentally, the Cambridge binding has the name of John Gunthorpe, whom Fox knew (as noted at n. 85–89 below) and who had died the previous year (1498), although I know of no evidence that this copy passed to Fox or Bishop Auckland. The *secundo folio* of Fox's copy of Cicero's *Epistolae* with commentary is given as 'qui cum imperio' which probably identifies it as Cicero, *Epistolae*, with commentary by Ubertino Clerico (Venice: Baptista de Tortis, 24 May 1485), where the second folio of the text and commentary proper (after the dedicatory epistles) begins 'Qui cum imperio' (sig. a4r). A copy of this work owned by Fox is now Oxford: Corpus Christi College, printed book Φ.C.5.8, though it is not bound with Silius Italicus. D. E. Rhodes, *A Catalogue of Incunabula in All the Libraries of Oxford University outside the Bodleian* (Oxford, 1982), nos 546, 547, 552 lists this and two other incunables of Cicero's *Epistolae* now at Corpus Christi College, one bound with the works of Cyprianus (Rhodes, *Catalogue*, no. 647). I thank Joanna Snelling and James Willoughby for their kind assistance in confirming the details of these books at Corpus Christi College, which I was unable to consult myself.

[6] D. Wakelin, *Humanism, Reading & English Literature 1430–1530* (Oxford, 2007), pp. 144–45.

Such evidence of humanism looks meagre, in particular, from the vantage point of the book which has hitherto offered the best insight into this subject: that of Roberto Weiss's *Humanism in England during the Fifteenth Century*. In that book Weiss espies innumerable rich details of humanist reading and writing but nonetheless claims that 'Pure humanists did not exist in England'. He argues that 'modest and amateurish' English humanists in the fifteenth century were interested only in style rather than deeper ideas and that they diluted their studies of antiquity with 'co-operation [. . .] with scholasticism' and with 'utilitarian ideals' of using the studies for statecraft or churchcraft.[7] This could well describe the offering of Cicero by Fox to the church of Bishop Auckland. The contrast between Weiss's glittering panorama and his disdainful regard has been noted before (as David Rundle comments in his introduction to the fourth edition of *Humanism in England*), and the influence of his disdain is considerable.[8] On the one hand, Weiss's dismissals – of impure humanism, of dilution with scholasticism, of banausic utility – lie behind the still-repeated claims that there was little humanist influence in fifteenth-century English culture. On the other hand, it may be that the few more brilliant examples of humanism that Weiss shone light on have blinded us to signs of humanism in the shadows.

For the most distinguished studies since Weiss's have also tended to focus on the most distinguished humanists: royal or noble patrons who received copious books, dedications and letters; cardinals, bishops and other well-heeled and well-connected churchmen who had access – often as ambassadors – to books and ideas from abroad; a few inventive writers of voluminous marginalia or dialogues. The story customarily begins with Humfrey, duke of Gloucester, uncle of Henry VI, who began patronizing Italian scholars and buying Italian copies of classical and new humanist texts in bulk in the 1430s and early 1440s. The story then proceeds through the scholars

---

[7] Weiss[4], pp. 275, 276.

[8] Weiss[4], pp. 9–10.

inspired by his books as they became available in Oxford (such as John Farley, Thomas Chaundler) and who undertook their own pilgrimages to study or buy books in Italy (John Tiptoft, John Gunthorpe). It concludes with a further set of cliques or influential people in various ecclesiastical ivory towers: a handful of bishops (William Gray, Thomas Bekynton, John Russell, James Goldwell), abbots (William Sellyng, perhaps John Whethamstede) and their secretaries or foreign scribes (John Free, Thomas Candour, Theoderic Werken, Pieter Meghen). Their humanist studies blossomed into the mastery of *littera antiqua*, the annotation of recherché classical works in Italian manuscripts and (later) Continental printed editions and the composition of Latin letters among themselves and their Italian correspondents. Their books are often gorgeous – in their Florentine illuminations; their words are sometimes charming – especially in a few playfully flattering letters; they are sometimes tinglingly alert to political turmoil – in a few annotations. This is the story told with brilliance by Roberto Weiss and still, in essence, retold in recent surveys of humanism in English intellectual life.[9]

Seventy years of research since Weiss wrote have uncovered further riches – have, for example, uncovered just how very many humanist books were circulating at the University of Oxford.[10] The riches found there and elsewhere belie Weiss's gloomy observation that 'Pure humanists did not exist in England'. Yet this is still Weiss's story; and as much as Weiss's dismissal might obscure the humanist influences in fifteenth-century England, so might these riches throw them into shadow. Firstly, it would be easy to dismiss this story as one of élite people and élite books in a tightly woven clique – irrelevant

[9] J.B. Trapp, 'The humanist book' in *The Cambridge History of the Book in Britain, III: 1400–1557*, ed. L. Hellinga and J.B. Trapp (Cambridge, 1999), pp. 285–315, esp. pp. 292–302, and D. Gray, *Later Medieval English Literature* (Oxford, 2008), pp. 74–79, give excellent summaries.

[10] R. M. Thomson, 'The Reception of the Italian Renaissance in Fifteenth-Century Oxford: The Evidence of Books and Book-Lists', *IMU*, xlvii (2007), pp. 59–75.

to understanding the rest of fifteenth-century culture and perhaps irrelevant to our own 'post-humanist' age. Yet, secondly, a narrow focus on the most élite activity might blinker us to the range, different depths and significance of humanism in fifteenth-century England. To counteract that, much interesting recent research has begun to broaden Weiss's field of vision. One line of enquiry has been to look for evidence of humanist scholarship among a wider personnel: most importantly, David Rundle has shown the dangers of 'magnate attraction', the attraction to a few scholarly heroes – mostly royal or noble magnates such as Humfrey, duke of Gloucester – whereas it is possible to find people of lesser rank and wealth engaged in the *studia humanitatis* – before, or in milieux far from, Humfrey, duke of Gloucester.[11] In another line, various people have explored humanist influences on less obviously humanist elements of fifteenth-century English culture – especially on political ideas.[12] And other elements might also yield evidence of humanist influences – the study of history, geography and medicine; the growing use of English for literary

[11] D. Rundle, 'Humanism before the Tudors: on nobility and the reception of the *studia humanitatis* in fifteenth-century England' in J. Woolfson ed., *Reassessing Tudor Humanism* (Basingstoke, 2002), pp. 22–42, with quotation at p. 23. For fuller information, see D. Rundle, 'Of Republics and Tyrants: aspects of *quattrocento* humanist writings and their reception in England, *c.* 1400–*c.* 1460' (unpublished D.Phil. thesis, University of Oxford, 1997), with a summary in his 'On the Difference between Virtue and Weiss: humanist texts in England during the fifteenth century' in D. E. S. Dunn ed., *Courts, Counties and the Capital in the Later Middle Ages* (Stroud, 1996), pp. 181–203.

[12] D. Rundle, 'Was There a Renaissance Style of Politics in Fifteenth-Century England?' and J. Watts, '*The Policie in Christen Remes*: Bishop Russell's parliamentary sermons of 1483–84', both in G. W. Bernard and S. J. Gunn ed., *Authority and Consent in Tudor England: essays presented to C. S. L. Davies* (Aldershot, 2002), pp. 15–59; P. Strohm, *Politique: Languages of Statecraft between Chaucer and Shakespeare* (Notre Dame, IN, 2005), pp. 17–18; Wakelin, *Humanism*, pp. 19–21, 89–92, 111–124, 149–57, 192–93; D. Starkey, 'England' in R. Porter and M. Teich ed., *The Renaissance in National Context* (Cambridge, 1992), pp. 146–63 at pp. 160–61.

and official purposes; the numerous new schools and colleges; shifts in theology and in the more practical processes of churchmanship.[13] We can look beyond the dedicated scholars of the *studia humanitatis* for people who engaged in such studies less concertedly, or beyond classical scholarship closely defined, to humanist influences in scattered art-forms, styles, places.

To sample just one region: in the mid-fifteenth-century in East Anglia there was a translation by a Suffolk poet of Claudian's hexameters into unrhymed English verse; there was a garden plotted in the new Italianate manner in the Cambridgeshire countryside; there was a tapestry of Camillus and the Siege of Falerii in a Norfolk manor. Yet it would be easy to miss these imitations of antiquity in English literature, landscape and the decorative arts, for each survives in only slender evidence: the translation of Claudian survives in only one manuscript; the Italianate garden, which might have belonged to John Tiptoft, earl of Worcester, is visible only to aerial photography; the tapestry in the castle of Sir John Fastolf at Caister is recorded only, and misspelled, in an inventory –and perhaps alluded to in an English political treatise by Fastolf's secretary, William Worcester.[14] Moreover, each imitation of antiquity is diluted among other things: the translation of Claudian was made in a house of Augustinian friars, probably by a poet who more voluminously composed saints' lives; the tapestry of Fastolf is less famous than his military and legal exploits. Only Tiptoft's garden fits the common impression of

---

[13] On many of these influences, still vital is D. Hay, 'England and the Humanities in the Fifteenth Century' in id., *Renaissance Essays* (London, 1988), pp. 169–231.

[14] Respectively Wakelin, *Humanism*, pp. 67–80; S. Oosthuizen and C. Taylor, '"John O'Gaunt's House", Bassingbourn, Cambridgeshire: a fifteenth-century landscape', *Landscape History*, xxii (2000), pp. 61–76 at p. 72; A. Hawkyard, 'Sir John Fastolf's "Gret Mansion by me late edified": Caister Castle, Norfolk' in L. Clark ed., *Of Mice and Men: Image, Belief and Regulation in Late Medieval England* (Woodbridge, 2005), pp. 39–68 at p. 60.

its owner's humanist predilections, but it has been little noted amid studies of his collection of books.

However, such chaotic and fragmented evidence is important, because it suggests that we might look for the study and imitation of antiquity in less obvious records or sources like the note of Fox's donation to Bishop Auckland: terse wills and inventories, letters in English, conventional obituaries, cathedral records. They all need to be scrutinized closely – and sometimes interpreted speculatively. For we might well ask whether a tapestry or garden which we cannot see for ourselves could be reliable evidence of humanist influence. Moreover, we might worry that such evidence also suggests that humanism flourished in fifteenth-century England not only in pure-bred form but in hybrid varieties, grafted onto other intellectual trends. We are less clearly looking at the 'Pure' *studia humanitatis*. We might ask whether a poem in English, rather than Latin or Greek, is truly the concern of a humanist, or merely of a popularizer who was, as Weiss puts it, 'utilitarian' in using his studies for common purposes. So this chapter looks beyond the evidence of more clearly defined humanism to the blurred edges where we see the *studia humanitatis* in dilution, but thereby in much wider diffusion. For it is in hybrid and dispersed forms that humanism is important in England.

Defining humanism

Oddly, both the breadth of the influence and the hybridity of it are betrayed by the more familiar records of humanism in its more focused, élite varieties and so it is to them that this chapter first digresses. The Italian authors who introduce the *studia humanitatis* for English patrons or readers often define those studies in a circumscribed way, because such authors are the specialists, and because they need to make clear to patrons what they are introducing. And, as these authors also boast that their studies are novel, they often thereby imply that humanism is rare in England, unfamiliar to their patrons. These implications of circumscription and rarity arise most influentially in the letters to Humfrey, duke of Gloucester. The writers around

Humfrey have a clear motive, in seeking his patronage, to portray their scholarship as somehow distinctive and new. Yet, as they are addressing a powerful duke, there is also a need to flatter him by hinting that humanism is not so new to *him*, and so their letters which introduce humanist texts to Humfrey curiously suggest more familiarity with such things than a letter of introduction might. For example, when PIER CANDIDO DECEMBRIO offers his translation of Plato's *Republic* to Humfrey in 1437, he seems to claim that humanist scholarship will introduce something novel and distinct:

> Quo quidem opere nil excellentius, nil utilius, nil preclarius te unquam vidisse confiteberis, aut legisse et vere nosces non frustra tanti philosophi nomen in ore Ambrosii, Hieronimi, Augustini percrebuisse, non frustra etiam antiquis et eruditis viris fuisse cordi. Nam si eloquentiam queris, hic lacteus est fons [. . .]¹⁵

> You will grant that you have never seen or read any work more excellent, useful or outstanding than this one, and you will truly realise that it was not for nothing that the name of so great a philosopher was often on the lips of Ambrose, Jerome or Augustine and not for nothing was it dear to the heart of ancient and learned men. For if you seek eloquence, here is the milky spring [. . .]

Yet this letter also hints that the *studia humanitatis* might not be that fresh, as one of the most important classical texts is introduced as something familiar from Christian theological ones: Plato's ideas could already be found by the Greekless in the works of the Fathers. This letter is not unique in making such a connexion: for example, another Italian mediating between Humfrey and Decembrio suggested that translating Plato could be a mere trial for something translated 'more loftily' ('altius') from a Christian text – and he commended Humfrey

---

[15] A. Sammut, *Unfredo duca du Gloucester e gli umanisti italiani* (Padua, 1980), pp. 181 (ll, 28–32). J. Hankins, *Plato in the Italian Renaissance*, 2 vols (Leiden, 1990), i, pp. 119–29, Rundle, 'Of Republics and Tyrants', i, pp. 194–229, and S. Saygin, *Humphrey, Duke of Gloucester (1390–1447) and the Italian Humanists* (Leiden, 2002), pp. 218–32, give various contexts.

for extirpating heresy.[16] Observing this connexion between Plato and the Church Fathers was perhaps a defensive response to criticisms of Plato's immorality by other Italian scholars.[17] More positively, the observation suggests that not all the humanist studies Humfrey sponsored were distinct from the theological learning of the day.[18] As several examples below suggest, the study of the Fathers served as a Trojan horse for the *studia humanitatis*, and the classical studies advanced theology.

Nor were these studies unfamiliar to the patron himself, for Decembrio asserts that Humfrey is already aware of their benefits: he dedicates his rendering of Plato to Humfrey not because Humfrey is ignorant of Greek philosophy but because Humfrey has had some difficult experience with it: LEONARDO BRUNI had (Decembrio claims) promised to dedicate his translation of Aristotle's *Politics* to the duke but had then failed to do so; it is this slight which Decembrio insists he will put right.[19] And Decembrio opens his letter with the necessary courtesy that already 'the glittering fame of the Duke's virtues has shone forth among all Italians' ('Clarissima apud Italos omnes virtutis tue fama percrebuit)'. That he uses same verb – 'percrebuit', 'percrebuisse' – of Humfrey and Plato makes them sound similar in renown.[20] So Humfrey is said already to be

---

[16] Sammut ed., *Unfredo*, p. 178 (ll, 28–6). Humfrey did also later receive translations of St Athanasius' writings against heretics from Greek into Latin by ANTONIO BECCARIA in the 1440s: see D. Rundle, 'From Greenwich to Verona: Antonio Beccaria, St Athanasius and the translation of orthodoxy', *Humanistica*, v (2010), pp. 109–19.

[17] On which, see Hankins, *Plato*, i, pp. 130–38.

[18] As noted by J. I. Catto, 'Conclusion: Scholars and Studies in Renaissance Oxford' in *The History of the University of Oxford, II: Late Medieval Oxford*, ed. J. I. Catto and R. Evans (Oxford, 1992), pp. 769–83 at p. 772; J. Summit, *Memory's Library: Medieval Books in Early Modern England* (Chicago, 2008), pp. 20, 29–31.

[19] Sammut ed., *Unfredo duca du Gloucester*, p. 181 (ll. 21–28); see also p. 177 (ll. 22–40).

[20] Sammut ed., *Unfredo duca du Gloucester*, p. 180 (l. 5).

informed about humanism, even as the eager Italian tries to introduce him to it.

This suggestion has relevance for the debate about how well-informed Humfrey was as a patron, a debate continued in several recent accounts.[21] Yet this suggestion – that the person to whom one introduces humanism already knows of it – recurs in other works by Italians for English patrons, such as the interesting prose treatise *De Institutionibus boni viri* by STEFANO SURIGONE dedicated to the prior of Great Malvern, one Richard Dene, perhaps in the late 1450s. This dedicatee is curious, for though Dene is recorded as a notable patron, it is of a different art-form: painted glass, as during his priorate Great Malvern acquired a near complete set of lovely windows.[22] There is otherwise no evidence of Dene's scholarly or artistic credentials, and Surigone's prologue sounds uncertain whether his work will be to Dene's taste.[23] Nevertheless, Surigone claims elsewhere in the prologue that Dene does already follow the ancients in virtue and learning and has become a 'speculum' or mirror to other men.[24] This flattery makes perfect sense – financial or friendly – but, if Dene is a good humanist already, then the text offered to him serves an odd purpose:

> Qui enim per se optima studia sequitur (vt facis) eundem consentaneum est alios qui ad virtutem et probitatem

---

[21] David Rundle's forthcoming book on Humfrey will be the fullest evaluation. Other recent evaluations are Saygin, *Humphrey*, A. Petrina, *Cultural Politics in Fifteenth–Century England: the Case of Humphrey Duke of Gloucester* (Leiden, 2004), and Wakelin, *Humanism*, pp. 26–55.

[22] Many bearing what seems to be his motto 'Letabor in misericordia' (Psalms 31:7: 'I will rejoice in your mercy'): A. C. Deane, *A Short Account of Great Malvern Priory Church* (London, 1914), pp. 18–19, 72, 75; G. McN. Rushforth, *Medieval Christian Imagery as illustrated by the painted windows of Great Malvern Priory Church Worcestershire* (Oxford, 1936), pp. 3, 247, 409. He was prior from at least 1457 to at least 1491: see *Records of Convocation VI: Canterbury 1444–1509*, ed. G. Bray (Woodbridge, 2005), pp. 104, 371 and *passim*.

[23] Rundle, 'Of Republics and Tyrants', ii, p. 332.

[24] Cambridge: Trinity College [hereafter TCC], MS. B.14.47, fol. 13^{r-v}.

adhortentur libenter audire. Quid enim viro claro prestantius esse potest quam in hominum vita ita se comparare, vt doctrine ac scientie speculum ceteris esse videatur[25]

Because it is fitting for whoever himself pursues the best studies (as you do) to listen freely to other men who encourage virtue and honesty. For what could be more glorious for an illustrious man than to compare himself thus with the life of other human beings, so that he might seem to be a mirror of learning and knowledge to others.

So men already trained in the best studies like to listen to other men's exhortations to such studies.[26] Removed from the pressures of prince-pleasing Humfrey, Surigone's work exemplifies the ongoing attempts of Italian humanist scholars to introduce their taste to English readers, and yet exemplifies their claims that what they offer might already have been familiar to those Englishmen – whether because of their contiguity to other studies, or because – as they are introduced to successive generations, Humfrey, Dene and then others – they very soon needed no introduction.

Dispersing humanism

Moreover, the similar way in which humanists imagined both the well-known Humfrey and the little-known Dene suggests that humanist works were familiar not solely to patrons with the

---

[25] TCC, MS. B.14.47, fol. 4ʳ. In all quotations from manuscripts I have expanded abbreviations silently and have modernized punctuation and capitalization; the marks ⌐ and ¬ identify words added in different ink or between the lines. Surigone's pairing of 'virtutem et probitatem' is found in Cicero, *De Amicitia*, VIII.28, although there describing how others' virtues elicit our friendship. Surigone later makes a similar point about role-models, echoing this wording at TCC, MS. B.14.47, fol. 55ᵛ: 'qui per se ipsum (vt tu facis) optima viuendi prosequitur officia conueniens est vt is alios quoque qui ad virtutem at probitatem adhortentur libenter audire'.

[26] David Rundle suggests to me that this might be modelled on Lucius Annaeus Seneca, *De Clementia*, ed. S. M. Braund (Oxford, 2009), pp. 94–95 (1.1.1) and 142–43 (2.2.2), which tells Nero that the work will give pleasure by reflecting his own virtues back to him.

deepest pockets, largest book collections and grandest reputations. So even if we look for *intellectual* selectiveness and élitism, or Weiss's 'Pure' humanist scholarship, we do not always find *social* élitism; we find the use of humanist books by people lower in the secular and ecclesiastical hierarchies too, below the princes and bishops. One important recent study stressed the importance of the influence of 'particular individuals', but also stressed that there was a 'wider spread [...] than has hitherto been realized' of access to humanist books among Englishmen.[27] The repute of the books of certain princes, lords and bishops was considerable in the fifteenth century and properly remains so: that is true, for example, of William Gray, bishop of Ely, who built a great book-collection – albeit of the Church Fathers (again) as well as the classics – and a great reputation in Italy; it is true, too, of John Tiptoft, earl of Worcester, whose surviving marginalia suggest that he not only gathered books with care, but also read them.[28] Yet we might look beyond these *principes* of church and state and consider the bibliophiles and scholars lesser in purchasing power but perhaps not lesser in passion, and find humanism dispersed among ever wider circles of people.

For example, besides the fine collections of Tiptoft and Gray, we might compare the smaller collection of someone who sought their patronage, John Free. He translated one of Synesius' Greek works, a short treatise in praise of baldness, for Tiptoft, 'in whom all liberal learning worthy of a noble man has been recognized', he said ('a quo omnis liberalis et digna homine

---

[27] Thomson, 'Reception of the Italian Renaissance', pp. 74–75, and cf. pp. 66–67. Wakelin, *Humanism*, pp. 37–38, analogously stresses that vernacular books for princes were not only for princes.

[28] On Gray, see R. A. B. Mynors, *Catalogue of the Manuscripts of Balliol College* (Oxford, 1963), pp. xxiv–xlv. On Tiptoft, see R. J. Mitchell, *John Tiptoft (1427–1470)* (London, 1938), with the fullest list of Tiptoft's books and annotations on David Rundle's blog at http://bonaelitterae.wordpress.com/david-rundles-research-projects/tiptoft/ [accessed 2nd December 2011].

nobili percepta doctrina est').²⁹ He wrote to Bishop Gray with the pledge that he 'will try to translate something Greek into Latin in your honour' ('tentabimus [...] aliquam tuo nomine e greco in latinam vertere').³⁰ Seeking even higher, he also translated another work of Synesius, *De insomniis*, for Pope Paul II. Free's service of various loftier men could suggest that humanist studies were somehow centripetal: the humanist was a prince-pleaser, and humanism was therefore an élite activity in a social sense. But it is important to note that Free's humanist reading does not seek out any one centre; it does not serve only one élite, hierarchy or institution: he serves a secular lord, Tiptoft, but he also serves one bishop, Gray, another bishop, Thomas Bekynton (to whom he dedicated one copy of his translation of Synesius' work on baldness), and the Pope; and in his letters too he reveres another authority, his teacher GUARINO DA VERONA, as well as the other scholars such as LORENZO VALLA, ÆNEAS SILVIUS PICCOLOMINI – who became a pope – and LUDOVICO CARBONE.³¹ Free's scholarship seems, then, to be centrifugal, spreading out through various networks, allegiances and hierarchies. It has been suggested that this is the typical quality of fifteenth-century English culture, where 'power was decentralized and dispersed across a series of institutions'.³²

---

[29] R. Weiss, 'A Letter-Preface of John Free to John Tiptoft Earl of Worcester', *Bodleian Quarterly Record*, viii (1935–38), pp. 101–3 at p. 102, translated by R. J. Mitchell, *John Free: From Bristol to Rome in the Fifteenth Century* (London, 1955), p. 143.

[30] Oxford: Bodleian Library [hereafter Bod.], MS. Bodley 587, fol. 161ᵛ, printed in G. R. Stephens, *The Knowledge of Greek in England in the Middle Ages* (Philadelphia, 1933), p. 139, and translated by Mitchell, *John Free*, 142; R. Weiss, 'New Light on Humanism in England During the Fifteenth Century', *Journal of the Warburg and Courtauld Institutes*, xiv (1951), pp. 21–33 at pp. 27–31.

[31] Bod., MS. Bodley 587, fol. 159ʳ, 164ʳ, 165ᵛ, printed in Stephens, *The Knowledge of Greek*, pp. 138, 141, 143.

[32] J. Simpson, *The Oxford English Literary History: Volume 2: 1350–1547: Reform and Cultural Revolution* (Oxford, 2002), p. 38, and cf. p. 55.

The unifying point in this dispersal is not the expertise of his patrons, Bishop Gray or the Earl of Worcester, but Free's own expertise. So in several books owned by Tiptoft there is Free's hand copying, annotating or correcting: for example, in a copy of Suetonius' incomplete *De grammaticis*, Free notes that 'Here the most ancient exemplar ends and seems to be incomplete' ('Hic antiquissimum exemplar finit et non integrum videtur').[33] Such exercises might look like those of a servant; is he serving Tiptoft by telling him about the missing end of Suetonius, and is he doing so nervously, self-defensively? Is he merely a servile textual analyst, considering Suetonius' fragmentary form but not his content? It would be possible to criticize Free's humanist studies in such moments thus, as socially and intellectually narrow.[34] But these textual exercises need not be servile. After all, Suetonius' own work distinguishes the 'lettered' or *litteratus* man from the mere grammarian only in having yet greater skill – and Free highlights this passage.[35] Free's textual meticulousness, then, might be as honourable as Tiptoft's gentlemanly dilettantism. And Free's letters seem to cultivate his own reputation as a scholar, as much as they flatter his paymasters and teachers. When he translates Synesius' *De laudibus calvitii* for Tiptoft, he says that he chose the text because it was

---

[33] Quoting BL, MS. Harley 2639, fol. 14ᵛ. See the manuscripts listed by [Bodleian exhibition catalogue], *Duke Humfrey and English Humanism* (Oxford, 1970) [hereafter *DH&EH*], nos. 70–71; [Bodleian exhibition catalogue], *Manuscripts at Oxford: An Exhibition in Memory of Richard William Hunt* (Oxford, 1980), no. XXII.9; and on David Rundle's blog at http://bonaelitterae.wordpress.com/david-rundles-research-projects/tiptoft/, see nos 13, 26, 27, 30, 31.

[34] A. Grafton and L. Jardine, *From Humanism to the Humanities: Education and the Liberal Arts in Fifteenth- and Sixteenth-Century Europe* (London, 1986), pp. 14–15, use some of Free's notes as evidence of the intellectual shallowness of humanism.

[35] BL, MS. Harley 2639, fol. 3ᵛ; C. Suetonius Tranquillus, *De Grammaticis et Rhetoribus*, ed. and trans. Robert A. Kaster (Oxford, 1995), cc. 4.1–4.3.

especially difficult to do.³⁶ When he offers to write for Gray, he offers (as mentioned) 'to translate something Greek into Latin in your honour' ('aliquam tuo nomine e greco in latinam vertere'): the specificity of a translation from Greek and the lack of specificity about exactly what will be translated ('aliquam', *something*) suggests an odd attempt to imitate the working processes of other humanist translators for the sake of the process and not for any request from the patron. And he uses this offer to translate something as a pretext to ask for money to buy Greek books for himself, as though the grand patronage of Gray were a pretext for advancing Free's own scholarship.

Furthermore, the diffusion of humanism does not only proceed from patron – or indeed multiple patrons – to client; in Free's case the network extends again: Tiptoft's scholarship feeds Free's and Free's feeds smaller fry's in turn. This is evident because some of Free's books survive, but they seem to do so only because other scholars preserved them. For example, a book which Free did manage to acquire in Greek – a volume containing works by Sophocles, Euripides, Theocritus, Hesiod and Pindar – came into the possession of William Worcester, the former secretary of Sir John Fastolf (who owned the aforementioned tapestry of Camillus at the Siege of Falerii).³⁷ Worcester also took possession of Free's extracts from Pliny's *Naturalis historia*, bound now with his copy of Diodorus Siculus' Greek *Bibliotheca historica* in POGGIO BRACCIOLINI's Latin version.³⁸ And he acquired twenty-one folios with rough lecture-notes in Free's handwriting, many of them commentary on the epigrams of Martial, and bound them into his notebook.³⁹ Worcester was not the only beneficiary of Free's

---

[36] Weiss, 'A Letter-Preface of John Free', p. 102, translated by Mitchell, *John Free*, pp. 142–43.

[37] Bod., MS. F. 3. 25, on which see *DH&EH*, no. 85.

[38] Oxford: Balliol College, MS. 124, on which see Mynors, *Catalogue*, pp. 102–3.

[39] BL, MS. Cotton Julius F. vii, fol. 221ʳ–231ʳ, with Martial on fol. 220ʳ–225ᵛ, 228ʳ–231ᵛ; J. Delz, 'John Free und die Bibliothek John Tiptofts', *IMU*, xi (1968), pp. 311–16 at p. 315, n.1.

books: more of Free's lecture notes from the school of Guarino and the rough drafts of his letters to Gray and to Italian scholars are now bound into a manuscript with draft diplomatic speeches by John Gunthorpe, another student in Italy, who was soon to be the dean of Wells Cathedral.[40] So Free's letters composed to dazzle Bishop Gray also circulated through a horizontal social network, of a fellow junior clergyman and a secretary, both of whom could have been inspired by the epistles they came to own.[41] We know about Free's specialized scholarship because his books and humanist studies were dispersed among further people in turn.

Yet as Free's notes from Pliny and from Guarino's lectures also circulated horizontally, to the learned secretary Worcester, what effect did they have? As humanist scholarship disperses, does its strength remain, or does it get diluted? Worcester is often characterized as untouched by humanism, because his handwriting and Latin are ropey.[42] But these books reveal that he was touched by humanism, even if he was not fully transformed. For example, Worcester showed some interest in Greek, for among the notes in Free's hand which he acquired are some on Greek, and in the same notebook of Worcester's are other notes on Greek from William Sellyng in 1471.[43] But in Free's manuscript of Greek plays and poems, Worcester writes an *ex libris* but no notes which suggest that he could read the

---

[40] Bod., MS. Bodley 587, fol. 137^r–166^v, on which see *DH&EH*, nos 82 and 95, and n. 90 below. On Gunthorpe, see in general n. 85, 89–91, 93 below.

[41] We might wonder whether Free's draft letters, some of which look as though they might have once served as fair copies, inspired Gunthorpe's decision to draft diplomatic orations (Bod., MS. Bodley 587, fol. 73^r–93^r) on pages the same size as Free's (after cropping at least) and to keep those pages for posterity, some duly marked up with notes of their occasion.

[42] Mitchell, *John Free*, pp. 12–14; Weiss⁴, pp. 267–70; cf. Wakelin, *Humanism*, pp. 93–125.

[43] BL, MS. Cotton Julius F. vii, fol. 118^r (from Sellyng in 1471), 118^v (perhaps from one Dr Usk), 123^r (on a page dated 1471), 216^v and 219^{r-v} (in Free's hand).

Greek texts. So what can have been his interest in them? There is an illustrated zodiac at the front of this book and, as Worcester was interested in astronomy, it is tempting to wonder whether he acquired the book not for its Greek plays but for this zodiac; after all, it is under this that he puts his *ex libris*. The rough notes of Free which Worcester owned also include verses describing the zodiac, and Worcester also spots a reference to the zodiac in Free's extracts from Pliny.[44] So is Worcester undertaking humanist reading, or astrological reading? The two interests seem to co-exist, and to encourage each other.

Some other scholars in fifteenth-century England did study Pliny's text with the humanist methods of textual criticism.[45] Similarly, though more amateurishly, elsewhere in reading extracts from Pliny, Worcester too evinces a more 'Pure' humanist interest in antiquity: he most often notes ancient history, sometimes measured in years from the foundation of Rome ('A Rome condita .129' and so on). But other notes by Worcester continue to show classical studies converging with other studies once more. It is a common feature of marginalia to resist any attempt to be categorized neatly. For example, in Free's extracts from Pliny, Worcester also takes notes on islands in the Atlantic and eastern Mediterranean, and he adds at the end a longer note about Crete, cross-referring to another geographical text in his possession.[46] Is this the humanist study of history? It seems more as though Worcester absorbs Free's

---

[44] Bod., MS. Auct. F. 3. 25, fol. 1^v; BL, MS. Cotton Julius F. vii, fol. 211^{r-v}; Oxford: Balliol College, MS. 124, f. 2^r (Pliny, *Naturalis historia*, II.8), as well as a reference to measuring the lunar year on fol. 157^v (Diodorus Siculus, *Bibliotheca historica*, I.26).

[45] M. Davies, 'Making Sense of Pliny in the Quattrocento', *Renaissance Studies*, ix (1995), pp. 240–57 at p. 257.

[46] Oxford: Balliol College, MS. 124, ancient history: fol. 2^r, 63^r (twice), 78^r, 82^v, 84^v (twice), 85^r, 88^v, 89^r (Pliny, *Naturalis historia*, II.8, X.20 x 2, X.22, XII.11, XIII.3, XIII.13 x 2, XIII.16, XIV.11–12, XIV.14); islands: fol. 18^v, 29^v, 84^r, 86^r (IV.16, VI.12, XIII.11, XIII.25); and fol. 242^v (on Crete). Worcester also entitles the manuscript 'De cosmografia mundi necnon ⌐de speris celestibus¬' (f. 1r, adding the last three words later).

humanist reading into a slightly different interest in geography. For Worcester is best known for a notebook (often given the title *Itineraries*) recording journeys round England and, in just a few teasing pages, the discovery of new islands in the Atlantic – and, intriguingly, Worcester's brother-in-law was involved in attempts to find further islands in the Atlantic in 1480.[47] Worcester's reading of Pliny, then, could seem part of some general interest in seafaring or geography, reflecting his connexions more with Bristol sailors than with Free the humanist. Yet the interest in charting places does have some humanist influence: into his notebook of travels, Worcester also compiles extracts from the aforementioned geographical text on Crete, which he cited in the margin of Free's book; and that text turns out to be one about the isles of the Greek archipelago, Cristoforo Buondelmonti's *Liber archipelagi insularum*.[48] This work, if its Latin is not always perfect, does reflect an Italian humanist zeal for antiquities and Greek culture. Then, in another notebook, Worcester compiles his own extracts from Pliny, many of them repeating notes taken by Free, running

[47] J. A. Williamson ed., *The Cabot Voyages and Bristol Discovery under Henry VII* [Hakluyt Society, 2nd series, cxx] (Cambridge, 1962), pp. 14, 19–20, 175, 187–88.

[48] Cambridge: Corpus Christi College, MS. 210, calendared in William Worcestre [*sic*], *Itineraries*, ed. J. H. Harvey (Oxford, 1969), pp. 306–11, 372–77. But Harvey re-orders the notebook and brings the notes from Buondelmonti's work, which form a distinct and coherent quire (MS. 210, paginated as pp. 279–94, quire XXII) next to scattered notes on Atlantic islands (MS. 210, p. 185, pp. 305–6, in quires XVII and XXIII). Quire XXII has completely different watermarks from XVII and XXIII. Worcester evidently consulted a finely illustrated copy of Buondelmonti's work, as his notebook describes in detail the illustrations often found with this text. His descriptions could fit the illustrations in, for example, Holkham: Holkham Hall, MS. 475, an Italian manuscript which has an initial in what looks like an English style (to which Suzanne Reynolds kindly drew my attention). Worcester's quotations are often very close to the text of Holkham Hall, MS. 475, but not perfectly identical; nor are there signs of annotation by him in this manuscript, whereas he annotates other books often heavily.

from the cosmos (given its Greek etymology: 'grece nomine ornamentum') through the three continents and seven segments of the globe, to separate paragraphs on the islands of the Atlantic, Britain and Thule, the latter extracts being ones Worcester annotates in Free's book too.[49] The mixture of classical and geographical studies is not only Worcester's, of course; Free's own studies make this mixture possible, so it is not the case that humanism has been diluted *only* as it has dispersed through wider social networks. But the point to stress is that it is a mixture, it is blended: though there are humanist sources for Worcester's enquiries, there might not be a 'Pure' humanist purpose, but rather might be other 'utilitarian' concerns, as Weiss called them. Furthermore, as humanism gets dispersed from Tiptoft to Free to Worcester, it then threatens to disperse. Moreover, in this case it threatens to disperse not just through England but beyond it, as it converges with dreams of exploration and colonisation, which will allow humanism to stir the settlement of Ulster, Virginia and Massachusetts.[50]

Tracing humanism

This dispersal and diffusion of Tiptoft and Gray's patronage through Free's activities ultimately to Worcester's interest in exploration might stand for multiple stories of dispersal and diffusion. English humanists' books and ideas seldom move in

---

[49] BL, MS. Cotton Julius F.vii, fol. 143^r–144^v, 147^r (Pliny, *Naturalis historia*, II.v.22–26, II.vi.28–29, VI.xxxviii.210–219, IV.xvi.102, IV.xvi.104), the latter annotated in Oxford: Balliol College, MS. 124, fol. 18^v–19^r. Intervening on BL, MS. Cotton Julius F.vii, fol. 145^r–146^v, are some notes from Pliny, *Naturalis historia*, VII.xxx.116–117, VII.xxv.91, VII.xxxi.119, VII.xxxiv.120, VII.xxxvii.123–24) on classical heroes and inventors. M. Small, 'From jellied seas to open waterways: redefining the northern limit of the knowable world', *Renaissance Studies*, xxi (2007), pp. 315–39 at pp. 322–24, notes the importance of Pliny for ideas about exploration.

[50] As argued by A. Fitzmaurice, *Humanism and America: an Intellectual History of English Colonisation, 1500–1625* (Cambridge, 2003), esp. pp. 7–9; also relevant are pp. 14–18, which debate how far élite scholarly ideas affected the large-scale social movement of colonization.

tightly drawn circles with defined circumferences. Rather, some less eloquent and less distinctly humanist sources – such as letters, bequests in wills, Patent Roll entries, rough notebooks – all reveal the humanists not in a self-contained circle but in something like circles in the water, moving constantly outward, expanding and overlapping with other circles or networks. Yet as humanism disperses thus, how does it diffuse its influence? Does it have a sort of homeopathic transformative power, or does it dissolve to nought? Something between the two: like water, it affects, but does not alter completely, various fields of English culture. The briefer, less specialized sources that reveal the humanists connected to less focused, less specialized scholars also reveal the *studia humanitatis* themselves having an influence in less focused, less specialized forms. Besides Worcester's geography, we could find these influences in many other sectors of English culture. Given the religious upheavals of England during the sixteenth century, and the vibrancy of England's devotional life in the fifteenth century, it is most important to consider what some of the short and seemingly unpromising records show us of the dispersal of humanism among English churchmen, and of its diffusion through their theology and practice.

The dilution and diffusion revealed by such records are well exemplified in a will which has often been scoured for evidence of humanism of the more thoroughbred sort – evidence of the study of Greek by William Sellyng and Thomas Linacre. It is the will of John Morer, the vicar of Tenterden in Kent, who died in 1489. Among his varied bequests, including forty-eight books in total, Morer bequeathed some seven books which would serve the *studia humanitatis*.[51] He left to various men

---

[51] Kew: National Archives, PCC Will Registers, PROB 11/8 (20 Milles), fol. 161ᵛ–162ᵛ, transcribed and contextualized by J. W. Bennett, 'John Morer's Will: Thomas Linacre and Prior Sellyng's Greek Teaching', *Studies in the Renaissance*, xv (1968), pp. 70–91 at pp. 89–91. N. Ramsay and J. M. W. Willoughby ed., *Hospitals, Towns, and the Professions* [Corpus of British Medieval Library Catalogues, xiv] (London, 2009), pp. 114–15, note one of Morer's other bequests to the

Cicero's *De Officiis*, Virgil's *Aeneid* and a work by Lorenzo Valla, the recent arbiter of style, and he left to Thomas Linacre five books, four of which would suit his humanist studies: *Rhetorica ad Herennium*, which was then thought to be by Cicero, Thucydides, a 'printed Greek book' and a 'Greek book written on parchment'; he also left 'money to Thomas Linacre, studying in Florence, to be transferred [. . .] by the prior of Christ Church, Canterbury', that prior being William Sellyng ('domino Thome Lynaker studenti Fflorence x li legalis monete tradendas [...] honorabili patri domno priori ecclesie Cant.'). Greek, Cicero, new ideas about Latin, study in Florence: all vital elements of Weiss's 'Pure humanism'.

Yet records such as this will, or Fox's donation of books (with which the chapter opened), need to be read closely and carefully. Do such cursory and ineloquent sources reveal humanism as a major or minor note in this vicar's cultural life? And as a distinct and clear strain or as a whisper muffled in the background of his intellectual life? In some ways, this will casts humanism as something distinct and special: Morer or those round his death-bed have singled out Linacre, by giving him four of the seven classical or Italian humanist texts. The bequest seems, with hindsight, perceptive of Linacre's distinctive taste; but it might not be recording Linacre's taste itself, as recording others' perception of his taste – or even forging that perception for anybody who would read the will later. After all, although he was studying in Florence, Linacre had not yet in 1489 published the translations from Greek which would foster his repute.[52] So were Morer's bequests accurate records of Linacre's taste – or of that of the three other men who received classical or

Hospital of St Thomas of Acre, London, which also had some humanist connexions by the early sixteenth century.

[52] C. H. Clough, 'Thomas Linacre, Cornelio Vitelli and Humanistic Studies at Oxford' in F. Maddison et al. ed., *Essays on the Life and Work of Thomas Linacre c. 1460–1524* (Oxford, 1977), pp. 1–23 at pp. 7–8, describes Morer's knowledge of Linacre's Greek studies; G. Barber, 'Thomas Linacre: A Bibliographical Survey of his Works' in Maddison ed., *Essays on Linacre*, pp. 290–336 at pp. 331–36, lists Linacre's books.

classicizing books – or were they self-fulfilling prophecies? Even if they were accurate records – which they quite possibly were – nevertheless they were partial records, leaving unmentioned Linacre's medical learning, say, or other aspects of his personality or of the personalities of the other men who received humanist books in this bequest. Furthermore, in presenting humanist study as something distinct and special, the will also presents it, as letters to Duke Humfrey do, as something therefore limited to one or two fanatics. Indeed, Morer or his executors could not specify what the Greek books were, and merely distinguished their material forms, as print or on parchment; but they felt that these books would suit Linacre, while illegible to themselves. So if we go looking for 'Pure' humanism from sources such as this will, or similar sources, we could find deep scholarship – Greek and Cicero – but in narrow compass – just one scholar, and one quitting England for Florence too. Humanism does something distinctive but nothing of much importance for England, it seems.

But the lack of special focus on humanism and the large circle of connexions in this will mean that it in fact betrays not the distinctness and circumscription of humanism but the hybridity and diffusion of it. Firstly, the will reveals the special interests not only of Linacre and Sellyng, those travellers in Italy or inhabitants of priories with well-stocked libraries at Canterbury; it reveals how widely through geography and society humanist influences were dispersed: among country parsons such as Morer too. The dispersal follows recognisable routes: Morer had formerly been a Fellow at New College in Oxford, which nurtured so many students of the humanities, so the coming of Valla to his village seems explicable.[53] As well as Tenterden in the Weald, or the East Anglian villages with poems by Claudian, one could list all manner of places in which humanist influences were found. (Note in this chapter the

[53] Bennett, 'John Morer's Will', 82–83. On New College, see *DH&EH*, pp. 15–23, and G. F. Lytle, '"Wykehamist Culture" in Pre-Reformation England' in R. Custance ed., *Winchester College: Sixth-centenary Essays* (Oxford, 1982), pp. 129–66.

mention not only of well-known places of humanist learning such as Wells or Canterbury but also of Great Malvern or Bishop Auckland.)[54] Secondly, and more importantly, Morer's will reveals that humanist studies were not always exclusive in the lives of their adherents. As in Fox's gift to Bishop Auckland ten years on, here the *studia humanitatis* occur alongside quite different intellectual trends and institutional activities – the liturgy and theology of a parson. Only seven of Morer's forty-eight books might be securely tied to the study and imitation of classical antiquity, and Morer also made bequests to his church of pastoral manuals or to William Sellyng's priory of theology. Moreover, even his humanist bequests were hybrids: he left to Linacre not only Cicero and Greek books but Peter Lombard's *Libri sententiarum*, or perhaps a commentary on it; and the copy of Valla's work was bound 'with a certain tract on judicial order' ('quodam tractatu De ordine judiciario') which sounds like a work on canon law.[55] These bequests suggest scholasticism in happy co-existence with humanism as synchronic rather than diachronic trends. Humanist influences seem, then, not distilled and totalizing, but more diluted or diffuse – merely a thin trace in the water.

Yet they do seem, thereby, to be diffused widely. For while there are fewer signs of complete humanist influence there are more common signs of it – signs more sketchy, but more numerous, than seven bequeathed books. Some of these signs might not be recognized until seen in the context of others. For example, Morer bequeaths several copies of Jerome's and Augustine's works, and while the study of the Church Fathers was neither reserved to, nor new with, those who liked the *studia humanitatis*, nor was it alien to them; they cultivated the

---

[54] David Rundle's forthcoming book will have a chapter on the geography of English humanism.

[55] Bennett, 'John Morer's Will', pp. 90–91, with suggested identifications on p. 71. The text on canon law could be the *Ordo iudiciarius* ascribed to one Ricardus Anglicus now sometimes identified as Richard de Mores: see R. Sharpe, *A Handlist of the Latin Writers of Great Britain and Ireland before 1540* (Turnhout, 1997), pp. 494–95.

study of patristic authors and the history of the early Church.[56] So could bequests of the Fathers be a sign of humanist tendencies, as much as bequests of Thucydides? A will can tell us little about how Morer read these things. But the general lesson is that there might be more fleeting but more frequent humanist influences hidden in unexpected details of fifteenth-century English intellectual life. Moreover, even less scholarly things might turn out to hide humanist influences. For example, the supposed pioneer of England's Greek studies, William Sellyng, appears in this will only as 'the prior of Christ Church, Canterbury'; he, Sellyng, had also held the right of advowson when Morer was made vicar of Tenterden in 1479.[57] Thus, documents which attest to unpromising things such as money-transfers, priorates or advowsons, might sometimes attest to the networks of humanist 'knowledge transfers'.[58] And as Robert Lutton has noted in a subtle response to Morer's will, there might even be signs of humanist influence in unexpected elements of the devotional life of Morer's parish.[59] The documents which record fifteenth-century life in general need close reading for such signs of the unrolling of humanist influence through diverse social and cultural spheres – and not only in the distinct but limited world of Linacre and his Greek books.

---

[56] Thomson, 'Reception of the Italian Renaissance', pp. 72–73; C. Stinger, 'Italian Renaissance Learning and the Church Fathers' in I. Backus ed., *The Reception of the Church Fathers in the West: From the Carolingians to the Maurists*, 2 vols (Leiden, 1997), ii, pp. 473–510; and see n. 68–69 & 100 below.

[57] R. Lutton, *Lollardy and Orthodox Religion in Pre-Reformation England: Reconstructing Piety* (Woodbridge, 2006), pp. 189–90.

[58] On social networks and intellectual diffusion, see P. Burke, *A Social History of Knowledge from Gutenberg to Diderot* (Cambridge, 2000), p. 8.

[59] Lutton, *Lollardy and Orthodox Religion*, p. 193.

Diluting humanism

There are many such spheres in which this dispersal and diffusion show their influence – such as England's ideology of the *res publica*, or its interest in colonization – in the fifteenth century and into the sixteenth.[60] But this diffusion of humanism through theology and ecclesiastical life, as in Morer's world, was among the most important. This diffusion occurred in a world in which most people in England were not full-time 'humanists': few were paid to teach specifically humanist studies before the late 1470s, and still few until the 1510s. For example, an Italian friar called LORENZO TRAVERSAGNI lectured at Cambridge in the late 1470s on Cicero – but he also lectured on St Augustine and dedicated a Christological text to the bishop of Winchester, William Waynflete, before returning to prominence in his order back in Italy.[61] This career within the Church is typical of English humanist scholars too, for much of the history of humanism in England is part of ecclesiastical history (given that the *ecclesia* included most schools and colleges).

Astutely, therefore, Andrew Cole has recently surveyed how the service of the earthly parts of the institutional Church in England drew on humanist writing practices in flattery, oratory and counsel, especially in the universities and in certain bishoprics.[62] The humanist tastes of ecclesiasts led to their receipt of dedications of works of humanist Latin which

---

[60] For some of these later trends, see recently P. Withington, *Society in Early Modern England: The Vernacular Origins of Some Powerful Ideas* (Cambridge, 2010), pp. 139–44, 203–4.

[61] G. Farris, *Umanesimo e religione in Lorenzo Guglielmo Traversagni (1425–1505)* (Milan, 1972), pp. 11–12, 71–81; V. Davis, *William Waynflete: Bishop and Educationalist* (Woodbridge, 1993), pp. 97–98. The complete preface to Traversagni's *Triumphus amoris* is available as Weiss[4], Appendix, Text I.

[62] A. Cole, 'Heresy and Humanism', in P. Strohm ed., *Middle English* (Oxford, 2007), 421–37, and id., 'The Style of Humanist Latin Letters at the University of Oxford: On Thomas Chaundler and the *Epistolae Academicae Oxon. (Registrum F)*' in S. Gayk and K. Tonry ed., *Form and Reform: Reading the Fifteenth Century* (Columbus, OH, 2011), pp. 40–65.

considered the establishment of the Church: for example, Thomas Chaundler dedicated a dialogue about the episcopal cities of Bath and Wells to their bishop, Thomas Bekynton;[63] GIOVANNI GIGLI dedicated a treatise on canonization to Cardinal John Morton, linking it to Morton's interest both in 'governing realms and states' and in 'understanding the truth' ('⌐ad⌐ regnorum uel rerum publicarum gubernationem, aut ad ueri cognitionem').[64] Besides practical ecclesiology, humanism influenced the theology of English churchmen too, as fifteenth-century humanists – like those later following Erasmus – returned to the sources of Christian thought in antiquity. So Chaundler also gave Bekynton a dialogue which reconciled Lactantius' and St Augustine's ideas with Cicero's; later in the century the first book printed at Oxford, set from an Italian humanist manuscript and at the command of James Goldwell, the humanist-inclined bishop of Norwich, was a theological one, Rufinus' *Expositio symboli*.[65] Nor was it only bishops or

---

[63] Thomas Chaundler, *Libellus de laudibus duarum civitatum*, ed. George Williams, *Proceedings of the Somersetshire Archaeological and Natural History Society*, xix (1873), pp. 99–121, discussed by D. Rundle, 'Humanist Eloquence among the Barbarians in Fifteenth-Century England' in C. Burnett and N. Mann ed., *Britannia Latina: Latin in the Culture of Great Britain from the Middle Ages to the Twentieth Century* [Warburg Institute Colloquia, viii] (London, 2005), pp. 68–85 at pp. 70–71, and Wakelin, *Humanism*, pp. 163–65.

[64] BL, MS. Arundel 366, fol. 2ʳ (Gigli), on which see C. H. Clough, 'Three Gigli of Lucca in England during the Fifteenth and Early Sixteenth Centuries: Diversification in a Family of Mercery Merchants', *The Ricardian*, xiii (2003), pp. 121–47 at pp. 134–37. Gigli also dedicated a treatise on Lenten observances to Bishop John Russell and Bishop Richard Fox: BL, MS. Harley 336, as noted in P.S. & H.M. Allen ed., *Letters of Richard Fox 1486–1527* (Oxford, 1929), p. 5 (no.1), and D. R. Carlson, *English Humanist Books: Writers and Patrons, Manuscript and Print, 1475–1525* (Toronto, 1993), pp. 175–76, 209 (n. 29); and see further n. 87 below.

[65] On which, see respectively D. Wakelin, 'Religion, Humanism and Humanity: Chaundler's Dialogues and the Winchester *Secretum*' in V. Gillespie and K. Ghosh. ed., *After Arundel: Religious Writing in Fifteenth Century England* (Turnhout, 2012), pp. 225–44 at pp. 230–

secular clergy who were involved: humanism influenced members of the enclosed religious orders too, who drew on such studies to renew not only their power in the *saeculum* but also their faith. In the early and mid fifteenth century, a prominent abbot of St Albans, John Whethamstede, extended his house's longstanding learning to read some humanist works and make contact with some Italian scholars, even if only a small part of his voluminous scholarship showed signs of these influences; the same could be said – a little humanism, diffused to him, but not wholeheartedly embraced – of the response to works by Boccaccio or Coluccio Salutati by the poet and monk of Bury St Edmunds, John Lydgate.[66] The fifteenth-century Church in England, then, absorbed humanist influences widely but in tiny traces which complemented its usual activities.

Even if we turn to religious who are better known for their humanism, still we find humanist influences incorporated into the more customary studies and activities of the Church. This can be seen, for example, in the case of William Sellyng, the prior of Christ Church, Canterbury, who was remembered in John Morer's will, and who shared some Greek notes with William Worcester (as noted above). Sellyng had studied Valerius Maximus under the aforementioned Stefano Surigone, studied in Italy, delivered a humanist oration on an embassy to Rome, and translated a work from Greek into Latin, like John Free.[67] Yet what he translated from Greek was not Synesius' *jeu*

36; A. C. de la Mare and Lotte Hellinga, 'The first book printed in Oxford: the *Expositio Symboli* of Rufinus', *Transactions of the Cambridge Bibliographical Society*, vii (1978), pp. 184–244.

[66] On Whethamstede, see J. Clark, *A Monastic Renaissance at St Albans: Thomas Walsingham and his circle, c. 1350–1440* (Oxford, 2004), pp. 234–38; on Lydgate, see Wakelin, *Humanism*, pp. 31–43. As it happens, Whethamstede patronized Lydgate: see N. Mortimer, *John Lydgate's* Fall of Princes: *Narrative Tragedy in its Literary and Political Contexts* (Oxford, 2005), pp. 118, 140, 151.

[67] For some of these activities, see BL, MS. Cotton Cleopatra E. iii, fol. 127^r, 125^r–126^v, printed by U. Balzano, 'Un' ambasciata inglese a Roma', *Archivio della Società Romana di Storia Patria*, iii (1880), pp.

d'esprit on baldness but a sermon of St John Chrysostom.[68] Moreover, the choice of text for this translation in 1488 had neat precedents in Sellyng's earlier experiences of humanist piety, for in 1474, early in his priorate, Christ Church commissioned or received a two-volume copy of FRANCESCO GRIFFOLINI's Latin translation of Chrysostom's homilies on St John's gospel. Chrysostom's works were popular subjects for translation into Latin among humanists in Rome, a city Sellyng had visited in 1469, and in the 1474 manuscript the homilies are copied in an archaizing hand partly modelled on humanist script by Theodoric Werken, a German scribe who had worked for William Gray.[69] One prologue notes, with interesting historical relativism, that Chrysostom cites a different version of Scripture from that now standard; another compares the dedicatee to Cicero, Demosthenes and so on: patristics and classics meld as objects for historical and rhetorical enquiry.[70]

175–211 (esp. p. 202 for Surigone, whose name Balzano cannot transcribe), and in general, Weiss, *Humanism*, pp. 153–59.

[68] BL, MS. Additional 15673, then transcribed into MS. Additional 47675 (and thence into MS. Harley 6237 in the seventeenth or eighteenth century); J. B. Trapp, 'Notes on Manuscripts Written by Peter Meghen', *The Book Collector*, xxiv (1975), pp. 80–96, no. 17. Sellyng's translation has an ecclesiastical context, for it survives copied with Simon Islip's fourteenth-century treatise against plundering churches – a work also excerpted alongside Italian humanist translations by Henry Cranebroke, a monk from Christ Church, Canterbury, in BL, MS. Royal 10. B. ix, fol. 67^v.

[69] C. L. Stinger, 'Greek Patristics and Christian Antiquity in Renaissance Rome' in P. A. Ramsey ed., *Rome in the Renaissance: The City and the Myth* (Binghampton, NY, 1982), pp. 153–69, at p. 157, places Griffolini's work in context. Werken's copy, transcribed from the printed edition of 1470 [ISTC, no. ij00286000], now survives in two parts, as TCC, MS. B. 3. 21 and Cambridge: University Library, MS. Ff. 3. 10 (Chrysostom, copied from a printed edition of 1470), on which see M. B. Parkes, 'Archaizing Hands in English Manuscripts' in J. P. Carley & C. G. C. Tite ed., *Books and Collectors 1200–1700: Essays Presented to Andrew Watson* (London, 2007), pp. 101–141 at p. 110. On the scribe, see also n. 99 below.

[70] TCC, MS. B. 3. 21, fol. 1^{r-v}, 16^r–18^r.

However, despite the humanist influence on Sellyng's translation of 'something Greek', Chrysostom's content is unexceptionally devout and traditional: the sermon which Sellyng translated preaches the glory of suffering, the negligibility of the body, the need to fear not death but sin. Nor is such piety unique: when Sellyng received gifts of works from Robert Gaguin, a distinguished humanist who had recently served as a French ambassador to England, what he received were works on the Blessed Virgin and *De misera hominis conditione* (*On the Miserable Condition of Humanity*). Gaguin's accompanying letter hoped that these works would counterpoint the hostility between the princes for whom he and Sellyng were ambassadors and would preserve instead the amity proper to the clergy, the protectors of Christ's peace ('Nam etsi ambitiosa contentione principes digladientur, ii tamen qui Christo militant pacem sibi a suo rege relictam custodiunt').[71] Such works, and such words, offer a bracingly unworldly alternative to the secular service in which we might imagine humanist ambassadors, even humanist churchmen as ambassadors.[72] Thus Sellyng's piety is influenced by encounters with humanist scholars, scribes and orators, but the resulting piety seems not to be new in content – seems indeed to eschew worldly influences.

Moreover, if Sellyng's religious reading and piety were not completely transformed by humanism, sometimes they were not even touched by it. For example, when Sellyng's correspondence records him seeking out books, they are not even patristic but simply scholastic. In one letter, John Langdon, the

---

[71] Robert Gaguin, *Epistole et Orationes*, ed. L. Thuasne, 2 vols (Paris, 1903), i, pp. 383–84. See also Gaguin's earlier reference to Sellyng merely as 'that old man from Canterbury' ('Cantuarium illum senem': i, p. 334). On Gaguin, see pp. 211–12 above, and n. 87–88 below.

[72] On the importance of ambassadors as carriers of humanist and other books, see M. Lowry, 'Diplomacy and the Spread of Printing' in L. Hellinga and J. Goldfinch ed., *Bibliography and the Study of 15th-Century Civilisation* (London, 1987), pp. 124–46.

warden of Canterbury College in Oxford, is worried that Sellyng:

> [. . .] thynkyth me neclygente, as I parceyue, that I have nat purueyd for yow Dunse vpon the iij^de off senten*c*ys. [. . .] And I can nat thynke yt lykely that ther shall come ony moo of them yn prentys, as be that I here off them that selle such bokys. [. . .]⁷³

Sellyng, then, was keen to buy Duns Scotus' commentary on book III of Peter Lombard's *Sentences*. Another letter reveals Sellyng seeking out a text by Robert Grosseteste, whom he cites in an extant sermon.⁷⁴ Even responding to the newish technology of printed books ('prentys'), Sellyng seeks scholastic texts. Nor is he alone in that: if only Morer had already died, Sellyng might have been able to peruse some texts of interest: Morer bequeathed to Canterbury College, where Langdon was, a copy of the *Master of the Sentences* and to Thomas Linacre, the Greek scholar known to Sellyng, the *Sentences* themselves or perhaps again a commentary on it.⁷⁵ While within the life of Sellyng, or other such men, humanism had some influence, within that life any one reading-encounter might be less touched by humanism than others; scholasticism or other intellectual traditions could coexist, of course, within one person but at different moments.

Remembering the fragmentation of life into these moments is important when we examine the less promising records of

---

[73] Canterbury Cathedral Archives [hereafter CCA], MS. DCc–CantLet/I, no. 10, printed by W. A. Pantin ed., *Canterbury College Oxford*, 4 vols [Oxford Historical Society, new series, vi–viii & xxx] (Oxford, 1947–1985), iii, p. 121 (no. 147, dated 3 September *c*. 1478–82 or 1486–90).

[74] CCA, MS. DCc–ChChLet/II, no. 99, printed by Pantin ed., *Canterbury College*, iii, p. 118 (no. 144); CCA, MS. DCc–CantLet, no. 10 (Pantin ed., *Canterbury College*, iii, pp. 120–21, no. 147); BL, MS. Cotton Cleopatra, E. iii, fol. 109ᵛ ('lincolniensem nostrum ⌐alius grosted¬', 'our Bishop of Lincoln, alias Grosseteste'), printed by E. Fueter, *Religion und Kirche in England im fünfzehnten Jahrhundert* (Tübingen, 1904), p. 70.

[75] Bennett, 'John Morer's Will', pp. 71, 89–91.

fifteenth-century culture for evidence of humanism. For, if we only had letters such as these, it would be possible to doubt Sellyng's engagement with humanism at all. His letters reveal him in his day-job as prior, checking out miracles, disciplining monks, or haggling over his entitlement to pipes of wine. The wine seems his biggest concern. Even a letter to Sellyng from Giovanni Gigli is about such dull ecclesiastical stuff; or when Sellyng writes to Thomas Chaundler, his praise for Chaundler's *humanitas* is primarily praise for his financial generosity (which *humanitas* often means).[76] However, we might begin to find traces of humanism's diffusion in – and by means of – even these unpromising letters. Firstly, there are hints at humanist interests: for example, the bishop of Lincoln asks Sellyng to send a cash advance to some prospective servant, and writes this humdrum letter in humdrum English; yet that servant is a Greek and evidently a scholar, for he must head abroad 'for þe settyng of his bookes' which he has promised to bring back to England.[77] What looks like usual worry over payment and allegiances, then, may have a scholarly motive. More importantly, we cannot doubt Sellyng's engagement with humanist learning if we turn from the printed editions of his letters to the original missives, for this bishop and Sellyng himself use handwriting which imitates humanist script.[78] Other ecclesiastical archives have been found to contain influences of humanist handwriting.[79] Yet we need to keep in mind the limited significance of that accomplishment: Sellyng's

---

[76] J. B. Sheppard ed., *Christ Church Letters: A Volume of Mediaeval Letters Relating to the Affairs of Christ Church, Canterbury*, [Camden Society, new ser., xix] (London, 1877), pp. 35–36 (no. xxxii, from Gigli); Pantin ed., *Canterbury College*, iii, pp. 123–24 (no. 150, to Chaundler); and see also CCA, MS. Register/S, fol. 361ʳ, in which Sellyng and the chapter appoint Giovanni Gigli to act on their behalf.

[77] CCA, MS. DCc-ChChLet/II, no. 123.

[78] CCA, MS. DCc-ChChLet/I, nos. 11, 14, 17 (Latin), 18, 27, 61, 111; CCA, MS. DCc-ChChLet/II, nos. 89a–c (accounts), 91, 96.

[79] J. G. Greatrex, 'Humanistic Script in a Monastic Register: An Outward and Visible Sign?', *Studies in Church History*, xiv (1977), pp. 187–91.

letters in humanist handwriting are not in fine Ciceronian Latin but are all bar one in English and mostly handle his dull ecclesiastical business of rents, payments and building works, or are even just scrappy accounts. Humanist training did not sever somebody from the vernacular language or, as it were, vernacular or everyday activity.

Moreover, we might wonder about the extent of the influence of such humanist habits as a new style of handwriting. Among those who write back to Seyllyng or on his behalf, Giovanni Gigli, of course, and a few other people had also mastered this script, such as his chaplain Thomas Humfrey or his successor as prior Thomas Goldstone.[80] Yet some hands writing to and from his priory show a little humanist influence mixed with other influences from secretary script; even Sellyng himself on occasion lets his humanist handwriting show some influence from secretary, say in **w** or in splaying descenders on **y**, letters less often used in humanist Latin of course, or in otiose flourishes on word-final **d**.[81] So we might wonder how thoroughly humanist influences could transform one person's writing; and we might wonder how extensively it might transform a network of people. For the letters which survive in the records of Christ Church Priory reveal only these few, not very numerous other users of it. The register of the priory's business in Sellyng's day, for example, is kept in conventional late fifteenth-century handwriting, modelled on mixtures of

---

[80] CCA, MS. DCc-Shadwell/37; CCA, MS. DCc-ChChLet/I, no. 48 (Gigli); CCA, MS. DCc-ChChLet/II, no. 94 (Thomas Humfrey); CCA, MS. DCc-ChChLet/I, no. 34, and MS. DCc-ChChLet/II, nos. 99–100, 102, and CCA, MS. DCc-CantLet/I, no. 5 (Goldstone); CCA, MS. DCc-ChChLet/II, no. 123 (as in n. 77 above). Parkes, 'Archaizing Hands', pp. 110–11, 123, considers the origins of this humanist influence.

[81] CCA, MS. DCc-ChChLet/I, no. 111 (Sellyng: Pantin ed., *Canterbury College*, iii, p. 115, no. 141); CCA, MS. DCc-ChChLet/I, no. 16 (an amanuensis: Pantin ed., *Canterbury College*, iii, pp. 123–24, no.150); CCA, MS. DCc-ChChLet/II, no. 60 (Robert Gosebourne: Pantin ed., *Canterbury College*, iii, pp. 119–20, no. 146).

anglicana and secretary features.[82] Yet, even when an influence is not followed it can nevertheless be influential, for once that new influence is available, the status quo is no longer automatic or natural but is suddenly a choice. Some awareness of *not* following Sellyng's example might be evident in some other letters to Sellyng: correspondents express some worry that Sellyng has certain expectations in letters – whether for particular forms of Latin or for Italianate handwriting – and some worry about not meeting those expectations. They seek from him a pardon for writing 'so homelly' or for 'rude writyng'; the aforementioned Langdon apologizes in one of his letters for 'thys rude writing for your servantys tary nat with us'.[83] And Langdon's letters, unlike some others to Sellyng, are not in an Italianate hand but in a scruffy handwriting modelled on secretary.[84] This is unexceptional in the late fifteenth century: so what is he worrying about? It is tempting to wonder whether the rudeness he and others worry about is rudeness of epistolary style or of non-humanist handwriting. To understand the dispersal and dilution of humanism throughout English culture, beyond the most devoted adherents, it might be worth looking for some self-conscious awareness of the *lack* of such influence; for humanism might be present even when absent, as it were, as an opportunity knowingly missed.

Thus Sellyng's letters suggest ways to analyse records of fifteenth-century English culture which seem uninfluenced by humanism, but in which humanist influence lurks as a possibility. The clue can often be the interests of the people

---

[82] CCA, MS. Register/S, fol. 300ᵛ–393ʳ.

[83] Sheppard ed., *Christ Church Letters*, pp. 34–35 (no. xxxi), pp. 39–40 (no. xxxv); Pantin ed., *Canterbury College*, iii, p. 129 (no. 154). Langdon also apologizes for what sounds like the general content: 'have me excusyd that I wryte noon odyr wyse on to yow. For I haue been syke, soo that I myght nat kepe my study' (Pantin ed., *Canterbury College*, iii, p. 121 (no. 147).

[84] CCA, MS. DCc-CantLet/I, no. 10 (Pantin ed., *Canterbury College*, iii, p. 129, no. 154); CCA, MS. DCc-ChChLet/II, no. 59 (Pantin ed., *Canterbury College*, iii, p. 121, no. 147).

recorded in such sources. For example, when the aforementioned Richard Fox, when bishop of Exeter, writes to John Gunthorpe, dean of Wells, there seems to be no trace of humanist influence, even though both men are well known for collecting humanist books:

> Maister Dean, I recommaunde me vnto you. And for such besinesse as I haue now in hand about thies ambassadouris and other maters, I may not at this tyme write vnto you my mynde at large in all maters. Wherfore I hertly pray you that, in suche thinges as I haue commaunded my welbeloued seruaunt Edmunde Mill this berer to shew vnto you on my behalue, ye wille yeue vnto hym therin asmoche feith and credence as if I spake personally with you my selve. And here after at better leiser I shal write vnto you my selve. And thus I committe you vnto our lord. Writen at Windesore the v^{te} day of Septembre your lovyng broder R. Exoniensis.[85]

The letter is not of much practical use, for all it records is that the bearer, Edmund Mill, would report the important things in person rather than writing, and that Fox has no time to write of anything else. Yet the person keeping records in the *Liber Ruber* at Wells that year found something noteworthy in this letter, enough to copy it down in its entirety, rather than in the usual pithier digest which tracks the cathedral's other business; and he introduced this letter by noting that 'the wording of the letter follows and is like this' ('tenor sequitur et est talis'), as though the exact form mattered somehow.[86] Why would he care to

---

[85] Wells: Cathedral Archives [hereafter WCA], MS. CF/2/2 (the *Liber Ruber*), fol. 26^v–27^r; printed by Allen ed., *Letters of Richard Fox*, p. 12 (no. 5, dated September 1489), and W. H .B. Bird and W. P. Baildon ed., *Calendar of the Manuscripts of the Dean and Chapter of Wells*, 2 vols [Historical Manuscripts Commission, xii.2–3] (London, 1907), ii, p. 116.

[86] WCA, MS. CF/2/2, fol. 26^v (not printed in Bird and Baildon ed., *Calendar*, ii, p. 116), using *tenor* in its medieval Latin senses of 'wording or effect of document' or 'style, character, manner': R. E. Latham, *Revised Medieval Latin Word-List from British and Irish Sources* (London, 1965), *s.v. tenor*. The same wording introduces another document in the *Liber Ruber*: WCA, MS. CF/2/2, fol. 18^r (not printed in Bird and Baildon ed., *Calendar*, ii, p. 109).

record such a letter? It seems unexceptional not only in content but in style: it is in English, plainly composed, devoid of allusions or learning. Yet there is a trace of humanism, albeit a very diluted one, in Fox's words. Most tenuously, the gesture of disclaiming the leisure for writing might be influenced by humanist precedent – it was a gesture made, for example, three years earlier in a letter dedicating a book to Fox from Giovanni Gigli, who claims that both men could only retrieve a little leisure for literature from their occupations. The claim to be squeezing literature into an active life is a humanist feint; Gigli cites Cato (probably the Elder), Cicero, Julius Caesar, Caesar Augustus and Alexander as models for this.[87] It is also another amusing way in which people refer to humanism as a possibility they profess not to have taken – an absent presence again. Of course, in Fox's letter to Gunthorpe, the lack of leisure reflects real business, the recent visit of some 'ambassadouris'. Yet in this detail there is a further trace of humanism not present but occurring off-stage, as it were, for the ambassadors seem from the date to be the group on embassy from 21 August to 16 September 1489, which included Robert Gaguin, Sellyng's correspondent, whose 'splendid speech' ('luculentam orationem') and vicious verses excited some humanists in England, including Gigli, to compose epigrams and verses in response.[88] Fox refers to the ambassadors with the demonstrative

[87] BL, MS. Harley 336, fol. 67ᵛ, printed in Allen ed., *Letters of Richard Fox*, p. 6 (no. 2), and G. & G. Tournoy-Thoen, 'Giovanni Gigli and the Renaissance of the Classical Epithalamium in England' in *Myricae: Essays on Neo-Latin Literature in Memory of Jozef IJsewijn* [Supplementa Humanistica Lovaniensia, xvi] (Leuven, 2000), pp. 133–93 at p. 151 (esp. ll. 4–6). On Fox's patronage, see n. 64 above and D. Rundle, 'Filippo Alberici, Henry VII and Richard Fox: The English Fortunes of a Little-Known Italian Humanist', *Journal of the Warburg and Courtauld Institutes*, xlviii (2005), pp. 137–155 at pp. 146–48.

[88] D. Carlson, 'Politicizing Tudor Court Literature: Gaguin's Embassy and Henry VII's Humanists' Response', *Studies in Philology*, lxxxv (1988), pp. 279–304, esp. pp. 282, 284; L. Thuasne, 'Les Missions de Robert Gaguin', *Revue d'histoire diplomatique*, xxx (1916), pp. 456–91 at pp. 472–81; C. Giry-Deloison, 'Le Personnel Diplomatique au début

('*thies* ambassadouris') suggesting that Gunthorpe knew just who 'thies' men were. Perhaps plans were already underway for the return embassy to France in June 1490, in which both Fox and Gunthorpe would serve, as would Sellyng.[89] Gunthorpe also, though, had an interest in humanist oratory by ambassadors: he had written some himself and he had collected a speech from an Aragonese ambassador.[90] There are two things to stress here. On the one hand, this is not a humanist letter, and reveals other aspects of the ecclesiastical and political careers of Fox and Gunthorpe, such as their involvement as educated clerics in diplomacy.[91] Yet humanist studies are present here even as something deferred, and by not referring to humanism pointedly, but almost casually in a trope of *otium* and *negotium*, Fox seems less self-conscious about humanism than were, say, the Italian show-offs Decembrio or Surigone; he seems more unthinkingly to be taking 'thies' Latin-spouting humanist

---

du XVIe siècle', *Journal des savants* (1987), pp. 205–253, esp. p. 251; Bernard André, *Historia Regis Henrici Septimi*, ed. J. Gairdner [Rolls Series, x] (London, 1858), pp. 55–56. One other respondent to Gaguin, PIETRO CARMELIANO, was also made a canon of Wells: see WCA, MS. CF/2/2, fol. 57[v] (Bird and Baildon ed., *Calendar*, ii, p. 143).

[89] For dates and personnel, see Giry-Deloison, 'Le Personnel', pp. 246–29; Howden ed., *The Register of Richard Fox*, p. xxv. Fox was later appointed bishop of Gunthorpe's cathedral: see Fox's register in E. Chisholm-Batten ed., *The Register of Richard Fox, while Bishop of Bath and Wells A.D. MCCCCXCII–MCCCCXCIV* (London, 1889), with references to Gunthorpe on pp. 25, 51, 64, 111 of the register.

[90] Bod., MS. Bodley 587, fol. 73[r]–93[r], with the Aragonese speech on fol. 81[r]–83[v], and Gunthorpe's speeches, but not his notes, printed by P. Chaplais ed., *English Medieval Diplomatic Practice*, 2 vols (London, 1982), i, pp. 234–53 (nos 138–40); they are bound with Free's letters (n. 40 above; *DH&EH*, nos 82, 95). On diplomatic interest in Spanish affairs, see Chisholm-Batten ed., *Register of Richard Fox*, p. 25.

[91] A. C. Reeves, 'John Gunthorpe: Keeper of Richard III's Privy Seal, Dean of Wells Cathedral', *Viator*, xxxix (2008), pp. 307–44 surveys Gunthorpe's career very thoroughly – though only spends two pages on his books and his lack of 'original, creative scholarship' (pp. 339–41).

ambassadors for granted as part of England's intellectual and political scene.

If humanism is both diluted till almost untraceable and yet diffused so that people take it for granted, then we might expect to find less explicit mention of it hidden in other records of the fifteenth-century English Church. To linger in Wells with Gunthorpe, for example, in one letter by the dean and chapter under Gunthorpe's tenure, the words *profits* and *fruits*, which English scribes most often spelled suggesting a pronunciation like ours, have the letter *c* in them ('all maner comodities, profectez and fructez'). Do these spellings suggest a scribe interested in the words' etymologies in Latin *profectus* and *fructus* – the sort of interest in etymological spelling found in classicizing texts of the sixteenth century?[92] Or to take another deliberately tendentious example: Gunthorpe donated to his cathedral in Wells an image of the Virgin in silver ('vnam ymaginem gloriose virginis marie de argente et deauratam'), and the vestments for his commemorative altar were 'damaskis' decorated 'with angellis'.[93] Were the ornaments in the style of Italian quattrocento church fittings of a classicizing sort? Quite likely not, but we cannot be sure; for the bureaucratic records of the age seldom even mention the mindset or motive of donations, let alone their artistic style or other aesthetic things.[94]

---

[92] WCA, MS. CF/2/2, fol. 67ʳ (Bird and Baildon ed., *Calendar*, ii, p. 149, dated likely late 1497); and 'profecte' recurs on fol. 18ʳ (Bird and Baildon ed., *Calendar*, ii, p. 109). *The Middle English Dictionary* (http://quod.lib.umich.edu/m/med/lookup.html [accessed 2nd December 2011]), has *fruit* (n.), spelled as *fruct–* in only in two of its 165 illustrative quotations, and *profite* (n. 1), spelled with *profect–* in only four of 197. Both words entered English centuries earlier, through French, without Latin's *c*. On etymological spelling, see V. Salmon, 'Orthography and punctuation' in R. Lass ed., *The Cambridge History of the English Language, Volume III: 1476–1776* (Cambridge, 1999), pp. 13–55 at p. 25, 27–28.

[93] WCA, MS. CF/2/2, fol. 13ᵛ, 177ʳ (Bird and Baildon ed., *Calendar*, ii, pp. 106, 221).

[94] M. Wyatt, *The Italian Encounter with Tudor England: A Cultural Politics of Translation* (Cambridge, 2005), pp. 43–44, suggests that the

For example, a long obituary for Sellyng from Christ Church focuses on his building works on the priory's manors, and his building of a library.[95] Such building works would look like the usual concerns of any bustling prior over the centuries and need not reflect humanist concerns; other monks are praised for supporting libraries and scholars or for their learning.[96] However, when the obituary is Sellyng's, the significance of this library might be different: this long obituary begins with a specific reference to his learning not only in divine but also secular books, Latin and Greek; another, shorter obituary of him also highlights his erudition in Greek and Latin and his excellent delivery of an oration before the Pope.[97] The longer obituary also begins with a lovely initial in Italianate style.[98] In such a life, in such an obituary, building a library might look like an imitation of the Vatican Library, Pisistratus' library in Athens, Caesar's in Rome. These three were, interestingly, all mentioned in GIOVANNI ANDREA BUSSI's preface to a copy of Jerome's works which was perhaps bought for Christ Church

---

earliest Italian artistic influences came from manuscript illuminations, and notes that the first Italian sculptors arrived in England in the 1500s.

[95] BL, MS. Arundel 68, fol. 4^{r-v}.

[96] BL, MS. Arundel 68, fol. 5^r (Thomas Goldstone, on whom see n. 80 above); and in general on praise for learning in obits from Christ Church, see M. Connor, 'Fifteenth-Century Monastic Obituaries: The Evidence of Christ Church Priory, Canterbury' in C. M. Barron and C. Burgess ed., *Memory and Commemoration in Medieval England: Proceedings of the 2008 Harlaxton Symposium* (Donington, 2010), pp. 143–62 at p. 150–51.

[97] CCA, MS. CCA-LitMs/D/12, fol. 31^v, with an earlier rough draft on fol. 27^v; on this manuscript, by Thomas Cawston, see Connor, 'Fifteenth-Century Monastic Obituaries'.

[98] BL, MS. Arundel 68, fol. 4^{r-v}; on the archaizing hand of the scribe Jacques Neele, see Parkes, 'Archaizing Hands', p. 111. Sellyng himself wrote at least one letter about building works in his humanist cursive: CCA, MS. DCc-ChChLet/I, no. 61 (Sheppard ed., *Christ Church Letters*, pp. 61–62, no. lviii).

under Sellyng's tenure.[99] We could even wonder about Richard Dene hiring the glass-painters at Great Malvern: was his adornment of the church just conventional piety or inspired by some favour for the arts among educated humanists?[100] Even when a monk hires a builder or glass-painter, seemingly unhumanist endeavours, he might be imitating antiquity under humanist influence.

Such evidence is widely dispersed and heavily diluted, and often reliant on debatable interpretations too. It is therefore easy to miss and open to dispute. It is quite sensible to focus on the 'Pure' humanist programmes preached and practised in England. Yet in the fifteenth century, as in the sixteenth and seventeenth centuries, it might be a sign of the prevalence and absorption of humanist influence that English scholars, scribes and bureaucrats do not always need to blazon their humanist studies so loudly; real scholars need not show off *all* the time. Our due attention to more thoroughbred and thoroughgoing humanist activities must not let us overlook other oblique, scattered moments of humanist activity – the snippets of Buondelmonti feeding a zeal for exploration, 'thies ambassadouris' coming and going, the building projects inspired by Roman magnificence, the gift of books by a bishop with just a few volumes of Cicero among the canon law. Once these stray references are spotted, and their interpretation is hazarded, then humanism appears as more widespread – both spread out and

---

[99] TCC, MS. R.17.4, fol. 1ʳ. This manuscript and its other half, MS. R.17.5, were copied by Theoderic Werken in 1477–78, from the 1468 edition of Jerome's letters [ISTC, no. ih00161000], on which see Giovanni Andrea Bussi, *Prefazioni alle Edizioni di Sweynheym e Pannartz, Prototipografici Romani*, ed. M. Miglio (Milan, 1978), pp. 3–11 at p. 3. R. A. B. Mynors, 'A Fifteenth-Century Scribe: T. Werken', *Transactions of the Cambridge Bibliographical Society*, i (1950), pp. 97–104 at p. 103, notes that the evidence that these books were direct commissions by Sellyng is only circumstantial. Interestingly, John Morer also bequeathed Jerome's letters to the students of Christ Church, Canterbury (Bennett, 'John Morer's Will', p. 89). On Werken, see n. 69 above.

[100] See n. 22 above.

spread thinly, but no less powerfully pervasive for that. This is unsurprising, for England's culture would, until the seventeenth century, be profoundly influenced by humanism. Yet those influences were profound in the sense of being deeply transformative, but also deeply buried. For example, though colonialism sprang from other economic and pious motives too, it did also spring from deep-seated classical ideas about travel, conquest and settlement, as noted in Worcester's use of Pliny to chart the Atlantic. Or, similarly, it might be said that humanist political enquiry in England did not produce Machiavelli's *Discorsi* but it did – so Hobbes, for one, thought – stir up a republican revolution;[101] and when the humanists transformed grammar-schools in England they produced few scholars like Scaliger; but they did instil small Latin, if less Greek, into Shakespeare's plays. One critic has described the influence of the humanist study of Roman drama on English drama as showing 'diffuseness', and diffuseness is just the right word.[102] For if humanism has dissolved until it is difficult to trace, it is nevertheless everywhere in diluted strains – and that diffusion, more than élite scholarship and close-knit magnate affinities, is what is important in the long run about humanism in England.

---

[101] Thomas Hobbes, *Behemoth or the Long Parliament*, ed. P. Seaward [Clarendon Edition of the Works of Thomas Hobbes, x] (Oxford, 2010), pp. 110, 179–80.

[102] G. Braden, *Renaissance Tragedy and the Senecan Tradition: Anger's Privilege* (New Haven, CN, 1985), pp. 182 and, in general, pp. 171–82.

HUMANISM ACROSS EUROPE: THE STRUCTURES OF CONTACTS

DAVID RUNDLE

At some moment near the very mid-point of the fifteenth century, a Genoese merchant, based in France, received a letter from his compatriot, BARTOLOMEO FACIO. The latter, based in Naples at the court of Alfonso V of Aragon and, indeed, historian of that king, importuned his correspondent to tell him whether there were any among the French who knew the name and works of Facio. Not, he insisted, that he held out much hope – 'for', he said, 'eloquence has hardly ever been able to penetrate beyond the confines of Italy, frightened off, as I take it, by the height of the mountains and the shivering of the snow.'[1] The evidence gathered in this volume has surely done enough to disprove Facio's assumption: whatever the magnitude of mountains and however distant the destination within Christendom, eloquence was not daunted: humanism travelled. International engagements were a repeated occurrence in the history of humanism, but they were not simply that – I would argue that they were fundamental to the self-definition of the humanist enterprise.

---

[1] G.-B. Mittarelli, *Bibliotheca codicum manuscriptorum monasterii S. Michaelis Venetiarum prope Murianum...* (Venice, 1779), col. 376. The manuscript from which Mittarelli transcribed is now Venice: Biblioteca Marciana, MS. lat. XI 80 (3057), on which see G. Albanese and M. Bulleri, 'L'Epistolario' in G. Albanese ed., *Studi su Bartolomeo Facio* (Pisa, 2000), pp. 133–214, esp. pp. 169–71 and pp. 185, 186 & 206 dating the correspondence to 1449 / 50, a date corroborated by the likelihood that the reference to unrest in London [col. 374] relates to Jack Cade's rebellion of 1450.

We are already adept at appreciating the *studia humanitatis* as grounded, as highly conscious of its Italian locales. The oft-cited *locus classicus* is LEONARDO BRUNI's celebration of his adoptive city of Florence in his earliest publications. The humanist who styled himself 'Leonardus Aretinus' opens his *Dialogi ad Petrum Paulum Histrum* deploring the decline of his home-town, Arezzo, but consoling himself by the fact that he lives in a *civitas* – and here he echoes his own *Laudatio Florentinae Urbis* – with such a bustle of people, a splendour of buildings, and a greatness of deeds already done that it is the most flourishing city.[2] Yet, even this preface, with its emphasis on the author's physical presence, is defined also by a sense of absence.[3] As the work's title emphasises, it is addressed to PIER PAOLO VERGERIO, a native of the Venetian Balkan dependency of Capodistria; he had been a member of the same coterie in Florence but had, by the time Bruni came to write his *Dialogi*, taken up employment in the papal curia at Rome.[4] Like Facio later imagining the Alps as a barrier to contact, Bruni bemoaned that 'mountains and valleys separate your body from us' but, he went on, Vergerio remained with them in their memory. That memory was not merely a mental faculty, since it gained some sort of lasting real presence through the written word – and this, of course, was the secular miracle at the centre of the humanist

---

[2] Leonardo Bruni, *Dialogi ad Petrum Paulum Histrum*, ed. S. U. Baldassarri (Florence, 1994), p. 235 (1, ll. 7–12); cf. Leonardo Bruni, *Laudatio Florentine urbis*, ed. S. U. Baldassarri (Florence, 2000). As James Hankins points out to me, Bruni came to designate himself 'Leonardus Arretinus', insisting on the double-r in the loconym.

[3] I concentrate in the next sentences on an acknowledged absence; there is another, silent but defining, absence at the heart of the work, if we accept the persuasive argument of R. Fubini, 'All'uscita dalla scolastica medievale: Salutati, Bruni e i "Dialogi ad Petrum Histrum"' in id., *L'Umanesimo italiano e i suoi storici* (Milan, 2001), pp. 75–103 [reproduced from *Archivio storico italiano,* cl (1992)].

[4] On Vergerio, see D. Robey, 'P. P. Vergerio the Elder: republicanism and civic values in the work of an early humanist', *Past & Present*, lviii (1973), pp. 3–37; J. McManamon, *Pier Paolo Vergerio the Elder: humanist as orator* (Tempe, AZ, 1996), and p. 150 above.

enterprise: accomplishing a level of eloquence that could persuade not just those sitting in front of you, but even those miles from where you stood. Mountains were made low as perceived distance was smoothed away and as the potential for continuing friendships (and enmities) beyond the face-to-face was realised. It might fairly be pointed out that this was no new miracle; it is true that quattrocento humanists followed where previous scholars had ventured in their correspondence and circulation of their writings. But there was, for many, a determination to test the limits of their skill, to prove that their eloquence was not bounded by the borders of the Italian peninsula. Some of those international achievements have been delineated in this volume; from them, I would urge, we should draw the conclusion that the *studia humanitatis* were less about genius of place than mastery over space.

My remit in the following paragraphs is to consider the mechanics or the methods by which these long-distance contacts were achieved by Italian humanists and by others – how, in other words, Italian Renaissance humanism was forged as an international enterprise.[5] The most obvious means was for a humanist himself to travel beyond the Alps. Too often an assumption is made that, as the humanist movement overproduced, it was those who were less able that were pushed out of the home market (as if 'the invisible hand' could add intellectual discernment to its prodigious array of supposed competences). In some cases, it even seems as if the suggestion is that taking employment abroad could be the death-knell of a humanist's talent: Bruni's friend, Pier Paolo Vergerio, was most famous for his popular tract on education, *De ingenuis moribus*; in 1418, he entered the employment of the Emperor Sigismund, travelling with him to Buda and so, it is said,

---

[5] This is a subject that is more usually discussed through *obiter dicta* than sustained study; note, however, the characteristically insightful essay of P. O. Kristeller, 'The European Diffusion of Humanism' in id., *Studies in Renaissance Thought and Letters*, 4 vols (Rome, 1954–96), ii (1985), pp. 147–165 [first printed in *Italica*, xxxix (1962), pp. 1–20].

'disappeared into obscurity'.[6] Vergerio himself might have been surprised to hear his promotion to imperial employment expressed in such terms; it is true that his translations of the Greek historian Arrian, undertaken in Sigismund's household, did not meet the standards expected by the next generation of scholars but that he produced them reminds us that his departure from Italy was no farewell to scholarship: locations beyond the peninsula could be sites of humanist invention.[7] More generally, contemporaries may have been less sure of themselves than historians seem to be in ordering their peers into some sort of league table of humanists, but Pier Paolo Vergerio should stand alongside the likes of ÆNEAS SYLVIUS PICCOLOMINI and POGGIO BRACCIOLINI as evidence to counter the assertion that 'no first-rate humanist went to teach outside Italy or served at a foreign court'.[8]

It might also be noted that in at least two of the cases just mentioned – Poggio and Vergerio – their move abroad occurred before there was any over-supply of humanists in Italy itself. For each of them, there was a positive decision to seek long-term employment with a foreign prince; they, as it were, jumped at the chance rather than being pushed to it. Yet, long-term residence at a court far from their hometowns could have its disadvantages: it not only placed them beyond the face-to-face

[6] George Holmes in J. R. Hale ed., *The Thames and Hudson Dictionary of The Italian Renaissance* (London, 1981), p. 331. On his time in Buda, see McManamon, *Vergerio the Elder*, pp. 153–67.

[7] On this translation, see P. A. Stadter, 'Arrianus' in *CTC*, iii (1976), pp. 1–20 at pp. 3–6, and for its fortuna, also my *England and the Identity of Italian Renaissance Humanism* (forthcoming). Note that Vergerio also produced two works, now lost: see Z. Kiséry, 'Vergerio et Sigismond de Luxembourg' in I. Takács ed., *Sigismundus Rex et Imperator. Art et culture au temps de Sigismond de Luxembourg 1387–1437* (Mainz, 2006), pp. 292–94.

[8] R. Weiss, 'Italian Humanism in Western Europe' in E. F. Jacob ed., *Italian Renaissance Studies. A tribute to the late Cecilia M. Ady* (London, 1960), pp. 69–93 at p. 70; cf. P. Burke, 'The Spread of Italian Humanism' in A. Goodman & A. MacKay ed., *The Impact of Humanism on Western Europe* (London, 1990), pp. 1–22 at p. 5.

contact possible in their earlier urban context – a practical counter-balance to their rhetorical confidence that, however far away they were, their eloquence could keep them present – but it also concentrated their attention on their prince and those around him. Humanists often supplemented their income by cultivating a plurality of patrons – a strategy that few of those in foreign courts imitated, with the result that their lifestyle may have been comfortable but inconspicuous.[9] Others who sought work abroad eschewed such a focused allegiance, preferring a more nomadic existence. For instance, STEFANO SURIGONE has been mentioned in the pages above for his time in England, where he produced writings in prose and verse, but his career was by no means confined to north of the Channel: between the 1450s and 1470s, this Milanese member of the Humiliati travelled between the university towns of Oxford, Louvain and Cologne, in all places presumably making his living primarily by teaching.[10]

Yet more extensive were the slightly later travels of GIROLAMO BALBI, though his movements were inspired as much by rivalry among Italians as by wanderlust.[11] Along with FAUSTO ANDRELINI and CORNELIO VITELLI, he taught at the University of Paris in 1489, but relations between the three were no advertisement for the internal harmony of an ex-pat community; their squabbling not only pushed Vitelli to move to England, where he had already been, but also sent Andrelini

---

[9] For discussion of some of these strategies, see my *England and Identity of Humanism*.

[10] On Surigone, see pp. 275–76 above. See also Weiss[4], pp. 211–213. The evidence for Surigone's time on the continent comes primarily from his poems, preserved at London: BL, MS. Arundel 249, fol. 94–117ᵛ.

[11] On Balbi, P. S. Allen, 'Hieronymus Balbus in Paris', *English Historical Review*, xvii (1902), pp. 417–28 remains fundamental; see also *CE*, i, pp. 88–89, and the articles of Gilbert Tournoy: 'L'œuvre poétique de Jérôme Balbi après son arrivée dans le Saint-Empire Romain' in *L'Humanisme allemand (1480–1540)* (Munich, 1979), pp. 321–337, and id., 'The literary production of Hieronymus Balbus at Paris', *Gutenberg-Jahrbuch*, [liii] (1978), pp. 70–77.

off to teach in Toulouse and Poitiers, only for him to return, and force Balbi himself to leave; while Andrelini found favour at the French court, Balbi (after his own brief spell in England) sought advancement further east, first at the University of Vienna and then at the court of Ladislaus II Jagiellon (1471–1516) in Prague.[12] Balbi's career might be read as an example of how one might progress from itinerant teacher to an insider at court, or it could be taken as evidence of how a humanist could retreat from a place more visited to a corner which they could make their own. There was, in short, more than one route open to the cosmopolitan humanist.

The examples that I have mentioned here could be grouped into three categories, forming a sort of sliding scale of mobility: the émigré, who settles in one place (Vergerio); the migrant, whose career involves movement between a few foreign locations (Surigone), and the instinctively migratory, for whom travel itself becomes a lifestyle. Often given a brief name-check in this last category is the poet known as JOHANNES MICHAEL NAGONIUS, whose wanderings, perhaps at times paid for as diplomatic trips, gave him opportunity to produce manuscripts in order to seek royal favour in cities as far apart as London and Buda.[13] An earlier example of the migratory could be TITO

---

[12] On Andrelini, see *CE*, i, pp. 53–56 and G. Tournoy-Thoen, 'Fausto Andrelini et la cour de France' in *L'Humanisme français au début de la Renaissance* (Paris, 1973), pp. 65–79. On Vitelli, see R. Weiss, 'Cornelio Vitelli in France and England', *Journal of the Warburg Institute*, ii (1939), pp. 219–26; C. Clough, 'Thomas Linacre, Cornelio Vitelli, and Humanistic Studies at Oxford' in F. Maddison et al. ed., *Linacre Studies. Essays on the life and work of Thomas Linacre c. 1460–1524* (Oxford, 1977), pp. 1–23 and id., 'New Light on Cornelio Vitelli and Humanistic Studies at Oxford University in the late Fifteenth Century', *The Ricardian*, xii (2000), pp. 94–119.

[13] Nagonius is mentioned, for instance, by P. O. Kristeller, 'European Diffusion', p. 153. For full discussion, see now P. Gwynne, *Poets and Princes. The panegyric poetry of Johannes Michael Nagonius* (Turnhout, 2012); see also id., '"Tu alter Caesar eris": Maximilian I, Vladislav II, Johannes Michael Nagonius and the *renovatio imperii*', *Renaissance Studies*, x (1996), pp. 56–71.

LIVIO FRULOVISI, who seemed to prefer to be outside Italy rather than in it: he is best known for his time as secretary to Humfrey, duke of Gloucester, but after his English employment ended and he had returned to his homeland, he did not stay long, his later career as a medical doctor taking him to Toulouse and Barcelona.[14] Like Balbi, his travels might not have been entirely directed by his own choice and this should remind us how contingent – or (as they might have put it themselves) subject to fortune – humanists' travels were. We record the dates and places of those that occurred but have to overlook those journeys that were cut short or did not take place: what would have happened to Poggio if, on his return to Italy from England, he had attained the Hungarian employment it seems he hoped to gain?[15] How different would the fortunes of AURELIO BRANDOLINI been if Matthias Corvinus had not died soon after his own arrival in Buda?[16]

Instead of dwelling on the counter-factual, however, let us emphasise an obvious truth: those humanists who did experience Europe beyond the Alps were a minority. For others, there may have been a simple practical disincentive to following their example: travel could be life-threatening. Piccolomini told

---

[14] I outline his career in D. Rundle, 'Tito Livio Frulovisi, and the place of comedies in the formation of a humanist's career', *Studi Umanistici Piceni*, xxiv (2004), pp. 193–202; see also id., 'The Unoriginality of Tito Livio Frulovisi's *Vita Henrici Quinti*', *English Historical Review*, cxxiii (2008), pp. 1109–31.

[15] M. C. Davies, 'Poggio as Rhetorician and Historian: unpublished pieces', *Rinascimento*, 2nd ser., xxii (1982), pp. 153–182, esp. pp. 167–68.

[16] Nowadays his best-known work is *De comparatione rei publicae et regni*, which is available in Aurelio Lippo Brandolini, *Republics and Kingdoms Compared*, ed. J. Hankins [IRTL, lx] (Cambridge, 2009); for his biography, the seminal work remains E. Mayer, *Un umanista italiano della corte di Mattio Corvino. Aurelio Brandolini Lippo* [Biblioteca dell'Accademia d'Ungheria di Roma, xiv] (Rome, 1938), but see also S. M. Mitchell, 'The *De comparatione rei publicae et regni (1490) of Aurelio Brandolini* (unpublished M.Phil. thesis, Warburg Institute, University of London, 1985), pp. 22–58.

in writing of his misfortunes en route to (and within) Scotland, though they did not stop his perambulations around northern and central Europe.[17] On the other hand, GUINIFORTE BARZIZZA, son of the famous teacher, Gasparino, having accompanied his master, Alfonso the Magnanimous, from Aragon to Tunisia and then gone on to Milan, fell into such ill health he could not return to his master; henceforth, his career was to be less adventurous.[18] With such examples before them, we may have sympathy for those humanists who decided that they could more safely cultivate international contacts from the comfort of their desk, and that is what many did. The long life of the leading Milanese humanist PIER CANDIDO DECEMBRIO, for example, involved few journeys beyond the Italian peninsula but his desire for patronage was not as confined as his travel patterns.[19] Indeed, he made a point of announcing how his works had reached as far away as Spain and even the ends of the

---

[17] Piccolomini's comments on Scotland are most usefully collected together in Pius II, *De Europa*, ed. A. van Heck [Studi e Testi, cccxcviii] (Vatican City, 2001), pp. 184–87.

[18] These years of Guiniforte's life are reconstructed by A. Sottili, 'Note biografiche sui petrarchisti Giacomo Publicio e Guiniforte Barzizza e sull'umanista valenziano Giovanni Serra' in F. Schalk ed., *Petrarca 1304–1374. Beiträge zu Werk und Wirkung* (Frankfurt, 1975), pp. 270–86 at pp. 277–82. For the intellectual continuities from the father Barzizza to his son, see G. Albanese, 'I "Commentarii in Epistolas Senece" di Gasparino Barzizza' in L. Gualdo Rosa ed., *Gasparino Barzizza e la rinascita degli studi classici: fra continuità e rinnovamento* [Annali dell'Istituto universitario orientale di Napoli, xxi] (Naples, 1999), pp. 9–83 at pp. 46–53.

[19] On Decembrio, the works of Vittorio Zaccaria remain fundamental, particularly his 'Sulle opere di Pier Candido Decembrio', *Rinascimento*, 1st ser., vii (1956) pp. 13–74, and id., 'L'Epistolario di Pier Candido Decembrio', *Rinascimento*, 1st ser., iii (1952), pp. 85–118. Decembrio made at least one journey to northern Europe: in the autograph copy of his *volgare* translation of another humanist's biography of a barbarian prince, the aforementioned Frulovisi's *Vita Henrici Quinti*, Decembrio adds a marginal note, reading 'Questo philippo [of Burgundy] e lo ducha presente dal quale fu mandato io candido in 1434 da philippo maria a praticare de farlo Imperatore...' [ÖNB, MS. 2610, fol. 46].

world – that is, England – and that was not without, it should be said, his own assistance.[20] He sought out associations both with Humfrey, duke of Gloucester and with Juan II, king of Castile, to mention only the most distinguished of his foreign dedicatees.[21] Decembrio was far from alone in wanting to proclaim the wide extent of his fame. During his few years at the papal curia, one of his colleagues was FLAVIO BIONDO, who associated his own identity most particularly with the city of Rome – with the physical remains of its past greatness and with its present renaissance, of which (he said) the throng of visitors who daily clustered in Christendom's centre provided evidence.[22] At the same time, it was also to Biondo's purpose to emphasise how his works reached far beyond his own location. In 1461, he boasted of his *Roma Triumphans* that 'England, France, Spain, and a range of cities in Italy already have highly embellished copies of the work'.[23] It was his claim that he had overseen a group of scribes who had quickly produced

---

[20] A. Sammut, *Unfredo duca di Gloucester e gli umanisti italiani* (Padua, 1980), p. 191, ll. 40–44; cf. M. Borsa, 'Pier Candido Decembri e l'umanesimo in Lombardia', *Archivio storico lombardo*, 2nd ser., x (1893), pp. 5–75 & 358–441 at p. 432.

[21] On his relations with Humfrey, see Weiss[4], pp. 85–95; I discuss the subject in *England and the Identity of Humanism*; see also pp. 273–75 above. On Decembrio and Juan II, see C. Fabiano, 'Pier Candido Decembrio traduttore d'Omero', *Aevum*, xxiii (1949), pp. 36–51; Zaccaria, 'Sulle opere', esp. pp. 22–24; P. S. Suarez-Somonte and T. Gonzalez Rolan, 'Sobre la presencia en España de la versión latina de la "Ilíada". Edición de la "Vita Homeri" y de su traducción castellana', *Cuadernos de filología clasíca*, xxi (1988), pp. 319–44, and M. Pade, 'The *Fortuna* of *Leontius Pilatus's* Homer. With an Edition of Pier Candido Decembrio's "Why Homer's Greek Verses are rendered in Latin Prose"' in F. T. Coulson and A. A. Grotans ed., *Classica et Beneventana. Essays presented to Virginia Brown on the occasion of her 65th birthday* (Turnhout, 2008), pp. 149–71 at pp. 160–61 & 168–72. See also p. 1 above.

[22] See, in particular, F. Biondo, 'Roma Instaurata' in id., *Opera* (Basel, 1531), pp. 222–272 at p. 272.

[23] B. Nogara, *Scritti inediti e rari di Biondo Flavio* [Studi e Testi, xlviii] (Rome, 1927), p. 208.

manuscripts of his new book so it could achieve such a wide dissemination.

We might ask why these humanists and others – for the examples could be multiplied – bothered to strive to reach foreign audiences. After all, as both Decembrio and Leonardo Bruni found when seeking the patronage of the same English royal duke, the process was both costly and fraught with practical difficulties; the methods of contact, sending manuscripts via trading ships or in diplomatic baggage, did not provide an efficient or even a reliable form of communication.[24] That they and others did try might suggest they perceived the outlay to be worth it – that there were, in other words, rich pickings on the horizon. If, though, they imagined their rewards were to be pecuniary, they would often have been disappointed as such long-distance financial transactions could prove elusive. Yet, there was perhaps another non-financial incentive, one related to a humanist's cultural capital. As I suggested earlier, at the heart of the humanist enterprise was a determination to demonstrate the power of one's eloquence, and long-distance communications could well prove that ability. But this was distance measured not just by miles, horizontally across space, but also vertically across cultural divides, in which the Italian humanists depicted themselves as of more worthy stock than the barbarian peoples elsewhere in Europe.[25] The advantage, then, of foreign contacts was that they could present a humanist as reaching both out and down, beyond and below, creating a fame that they could claim was wide and deep. By those

[24] I highlight this in *England and Identity of Humanism*.
[25] E. Garin, 'La cultura fiorentina nella seconda metà del '300 e i "barbari britanni"', *La Rassegna della letteratura italiana*, lxiv (1960) pp. 181–195; see also P. Boitani, 'Petrarch and the "barbari Britanni"' in M. McLaughlin and L. Panizza ed., *Petrarch in Britain. Interpreters, imitators, and translators over 700 Years* [Proceedings of the British Academy, cxlvi] (Oxford, 2007), pp. 9–25, and, for some of the later history of the concept, D. Hay, 'Italy and Barbarian Europe' in id., *Renaissance Essays* (London, 1988), pp. 353–73 [first published in E. F. Jacob ed., *Italian Renaissance Studies. A tribute to the late Cecilia M. Ady* (London, 1960), pp. 48–67].

contacts, they could demonstrate that their eloquence had purchase not just among their peers but even with those they deemed less civilised – while, of course, in reality, they were most often approaching their social betters. Consequently, competing rhetorics of submission, of 'friendship' and of superiority can sometimes been seen to jostle for space in their letters – letters which often would not just be sent to their recipient abroad but would also circulate among colleagues within Italy. Foreign connexions, then, could be valuable to a local persona, assisting the self-construction of a humanist's reputation as international to impress those close to home.

The far reach of one's fame was, therefore, a humanist topos of praise; it could be facilitated by advances to foreign patrons but it had a further variant. The alternative was to celebrate how a humanist's repute proved an irresistible pull to foreigners, impelling them to traverse Europe to be in his presence. As Biondo praised the city of Rome for the attraction it held to the peoples of Europe and beyond, so others lauded an individual scholar for a fame or charisma that brought barbarians to sit at his feet. The scholar in question was most often GUARINO DA VERONA, the school-master and lecturer whose later years were spent in the d'Este city of Ferrara. Around him there seems to have developed a particular cult which celebrated not only his ability, as LUDOVICO CARBONE put it, to liberate foreigners from their barbarity, but also his international fame that drew the distant peoples to him.[26] So, Janus Pannonius declared how men came 'from all the ends of the earth' to Ferrara in order to hear Guarino – and he goes on to demonstrate his grasp of arcane Latin geographical terms as he lists the regions, from Dalmatia to Britain (via Rhodes and Crete), that have become enthralled by this humanist.[27] Historians, it must be said, have tended to read such praise ingenuously, taking it as evidence of

---

[26] *Prosatori latini del quattrocento*, ed. E. Garin (Milan, 1952), p. 398.

[27] *Panegyricus in Guarinum* in I. Thomson, *Humanist Pietas: the panegyric of Ianus Pannonius on Guarinus Veronensis* (Bloomington, 1988), p. 148 (ll. 473–486). On Pannonius, see pp. 146–48 and 160–62 above.

the esteem in which Guarino was already held but I wonder whether we would be better advised to see it as constructing and moulding that esteem.[28] It is notable that those who praise him were, in the first place, his students, men like Pannonius or the Englishman John Free. As the latter wrote to Guarino when claiming the reason he had travelled to Italy was the humanist's fame, it is the duty of every liberal man to praise the deserving – a mark of good manners that presumably he learnt from Guarino himself.[29]

Whether or not the barbarians peacefully invaded Italy in the mid-fifteenth century in order to submit themselves to Guarino's teaching, it is certainly the case that there were foreigners in the peninsula who became active participants in the humanist agenda. This is the counter-balance or the complement to considering the presence of the *studia humanitatis* in lands beyond Italy: humanist activities, even in its homeland, were a cosmopolitan enterprise. I leave aside the issue of the Greeks, who held a special status as the source of precious knowledge but whose cultural role, as John Monfasani has shown, should not be seen solely in terms of humanist interests.[30] It might similarly be said that we cannot adduce from the mere fact of their presence at an Italian university that a foreign student was bound to be infected (to use Stephen Milner's virus metaphor) by any strain of humanism.[31] Yet, as previous chapters have shown, there were non-Italians whose time in the peninsula contributed to or inspired their literary studies. I want briefly to highlight a particular group of foreigners, that is those who were humanist collaborators by

---

[28] I expand on this point in D. Rundle, 'Beyond the classroom: international interest in the *studia humanitatis* in the university towns of Quattrocento Italy', *Renaissance Studies*, xxvii (2013), pp. 533-48.

[29] J. E. Spingarn, 'Unpublished Letters of an English Humanist', *Journal of Comparative Literature*, i (1903), pp. 47–65 at p. 55.

[30] See pp. 31–57 above.

[31] See p. 4 above.

adopting the script and style of manuscript presentation favoured by the humanists.

It was Poggio Bracciolini who first constructed the archaising bookhand that was to become known as *littera antiqua* – a style of script that, adopted and adapted in print, was to remain with western civilisation for centuries; it belies its classicising origins in the designation sometimes used for it of 'Roman'.[32] It – and the accompanying style of *bianchi girari* ('white vine-stem') illumination – became, as it were, the face of Renaissance manuscripts, so much so that we are inclined to consider them particularly 'Italian'. From the start, however, the producers of humanist script were not only Poggio's countrymen: his first student of *littera antiqua* was the person he described as the 'good French scribe'.[33] The name of that Gallic pioneer is now lost to us, but he had many successors. In a survey of just over four hundred copyists who signed and dated humanist manuscripts they produced in Italy, a sixth of the scribes is identifiably non-Italian.[34] The evidence holds out the prospect of being able to quantify these partners in the humanist enterprise by geographical origin, broadly defined:

German	35	50%
Netherlandish	19	27%

[32] B. L. Ullman, *The Origin and Development of Humanistic Script* (Rome, 1960); A. C. de la Mare, *Handwriting of the Italian Humanists*, i / 1 (Oxford, 1973).

[33] On whom, see de la Mare, *Handwriting*, pp. 82–84, with a tentative identification of the scribe.

[34] I base the data on A. Derolez, *Codicologie des manuscrits en écriture humanistique sur parchemin*, 2 vols (Turnhout, 1984), i, pp. 124–63. The full details are as follows: Bohemian (scribe 289); Dalmatian (138); French (158, 159, 180, 193, 218, 300, 367); German (8, 50, 90, 91, 123, 133, 137, 149, 155, 165, 182, 185, 187, 189, 202, 209, 214, 215, 217, 219, 221, 227, 234, 238, 247, 248, 253, 260, 288, 298, 301, 321, 327, 352, 401); Greek (26, 251); Netherlandish (51, 124, 141, 147, 148, 162, 164, 170, 211, 213, 222, 225, 245, 262, 307, 322, 353, 357, 391); Scottish (136); Spanish (12, 125, 145); unidentified foreigner (146).

French	7	10%
Spanish	3	4.25%
Greek	2	3%
Bohemian, Dalmatian & Scottish	1 each	4.25% in all
Unidentified	1	1.5%
TOTAL	70	

Such bald percentages obviously have to come with several caveats. In the first place, the overall figure hides variation from city to city. The papal capital of Rome was well-known for its cosmopolitan nature and something near a half of its scribes may have been from outside the peninsula.[35] At the other extreme, Florence, the hometown of *littera antiqua*, could supply its needs mainly through local copyists, though, even there, about one in ten named humanist scribes were foreign, with the largest proportion (once again) being German.[36] Given the extent of the German-speaking lands, it would be natural for the greatest number to hail from there, but there may be other factors in play. The data we have is self-selecting: it depends on the scribe deciding to reveal their identity, and many chose not to; the

---

[35] For a discussion of this international milieu in Rome, see E. Caldelli, *Copisti a Roma* (Rome, 2006), pp. 25–32, esp. p. 28 (n. 19); her precious listing of scribes in Rome, identified via explicitly localised manuscripts, does not, however, distinguish between humanist and non-humanist scribes.

[36] A. C. de la Mare, 'New Research on humanistic scribes in Florence' in A. Garzelli ed., *Miniatura fiorentina del Rinascimento*, 2 vols (Florence, 1985), i, pp. 393–600. In her list of seventy-two named scribes, there are eight foreigners: one French (scribe 33), five German (32?, 34, 35, 56, 69), one Netherlandish (63) and one Spanish (31).

choice might be personal or might be a cultural habit.[37] None in the lists of humanist copyists who signed themselves was, for instance, English and, while there were only a few, we know some were active, like Thomas Candour, who never announced his name in the colophons to his manuscripts.[38] This also alerts us to a wider truth: the identification of a humanist manuscript as by a non-Italian scribe requires explicit evidence and, in the absence of that, the tendency is to assume its creator was indeed Italian. The level of foreign engagement with these practices suggests that tendency might not always be wise. It also suggests that the evidence we have to date provides estimates closer to the minimum than the maximum of foreign engagement with 'Roman' script.

Copying texts in a humanist book-hand might be said not to make one a humanist, and it is certainly the case that many fashionable scribes – Italian or not – were less interested in textual accuracy than the *studia humanitatis* should have hoped. But even if we may, in some cases, doubt the scribe's personal commitment to the intellectual programme that found visual expression in the 'antique' mise-en-page, we cannot deny that the patrons who were often their employers and who were often themselves Italian patently did not see the practice of humanist book production as being a closed shop from which any non-Italian was excluded. Nor were the other activities that characterise humanism confined, even in the peninsula of its birth, to those who were also born there. Previous chapters have mentioned the likes of Rudolf Agricola, some of whose translations from Greek into Latin were produced while he was employed in Ferrara, and John Free, all of whose œuvre was composed while he was in Padua or in Rome, the place of his

---

[37] A. Derolez, 'Pourquoi les copistes signaient-ils leurs manuscrits?' in E. Condello & G. De Gregorio ed., *Scribi e Colofoni* (Spoleto, 1995), pp. 37–56.

[38] D. Rundle, 'The Scribe Thomas Candour and the making of Poggio Bracciolini's English reputation', *English Manuscript Studies 1100–1700*, xii (2005), pp. 1–25.

premature death.[39] The geographical range could be stretched further, to include both the rather obscure Portuguese scholar 'Valascus Lisbonensis' and the better-known Dalmatian humanist and bishop, Nicholas of Modrus (c. 1427–1480), book-collector and historian of the Goths.[40] Each of these may be considered exceptional but together and alongside the humanist scribes just mentioned, they remind us that, not only beyond Italy but also within it, humanism could not avoid being an international enterprise.

So far in this chapter, I have discussed humanist activities in courtly and civic contexts, but not in congresses, those international diplomatic gatherings that could greatly swell a town's population for weeks or months or years. One specific type of congress is often given a privileged position in narratives of the success story of humanism: the General Councils of the Church that met in the first half of the fifteenth century, intent on healing a disunited church and then on reforming it nearly to the point of renewed disunity. Of these Councils – Pisa (1409), Constance (1414–18), Pavia–Siena (1423–24), Basel (1431–49), Ferrara–Florence (1438–39) – Constance is particularly mentioned, most often for the escapades of Poggio Bracciolini. It was on a trip away from the main business of the Council that he and his colleagues famously 'liberated' the complete text of Quintilian's *Institutes of Oratory* from its 'dungeon' in the monastery of St Gall; it was at the Council that he made a display of Ciceronian eloquence, orating on the death of Cardinal Francesco Zabarella; it was from there that he

---

[39] See pp. 83 and 277–81 above.

[40] On the first, see A. de la Mare, 'Notes on Portuguese Patrons of the Florentine Book Trade in the Fifteenth Century' in K. J. P. Lowe, *Cultural Links between Portugal and Italy in the Renaissance* (Oxford, 2000), pp. 167–81 at pp. 171–72. On Nicholas of Modrus, we look forward to the study by Luka Špoljarić (Central European University, Budapest); for the time being, see G. Mercati, 'Notizie varie sopra Niccolò Modrussiense' in id., *Opere minori*, 6 vols [Studi e testi, lxxvi–lxxx & ccxcvi] (Vatican City, 1937–84), iv (1937), pp. 205–67.

entertained friends back in Italy with tales of his adventures, both intellectual and earthier.[41] A Council like Constance could also act as a stimulus to textual exchange, a nodal point for the circulation of books.[42] These works could include refound classical texts, like Quintilian, or witnesses to the *studia humanitatis*, like Poggio's oration on Zabarella, but this humanist element – we should remember – was only ever one small part in the welter of cultural activities which were the stuff and show of these events: the ceremonies, the services, their music, their physical setting, the acts of cultural display, let alone the intellectual debates that defined their sessions. The vast majority of the orations at Constance, for instance, while they may have been eloquent and persuasive, were certainly not given in the style which was being promoted by Leonardo Bruni and his fellow trailblazers.[43] This is not to deny the possibility that the content or presentation of humanist rhetoric may have had some influence on non-humanist speeches at such an occasion – a point that demonstrates that Daniel Wakelin's distinction in this volume between pure and diffuse

[41] Poggio's finds at St Gall – in the company of Cencio de' Rusticci and Bartolomeo da Montepulciano – can be best read in his own words: *Lettere*, ed. H. Harth, 3 vols (Florence, 1984–87), ii, pp. 153–56 (and cf. pp. 444–447); see also R. Sabbadini, *Le Scoperte dei codici latini e greci ne' secoli xiv e xv* (Florence, 1905), pp. 77–79. On his Zabarella oration, see J. McManamon, *Funeral Oratory and the Cultural Ideals of Italian Humanism* (Chapel Hill, NC, 1989), pp. 11–12. For his letters from Constance, see also Poggio, *Lettere*, ed. Harth, i, pp. 128–35 & ii, pp. 157–63. The relevant letters are accessible in English translation: *Two Renaissance Book Hunters. The letters of Poggius Braccolini to Nicolaus de Niccolis*, trans. P. W. Goodhart Gordon (New York, 1974), pp. 24–31 and 187–213.

[42] See, for instance, D. Marcotte ed., *Humanisme et culture géographique à l'époque du Concile de Constance autour de Guillaume Fillastre* (Turnhout, 2002).

[43] A most useful relevant resource now available is the website by C. Nighman and P. Stump, 'A Bibliographical Register of the Sermons and other Orations delivered at the Council of Constance (1414–1418)', available on-line at http://www.bibsocamer.org/BibSite/Nighman-Stump/index.html [accessed 21st September 2011].

humanism has relevance far beyond the English examples which are his remit here.[44] But, while events that took place at Constance or other General Councils may have been important for the self-identity of the *studia humanitatis*, humanism was hardly essential to the Councils. Furthermore, these gatherings may have been the largest and the most cosmopolitan – a cosmopolitanism which could reach beyond western Europe to the Greeks and yet further, to embrace, for instance, Ethiopians – but they are best considered as one subset of those international congresses that were seen as useful recourse in attempting to resolve contention, secular as well as ecclesiastical.[45] So, in this definition are to be included not only Pius II's vain attempt at Mantua in 1459 to rally European princes to a new crusade, or those imperial Diets where the Ottoman threat was high on the agenda (for instance at Frankfurt in 1454 or Regensburg in 1471), but also those events occasioned by other conflicts, like the meetings designed to end the Hundred Years War, most notably the Congress of Arras (1435).[46] For all of these, we might find the general pattern to involve the presence of some humanists and the sound of some Ciceronian oratory but always subsumed within

---

[44] See pp. 289–306 above. For an example of this 'diffusion', see C. L. Nighman, 'Reform and Humanism in the Sermons of Richard Fleming at the Council of Constance (1417)' (PhD thesis, University of Toronto, 1996) which is available on-line at: https://tspace.library.utoronto.ca/handle/1807/12882 [accessed 21st September 2011].

[45] On the Council of Ferrara–Florence, see pp. 43-44 above, with the bibliography there. For the presence of Greeks and Ethiopians not only there but at Constance as well, see J. Gill, *The Council of Florence* (Cambridge, 1959), pp. 21–22 and cf. pp. 321–328.

[46] For the uncertain possibility that it was at Frankfurt that Piccolomini caught sight of the first printed Bibles, see M. C. Davies, 'Juan de Carvajal and Early Printing: the 42-line Bible and the Sweynheym and Pannartz Aquinas', *The Library*, 6th ser., xviii (1996), pp. 193–215; at Regensburg, the papal delegation, led by Francesco Todeschini–Piccolomini, included Giovanni Antonio Campano. I discuss the Congress of Arras in my *England and the Identity of Humanism*.

a wider range of cultural display, and usually frankly marginal to the intellectual exchange that was the purpose of the event.

Congresses were also, of course, by their nature exceptional occasions; I would like, before closing this chapter, to draw attention to a more humdrum, quotidian factor that is given less consideration than it should be. Half a century ago, Paul Oskar Kristeller noted that, in the exchange of persons that facilitated the movement of humanist activities, a role was played by Italian 'bankers and businessmen' abroad, many of whom 'had scholarly interests and contacts'.[47] He himself cited one example of this phenomenon which he had studied himself: Francesco Tedaldi (d. 1518), Florentine silk merchant who was also a correspondent of MARSILIO FICINO and who, during his long sojourn in France (in places as disparate as Brittany and Avignon), found time to pen a short novella in humanist Latin.[48] Few have followed up Kristeller's suggestive general comment, perhaps under the impression that hard-nosed capitalists far from their homeland would have little use for the fashionable Latin being paraded by the literati in their native towns. Yet, learned contact is often a parasite travelling on the back of international commerce, and merchants at times did assist the humanist enterprise, not only by being conduits but also by being correspondents and collaborators in it. Let me give three examples.

The first involves an Englishman who, when he travelled in Italy, was fêted as a member of the royal family, though his

[47] Kristeller, 'European Diffusion', p. 151.

[48] P. O. Kristeller, 'Una novella latina e il suo autore Francesco Tedaldi, mercante fiorentino del quattrocento' in id., *Studies*, ii, pp. 385–402 [first published in *Studi Letterari. Miscellanea in onore di Emilio Santini* (Palermo, 1956), pp. 159–80]. For his correspondence with Ficino, in which the latter berates Tedaldi for his travelling and alludes to a philosophical work, apparently of Tedaldi's, 'in quo occidentalium philosophorum disputationes de anima recensentur', see Marsilio Ficino, *Opera omnia* [reprint of the Basel edition of 1576], 2 vols in 4 (Turin, 1959), i / 2, pp. 635, 653 [English translation available in *The Letters of Marsilio Ficino*, 8 vols to date (London, 1975–2009), i (1975), pp. 99 & 148–49].

genealogy gave him little reason to make that boast. William Gray (c. 1414–78), later to be bishop of Ely, was a student at Padua and Ferrara (sitting at Guarino's feet) and then the English royal proctor in Rome.[49] He certainly deported himself so as to appear princely, travelling with a large retinue and opening his house to scholars like NICCOLÒ PEROTTI.[50] It begs the question: how did he come by the money with which he was lavish? We can at least have some sense of how he avoided cash-flow problems: it appears that he arranged transfers of money from London via the Venetian bank of Giovanni Marcanova, who had himself been based in England for some years.[51] This was not the only Venetian of that name known to Gray: one of the witnesses at his academic ceremonies in Padua in September 1445 was Giovanni Marcanova, humanist and cousin to the banking merchant.[52] Marcanova was an already established figure at the University but it is surely legitimate to wonder whether the financial association that Gray had with his family oiled the acquaintance the Englishman developed with him. We are aware of merchants as conduits in the sense of carrying books in their bags or being used as diplomatic couriers, but this example might suggest more active personal agency, a merchant consciously facilitating humanist contacts.

The second example comes from later in the century and involves another English cleric: William Sellyng, monk and later

---

[49] I discuss the 'pretensions' of William Gray in *England and Humanism*. See also Weiss[4], pp. 132–48, and R. A. B. Mynors, *Catalogue of the Manuscripts of Balliol College Oxford* (Oxford, 1963), pp. xxiv–xlv.

[50] On Perotti in Gray's household, see Mynors, *Catalogue of the Manuscripts of Balliol*, p. xxx.

[51] E. Barile, P. C. Clarke and G. Nordio, *Cittadini veneziani del quattrocento: I due Giovanni Marcanova, il mercante e l'umanista* (Venice, 2006), pp. 22 and 333–34, discussing Giovanni Marcanova's tax return of 1446. This is a uniquely rich document for Marcanova's activities; it is reasonable to assume Gray made more frequent use of this method to transfer money from London to north-east Italy.

[52] *Acta graduum academicorum gymnasii Patavini ab anno 1406 ad annum 1450*, ed. C. Zonta & G. Brotto (Padua, 1922), no. 1968, noted by Weiss[4], p. 136.

prior of Christ Church, Canterbury, about whom – including his teaching by Stefano Surigone – much has already been said in this volume.[53] Some years later, around 1470, Sellyng was in contact with another Italian, Umfredo Gentili, a Lucchese merchant based in London. His purpose in writing, in fashionable Latin, was to prevail upon Gentili's *humanitas* so that he would show a friend the copy of Livy's *Decades* that he owned.[54] Gentili, then, was a manuscript-owner of classical works whom others thought it appropriate to importune in humanist tones; we seem to be getting close to an example of a merchant as humanist collaborator.[55]

This is all the more evident with our final example, which returns us to the opening of this chapter. We saw Bartolomeo

---

[53] See pp. 293–302 above.

[54] W. A. Pantin, *Canterbury College, Oxford*, 4 vols [Oxford Historical Society, new series, vi–viii & xxx] (Oxford, 1947–85), iii (1950), p. 109, transcribing from London: BL, MS. Cotton Julius F. vii, fol. 205 (notebook of William Worcester). Given the provenance of the manuscript, the suggestion that the unnamed friend was Worcester is attractive but unlikely since he was not, at this point, 'cuiusdam venerabilis viri familiaris', as described in the letter: for the suggestion, see C. Clough 'Selling, William (c. 1430–1494)' in the on-line *Oxford Dictionary of National Biography* [accessed 30th November 2011]. Gentili's identity as a merchant is revealed by the 1472 pardon to him enrolled at Kew: National Archives, C66 / 528, membrane 4, calendared at *Calendar of Patent Rolls 1467–77* (London, 1900), p. 312.

[55] The *terminus post quem non* of Sellyng's letter (which, as he signs himself 'monachus', is September 1472, when he was made prior) makes it impossible entirely to exclude the possibility that Gentili's Livy was one of the incunables printed in Italy in 1469 and 1470 [ISTC, nos il00236000, il00237000 and il00238000], but the phrasing of the letter certainly implies that Gentili's ownership of the volume was not part of the trade in printed books then beginning; on that trade see L. Hellinga, 'Importation of Books Printed on the Continent into England and Scotland before c. 1520' in S. Hindman ed., *Printing the Written Word. The social history of books, circa 1450–1520* (Ithaca, 1991), pp. 205–224, and the comments I make in D. Rundle, 'English books and the continent' in D. Wakelin and A. Gillespie ed., *The Production of Books in England 1350–1500* (Cambridge, 2011), pp. 276–91.

Facio writing to a Genoese merchant, who was then in France, but this was not a one-sided correspondence. We have letters from the merchant, Gian Giacomo Spinola, and they show him matching Facio in their style of Latin. He opens one letter, for instance, in good humanist style, begging his correspondent to attribute his silence 'curae mercaturae nostrae, quae nullam habet intermissionem ... potius quam negligentiae' ('to our mercantile business, which gives no let-up, rather than to neglect'). However, it is not only in his Latin style that Spinola wants to match Facio; he goes on in his letter, interspersing news about his family with a description of his own pastimes:

> Nulli aut perpauci sunt apud hos Gallos qui eloquentiae studiis delectentur, aut iis operam dent. Multi autem Italici fuerunt, qui Ciceronis opera, maxime *de re publica*, summa diligentia quaesierunt, sed frustra. Ego quidem semper dedi operam, ut aliquid novum invenirem, sed nihil reperi in eloquentia.[56]

> There are none or very few among these French who are interested in the study of eloquence or give effort to it. On the other hand, there have been many Italians who have searched very hard for the works of Cicero, particularly his *De re publica*, but in vain. I, indeed, have always put in the effort so that I might find something new, but I have found nothing of eloquence.

He was a merchant, in other words, who, in what few hours business allowed, liked to act out the humanist activity of searching for lost classical manuscripts. Nor, clearly, did his association with the *studia humanitatis* end when he crossed over from Italy to France. It might fairly be said that Spinola was no petit bourgeois salesman: a member of one of the leading families of Genoa, he was both a former student of Facio and a dedicatee of some of the humanist's works.[57] However, while he

---

[56] Mittarelli, *Bibliotheca ... monasterii S. Michaelis Venetiarum prope Murianum*, col. 374.

[57] On him, see F. Gabotto, 'Un nuovo contributo alla storia dell'umanesimo ligure', *Atti della Società Ligure di Storia Patria*, xxiv (1892), pp. 5–331 at pp. 22–25, and G. Albanese and D. Pietragalla, '"In honorem regis edidit": lo scrittoio di Bartolomeo Facio alla corte

may have been outstanding in his status and his literary pretensions, similar interests were certainly shared by others among the Genoese mercantile community.[58] None of this, however, is to claim that his affectations may have been displayed to his French hosts: his correspondence with Facio could be an example of what I have dubbed the 'ex-pat problem', where those of one nation in a foreign land communicate with each or with those back home at the expense of cultural intercourse with the locals.[59] Moreover, Spinola laces his rhetoric with that disdain for the intellectual aptitude of foreigners which is a humanist trope and which later scholarship has all too often found persuasive: it should not blind us to the reality of humanism's identity as an international enterprise in which the uses of 'beyond Italy' included its potential for providing not just employment or audiences for humanists but also locales in which their creativity could occur.

Yet, even stereotypes, remarkably resilient though they are in the face of facts, are not immutable. They can develop in response to their own logic, so that humanist *prepotenza* towards barbarian foreigners inspired its own backlash: the Italians stood accused of arrogance in the eyes of Rudolf Agricola and others.[60] Or stereotypes could succumb to the force of changing circumstances: as John Flood has shown, in the last third of the fifteenth century German inventiveness became a humanist topos of praise, thanks to the printing press.[61] This may seem to us so common-sensical that we fail to consider why authors like Ludovico Carbone made such a strong linkage between the Germans, print and learning. Certainly, movable type was not

napoletana di Alfonso il Magnanimo' in Albanese, *Studi su Facio*, pp. 1–44 at p. 4.

[58] I give further examples in *England and the Identity of Humanism*.

[59] I briefly discuss the 'ex-pat problem' in D. Rundle, 'Polydore Vergil and the *Translatio studiorum*: the tradition of Italian humanists in England' in R. Bacchielli ed., *Polidoro Virgili e la cultura umanistica europea* (Urbino, 2003), pp. 53–74 at pp. 62–63.

[60] See pp. 87–88 above.

[61] See pp. 105–16 above.

only born in Mainz, it was also exported to most other countries by Germans, with Italy being no exception. The clerics Conrad Sweynheym and Arnold Pannartz first set up their press in the monastery of Subiaco, some forty miles east of Rome, in 1465, and, two years later, moved into the papal city itself.[62] Their publications were to include humanist, patristic and classical texts, some edited by GIOVANNI ANDREA BUSSI, but the new technology had no particular affection for humanist eloquence; on the contrary, the commercial calculations that needed to drive a successful printing house favoured works less learned and more popular than those provided by the *studia humanitatis* – as several early printers, including Sweynheym and Pannartz and, later, ALDUS MANUTIUS learnt only when the spectre of bankruptcy overshadowed them.[63] Nor did print create *ex nihilo* a book-trade on which humanism could capitalise: publication was certainly possible in manuscript culture, as the example of Flavio Biondo already mentioned demonstrates; hand-written codices could also, as we have seen, cross Europe in diplomatic bags or a ship's cargo; and speculative production of volumes could occur, as when Vespasiano da Bisticci compromised quality for speed in producing supplies that he hoped to sell at the Congress of Mantua.[64] However, what was unprecedented was the quantity of copies that print made possible to be transported, turning the book

---

[62] On Sweynheym and Pannartz, see E. Hall, *Sweynheym & Pannartz and the Origins of Printing in Italy* (McMinnville OR, 1991). On their relations with Bussi, see *Prefazioni alle edizioni di Sweynheym e Pannartz prototipografi romani*, ed. M. Miglio (Milan, 1978).

[63] A point recently emphasised by A. Pettegree, *The Book in the Renaissance* (New Haven, CT, 2010), esp. 49–62.

[64] See pp. 315–16 above; A. C. de la Mare, 'Vespasiano da Bisticci as a Producer of Classical Manuscripts in Fifteenth-Century Florence' in C. A. Chavannes-Mazel & M. M. Smith ed., *Medieval Manuscripts of the Latin Classics: Production and Use* (Los Altos Hills, CA, 1996), pp. 166–207 at pp. 201–202.

into a relatively cheap commodity.⁶⁵ The book, that is to say, became more attractive to, and more reliant upon, the structures of commerce. From this, further changes flowed, at swift pace.

For humanists intent on forging the reputation of themselves as individuals and as coteries, print provided new possibilities. It may have been Erasmus in the early sixteenth century who was the most artful at constructing his charisma through the new medium but he was not the first.⁶⁶ For instance, the Dutch humanist himself is a witness to the fame of FILIPPO BEROALDO, a fame shaped by his use of the press, particularly in his hometown of Bologna, but also in Paris when Beroaldo was briefly there.⁶⁷ However, print was not only about promotion of oneself. It could also be an act of pietas, as when Iacopo Antiquari (1452/55–1512), a student of the late GIOVANNI ANTONIO CAMPANO, conceived a plan to have all his master's works published, resulting in the Roman edition of 1495, complete with a biography of Campano by Antiquari's friend, Michele Ferno (1465–1513), who also added indices and saw the work through the press; the edition was reprinted by Aldus Manutius in 1502.⁶⁸ This example, though, can also hint at the potential dangers of print: its ability to mould reputation was also one which decreased the author's own already-vulnerable control of the process. The living could also

---

⁶⁵ For insightful comment on the problematic status of book as commodity, J. L. Flood, '"Volentes sibi comparare infrascriptos libros impressos..." Printed books as commercial commodity in the fifteenth century' in K. Jensen ed., *Incunabula and their Readers. Printing, selling and using books in the fifteenth century* (London, 2003), pp. 139–51.

⁶⁶ I allude, of course, to L. Jardine, *Erasmus, Man of Letters. The construction of charisma in print* (Princeton, NJ, 1993), on which see the review by Jill Kraye in *The Library*, 6ᵗʰ ser., xvii (1995), pp. 77–80. See also the methodical survey of Erasmus' engagement with the press given by K. Crousaz, *Érasme et le pouvoir de l'imprimerie* (Lausanne, 2005).

⁶⁷ Erasmus, *Epistolae*, ed. P. S. Allen, 12 vols (Oxford, 1906–58), v (1924), p. 244 [ep. 1347, ll. 220–224]. The printings from Beroaldo's time in Paris are ISTC, nos ib00488800, ic00552000, is00065000, and iv00160800. For his influence in Poland, see p. 140 above.

⁶⁸ The first edition is ISTC, no. ic00073000.

find that the image they wished to broadcast could be distorted by the hiss and hum of others' interventions, as Niccolò Perotti was to find when criticising the classical scholarship of DOMENICO CALDERINI.[69] More neutrally, the reputation of a humanist of an earlier generation could be re-fashioned by what went into print. A notorious example involves a text often now cited by scholars and mentioned at the beginning of this chapter, one which had a Europe-wide success in manuscript but which did not appear in print until the twentieth century: Leonardo Bruni's *Laudatio Florentinae urbis*.[70] Or consider Bruni's friend, Poggio, of whose writings the best-known now are probably his dialogues in Ciceronian style; like the *Laudatio*, these circulated internationally in manuscript but if we were to judge this humanist by his incunable identity, it would not be these well-crafted works that made his name.[71] Instead, the one

---

[69] See F.-R. Hausmann, 'Martial in Italien', *Studi medievali*, 3rd ser., xvii (1976), pp. 173–218 at pp. 201–216; id., 'Martialis' in *CTC*, iv (1980), pp. 249–96 at pp. 253–54 & 261–71. As the detail of that spat demonstrates, harsh criticism was not reserved solely for print in this incunable period; for a further set of examples, see V. Fera, 'Polemiche filologiche intorno allo Svetonio del Beroaldo' in A. C. Dionisotti et al., *The Uses of Greek and Latin* (London, 1988), pp. 71–87.

[70] Hans Baron provided the 'first printed edition' in his *From Petrarch to Leonardo Bruni* (Chicago, 1968), pp. 217–63 (noting its earlier lack of print fortuna at pp. 151–55); there had, in fact, been two partial editions produced in 1889: see Bruni, *Laudatio*, ed. Baldassarri, pp. xxiii–xxvii.

[71] Only two of the dialogues saw their way into print in the fifteenth century: there were two editions of *De infelicitate principum* [ISTC, nos ip00875300 (Paris, c. 1473) and ip00875500 (Louvain, c. 1480)], on which work, see the edition by Davide Canfora (Rome, 1998), with his listing of manuscript witnesses suggesting the international circulation of the work; and there was one of *De nobilitate* [ISTC, no. ip00877000 (Antwerp, 1489)]. Other dialogues, including *De avaritia*, had to wait until the early sixteenth century to receive a printed edition; I discuss the English interest in this work in D. Rundle, 'On the Difference between Virtue and Weiss: humanist texts in England during the fifteenth century' in D. Dunn ed., *Courts, Counties and the Capital in the Later Middle Ages* (Stroud, 1996), pp. 181–203 at pp. 195–201.

work of his that was frequently republished was his collection of ribald tales, the *Facetiae*, which received over thirty printed editions in the fifteenth century, not just in Italy but also in France, the Low Countries, Germany and Poland.[72]

Print, in other words, did not simply quicken the pace of circulation of works by certain humanists; in the process, it could contort a humanist's corpus, mis-shaping an identity previously presented. To the examples already given, let me add another: a work we often consider the classic quattrocento exposition of good Latin, the *Elegantiae* of LORENZO VALLA, secured a relatively modest circulation in hand-written copies, and only became something of a best-seller through the printing press.[73] First printed in 1471, there was a particular concentration of editions produced in Paris in the last decade of its fifteenth century; in the same years, a work entitled *Elegantiae terminorum* and announcing its debt to Valla was regularly printed in Deventer.[74] The popularity of Valla's work – and that of a work like AGOSTINO DATI's *Elegantiolae* – suggests another possibility that flowed from the increased availability of copies: reform of the teaching of Latin in schools beyond Italy.[75] As several chapters, particularly that of Jacqueline Glomski, have mentioned, the dominant pattern of fifteenth-century educational engagement with humanism was that individuals in particular establishments showed interest but

[72] L. Sozzi, 'Le "Facezie" e la loro fortuna europea' in *Poggio Bracciolini 1380–1980* (Florence, 1982), pp. 235–59; I have used the listing of printings in ISTC. The work is readily available in, for instance, Poggio Bracciolini, *Faciezie*, trans. M. Ciccuto (Milan, 1983).

[73] On the *Elegantiae* in England, see D. Rundle, 'Humanist Eloquence among the Barbarians in Fifteenth-Century England' in C. Burnett and N. Mann ed., *Britannia Latina. Latin in the culture of Great Britain from the Middle Ages to the twentieth century* (London, 2005), pp. 68–85 at p. 84. For a manuscript copy in Scotland, see p. 253 above.

[74] Paris editions: ISTC, nos iv00052000, iv00062500, iv00064000, iv00065500, iv00068200, iv00068300 (and see p. 1 above); the Deventer editions of *Elegantiae terminorum*: ISTC, nos ie00028800–ie00029150.

[75] On Dati, see pp. 139, 204 above.

this rarely translated into the sort of curricular reform that we are inclined to set as a litmus-test for the presence of the *studia humanitatis*. This, in turn, may seem justification for a narrative of the slow spread of humanism seeping out of its Italian strongholds – but only if we make what may be an unwarranted assumption about an early and widespread adoption of humanist methods in Italian schools and universities.[76] Instead, it would be better to recognise the development of humanist educational practice as more faltering in Italy and less resistant elsewhere than sometimes acknowledged. The last third of the fifteenth century saw increased possibilities for humanist education, partly because of the availability of suitable teachers but all the more because the products of the printing press made the wherewithal on which to base the teaching available. It was in this context that the activities of a Guillaume Tardif in Paris or John Anwykyll in Oxford could take place.[77]

This brings us finally to a question begged by the title of this volume: do the chronological boundaries of a century isolate a set of practices that form a unified and distinct identity? Was there, in short, fifteenth-century humanism? The patterns that emerge from the preceding paragraphs depict a tradition of travel and intellectual encounters which lasted through our period but was by no means confined to it. At the same time, those paragraphs do suggest that there are dividing points in the fifteenth century, albeit not the old ones of the fall of Constantinople of 1453 or the onset of the Italian Wars in 1494.[78] Instead, there would seem to be three phases: the

---

[76] R. Black, *Humanism and Education in Medieval and Renaissance Italy* (Cambridge, 2001), and see his 'Italian Renaissance Education: changing perspectives and continuing controversies', *Journal of the History of Ideas*, lii (1991), pp. 315–34 (and cf. pp. 335–37 & 519–20).

[77] On Tardif, see Craig Taylor's comments at pp. 223 and 225 above; on Anwykyll, see N. Orme, *Education in Early Tudor England: Magdalen College Oxford and its School 1480–1540* (Oxford, 1988).

[78] On 1453, see p. 33 above; on 1494, see Rundle, 'Polydore Vergil and the *translatio studiorum*'.

opening decade and a half in which Bruni and his colleagues moulded the *studia humanitatis* as a self-conscious break with the past was also overshadowed by the continuing Schism of the church; it was only with the outcome of the Council of Constance that Avignon finally lost much of the significance it had had in Petrarch's life-time and Rome could become something close to an unrivalled centre for ecclesiastical diplomacy. If, then, we see a shift originating in the mid-1410s, the next phase might be said to last for about half a century. The end of the 1450s saw, with the deaths of Valla, Poggio and Guarino, both the passing of a generation, and a change in intellectual interests; overset upon these was, from the middle of the 1460s, the transformative – I resist writing revolutionary – impact of print. When did that third phase close? Perhaps only with the new fissures and associations wrought by the confessional struggles that scarred Europe from the 1520s. The decades beyond that might be seen as the fulfilment of the potential of the preceding period, as the arrival in the Promised Land – or they could be seen as the age following The Fall, the bitter-sweet aftertaste left by the sharing of the fruits of humanist genius. From this perspective, this volume needs no epilogue: that is provided by the sixteenth century.[79]

---

[79] I would like to thank Oren Margolis and John Monfasani who gave sage advice on an earlier draft of this chapter.

BIOGRAPHICAL APPENDIX OF FIFTEENTH-CENTURY ITALIAN HUMANISTS

OREN MARGOLIS AND DAVID RUNDLE

This Appendix has a limited remit: it is intended to provide, in brief, basic information about those Italian humanists who have been mentioned in the preceding chapters. It privileges, therefore, those humanists who had international contacts, with the result that some significant scholars are not mentioned, while others often given less coverage are present. At the same time, at just over sixty entries, it does not pretend to be an exhaustive listing even of those humanists who did either spend time abroad or had contacts with foreign patrons.

The list is arranged alphabetically by baptismal name in its Italian form, unless the humanist is best known by a sobriquet, in which case that is used; alternative names are given on following lines after the heading. To search by surname, the reader can turn to the volume's index. Bibliographical references are not given here: they can be found at the relevant footnotes to the chapters that are the main part of this volume.

ÆNEAS SYLVIUS PICCOLOMINI   1405–1464
    Pius II

The eldest son of a noble but impoverished Sienese family, Æneas Sylvius attended the University of Siena, punctuated by two years studying the classics in Florence under FRANCESCO FILELFO. In 1432 he travelled to the Council of Basel as part of the opposition to Pope Eugenius IV. Soon becoming attached to Cardinal Niccolò Albergati (c. 1375–1443), he travelled on his patron's business in France, Scotland and England. He served as master of ceremonies of the conclave that elected Antipope Felix V and became Felix's secretary, but switched employers in 1442: he was crowned poet laureate by Emperor Frederick III, who appointed him secretary at the imperial chancery in Vienna, where, in 1446, he took holy orders. He accompanied and advised Frederick on his coronation journey to Rome in 1452. Made a cardinal by Calixtus III in 1456, he was elected as Pope Pius II two years later. His pontificate was dominated by plans for a crusade against the Turks, to which end he called the Congress of Mantua (1459). Pius is the only sitting pope to write his own memoirs: his *Commentaries* are modelled on Caesar's. His major historical works, *Historia rerum Frederici III imperatoris* (1452–58) and *Historia Bohemica* (1458), are testament to his experience north of the Alps. His writings also demonstrated his interest in geography, particularly in *De Europa* (1458), and he was known for his erotic epistolary novel, *Historia de duobus amantibus* (1444). Perhaps his most ambitious project was Pienza, the plan to rebuild his birthplace (formerly Corsignano) as an ideal town according to fashionable architectural principles. He died with the project unfinished, to the relief of those cardinals who had not shared his enthusiasm for his Tuscan retreat.

AGOSTINO DATI	1420–
Augustinus Datus (*or* Dactus, Dathus)	1478

Dati was born in Siena and studied under FRANCESCO FILELFO when the latter taught there after 1435. He went to teach in Urbino, but not long after Duke Oddantonio da Montefeltro was assassinated in 1444, he returned to his hometown, where he remained for much of his life, despite invitations to return to Urbino and to join Nicholas V in Rome. He taught rhetoric and theology at the university, and was appointed to a number of prestigious civic offices. He wrote histories of Siena and of Piombino, both published posthumously; his most widely circulated work, however, was the *Elegantiolae* (1470), a guide to elegant Latin style, which received over 110 incunable editions, printed in Italy, France, Spain, England, Germany and the Low Countries.

ALDUS MANUTIUS   c. 1450/52–1515
    Aldo Manuzio

Manutius gained a reputation fairly late in life as a printer of classical and humanist works; that was his second career. Born in Bassiano in southern Lazio, Aldus studied first in Rome, and, from 1475, in Ferrara under BATTISTA GUARINI; there he met PICO DELLA MIRANDOLA. In 1480, Manutius became tutor to Pico's nephews, the princes of Carpi, a position he held until 1489; he spent some months in Mirandola in 1482, making connexions with members of Pico's circle, like POLITIAN. His *Musarum panegyris* was likely published in Venice in 1489, just before he moved to that city, where his *Institutiones grammaticae Latinae* followed in 1493. It was in the mid-1490s that he made his career change from teacher to printer, setting up what was to become known as the Aldine Press. He boasted of making available learned texts in (relatively) inexpensive octavo editions, presented in a typeface that imitated the fashionable italic bookhand. His first focus was ancient Greek authors; after 1500 the number of Latin publications increased. He published translations of Euripides by Erasmus (1507), and the Dutch humanist's *Adagia* (1508). He produced illustrated works much less frequently, but one of those was the 1499 *Hypernotomachia Poliphili* of Francesco Colonna (1433/34–1527). Being highly regarded was not the same as being successful: Manutius fell into financial difficulties in 1505, but his business survived and, after his death, was continued by his sons, in particular Paolo (1512–1574).

ALESSANDRO GERALDINI   1455–1524
    Alexander Geraldinus

Born in Amelia (Umbria), he was half-brother to ANTONIO
GERALDINI and had a similar early career. Like Antonio,
Alessandro found employment at the court of the Catholic
Kings as a tutor to one of their daughters, Catalina (1485–
1536; Katherine of Aragon). Like his brother, he also acted as a
diplomat, travelling to Brittany in 1485 and, in 1501, to
England, with Catalina, the ill-fated bride of Henry VII's
son(s). Alessandro did not stay in England, though he
returned in the mid-1510s. By then, however, his attentions
were drawn elsewhere for, in 1516, he was named Bishop of
Santo Domingo, the first city of the 'New World'. He sailed to
his diocese in 1519; he died and was buried there in a Renaissance tomb.

AMBROGIO TRAVERSARI   1386–1439
    Ambrosius Camalduliensis

Born at Portico (Romagna), Traversari entered the Camaldolese
monastery of Santa Maria degli Angeli in Florence in 1400,
later (1431) becoming General of the Order. He studied
Greek with Manuel Chrysoloras, and his cell became a major
meeting place for the circle of POGGIO BRACCIOLINI, NICCOLÒ NICCOLI and Palla Strozzi. He encouraged FRANCESCO
FILELFO to come to Florence as well, but soon fell out with
him on account of the latter's bitter feud with Niccoli; he
traded invectives with LEONARDO BRUNI too. Traversari was
close to Cosimo de' Medici and also to Pope Eugenius IV,
whom Cosimo sustained financially. Traversari defended
Eugenius at the Council of Basel, and supported the pope
when he transferred the council to Ferrara and then to
Florence, where he drafted the decree of the union between
the Greek and Latin churches in 1439. Alongside the

theological treatises he wrote, Traversari translated and promoted many works by the Greek Church Fathers. Persuaded by Cosimo and Niccoli to translate the *Vitae philosophorum* of the pagan Diogenes Laertius, his work (1433) went on to influence the generation of Renaissance Platonists, including MARSILIO FICINO.

ANGELO DECEMBRIO ?1415–after 1467
    Angelus Camillus Decembrius

Angelo Decembrio was the youngest son of Uberto Decembrio (d. 1427) and so, among his elder brothers, he had to count PIER CANDIDO DECEMBRIO. Angelo was educated in Milan, by GASPARINO BARZIZZA, and then in Ferrara. Much of Angelo's career was spent in the d'Este city and he recorded – or rather idealised – the learned nature of the court culture in his dialogue, *De politia litteraria* (On Literary Polish), a version of which was dedicated to Pius II (ÆNEAS SYLVIUS PICCOLOMINI) in 1462. The title may be a joke at the expense of his estranged brother, who had given the title *Celestis politia* to his translation of Plato's *Republic*. After Leonello d'Este's death (1450), Angelo's career was peripatetic: he travelled to Spain, both as an ambassador and for his own scholarly interests; he was also sent to Burgundy by the Ferrarese rulers in 1466. After his return from that trip, he disappears from the records.

Angelo Poliziano *see*
    POLITIAN

Antonio Beccadelli *see*
    PANORMITA

ANTONIO BECCARIA c. 1400–
Antonius Becarius Veronensis 1474

Born in Verona, he attended the school of VITTORINO DA FELTRE at Mantua and, according to Vittorino's biographer, was one of his most gifted pupils. Beccaria's early career saw him travel across Europe to become secretary to the English prince, Humfrey, duke of Gloucester. Arriving probably in 1438 and replacing TITO LIVIO FRULOVISI in the duke's household, he stayed for about eight years. In England, he not only composed the duke's foreign correspondence but also translated into Latin works of Plutarch, Athanasius and Boccaccio. Beccaria returned to his hometown about 1446 and became a member of the circle of the local bishop, Ermolao Barbaro (1410–1471), being appointed cathedral treasurer in 1458. He continued to produce translations, as well some poetry and orations on poetry for a set-piece debate, in which his opponent was the son of FRANCESCO FILELFO, Gian Maria Filelfo (1426–1480).

ANTONIO BONFINI 1427 or 1434–
Antonius Bonfinius *(or* de Bonfinis*)* 1502 or 1503

From the village of Patrignone in the March of Ancona, Bonfini studied under Enoch of Ascoli, before becoming a teacher himself, tutoring for wealthy families in Ascoli, Florence, Padua, Ferrara and Rome. In 1476, he was part of the official welcoming party at Loreto for Beatrice of Aragon, future queen of Hungary, and, a decade later, he travelled to Hungary to seek employment at her court. In 1487, he was commissioned by Matthias Corvinus to translate into Latin the *volgare* architectural treatise of Filarete, which FRANCESCO BANDINI had introduced, and to write a humanist history of Hungary, *Rerum Vngaricarum decades*, on which he worked until 1496, after Matthias' death. Already official court historian, he was ennobled and crowned with the laurel by

King Ladislaus II in 1492. Bonfini made periodic trips back to Italy (including one in 1493 to Ferrara, where he taught Greek to the son of MARCANTONIO SABELLICO), but died in Buda.

Antonio Cortesi Urceo Codro *see*
    ANTONIO URCEO

ANTONIO GERALDINI (*or* Gerardini)   1448/9–1489
    Antonius Geraldinus

Born in Amelia (Umbria), he travelled around central Italy to receive his education. At the age of twenty, he accompanied his uncle, Angelo, bishop of Sessa Aurunca (1422–86), on a mission to Aragon, where, according to his own account, his poetic ability won him the laurel crown from the infante, Ferdinand. A few years later, he was again in Spain, being named in 1475 secretary to Ferdinand's father, John II (1458–1479) and employed by him as an ambassador to Brittany, Burgundy and England. He was subsequently secretary to the Catholic Kings, as well as tutor to their elder daughter, Isabella (1470–98). He was barely in his forties when he died; his half-brother, ALESSANDRO GERALDINI, was to have a longer career in Spanish service.

ANTONIO (Cortesi) URCEO   1446–1500
    Antonius Urceus Codrus

Born in Rubiera (between Modena and Reggio Emilia), Urceo took the Juvenalian sobriquet of Codrus. He remembered as his teacher BATTISTA GUARINI, who inspired his interest in Greek. His own career was as a teacher: first in Forlì, both publicly and privately, and, from 1482, in Bologna, where he was held in high regard by FILIPPO BEROALDO. Beroaldo's nephew – like Copernicus, a student of Urceo's – helped prepare his late master's works for publication in 1502; they included prolusions to his courses, letters and epigrams.

AURELIO BRANDOLINI   c. 1454–1497
Aurelius Lippus Brandolinus

Born in Florence but educated in Naples, Brandolini was half-blind from childhood. This made his skill as an extempore versifier all the more noticeable; he also gained a reputation as an author, in Latin and the *volgare*, in prose and verse. He moved to Rome about 1480 and, in 1489, he left Italy for Buda, in search of royal patronage. He dedicated to Matthias Corvinus a short work on suffering illness, *De humanae vitae conditione*, but his hopes for his next work, *De comparatione rei publicae et regni*, were twice thwarted by death: it was to be dedicated to Matthias but he died in April 1490, and, then, on the author's return to Florence, to Lorenzo de' Medici who similarly expired before the presentation could be made. Brandolini joined the Augustinian order, travelled as a preacher and himself died of the plague in Rome.

BARTOLOMEO FACIO (*or* FAZIO)   before 1405–1457
Bartolomeus Facius

Born in the Genoese dependency of La Spezia, Facio studied under GUARINO DA VERONA in the Veneto, and then seems to have spent some years travelling there and elsewhere in northern Italy, sometimes earning money as a teacher. In 1443, he was sent to Naples as Genoese ambassador to Alfonso V of Aragon; he stayed to become official historian and tutor to the king's son Ferrante, and so joined the likes of LORENZO VALLA and PANORMITA. Between Facio and Valla was no curial camaraderie: Facio's criticisms of Valla's history of their mutual employer sparked a ping-pong match of invectives. Facio's most significant work was his own *De rebus gestis ab Alphonso*

I, the ten volumes of which were completed in 1455. His other writings included *De vitae felicitate* (1445), a novella on the origins of the Hundred Years War (mid-1440s) and the short *De viris illustribus* (1456). This last, among other things, demonstrates the popularity of northern artists at Alfonso's court: Facio praises Jan van Eyck and Rogier van der Weyden as the greatest artists of his day, and mentions works by van Eyck then known in Italy which have not survived.

BATTISTA GUARINI   1434–1503
    Baptista Guarini

The tenth child of GUARINO DA VERONA was born in Ferrara, and studied there under his father. His first public appearance was in 1452, at the arrival in Ferrara of the Holy Roman Emperor Frederick III (1440–1493). In 1455–57 he taught rhetoric and poetry at the University of Bologna, before going to Verona, where he wrote his most important work, *De ordine docendi ac studendi* (1459), promoting the teaching methods of his father's school. When Guarino died in Ferrara in 1460, Battista was hired to replace him. He continued to work as a translator and an editor, and exchanged letters and writings with PICO DELLA MIRANDOLA, ANGELO POLIZIANO, and his old schoolmate Janus Pannonius. Battista was most famous, however, as a teacher: he was tutor to the children of Duke Ercole d'Este (1471–1505); and amongst his most celebrated students were Regiomontanus, Rudolf Agricola, and ALDUS MANUTIUS. Although he briefly sought Gonzaga patronage, he remained in Ferrara until his death.

Biondo Flavio *see*
    FLAVIO BIONDO

Callimachus Experiens *see*
FILIPPO BUONACCORSI

Codrus Urceus see
ANTONIO URCEO

CORNELIO VITELLI c. 1440–c. 1500
Cornelius Vitellius

Vitelli was credited by Polydore Vergil (c. 1470–1555) with introducing the *studia humanitatis* into England – a gross overstatement but, nevertheless, he was, after STEFANO SURIGONE and LORENZO TRAVERSAGNI, one of the first Italians to teach humanist eloquence in one of the English university towns. He was born in Cortona on the Tuscan / Umbrian border and he may have been educated in Rome under DOMENICO CALDERINI. His early career was in Padua and Venice. After teaching in Oxford in the period 1482–86, he went to the University of Louvain and, in 1488, to Paris. There his colleagues, GIROLAMO BALBI and FAUSTO ANDRELINI, turned into his enemies and he left France, returning eventually to Oxford. Little is known about his later years.

COSMA RAIMONDI 1400–1436
Cosmas Raimundus

Born in Cremona, Raimondi studied under GASPARINO BARZIZZA in Milan, where, in 1421, he was among the first to study the celebrated manuscript discovered by Gerardo Landriani (bishop of Lodi; d. 1445), containing the previously uncirculated rhetorical works of Cicero (*Brutus, De oratore*,

Orator). Around 1429, he composed in epistolary form a defence of Epicurus, the only known serious espousal of Epicurean philosophy before LORENZO VALLA. The next year, he moved to Avignon to teach law, though he did not give up on his humanist interests: it was there that he wrote his praise of eloquence (*De laudibus eloquentiae*). He later sought to return to Italy but never did; he committed suicide.

DOMENICO (or Domizio) CALDERINI   1446–1478
    Domitius Caldarinus

Born near Lake Garda and baptized Domenico, he classicized his name to Domitius in Rome, following the style of the circle around POMPONIUS LAETUS. Before he went to the papal city, he was educated in Verona and Venice; in Rome, he entered the service of Cardinal Bessarion, and seconded him in his dispute with George of Trebizond over Plato. Calderini travelled with Bessarion on his 1472 embassy to France, and claimed to have found classical manuscripts – but none of them definitely existed. Bessarion died soon after their return but by then Calderini had gained both patronage from Sixtus IV and a teaching position in the city's University. MARCANTONIO SABELLICO, PIETRO MARSO and ALDUS MANUTIUS were among his pupils. At the same time, he showed a penchant for securing enemies by criticizing others – including his former colleague, NICCOLÒ PEROTTI – in his commentaries on classical authors, which were published in both manuscript and print. Criticisms of his own scholarship were continued after the plague killed him, by ANTONIO URCEO and POLITIAN.

DONATO ACCIAIUOLI (or Acciaioli)   1429–1478
    Donatus Acciaiolus

Born to a famous Florentine family, Donato was also a relation of Giannozzo Manetti (1396–1459), who became a mentor to him. Along with other young patricians, Donato frequented the shop of the book-dealer Vespasiano da Bisticci, becoming his customer, secretary and friend. He was part of the group that in 1456 brought to Florence John Argyropoulos, whose lectures on Aristotle he attended. He also began to work on Latin translations of Plutarch's *Lives*. In 1461–2, he joined his father-in-law Piero de' Pazzi on a diplomatic mission to France, presenting his *Vita Caroli Magni* to Louis XI. After Piero's death in 1464, Donato became increasingly affiliated with the Medici, and eventually held a number of important offices for the regime. During these years, he produced commentaries on Aristotle's *Ethics* (1464) and *Politics* (1472), and an Italian translation (1473) of LEONARDO BRUNI's *Historia Florentini populi*, as well as his own pseudo-Plutarchan lives of Scipio and Hannibal (1467–8). Cleared of involvement in the 1478 Pazzi Conspiracy, Donato was dispatched to seek aid from the king of France, but he died en route in Milan.

FAUSTO ANDRELINI   c. 1462–
    Publius Faustus Andrelinus   1518
    Foroliviensis

Born in Forlì, he was educated at Bologna and then in Rome, where he was crowned poet by POMPONIUS LAETUS. He also sought the patronage of Ludovico Gonzaga, bishop of Mantua (1460–1511), and it was through him that he gained an introduction to Gilbert, count of Montpensier (1443–1496), the husband of Gonzaga's sister. Having arrived in France in 1488, he moved the next year to Paris and was appointed a teacher *in arte humanitatis* at the University, alongside CORNELIO VITELLI and GIROLAMO BALBI. The bickering of the three led each of them to quit Paris – Andrelini travelled to Toulouse and Poitiers, but, unlike the others, he returned to Paris and settled there, where his friends were to include Erasmus (in Paris in 1495) and his pupils, Beatus Rhenanus (1485–1547). He published his amorous verses (*Livia*, 1490) and also often produced poetry for the French kings. But this did not make his career a financial success: it appears that he died in Paris in poverty.

FILIPPO BEROALDO (the Elder)   1453–1505
   Philippus Beroaldus

Known as 'the Elder' to distinguish him from his nephew of the same name, who was also a humanist (1472–1518); the nephew was educated by ANTONIO URCEO, and provided the first edition of Tacitus' *Annals*. The uncle's place of birth, as well as the locale for much of his career, was Bologna. He was appointed a professor at the university in 1472, though he soon moved to Parma and, in 1476, to Paris. He was certainly back in Bologna by 1479, though he continued contact with his pupils in France, including Robert Gaguin. Beroaldo made sure his voice was heard not only from the lectern but also through the printing press, which published his copious commentaries on classical authors (in particular, Apuleius) and his own orations. He gained a fame that, as Erasmus attests, outlived him in his homeland, though some – like POLITIAN – were not persuaded of his scholarship.

FILIPPO BUONACCORSI   1437–1496
   Callimachus Experiens

Born in San Gimignano (Tuscany), Buonaccorsi began his career as a tutor in the house of a merchant family in Pesaro. In Rome from 1462, he obtained employment as secretary to the archbishop of Ravenna, Bartolomeo Roverella, as well as the protection of GIOVANNI ANTONIO CAMPANO. He also joined the 'Roman Academy' of POMPONIUS LAETUS, adopting the name Callimachus, and, in 1468, was one of Laetus' associates put on trial for conspiring against Pope Paul II: accusations against him included irreligion, anti-clericalism, and sodomy. Fleeing Rome in 1469, he travelled to Crete, Cyprus, Chios and Constantinople, before going to Poland at the end of that year, where he gained the protection of Gregory of Sanok, archbishop of Lwów, and subsequently of King Casimir IV Jagiellon (1447–1492). Buonaccorsi was pardoned following Paul II's death in 1471; in 1472, he was appointed tutor to the king of Poland's sons; two years later, he was made royal secretary, and a career as a Polish ambassador followed. After Casimir died, Buonaccorsi went to Vienna until the succession of Jan Olbracht was confirmed. He returned to Cracow, where he died in 1496. Alongside his diplomatic career, he engaged in philosophical disputes with MARSILIO FICINO and PICO DELLA MIRANDOLA, and participated in the Sodalitas Vistulana founded in Cracow by Conrad Celtis.

FLAVIO BIONDO 1392–1463
Biondo Flavio / Flavius Blondus

Though proud to be a native of Forlì, Biondo's humanist identity was to be associated primarily with Rome. He entered the papal curia only in his forties, already married (he eventually had ten children) and having acted as secretary to men like the Venetian Francesco Barbaro (1390–1454), as well as being a correspondent of scholars including GUARINO DA VERONA. Appointed a papal secretary in 1434, his writings both reflect the culture of the curia – his *De verbis Romanae locutionis* (1435) recalls a debate with LEONARDO BRUNI over whether Latin and Italian had both existed in classical Rome – and promote the celebration the papal city, in his *Roma instaurata* (1444–46) and *Roma triumphans* (c. 1453–1460). The first of these two works described the sites of ancient Rome and he later broadened that topographical interest in *Italia illuminata* (1447–53). He was also an historian, his major enterprise being his *Decades* on Roman history (begun in 1437): its title suggesting his self-presentation as following in Livy's footsteps, though his work covered the period after 410 A.D. His works gained an international circulation (praised, for instance, by Louis XI of France), but that did not bring him riches: in his last years, his economic situation remained precarious.

FRANCESCO BANDINI   d. after 1490
    Franciscus Bandinus

Born in Florence, Bandini was an enthusiastic follower of MARSILIO FICINO, and organised 'symposia' to celebrate Plato's birthday. But he may not have been in sympathy with Ficino's patron, Lorenzo de' Medici: Bandini's brother was later to take a leading role in the Pazzi Conspiracy (1478), and Francesco certainly spent some years in Naples. In 1476, he was sent from there to Hungary in the entourage of the new queen, Beatrice of Aragon. Bandini remained at the court of Matthias Corvinus, to whom he also acted as an architectural advisor. He maintained frequent correspondence with Ficino, whose works he helped make known at court, even trying to establish a 'Platonic Academy' in Buda.

FRANCESCO FILELFO   1398–1481
    Franciscus Philelphus

Filelfo's career was marked by both its length and its itinerancy within Italy. From Tolentino in the March of Ancona, Filelfo went to study under GASPARINO BARZIZZA in Padua, where he was made professor, aged eighteen. The next year he relocated to Venice, and in 1420, he went to Constantinople as secretary to the Venetian consul. While in Constantinople he studied Greek, in which language he became proficient; he returned to Venice in 1427 with both a large library of Greek books and a wife, Teodora, daughter of John Chrysoloras (nephew of Manuel Chrysoloras). After a brief stay in Bologna, Filelfo went to Florence in 1429. Allied to the Albizzi faction, he fell foul of the Medici: it was in this context that he feuded with NICCOLÒ NICCOLI and POGGIO BRACCIOLINI and also earned the enmity of AMBROGIO TRAVERSARI, all of whom were close to Cosimo. Having celebrated the expulsion of the Medici in 1433, the next year he fled the city after Cosimo's return and went to Siena, then Milan. Filelfo served at the courts of Filippo Maria Visconti (1412–47) and Francesco Sforza (1450–66). For the latter he wrote the 12,800-line *Sforziad*, which he never published. He took up a professorship in Rome in 1474, but fell out with Sixtus IV (1471–84) and went back to Milan. Reconciled with the Medici through their mutual hostility to Sixtus (who had supported the Pazzi Conspiracy in 1478), Filelfo returned to Florence to teach Greek in 1481, but died just two weeks later.

FRANCESCO GRIFFOLINI 1420–1488
    Franciscus Aretinus

He was born at Arezzo and used that Latin loconym – which has led to confusion with another Franciscus Aretinus, Francesco Accolti (c. 1416–1488) – even though, on his father's execution in 1431, his family was exiled. His education was in Ferrara, under GUARINO DA VERONA and Theodore Gaza, and in Rome, under LORENZO VALLA. He made his reputation as a translator of Greek texts into Latin, most notably the *Epistolae* of (Ps-)Phalaris, which circulated widely in manuscript and, thanks to Ulrich Han and GIOVANNI ANTONIO CAMPANO, in print. The cast-list of dedicatees of his works was international, including the French cardinal Jean Jouffroy (Chrysostom's *Homilies* on St John; re-dedicated in 1462 to Cosimo de' Medici) and the English earl,

John Tiptoft (Lucian's *De Calumnia* and *Declamationes* of Libanius, 1461). Through the assistance of PANORMITA, he gained employment in Naples as tutor to the future Alfonso II (1448–1495). It was there that he died from a fall from a horse.

FRANCESCO NEGRO   1452–mid-1520s?
    Pescennius Franciscus Niger

Born in Venice, but of Croatian parentage, Negro was to be a wandering scholar because of misfortune and patronage. Educated in the Veneto and a priest in Venice, he was arrested in 1483 and tortured on suspicion of treason. After his release and despite attempts to ingratiate himself to the authorities, he was no longer welcome in the Serene Republic; he travelled as a teacher, both in Italy and in Hungary. He found more stable employment as tutor to Cardinal Ippolito d'Este (1479–1520), in whose service he continued until 1505. Ippolito had been nominated archbishop of Esztergom (Hungary) at the age of seven; Negro went with him on his journeys to Hungary and also in Italy – on one trip to Rome, in 1497 or 1498, Negro was made apostolic protonotary. His later life is less clear: he moved around southern Italy, was in contact with Ippolito in 1515, and seems to have been still alive in the early 1520s. Negro's printed works were mainly grammatical and included the *Modus epistolandi* which aroused Erasmus' disdain but which, after its first printing in Venice in 1488, went through over 35 incunable editions, being printed in France, Germany and Spain, as well as in Italy.

GALEOTTO MARZIO   c. 1427–c. 1497?
    Galeottus Martius / Galeottus
    Narniensis

Born to a noble family from Narni (Umbria), Marzio studied at Ferrara under GUARINO DA VERONA, where he befriended the young Hungarian humanist Janus Pannonius. Andrea Mantegna painted a double portrait of the two when students at the University of Padua in the mid-1450s. After returning to Hungary, Pannonius arranged in 1465 for his old friend to come and teach at the newly founded Universitas Histropolensis (Bratislava). The relationship between the two soon grew more distant – fortunately for Marzio, as it probably helped him survive the fall-out of the failed 1471 rebellion against Matthias Corvinus, in which Pannonius participated. Marzio travelled to the court of Louis XI of France and then to Bologna, but he was arrested in 1477 on accusations of heresy in his treatise *De vulgo incognitis* (1477). He was freed on the intervention of Matthias, Lorenzo de' Medici and Pope Sixtus IV, and returned to Buda, where he served at court c. 1478–c. 1490, and wrote *De dictis ac factis regis Mathiae* (1485), dedicating it to Matthias' ill-fated son, John Corvinus. He later returned to France, visiting the court of Charles VIII.

GASPARINO BARZIZZA   c. 1360–1431
    Gasparinus Barzizius Pergamensis

Born near Bergamo (thus Pergamensis), Gasparino was to become, alongside GUARINO DA VERONA and VITTORINO DA FELTRE, one of the leading humanist educators of the early Quattrocento. Educated in Pavia and Padua, he went on to teach in both places; he was based in Padua from 1407–1421, after which he returned to the duchy of Milan. His pupils included sons of leading families of Venice – like Francesco Barbaro (1390–1454) – and Milan – like Zanone da Castiglioni, future bishop of Bayeux (d. 1459) – as well as the humanists LEON BATTISTA ALBERTI, ANGELO DECEMBRIO and FRANCESCO FILELFO. Alongside his teaching, he was a prolific author, producing commentaries on classical texts (particularly Seneca and Cicero) as well as orthographical works; the latter circulated across Europe, as did many of his orations and letters which were taken as models of style, though their Ciceronianism was autonomous of that developing in Florence around LEONARDO BRUNI. The memory of his teaching and intellectual interests was kept alive by his son, GUINIFORTE BARZIZZA.

GIOVANNI AURISPA   1376–1459
    Johannes Aurispa

A noted son of Noto in Sicily, he spent his early years in Naples and his later life in Ferrara. Between his periods of long residence, there were bouts of travelling in the eastern Mediterranean; he returned to Italy with both expertise in Greek – he was LORENZO VALLA's first teacher in the subject – and manuscripts of Greek texts previously unknown in the West. In this regard, his journey of 1423, laden with manuscripts, is particularly celebrated, though some of his contemporaries, including FRANCESCO FILELFO (himself not unmercenary) complained that Aurispa wished to make a profit from them. His manuscript hunting also extended to Latin texts; as POGGIO BRACCIOLINI had done at Constance, Aurispa used the opportunity of the Council of Basel to search German libraries and to uncover, in 1433, the ancient Latin panegyrics, headed by Pliny the Younger's. Aurispa was also a translator of Greek opuscula into Latin, and some of his translations received a Europe-wide circulation.

Giovanni Andrea Bussi 1417–1475
   Johannes Andreas Aleriensis

Born near Pavia, Bussi is said to have travelled to Paris for some of his education, before going to the school of VITTORINO DA FELTRE. He also learnt Greek from Theodore Gaza. He became a teacher in Genoa while also seeking ecclesiastical preferment, which culminated in his appointment to a Corsican bishopric (Accia, 1461, transferred to Aleria, 1466). From 1458, he was secretary to the German cardinal, Nicholas of Cusa (1401–1464); it was Bussi who claimed that Cusa was a supporter of the new technology of printing, and Bussi's own later years saw him collaborating with the German printers, Conrad Sweynheym (d. 1477) and Arnold Pannartz (d. 1476 / 78). In preparing texts for the press, he drew upon both his connexions with humanists (like Gaza, POMPONIUS LAETUS and LEON BATTISTA ALBERTI) and the manuscripts available in the papal library at the Vatican. He provided prefaces to many of their editions – to the disgust of NICCOLÒ PEROTTI, who added this to his criticism of Bussi's editorial work. Others, including FRANCESCO FILELFO, were less critical. In 1471, Bussi was appointed papal librarian.

Giovanni Antonio Campano 1429–1477
   Johannes Antonius Campanus

Born near Caserta (Campania) into a humble family, Campano completed his education in Perugia, where he studied Greek, wrote a life of the local *condottiere* Braccio da Montone (1368–1424), and, in 1455, was awarded the chair in rhetoric at the university. During the pontificate of Pius II (ÆNEAS SYLVIUS PICCOLOMINI), he gained curial patronage and was appointed a bishop. In Rome he was acquainted with both Cardinal Bessarion and POMPONIUS LAETUS. Campano gave a much-praised funeral oration for Pius and later wrote a biography of the pontiff (c. 1470). He remained in favour under Paul II, avoiding the persecutions that befell Laetus and much of that circle (despite his own barely-hidden homosexuality). At this time, Campano acted as editor of classical texts being printed in Rome by the German Ulrich Han, and then himself travelled to Germany in 1471 in the embassy of Cardinal Francesco Todeschini Piccolomini (Pius II's nephew, the future Pius III); he declared himself unimpressed by the Germans. Later, after falling out with Sixtus IV, he sought the support of King Ferrante, whose historian he failed to become, and of Federigo da Montefeltro, whose biography he completed in 1475.

GIOVANNI GIGLI 1434–1498
    Johannes Giglis

Gigli's birth reflects the success of Italian commerce, his career the development in diplomatic practice. He was born in Bruges, the son of a merchant then resident there who later lived in England; Giovanni himself may have been educated at Oxford. He entered the church and was based in the family hometown of Lucca, but was appointed papal collector to England in 1476. In England, he – like PIETRO DEL MONTE before him – combined his ecclesiastical duties with literary productions, in his case poems and religious treatises. He also proved a useful agent for both the papacy and the English crown; in 1490, he was appointed the first Italian resident ambassador for England in Rome, where, seven years later, he was consecrated bishop of Worcester. He did not live to visit his see, of which the next incumbent was Giovanni's relative, protégé and successor as English ambassador in Rome, Silvestro Gigli (1463–1521).

Giovanni Michele Nagonio *see*
    JOHANNES MICHAEL NAGONIUS

Giovanni Pico della Mirandola *see*
    PICO DELLA MIRANDOLA

GIROLAMO BALBI   c. 1450–after 1535
    Hieronymus Balbus

A Venetian, he was educated in Ferrara, Padua and in Rome (under POMPONIUS LAETUS). He travelled to France in 1484 or 1485, and in Paris soon proved his gift for squabbling. He publicly fell out with the local scholar, Guillaume Tardif (c. 1440–c. 1500); then, when two Italian humanists, CORNELIO VITELLI and FAUSTO ANDRELINI, arrived in his city and, in 1489, all three were licensed to teach humanities, he quarrelled in print with them too. The eventual result was that Balbi left France, first for England and then Vienna. In fact, even before his departure from Paris, he had been seeking patronage further east, producing a panegyric to the bellicose king of Hungary, Matthias Corvinus. In Vienna in 1493, he revised this for presentation to the Holy Roman Emperor Maximilian (1493–1519). In 1499, he moved to Prague as tutor to the off-spring of the new king of Hungary, Ladislaus II Jagiellon (1490–1516). He continued in royal service after Ladislaus' death, being sent on diplomatic missions, and appointed bishop of Gurk in 1522. He resigned his see in 1526 and spent his last years in Italy.

GREGORIO TIFERNATE / P. Gregorius   1414–1464
    Tifernas

Born in Città del Castello (Umbria), the ancient Tifernum, Gregorio left home to study in Perugia. He appears to have visited the Peloponnese and Constantinople at some point and studied with Gemistos Pletho. He went to Naples in the 1440s, where he befriended both LORENZO VALLA and PANORMITA, and was given a stipend by King Alfonso.

Moving to Rome in early 1453, he produced a number of translations of Greek texts for Nicholas V, including works by Aristotle, Theophrastus, and Strabo. After the pope's death in 1455, Tifernate left Rome, first for Venice, and then for Milan, where, in May 1456, he was granted a teaching position by Francesco Sforza. But in the autumn he left Milan and went to France, where soon he was teaching Greek at the University of Paris. Returning to Italy three years later, he hoped to return to Milan through the mediation of FRANCESCO FILELFO. These attempts came to nothing; instead, in 1460, on the recommendation of Pius II (ÆNEAS SYLVIUS PICCOLOMINI), Tifernate was hired by Ludovico Gonzaga to open a school in Mantua, where he remained until mid-1462. The last years of his life were spent in Venice.

GUARINO DA VERONA 1374–1460
    Guarinus Veronensis

The most celebrated humanist educator of his time, Guarino followed Manuel Chrysoloras to Constantinople in 1403, where he studied Greek. He remained there until 1409, when he returned to Italy, going first to Venice, and then to Bologna, where he met POGGIO BRACCIOLINI and LEONARDO BRUNI, who encouraged NICCOLÒ NICCOLI to invite him to teach Greek in Florence. Guarino stayed in Florence only until 1414, returning to Venice. He went back to Verona in 1419, where he lived and taught on and off until 1429, when he went to Ferrara to teach the young Leonello d'Este, and founded the school at which he taught until his death. An editor and translator as well as a teacher, Guarino also took part in some of the most high-profile humanist controversies of his day: he defended PANORMITA during the uproar that greeted his *Hermaphroditus* and engaged in a famous debate with Poggio over the relative merits of Scipio Africanus and Julius Caesar (1435). Guarino's reputation is largely the work of his many students, who spread their teacher's fame across Europe: his foreign students included Janus Pannonius and John Tiptoft, earl of Worcester; Italians included BARTOLOMEO FACIO, GALEOTTO MARZIO and NICCOLÒ PEROTTI, as well as his son BATTISTA GUARINI.

GUINIFORTE BARZIZZA 1406–1463
    Guinifortius Barzizius

The third son of GASPARINO BARZIZZA, whose intellectual legacy he kept alive, though (it is often said) he was not his father's equal. Educated by his father, he learnt Greek from GUARINO DA VERONA. He too became a teacher but in 1432, the year after Gasparino's death, he travelled to Catalonia, and entered the service of Alfonso V of Aragon. From Alfonso's household, he also made contact with Juan II, king of Castile (1406–54). He went on Alfonso's 1432 campaign in Tunisia and then, from Sicily, was sent by the king as an ambassador to his home city of Milan, where he was struck by illness that meant he could no longer travel. Instead, he received Visconti favour, teaching at the University of Milan, becoming a ducal secretary and producing a commentary on Dante's *Inferno*. He left Milan after the death of Filippo Maria Visconti (1447), and served various signori as an ambassador, going to the court of the Holy Roman Emperor Frederick III and also to Savoy. He eventually returned to Milan, as tutor to the heir to the duchy, Galeazzo Maria Sforza (1444–1476).

JOHANNES MICHAEL NAGONIUS fl. 1490s–
    Giovanni Michele Nagonio 1500s

The biography of the itinerant poet who called himself Nagonius is shrouded in inclarity. He was born near Pavia and seems to have had some association with the 'Roman Academy' of POMPONIUS LAETUS. His travels may have been occasioned by being in papal service. His first known work is an oration welcoming Pietr Wapowski, the representative of Cardinal Fryderyk Jagiellon (and uncle of Bernard Wapowski), to Rome in 1493. The following years saw him travelling across Europe – from England (1496) to Hungary (1497), and taking in also the courts of Louis XII of France (1499) and the Holy Roman Emperor Maximilian (1493 / 94). To each ruler, Nagonius had a manuscript prepared of his own poetry, sometimes recycling his compositions for the new dedicatee.

LEON BATTISTA ALBERTI 1404–1472
    Leo Baptista Albertus

For Jacob Burckhardt in the mid-nineteenth century, Alberti was the quintessential Renaissance man – on the basis of a description which, in fact, he wrote himself (probably in 1438). He may not be able to compare with LEONARDO BRUNI or GUARINO DA VERONA in terms of contemporary international reputation as a humanist, but, then, his scholarly achievements were only part of his accomplishments. The author of translations, comedies (*Momus*; 1443–50) and Lucianic dialogues, he was also an architect and artist, who wrote about those subjects in Latin and the *volgare* (*De Pictura*, 1435 / *Della Pittura*, 1436; *De re aedificatoria*, 1452). He was of a wealthy but exiled Florentine family and he, besides, was illegitimate. He was educated in Padua, by GASPARINO BARZIZZA, and in Bologna. He made his career in the papal curia, but also found patronage in Florence (thus his façades for Palazzo Rucellai and Santa Maria Novella) and elsewhere, including Mantua and also Rimini (where his design for Sigismondo Pandolfo Malatesta transformed the city's Franciscan church into the Tempio Malatestiano).

Leonardo Bruni   1370–1444
    Leonardus (Brunus) Aretinus

The pre-eminent humanist of the early Quattrocento and, indeed, the scholar who more than any other defined the agenda of the *studia humanitatis*. He styled his Latin name from the town of his birth, Arezzo, and some of his career was at the papal curia, but he was most associated with his adoptive city of Florence, which he praised in his early works and where he was to become Chancellor (1410–11; 1427–44). He arrived in the city as a young man, where the then Chancellor, Coluccio Salutati (1331–1406), was a mentor to him, as to Poggio Bracciolini, and where, alongside Niccolò Niccoli, he was one of the first to learn Greek from Manuel Chrysoloras. At the very start of the fifteenth century, he produced his first literary works: his *Dialogi ad Petrum Paulum Histrum* (that is, to Pier Paolo Vergerio) and his *Laudatio Florentinae urbis*, as well as translations from pagan and patristic Greek texts. As a translator, he became most associated with his new versions of the core texts of Aristotle–the *Ethics* (1416 / 17, dedicated to Martin V, 1419) and the *Politics* (1437) – which he claimed were necessary because the earlier medieval translations were both inaccurate and unreadable. Alfonso da Cartagena and Pier Candido Decembrio challenged his contention but their criticisms did not dampen the international success of these versions. He also turned his hand to history, particularly of Florence and, indeed, it was for his *Historia Florentini populi* that he was primarily venerated on his death by his fellow citizens.

Lorenzo Traversagni   1425–1503
    Laurentius Guilelmus Traversanus
    Savonensis

Born at Savona (Liguria), he became a Franciscan friar and was educated at the universities of Padua and Bologna. The next few decades saw him travelling further afield. He spent most of the 1450s in Vienna, as a student, writer and lecturer; in the early 1460s, he was teaching in Avignon and Toulouse, and, in the later 1470s, he was for several years in England. He taught at Cambridge and also wrote devotional and grammatical tracts; the first work of his to be printed was of the latter sort, the *Margarita eloquentiae*, produced by William Caxton in 1478. In the late 1470s and early 1480s, he moved between London, Cambridge, Paris and Bruges. He dedicated his *Triumphus amoris* to William Waynflete, bishop of Winchester (c. 1400–1486), in 1485; two years later, he was back in his order's convent in Savona, where he spent the rest of his life, continuing to write. His plans to print his collected works were foiled by death.

LORENZO VALLA   1407–1457
    Laurentius Valla

Valla was born in Rome to a family closely connected to the Curia. His philological approach and strident tone made him a lightning rod for controversy: encouraged by PANORMITA to move to Pavia and teach rhetoric in 1431, he was forced to flee two years later when his criticisms of Bartolus of Sassoferrato (1314–57) raised the ire of the jurists; entering into Alfonso of Aragon's service in 1435, he soon became involved in the king's feud with Eugenius IV, when he demonstrated that the Donation of Constantine, which justified the secular power of the Church, was a forgery (1439–40). His own feuds with BARTOLOMEO FACIO and POGGIO BRACCIOLINI spawned a series of bitter invectives, and he fell out with Panormita as well. He only made peace with Rome after Eugenius' death in 1447, becoming a papal secretary under Nicholas V in 1455. A prolific scholar, his works include numerous translations of Greek authors (Thucydides, Herodotus), annotations of Latin ones (Livy, Quintilian), and the provocative treatise *De voluptate* (1431), in which Valla closely associated

Epicureanism (rather than Stoicism) with Christianity. In the decades immediately after his death, he was best remembered for his *Elegantiae linguae Latinae* (1435–44; in print 1471), which became the most important manual for Latin usage across Europe.

LUCA MARINEO 1444–?1533
    Lucius Marineus Siculus / Lucio Marineo Siculo

Born in Catania, Marineo was both educated and, later, a teacher in Palermo. It was there that he met the son of the admiral of Castile, Fadrique II Enríquez and entered his service, travelling to his master's homeland in 1484; in the same year, he began a twelve-year stint teaching at the University of Salamanca. Other Italian humanists visited him there, including PIETRO MARTIRE D'ANGHIERA. In 1496, he produced *De laudibus Hispaniae*, a work which endured the ire of Antonio de Nebrija; in the same year, he left Salamanca for the court, to be a royal tutor alongside ANTONIO and ALESSANDRO GERALDINI. It was in that milieu that he became an historian, writing biographies of the Aragonese kings for Ferdinand (1479–1516) and a more general history of Spain for Charles I (1516–1556; Emperor Charles V).

LUDOVICO CARBONE 1430–1485
    Ludovicus Carbo Ferrariensis

Born of a poor Cremonese family, Carbone's self-identity was closely associated with the city of Ferrara. It was there that he was taught by GUARINO DA VERONA and by Theodore Gaza, there that he himself became a private teacher and, in 1456, a professor at the University. The student body was cosmopolitan and Carbone certainly had strong links with some of its English members: John Tiptoft, earl of Worcester

(1427–1470) suggested that he should join his service, an invitation that Carbone seriously entertained. However, late in 1460, Guarino died. Carbone, already known for his rhetoric, gave the funeral oration; his hope of succeeding Guarino as the centre-point of Ferrarese humanist activity led him eventually to reject Tiptoft's proposal. He was later invited by Matthias Corvinus to set up school in Hungary; Carbone again chose to stay at home, though he sent the king a work in his praise. Carbone continued in favour with the d'Este rulers of Ferrara; his oratory made him useful on diplomatic occasions, and he also dedicated some of his works – Latin dialogues and translations into the *volgare* – to them. And, yet, it seems the poverty into which he had been born plagued him again in his last years.

MARCANTONIO SABELLICO   1436–1506
Marcus Antonius Sabellicus

Sabellico was born Marcantonio Coccio in Vicovaro (Lazio), in the ancient land of the Sabines (or 'Sabelli'). He received his early schooling in his hometown, but then went to Rome, where he studied under POMPONIUS LAETUS and became one of his 'Roman Academy'. In 1473 he left Rome for a teaching position in Udine; it was there in 1482 that he wrote his first work of history, *De vetustate Aquileiae et Foriiulii libri VI*. Dismissed from his position the next year, Sabellico went to Vicenza, where he began to write a history of Venice, *Historia rerum Venetiarum*. He presented the first 22 (of 33) books to the Venetian doge and Senate in 1485; in response, he was appointed both as a lecturer in Venice and as librarian of the books left to the Republic by Cardinal Bessarion, which is one of the founding collections of today's Biblioteca Marciana. Sabellico remained in Venice for the rest of his career, and became the leading humanist propagator of its 'myth': his completed *Historia* (1487), *De Venetis magistratibus* (1488), *De Venetae urbis situ et vetustate* (1492) and his many orations glorified the city, its government, its environment and its past. He also wrote the life of his teacher Pomponius (1499), and a universal history, *Enneades*, which he dedicated to Doge Leonardo Loredan in 1504.

MARSILIO FICINO 1433–1499
   Marsilius Ficinus / Marsilius Feghinensis

Born in Figline Valdarno in the Florentine *contado*, Ficino went to Florence at a young age. The details of his early education are unclear, but by the 1450s he was already writing philosophical treatises and letters, showing particular interest in the works of Plato. He also caught the eye of Cosimo de' Medici, who bought for him a small villa at Careggi and appointed him tutor to his grandson, Lorenzo. A central figure in the leading intellectual and social circles of later quattrocento Florence, Ficino was a physician, a philosopher and a priest (ordained in 1473). He sought to bring together Platonic and Christian thought, to which end he wrote the *Theologia platonica* in 1469–74. He translated into Latin the complete works of Plato, published in 1482, and also wrote the *Commentaries on Plato* (1496). Ficino's corpus of philosophical treatises is extensive, and his network or 'academy' of students, followers and contacts (including Lorenzo de' Medici and Matthias Corvinus, as well as ANGELO POLIZIANO, PICO DELLA MIRANDOLA, FRANCESCO BANDINI and GIOVANNI ANTONIO CAMPANO) was vast. Associated with the Medici for most of his career, Ficino supported Girolamo Savonarola for a time upon the friar's arrival in Florence.

MATTEO PALMIERI   1406–1475
    Matheus Palmierius Florentinus

A Florentine of Medicean sympathies, Matteo followed his father's profession of apothecary and also served in political and diplomatic office for his city. His teachers included AMBROGIO TRAVERSARI and LEONARDO BRUNI's successor as Chancellor of Florence, Carlo Marsuppini (c. 1398–1453), whose funeral eulogy Palmieri later gave. Like LEON BATTISTA ALBERTI, he chose to write both in Latin and in the *volgare*. In the former language, his productions included a universal chronicle, *Liber de temporibus* (1448) – a medieval genre to which Palmieri brings some humanist elements – and a life of Niccolò Acciaiuoli (c. 1440; translated into Italian by DONATO ACCIAIUOLI). In the *volgare*, he produced a classical-style dialogue *Della vita civile* (1431–38), and a visionary poem indebted to Dante, *La città di vita* (1451–65).

NICCOLÒ NICCOLI   c. 1364–1437
    Nicolaus de Niccolis

An arbiter of taste rather than an original scholar, Niccoli was a major influence on Florentine humanism in the early Quattrocento. A protégé of Coluccio Salutati, he became a central figure in an intellectual circle that included AMBROGIO TRAVERSARI, LEONARDO BRUNI, POGGIO BRACCIOLINI, and the statesman-scholar Palla Strozzi (c. 1373–1462). The list of his enemies is nearly as distinguished as that of his friends; detractors (who included FRANCESCO FILELFO and GUARINO DA VERONA) regularly criticized his aptitude for both the classical languages, Latin and Greek. Niccoli wrote almost nothing: his only literary work was an Italian-language treatise on Latin orthography, which he quickly retracted and which does not survive. Yet he copied and collated the classical texts uncovered by his friend Poggio, and assembled what was at the time the second-largest library in Florence, bettered only by that of his friend Cosimo de' Medici, whose collection was built to Niccoli's recommendations. Niccoli is also credited with inventing the humanist cursive script (later to spawn the italic bookhand).

NICCOLÒ PEROTTI (*or* Perotto)   1429–1480
    Nicolaus Perottus

Born in Fano (Marche), Perotti studied under both VITTORINO DA FELTRE and GUARINO DA VERONA. In 1447, he travelled to Rome in the entourage of his fellow student William Gray, future bishop of Ely; in the papal city, he became secretary to Cardinal Bessarion. He taught rhetoric and poetry in Bologna in 1451–53, and was made poet laureate by Emperor Frederick III in 1452. Becoming secretary to Pope Calixtus III in 1455, he was soon ordained, and was made archbishop of Siponto (Manfredonia) in 1458. He regularly served as governor of towns in the Papal States, and as a diplomat in Italy and abroad. As a scholar, he became best known for his grammar, *Rudimentes grammatices*, which went through over 120 printed editions between 1473 and 1500. He also produced an encyclopaedic study of Martial (1478), whose works he had edited with POMPONIUS LAETUS. Perotti was highly critical of other scholars' work, regularly attacking them for their errors. His 1453 dispute with POGGIO BRACCIOLINI was on another level: he hired an assassin to kill the Florentine. The plot failed, and Perotti was forced to apologize.

PANORMITA   1394–1471
    Antonio Beccadelli

Born in Palermo (Latin: Panormus, hence his *nom de plume*), Panormita left Sicily around 1420 to study in Florence and Padua. Over the next decade he travelled between Florence,

Siena, Bologna, Rome and Genoa, during which time he earned a doctorate in law and wrote *Hermaphroditus* (1425/26) – a book of obscene verse following classical models like the *Priapea* – which he dedicated to Cosimo de' Medici. This book was publicly burnt by the future saint, Bernardino of Siena; it also won him the poet's laurels from Emperor Sigismund in 1432. Panormita took employment at Filippo Maria Visconti's Milanese court in 1429, before becoming attached in 1434 to Alfonso V of Aragon, king of Naples from 1442. The rest of his career was spent in service to Alfonso and his son Ferrante, as an ambassador and in various other offices; he also wrote *De dictis et factis Alphonsi regis* (1455). Panormita served as a mentor to Giovanni Pontano (1429–1503), but feuded with many other humanists over his long career, including PIER CANDIDO DECEMBRIO and his own former supporters LORENZO VALLA and GUARINO DA VERONA.

(Giovanni) PICO DELLA MIRANDOLA 1463–1494
Johannes Picus Mirandulanus

The youngest son of the signore of Mirandola (near Modena) proved a precocious intellect. In his philosophy he attempted to synthesize Christian and pagan, Aristotelian and Platonic knowledge, and showed an unusual interest in Arabic and Hebrew learning. Originally intended for an ecclesiastical career, he studied Latin and Greek at an early age, canon law in Bologna in 1477, and philosophy in Ferrara in 1479: in this last place he became a friend of BATTISTA GUARINI. He spent two years respectively in Padua (where he learned Hebrew and Arabic) and Pavia, before going to Florence and joining the circle of MARSILIO FICINO and POLITIAN. In 1485, he went to study at the University of Paris; he returned to Italy in 1486 and headed to Rome, where he proposed to defend his 900 theses (*Conclusiones philosophicae, cabalisticae et theologicae*) against all other scholars. Along with the theses, he published an oration on the dignity of man, which subsequently gained the title, *De hominis dignitate*. Innocent VIII called off the debate, condemning some of the theses as unorthodox. Although Pico retracted the offending theses, in 1488 he fled to France, where he was arrested on the pope's orders, and then freed through the intercession of Lorenzo de' Medici. He returned to Florence, where he dedicated his *De ente et Uno* (1492) to Politian. He became a follower of the austere Dominican friar, Girolamo Savonarola, who, on Pico's premature death, delivered the funeral oration.

Pier Candido Decembrio 1399–1477
Petrus Candidus Decembris

Pier Candido was the second son of the scholarly secretary, Uberto Decembrio (d. 1427), who was himself a friend of Manuel Chrysoloras and whose later career saw his family based in Milan. Pier Candido's humanist identity was, for most of his career, allied to his city, where he became, in 1419, secretary to Filippo Maria Visconti. He celebrated Milan in a *Panegyricus* that was a none-too-original riposte to the praise of Florence by LEONARDO BRUNI. However, he was ambitious for a reputation that stretched far beyond his homeland, seeking patronage as far afield as England and Castile. He presented himself as a translator both of Greek into Latin (though GUARINO DA VERONA doubted his competence), and of Latin into the *volgare*; examples of each are his renditions of Plato's *Republic* (on which his father had previously worked with Chrysoloras) and of the *Vita Henrici Quinti* by TITO LIVIO FRULOVISI. After Visconti's death and his own support for the short-lived Ambrosian Republic, Decembrio left Milan and sought employment at the papal curia of Nicholas V, then at the court of Alfonso V and ended his career in the service of the d'Este of Ferrara, where his estranged younger brother, ANGELO DECEMBRIO, had previously been resident.

PIER PAOLO VERGERIO (the Elder) 1370–1444
    Petrus Paulus Histrus

Born in the Venetian-ruled Dalmatian city of Capodistria (present-day Koper, Slovenia), Vergerio made his career as a curial humanist, in Padua, at the papal court and then, for over two decades, in Buda. Part of the coterie that sat at the feet of Manuel Chrysoloras in Florence, he was the dedicatee of LEONARDO BRUNI's *Dialogi*, the preface of which opens with an allusion to Vergerio's best-known work, *De ingenuis moribus* (c. 1402–3). That text was the first humanist advice-book on education, dedicated to Vergerio's masters, the Carrara of Padua. After the fall of that dynasty, he served at the Roman curia, in which capacity he travelled to the Council of Constance. There he met the Emperor Sigismund, whose employment he entered at the end of the Council, and so left Italy. He played a significant role as adviser to the Emperor, as well as also translating the Greek historians Arrian and Herodian into Latin. The latter of these, like Vergerio's life of Sigismund, is not known to survive.

PIETRO CARMELIANO 1451–1527
    Petrus Carmelianus Brixiensis / Pietro
    Fava

Born near Brescia with the family name Fava, his early career is unclear. The man who re-named himself Carmeliano claimed to have travelled for ten years in the eastern Mediterranean, perhaps on commercial business. But he changed directions, travelling in 1481 to France and then to England where, perhaps despite himself, he settled. He sought the patronage of the Yorkist royal family through his poems and, after 1485, was, along with GIOVANNI GIGLI and CORNELIO VITELLI, one of the so-called *grex poetarum* intent on currying favour with Henry VII; at the same time, he also worked with England's first printers, William Caxton and Theodoric Rood. He acted as secretary to both Henry VII and Henry VIII, producing diplomatic correspondence in his elegant italic script. These services helped him achieve ecclesiastical preferment, becoming eventually a canon of St Paul's, London.

PIETRO DEL MONTE c. 1400–1457
    Petrus de Monte Venetus

A Venetian, he was a student of GUARINO DA VERONA and of the University of Padua. His learning was primarily in canon law, though he also showed an interest in humanist studies. In 1435, he was appointed papal collector to England, a post he held for five years; while there, he presented a reworking of the *De avaritia* of POGGIO BRACCIOLINI (re-named *De vitiorum inter se differentia*, 1438) to Humfrey, duke of Gloucester, and also composed a contribution to the Scipio/Caesar controversy between Poggio and Guarino; he was also the dedicatee of a Plutarch translation from Humfrey's secretary, ANTONIO BECCARIA. In 1442, he was appointed bishop of Brescia and sent to France to negotiate issues of church privileges with Charles VII. He returned to Italy in 1445 and received further ecclesiastical appointments – but never the red hat for which it is said he craved. His later writings were legal, but with prefaces written in humanist style. After his death, most of his large book collection eventually became part of the Vatican library.

PIETRO MARSO 1441–1511
    Petrus Marsus

A commentator on classical texts, Marso was born in the Abruzzo but – apart from a short teaching stint in Bologna, 1478–80 – most of his career was in Rome, where his teachers included John Argyropoulos and DOMENICO CALDERINI. A cleric, he was also one of those arrested in 1468 for their involvement in the 'Roman Academy' of POMPONIUS LAETUS (for whom – as for Arygropoulos – he would later give a funeral oration). His first classical commentary, on the *Ibis* of Ovid, was printed in 1471 / 72. Around this time, he was also acting as a tutor, and later lectured at the University of Rome. As well as his commentaries, he was in demand as a preacher; one such sermon, given in 1488 on St Augustine, he had printed with a dedication to the Spanish Catholic Kings, Ferdinand and Isabella. This was not unique in Marso's œuvre in being directed to a foreign patron: Marso dedicated his 1508 commentaries on Cicero's *De natura deorum* and *De divinatione* to Louis XII of France and his wife, Anne of Brittany. It was, indeed, with his work on Cicero – his first commentary, on *De officiis*, had appeared in 1481 – that he earned his reputation, his commentaries often being reprinted outside Italy.

PIETRO MARTIRE D'ANGHIERA   1457–1526
    Petrus Martyr de Angleria

Born near Lake Maggiore (Anghiera is now Angera), he spent time in Milan and then in Rome, where he was known to the circle around POMPONIUS LAETUS. Despite his friends' discouragement, he took employment in the entourage of the representative in Rome of the Catholic Kings, Íñigo López de Mendoza (1440–1515), count of Tendilla and nephew of the marquis of Santillana, and so Pietro travelled to the Spanish kingdoms in 1487. He was involved in the renewed Reconquista, being present at the siege of the Moorish city of Granada, which fell in 1492. He entered royal service and was, in 1501, sent as an ambassador to Egypt, a journey which he recorded in the *Legatio Babylonica*. The best-known of his works, however, is now his description of the 'New World', the *Decades de orbe novo*, the first part of which was published (through the intervention of LUCA MARINEO) in Seville in 1511.

PIETRO RANZANO 1428–1492
    Pietro Ransano / Petrus Ransanus

A Sicilian, he went to Florence when twelve to be educated there (travelling to Tuscany in the company of Theodore Gaza, recently arrived in Italy). He entered the Dominican order at the age of sixteen; much of his career was spent in clerical administration and diplomacy. In 1476, he was appointed bishop of Lucera in Apulia. In literary terms, his life's work was the ambitious *Annales omnium temporum* (begun in 1450), sections of which imitated FLAVIO BIONDO in their style of geographical description. He devoted some of the work to an *Epithoma rerum Hungaricarum*, written while he was at the court of Matthias Corvinus, where he was sent in 1488 on a diplomatic mission by King Ferrante of Naples; he was there at the Matthias' death and gave the funeral oration. The *Annales* also included a history of Palermo, and a defence of the scandalous *Hermaphroditus* of his friend, PANORMITA.

Pius II *see*
    ÆNEAS SYLVIUS PICCOLOMINI

POGGIO BRACCIOLINI 1380–1459
    Poggius Florentinus

Born in the Florentine *contado*, his career was mainly at the papal curia (therefore Rome and Florence), with some years in England, but with a life-long attachment to his home city. A protégé of Coluccio Salutati (1331–1406), his first achievement was the invention of the humanist book-hand, *littera antiqua*, probably just before 1400. From 1403, he was employed at the Roman curia as a scriptor. He attended the Council of Constance and, on trips from there, made celebrated discoveries of classical texts like the full text of Quintilian. At the end of the Council, he became secretary to the English royal cleric, Henry Beaufort, bishop of Winchester, and travelled with him to the Lancastrian kingdoms. Poggio returned to the papal curia in 1423, where he was to become an increasingly influential political figure. Aside from his activity as a letter writer, his authorial career began with his dialogue, *De avaritia* (1428 / 29), which was followed by further works in this genre, all skilfully emulating the Ciceronian example. He strove to ensure his works circulated far away in England, and sought patronage in Hungary, Castile and Portugal. The antagonisms that developed between him and two other humanists – LORENZO VALLA and FRANCESCO FILELFO – were recorded in the invectives he wrote. His enemies mocked his private life (having abandoned his mistress, he became an old husband to a young wife) and his knowledge of Greek, which he gained only late in life and which resulted in his translations of Xenophon and Diodorus Siculus. In addition, over time, Poggio compiled a set of *Facetiae*, jokes, dirty stories and tales of monstrous births, which had an enduring and international popularity. In 1452, he retired from the curia and was appointed Chancellor of Florence, in which capacity he followed LEONARDO BRUNI in writing a *Historia Florentina*.

POLITIAN 1454–1494
   Angelo Poliziano / Angelo Ambrogini /
   Politianus

No humanist is more closely associated with Lorenzo de' Medici than Politian. He travelled to Florence from Montepulciano, Tuscany (Latin: Mons Politianus) before 1469. In 1473, he dedicated his Latin translation of the first two books of the *Iliad* to Lorenzo, and was taken into the Medici household; in 1475, he was appointed tutor to Lorenzo's son, Piero. He also wrote poems in Latin and the vernacular, including the *Stanze* (unfinished, 1475–78), the protagonist of which was Lorenzo's brother Giuliano. Giuliano was killed in the Pazzi Conspiracy (1478), and Politian produced the Medici regime's propagandistic history of the event. Appointed to the chair in Greek and Latin eloquence at the Florence *studio* in 1480, he continued to write Latin poetry and produce translations from the Greek; his *Miscellanea* (1489) is a series of 100 essays demonstrating his philological method. Politian's Latin style was erudite but eclectic and contrasted with the Ciceronianism of many of his contemporaries. In the wider circle of MARSILIO FICINO, he was particularly close to PICO DELLA MIRANDOLA. He is depicted in two frescoes in Florence by Domenico Ghirlandaio: in the Cappella Sassetti, Santa Trìnita (1483), and the Cappella Tornabuoni, Santa Maria Novella (1490).

POMPONIUS LAETUS   1425–
Giulio Pomponio Leto   1498

Likely born in Campania, the person who came to call himself Pomponius Laetus studied in Rome under LORENZO VALLA and learnt Greek from Theodore Gaza. He taught at the University of Rome and also brought together his protégés and friends in an 'academy', which he modelled on an ancient priestly college. Members – who included GIOVANNI ANTONIO CAMPANO, FILIPPO BUONACCORSI, MARCANTONIO SABELLICO, PIETRO MARSO and Bartolomeo Sacchi (Platina, 1421–1481) – adopted Latin names, and Laetus was recognized as *pontifex maximus*. In 1468, Laetus and others of this Roman Academy were arrested on the orders of Paul II, on charges of sodomy and encompassing the death of the pope. Laetus was tortured, but ultimately acquitted, and his Academy met again under Sixtus IV. In 1483, during a journey to Germany, the Holy Roman Emperor, Frederick III, gave him the power to confer the laurel crown for poetic achievement; among the first of his protégés to receive this was FAUSTO ANDRELINI. Renowned as a teacher, Laetus' written scholarship concentrated on philological studies and commentaries on classical authors.

ROLANDO TALENTI   d. 1473
    Rolandus de Talentis

Milanese by birth, he may have been educated by GASPARINO BARZIZZA; he certainly corresponded with GUINIFORTE BARZIZZA. Much of his career was spent as secretary to another Milanese, Zanone da Castiglioni (d. 1459), nephew of Cardinal Branda da Castiglioni (d. 1443), whose English contacts gained Zanone bishoprics in Lancastrian Normandy – first Lisieux (1424) and then Bayeux (1432). Both Rolando and his brother Antonio were resident in France, and both became canons of Bayeux (Rolando in 1434). Rolando did not lose contact with his homeland and, indeed, was a correspondent of PIER CANDIDO DECEMBRIO, being one of the channels by which Decembrio hoped to gain the patronage of Humfrey, duke of Gloucester. The declining fortunes of the Lancastrian regime led both bishop and canon in 1450 to change allegiance to the winning side; the next year, Talenti importuned Charles VII of France to crusade against the Turks. He died in Bayeux.

STEFANO SURIGONE   fl. 1450s–1480s
    Stephanus Surigonus

Surigone was from Milan and was a member of the religious order of the Humiliati. The first tentative evidence for his career comes from England; he was in Oxford soon after the middle of the century, where he taught privately – William Sellyng (c. 1430–1494) was among his students – and also composed a prose tract *De institutionibus boni viri*. Most of his writings, however, were in verse; his epigrams show that he was in Cologne – he studied there in 1471 – and that he taught in Strasbourg and Louvain. He returned to England, graduating at Cambridge, writing for William Caxton an epigram on Geoffrey Chaucer, which was printed in 1478, and apparently teaching once more in Oxford; John Claymond (1467/8–1536), first President of Corpus Christi College, Oxford, later recalled sharing verses with this 'greatest poet and orator'.

TADDEO UGOLETO (Ugoletto, Ugoletti) c. 1448–c. 1514
    Thaddeus Ugolettus

Born in Parma to a family that became involved in the trade in manuscripts and, later, print, Ugoleto studied in Milan and taught in Reggio Emilia, before travelling to the court of Matthias Corvinus in Hungary in 1477. Ugoleto became chief librarian to the king, a position that involved purchasing new volumes from abroad. To that end, in 1487–8, he travelled to Florence and while there met POLITIAN. A central figure for over twenty years at the court that included GALEOTTO MARZIO and ANTONIO BONFINI, Ugoleto also tutored Matthias' illegitimate son John. He returned to Parma after Matthias' death (1490), and, in collaboration with his brother Angelo, a printer, he published a number of the ancient authors whose books he had earlier purchased for the king, including Claudian, Ausonius, Quintilian and Plautus. He became a professor of humanities at the Parma *studio*, and also served as a member of the civic government.

TITO LIVIO FRULOVISI fl. 1420s–1450s
    Titus Livius Frulovisius

His surname suggests an association with Forlì, but his career was peripatetic, taking him from Venice to Ferrara, then

London and later to Toulouse and Barcelona. In Venice in the late 1420s he was a school-teacher experimenting in having his pupils perform Latin comedies of his own composition. He may have written at least one of his comedies for presentation to the d'Este rulers of Ferrara, to whom he certainly dedicated his dialogue on political thought, *De re publica*. He travelled to northern Europe and became 'poet and orator' to Humfrey, duke of Gloucester, producing for him a verse epic (the *Humfrois*) and a biography of Humfrey's late brother, Henry V. The *Vita Henrici Quinti* – itself derived from an Anglo-Latin biography – was later translated into Italian by PIER CANDIDO DECEMBRIO. Frulovisi was resident in England between probably 1436 and 1440; he was succeeded as Humfrey's secretary by ANTONIO BECCARIA. Frulovisi's later life is less known; he appears to have become a doctor in France, travelled to Catalonia, returned to Venice in the 1450s and probably died there, perhaps around 1464.

VITTORINO (Rambaldoni) DA FELTRE   1378–1446
    Victorinus Feltrensis

Remembered as one of the inspirational teachers of the early Quattrocento, Vittorino came from humble origins from Feltre (northern Veneto). He both studied and taught at the University of Padua, where GUARINO DA VERONA may have been a fellow student and GASPARINO BARZIZZA was a colleague and influence. He moved from there to teach in Venice and, in 1423, was invited by Gianfrancesco Gonzaga (1395–1444) to establish a school in Mantua. It was there that he remained for the rest of his career. His students included scholars like ANTONIO BECCARIA, GIOVANNI ANDREA BUSSI and NICCOLÒ PEROTTI, and more active characters among whom were Federigo da Montefeltro and the children of the Gonzaga dynasty. He himself was not an author but his name was kept alive by his students, in particular by the biography written by Francesco Prendilacqua (b. c. 1422).

INDEX OF NAMES

Page references in bold mark entries
in the Biographical Appendix.

Aberdeen, University of   240–41, 246, 254–55
Acciaiuoli, Donato   211, **348**, 367
Acciaiuoli, Niccolò   367
Accolti, Francesco   352
Adramyttenos, Emmanuel   70
Æschylus   25
Æsticampianus, Johannes (Sommerfeld) the Elder   139
Agricola, Rudolf (1443/44–1485)   83, 87–88, 321, 329, 345
Agricola, Rudolf, junior (d. 1521)   132, 142–46
Ailly, Pierre d', cardinal   206–7, 220, 222, 224, 234
Albergati, Niccolò, cardinal   210, 337
Albertano da Brescia   13
Alberti, Leon Battista   257, 355, 356, **361**, 367
Alciati, Andrea   170
Alcuin of York   214
Alderotti, Taddeo   13
Aldus Manutius *see* Manutius, Aldus
Alexander Cretensis *see* Cretensis, Alexander
Alexandros, George of Crete   62
Alexios, Greek scribe   65
Alexios, John, Greek scribe   68
Alfonso II, king of Naples   353, 358
Alfonso V, king of Aragon (Alfonso the Magnanimous)   180, 208, 307, 314, 344–45, 360, 362, 363, 369, 370
Allachi, Leone (Leo Allatius)   57
Ambrose, St   273

Amelia (Umbria)   340, 343
Amiroutzes, George   44
Ancona (Marche)   342
Andrelini, Fausto   241, 258–59, 311–12, 346, **348–49**, 358, 377
Andronicus Callistus *see* Callistus, Andronicus
Anghiera, Pietro Martire d'   194, 198, 364, **373–74**
Anselm of Canterbury   38
Antiquari, Iacopo   331
Antoninus, St, archbishop of Florence   160
Anwykyll, John, schoolmaster   334
Apollonius of Rhodes   73
Apostolis, Michael   50, 51, 63
Apostolos, Aristoboulos (Arsenius)   64, 70
Appian (Appianus)   250
Apuleius (Lucius Apuleius)   256, 349
Aquarubea, Thomas   237
Aquinas, Thomas   37, 38–39, 44
Aragon, Beatrice of, *see* Beatrice
Aragon, Katherine of, *see* Katherine
Arezzo   9, 207, 308, 352, 362
Argyropoulos, John   39, 42, 45–46, 62, 70, 75, 247, 348, 372
Aristophanes   85
Aristotle (Aristoteles)   13, 25, 38, 56, 85, 141, 196, 229, 233, 242, 348, 359
   Analytica priora et posteriora   75;
   De anima   39, 74–76; *De animalibus* 48, 55, 74, 78; *De caelo* 74; *De generatione et*

corruptione 73–74; *De interpretatione* 75; *Ethica ad Nicomachum* 25, 74, 247, 348, 362; *Metaphysica* 48, 73; *Physica* 74, 75; *Politica* 25, 247, 348, 362; *Problemata* 48, 55, 74, 78; *Praedicamenta* 75; *Rhetorica* 48, 74
Aristotle, Ps., *De mirabilibus auscultationibus* 76; *De virtutibus et vitiis* 74, 78; *Oeconomica* (Economics) 25, 247; Letter to Alexander the Great 75
Arras 210
  Congress of 324–25
Arrian (Lucius Flavius Arrianus 'Xenophon') 77, 310, 371
Ascoli (Marche) 342
Asconius (Quintus Asconius Pedianus), *Commentarii in orationes Ciceronis* 250
Athanasius, St 274, 342
Athenaios, Alphonsus Doursos, scribe 60
Athenaios, Antonius, scribe 61
Athenaios, Harmonius, scribe 62, 70
Atramyttinos, Emmanuel, scribe 61
Atrapes, Leo, scribe 63
Atrapes, Manuel, scribe 63
Atumanos, Simon 41, 78
Augsburg 83, 100
Augustine, St 39, 223, 228–29, 273, 289, 290, 291, 373
Aurelius Victor 256
Aurispa, Giovanni 25, 55, 208, **355**
Ausonius (Decimius Magnus Ausonius) 378
Aventinus, Johannes Turmair 101
Avignon 21, 205–6, 214, 217–18, 224, 230, 325, 335, 347, 363
Bachelor, James, vicar 256
Bade, Josse 256
Baena, Juan Alfonso de 181

Balbi, Girolamo 241, 311–13, 346, 348, **358**
Baldung, Hieronymus 100
Baleris, Basil, scribe 65
Bandini, Francesco 146, 149, 342, **351**, 366
Barbaro, Ermolao, bishop of Verona (1410-71) 342
Barbaro, Francesco (1390-1454) 350, 354
Barcelona 313, 379
Bardejov (Bártfa) 143
Bareles, Hippolytus, scribe 66
Barlaam of Calabria 40, 52
Bartolus of Sassoferrato, jurist 363
Barzizza, Gasaparino 130, 204, 314, 341, 346, 351, **354–55**, 360, 361, 377, 379
Barzizza, Guiniforte 314, 355, **360**, 377
Basil the Great, St 53, 72, 73, 74, 75, 160
Basilicos, George, scribe 66
Basel 82, 126–27
  Council of 80, 82, 86, 114, 121, 122, 126–31, 176, 322, 340, 355
Bassiano (Lazio) 339
Baye, Nicolas de 232
Bayeux 377
Beatrice of Aragon, queen of Hungary 342, 351
Beatus Rhenanus 91, 101, 349
Beaufort, Henry, bishop of Winchester 375
Beauvau, Louis de, seneschal of Anjou and of Provence 209–10, 231
Bebel, Heinrich 94, 100–1
Beccadelli, Antonio *see* Panormita
Beccaria, Antonio 251, 274, **342**, 372, 379
Bekynton, Thomas, bishop of Bath and Wells 269, 278, 291
Bel, Matthias 158, 168
Bellenden, John 260

INDEX OF NAMES

Bembaines, Emmanuel, scribe 66
Bembaines, George, scribe 62
Bembo, Pietro 199–200
Benedict XIII, pope 205, 218
Bergicios, Peter 68
Bergicius, Angelus 65, 72
Bernard of Clairvaux 14
Bernardino of Siena 369
Beroaldo, Filippo (the Elder) (1453–1505) 142, 241, 331, 343, **349**
Beroaldo, Filippo (the Younger) (1472 – 1518) 344, 349
Bersuire, Pierre 230
Bessarion, cardinal 34–35, 38–39, 42, 45–48, 53–55, 57, 61, 73, 104, 194, 207, 347, 356, 365, 368
Biondo, Flavio 99, 315–17, 330, **350–51**, 374
Bishop Auckland (Co. Durham) 265–67
Bisticci, Vespasiano da 26, 156, 330, 348
Blar, Albert (Brudzewski, Albert) 132
Blastos, Nicholas, scribe 64
Boccaccio, Giovanni 19, 33, 37, 46, 102, 205, 207, 209, 230–32, 258–59, 260–61, 292, 342
Boece, Hector 241, 246–47, 254–55, 260
Boethius (Anicius Manlius Severinus Boëthius) 9, 13, 38, 141, 266
Bologna 9, 15, 19, 21, 90, 331, 343, 348, 349, 352, 359, 361, 368, 369, 372
University of 84, 345, 348, 362
Bonfini, Antonio 149–50, 158, 166–67, 168, **342–43**, 378
Bordeaux 257
Borgo San Sepolcro, Dionigi di 230
Boucer, George, Greek scribe 66
Bower, Walter 249–50
Bracciolini, Poggio 7, 55, 84, 89, 129–30, 212, 218, 258–59, 280, 310, 313, 319, 322–23, 333, 335, 340, 352, 355, 359, 360, 362, 363, 367, 368, 372, **374–75**
Brandolini, Aurelio 313, **344**
Brant, Sebastian 110, 113, 115
Brassicanus, Johannes Alexander 165
Bratislava, Universitas Histropolensis 153, 161, 354
Brenner, Martin 166
Brescia (Lombardy) 371–72
Brest, Union of 43
Brittany 325, 340
Brodericus, Stephanus 165, 168
Brudzewski, Albert, see Blar, Albert
Bruges 357, 363
Bruni, Leonardo 7, 16, 22–23, 25, 38, 55, 84–85, 160, 176, 177–78, 186–87, 191, 194, 247, 274, 308–9, 316, 323, 340, 350, 355, 359, 361, **362**, 367, 370, 376
De militia 177, 187; *Cicero novus* 178, 213; *Commentary on the first Punic war* 235; *Dialogi ad Petrum Paulum Histrum* 308; 362, 371; *Historia Florentini populi* 348, 362; *Laudatio Florentinae urbis* 308, 362
Buda Chronicle see *Chronica Hungarorum*
Buda 135, 143, 147, 156, 157, 158, 160, 171, 309–10, 312–13, 343, 344, 351, 354, 371
Budé, Guillaume 219
Buonaccorsi, Filippo (Callimachus) 121–22, 132–40, 146, 156, **349–50**, 376
Buondelmonti, Cristoforo 283
Burgos, Diego de 178, 187
Burgundy 341, 343
Buschius, Hermann 100
Bussi, Giovanni Andrea 106, 257, 303, 330, **356**, 379
Byzantios, Nicholas *see* Nicholas (Byzantios?)
Byzantium *see* Constantinople

Cabaces, Manuel, scribe 64
Cabasilas, Nicholas 52
Caen, University of 223
Caesar, Julius 155, 251, 256, 300
Caister (Norfolk) 271
Calciopoulos, Leo, scribe 63
Calderini, Domenico (or Domizio) 249, 332, 346, **347**, 372
Calecas, Manuel 38, 60
Calophrenas, George, scribe 62
Calixtus III, pope 338, 368
Callimachus Experiens *see* Buonaccorsi, Filippo
Callistus, Andronicus 45–46, 51, 60, 69, 73
Calophonos, George, scribe 62
Camariotes, Matthew, scribe 63
Cambridge 79, 290, 363
Campano, Giovanni Antonio 93, 331, 350, 352, **356–57**, 366, 376
Campensani, Benvenuto 19
Candour, Thomas, scribe 269, 321
Cantactuzenos, Demetrius, scribe 61
Canterbury 79, 295
  Christ Church 286, 289, 292–93, 297, 303–4, 327
Capodistria (Dalmatia) 308, 371
Carabelos, Phanourios, scribe 65
Carbone, Ludovico 106, 278–79, 317, 329–30, **364–65**
Carmeliano, Pietro 301, **371–72**
Carnabacas, Peter, scribe 68
Carnedes, Peter, scribe 68
Cartagena, Alfonso de, bishop of Burgos 176, 177, 182, 188, 189–94, 197–98, 362
Caryophyllos, John Matthaios 68, 71
Caserta (Campania) 356
Casimir IV Jagiellon, king of Poland 122, 124, 133–34, 148, 350
Castiglione, Baldassare, *Il Cortegiano* 185, 197
Castiglioni, Branda da, cardinal 377

Castiglioni, Zanone da, bishop of Bayeux 224, 354, 377
Castrenus, Demetrius, scribe 61, 70
Catania (Sicily) 364
Catelos, John, scribe 66
Cato (Marcus Porcius Cato) 258, 300
Cavaces, Demetrius Rhaoul, scribe 61
Cavalca, Domenico 13
Cawston, Thomas, monk 303
Caxton, William 92, 363, 372, 378
Ceffi, Filippo 13
Celadenus, Alexius 47
Celtis, Conrad 80, 85, 88–90, 93–103, 107–9, 111–15, 121–22, 132, 139–42, 164–65, 350
Chalceopoulos, Athanasius 47, 61, 73
Chalceopulos, John, scribe 62
Chalcondyles, Demetrius 48, 61, 64, 70
Champier, Symphorien 219
Charlemagne, Holy Roman Emperor 7, 214
Charles, duke of Orleans 229
Charles IV, Holy Roman Emperor 79, 102
Charles V, Holy Roman Emperor 85, 170, 364
Charles V, king of France 210, 228–30, 233
Charles VI, king of France 206, 220, 229
Charles VII, king of France 377
Charles VIII, king of France 203, 207, 212, 354
Chartier, Alain 212
Chaucer, Geoffrey 378
Chaundler, Thomas 269, 290–91, 296
Chepman, Walter, printer 253
Chios 57, 350

INDEX OF NAMES

Choniates, John, scribe 66
Choniates, Nicholas, scribe 67
Choquart, Anseau 214–15
Chronica Hungarorum 159
Chrysoberges, Maximus, scribe 60
Chrysoloras, John 25, 352
Chrysoloras, Manuel 25, 34, 37,
  42, 45, 46–47, 57, 60, 69, 76, 340,
  352, 359, 362, 370, 371
Chrysostom, St John 75, 293–94,
  352
Cicero (Marcus Tullius Cicero) 13–
  14, 17, 39, 52, 81–82, 84, 142,
  144, 176, 205, 212, 216, 218,
  221, 228, 242–43, 245, 250–52,
  258, 286–90, 293, 297, 328, 355
  Brutus 346; *De amicitia* 231,
  232, 267, 276; *De divinatione*
  373; *De inventione* 8–9; *De
  natura deorum* 373; *De officiis*
  188, 266–67, 286, 373; *De oratore*
  347; *De re publica* 328; *De
  senectute* 231, 267; *Epistolae ad
  familiares* 267; *Orator* 347;
  Paradoxa 267; *Pro archia* 6; *Pro
  Murena* 212; *Tusculan Disputations* 256
Cicero, Pseudo, *Liber de proprietatibus terminorum* 253; *Rhetorica
  ad Herennium* 286;
Ciołek, Erazm, bishop 138
Città del Castello (Umbria) 358
Clados, Franciscus, scribe 66
Clamanges, Nicolas de 206, 212,
  217, 220, 222–28, 232, 234
Claudian (Claudius Claudianus)
  271, 378
Claymond, John, president of Corpus Christi College, Oxford 378
Clement V, pope 205
Clement VII, pope 205
Clerico, Ubertino 267
Cluny 212, 213
Cocolos, George, scribe 66
Cocolos, Nicholas, scribe 67

Codrus Urceus, *see* Urceo, Antonio
Coimbra 257
Col, Gontier 205–6, 223, 232
Cola, Rienzo di 21–22
Coletes, Peter, scribe 68
Cologne 79–80, 92, 93, 241, 311,
  378
Colonna, Francesco, *Hypernotomachia Poliphili* 339
Constance 128, 355
  Council of 26, 128–29, 206,
  217, 322–24, 335, 355, 371, 375
Constantine, collaborator of
  Demetrius Zenos 66
Constantinople 32–35, 39, 41–44,
  53, 134, 151, 350, 351, 359
  Fall of (1453) 32, 38, 43, 335
Constantinople, Emmanuel of,
  scribe 61
Contaleon, Michael, scribe 67
Copernicus, Nicolaus 132, 343
Cornelius Nepos 251
Corogonas, Nicetas, scribe 67
Cortesi, *see* Urceo, Antonio Cortona
  (Tuscany) 346
Corvinus, Laurentius 140–42
Cosmas (Trapezuntios) of Crete 61
Cossa, Giovanni 209
Coucy, Enguerrand de 207
Cox, Leonard 129, 132, 142, 143
Cracow 93, 119–145, 350
  Bursa Hungarorum 139
  Jagiellonian University 120–21,
  124, 126–30, 139
  Sodalitas Vistulana 122, 140, 350
Cranebroke, Henry, monk 293
Cranston, Thomas, canon of St
  Andrews 255
Crates, Cynicus Pseudo, *Epistolae*
  73
Cremona (Lombardy) 346
Crete 350
Crete, Peter of, scribe 64
Cretensis, Alexander 70

Creussner, Friedrich 90
Crosnensis, Paulus *see* Paul of Krosno
Cuspinian, Johannes 103
Cydones, Demetrius 36–38, 39, 52–53, 57, 60
Cyprian, St 267
Cyprus 350
Cyril of Alexandria 75
Dąbrówka, John (Jan) 129
Dalberg, Johannes von 83
Damascenos, John, scribe 66
Damescenos, Michael, scribe 63
Damilas, Antonius, scribe 64
Damilas, Demetrius, scribe 64
Dante (Dante Alighieri) 13, 360, 367
Dantiscus, Johannes 145
Darmarius, Andreas 49, 65
Dati, Agostino 82, 139, 204, 253, 333, **338–39**
Daudin, Jean 228–29, 233
Debares, Matthew, scribe 67
Debares, Petrus, scribe 68
Decembrio, Angelo 194, **341**, 355, 370
Decembrio, Pier Candido 89, 151, 178, 186, 194, 250, 273–75, 314–16, 341, 362, 369, **370**, 377, 379
Decembrio, Uberto 46, 341, 370
Decius, Justus Ludovicus 145
Del Monte, Pietro 357, **372**
Delle Colonne, Guido, *Historia destructionis Troiae* 186
Demetrius of Phalerum, *Septem sapientium apophthegmata* 74
Demosthenes 73, 75, 77, 78, 85, 293
Dene, Richard, prior 275–76, 304
Deventer 333
Diassorinos, Iacobus, scribe 66
Diluvium, Iohannes 79
Diocles of Carystus, *Epistola ad Antigonum regem de tuenda* 76
Diodorus Siculus 26, 56, 90, 280–82, 375

Dionysius of Halicarnassus 78
Dionysius the Areopagite 55
Dizomaios, Antonius, scribe 65
Długosz, John (Jan) (Johannes Dlugossius) 122–26, 138
Donatus, Ælius 218, 253–54, 257
Donos, Andreas, scribe 64
Dositheos (Dramas), scribe 61
Douglas, Gavin 238, 257–62
Dracopoulos, John, scribe 66
Dürer, Albrecht 85
Drzewicki, Matthias (Maciej) 138
Ducas, Demetrius, teacher 71
Duns Scotus 295
Durham 265
Eberhard of Béthune 261
Eberlin von Günzburg, Johann 91, 99
Eck, Valentin 142–43
Elgot, John (Jan) 126
Elizabeth, queen, wife of Henry VII 245
Elphinstone, William, bishop 240, 246, 247–48, 252–53
Encina, Juan del 180
Enoch of Ascoli 342
Enrique IV, king of Castile 192
Enríquez, Fadrique II 364
Eparchos, Antonius, scribe 64
Ephesus, Michael of 77
Epicurus 347, 364
Episcopopoulos, Benedictus, scribe 65
Episcopopoulos, Iacobus, scribe 66
Episkopoulos, Antonius, scribe 65
Érard, Guillaume 224
Erasmus (Desiderius Erasmus Roterodamus) 54, 120, 142, 165, 241, 331, 339, 349, 353
Erfurt 80–83, 93
Este, Ercole d', duke 345, 370
Este, Ippolito d', cardinal 353
Este, Leonello d' 341, 359, 379

INDEX OF NAMES

Estouteville, Guillaume d', cardinal 225
Esztergom (Gran) 143
Eugenicos, John 62
Eugenius IV, pope 127, 337, 340, 363
Euripides 76, 280, 339
Eurippiotes, John, scribe 66
Eusebius of Caesaria, *Preparatio Evangelica* 75
Eustratios, Leontius, scribe 67
Exeter 299
Eyck, Jan van 345
Facio, Bartolomeo 193, 307, 328, **344–45**, 360, 363
Falcutius, Nicholas, *Sermones medicinales* 249
Fano (Marche) 368
Farley, John, scribe 269
Fastolf, Sir John 271, 280
Fava, Guido (Guido Faba) 9
Fazio, Bartolomeo *see* Facio, Bartolomeo
Felix V, anti-pope 338
Ferdinand I, Holy Roman Emperor 165, 170
Ferdinand II, king of Aragon 150, 181, 343, 364
Ferdinand of Naples *see* Ferrante, king of Naples
Fernández de Velasco, Pedro, count of Haro 197, 198
Fernández de Palencia, Alfonso 196
Ferno, Michele 331
Ferrante, king of Naples 203, 357, 369, 374
Ferrara 25, 148, 321, 326, 339, 340, 342, 342–43, 345, 353, 354 355, 358, 359, 364–65, 369, 378–79
Ferrara–Florence, Council of *see* Florence, Council of
Fichet, Guillaume 204, 206, 223, 225, 235

Ficino, Marsilio 37, 137, 144, 150, 254–55, 260, 325, 341, 350, 351, **366**, 369–70, 376
Filarete 342
Filelfo, Francesco 25, 144, 337, 340, 342, **351–52**, 355, 356, 359, 367, 375
Filelfo, Gian Maria 342
Fillastre, Guillaume, cardinal 206, 213
Fioravanti, Aristotile 154
Fiorentino, Francesco 145
Flamenc, Pierre 224
Flavio Biondo *see* Biondo, Flavio
Florence 13, 19, 23–25, 34, 38, 45, 47, 207, 212, 286, 320, 337, 340, 342, 348, 352, 355, 361, 362, 366, 368, 369, 370, 374, 375, 376, 378
  Biblioteca Laurenziana 35
  Council of 53, 77, 324, 340
  Pazzi Conspiracy 351, 352, 376
  Santa Maria degli Angeli, monastery of 38, 340
Florus 144, 251
Fordun, John of, *Chronicles* 249
Forgách, Ferenc (Franciscus), bishop of Várad 166, 168
Forlì (Romagna) 343, 348, 350, 378
Forman, John, vicar 256, 263
Foullis, James 259
Fox, Richard, bishop of Winchester 265–68, 291, 299–301
Fracastoro, Girolamo 4
Francesco Negro 144, 353
Frankfurt am Main 91, 99, 106, 149, 324
Frankfurt an der Oder 80
Frederick I Barbarossa, Holy Roman Emperor 100
Frederick III, Holy Roman Emperor 83, 86, 102, 104, 107, 135, 148, 209, 338, 345, 360, 368, 376

Frederick the Wise, elector of Saxony 102
Free, John 269, 277–84, 301, 318, 321
Freiburg 80
Friburger, Michael 204
Frontinus (Sextus Julius Frontinus) 231, 257
Frulovisi, Tito Livio 313–14, 342, 370, **378–79**
Fulda, monastery of 89
Fulgosus, Baptista 106
Fusilius *see* Gossinger, Sigismund
Gaguin, Robert 211–12, 219, 223, 225, 235, 241, 294, 300–1, 349
Galen 85
Galesiotes, George Disypatos, scribe 62
Galiziotes, Andronicus 61, 70
Gallierges, Zacharia, scribe 65
Garcilaso de la Vega 199
Gaza, Theodore 39, 42, 65, 47, 55, 64, 70, 78, 352, 356, 364, 374, 376
Gennadius II (George Scholarius) 40, 42, 52, 62, 73
Genoa 328, 356, 369
Gentili, Umfredo, merchant 327
Geoffrey of Vinsauf 9
George Gemistus Pletho *see* Pletho, George Gemistus
George of Trebizond 38, 42, 45, 46, 49, 54, 57, 62, 70, 74, 347
George Scholarius *see* Gennadius II
Geraldini, Alessandro 194, **340**, 343, 364
Geraldini, Angelo, bishop of Sessa Aurunca 343
Geraldini, Antonio 194, 340, **343**, 364
Gerardus of Patras, scribe 62
Geri d' Arezzo 16
Gering, Ulrich, printer 204

Gerson, Jean 206, 216–17, 220–21, 223, 224, 227–8, 229, 230–31, 235
Ghent 173
Ghirlandaio, Domenico 376
Gibbon, Edward 32 - 33
Gibson, Henry, notary 256–57
Gigli, Giovanni, bishop of Worcester 291, 296–97, 300, **357**, 371
Gigli, Silvestro, bishop of Worcester 357
Gilbert, count of Montpensier 348
Giles of Rome, *De regimine principum* 230–31
Giovio, Paolo 170, 199
Glasgow, University of 240–41
Gloucester, Humfrey, duke of *see* Humfrey, duke of Gloucester
Glynzounos, Manuel, scribe 67
Gmunden, Johann von, mathematician 104
Goldstone, Thomas, monk 297, 303
Goldwell, James, bishop of Norwich 269, 291
Gonzaga, Gianfrancesco, marchese of Mantua 379
Gonzaga, Ludovico, bishop of Mantua 348, 359
Gosebourne, Robert, monk 297
Gossembrot, Sigmund, merchant 83
Gossinger, Sigismund 141
Graecus, John Franciscus 66
Granada, siege of 373
Gray, William, bishop of Ely 269, 277–78, 280–81, 293, 326, 368
Great Malvern (Worcestershire) 275
Gregoropoulos, John 64, 71
Gregory III Mammas, patriarch of Constantinople 43
Gregory Nazianzenus 75, 76, 85
Gregory of Nyssa 73, 75

INDEX OF NAMES

Gregory of Sanok (Gregorius Sanocensis), archbishop of Lwów 132, 137, 350
Gregory XI, pope 206
Gregory XIII, pope 47
Greifswald, University of 80
Griffolini, Francesco 293–94, **352–53**
Grosseteste, Robert 295–96
Guarini, Battista 339, 343, **345**, 360, 369
Guarino da Verona 25, 84, 130, 148–49, 197, 204, 209, 211, 219, 235, 253, 278, 281, 317–18, 326, 335, 344, 345, 350, 352, 354, **359–60**, 361, 364–65, 367, 369, 370, 372, 379
Gunther of Pairis 100
Gunthorpe, John, dean of Wells 244, 267, 269, 281, 299–302
Gutenberg, Johannes 105–6, 113, 115
Guthrie, David, canon of Aberdeen 254
Haldane, Gilbert, rector of Dalry 253
Han, Johannes 161
Han, Ulrich, printer 352, 357
Haro, count of *see* Fernández de Velasco, Pedro
Heere, Lucas d' 173
Heidelberg 79, 81–83, 93, 114
Heimburg, Gregor 87
Heinrichmann, Jacob, grammarian 144
Heltai, Gáspár, printer 168
Henry VI, king of England 266
Henry VII, king of England 244–45, 372
Henry VIII, king of England 372
Henryson, Robert 242, 260–62
Herburt, Jan Szczęsny 125
Hermonymos, Charitonymus, scribe 61
Hermonymos, George, scribe 64, 70, 74
Hero Byzantius, *Poliorcetica* 78
Herodian 371
Herodotus 363
Hesdin, Jean de 215
Hesdin, Simon de, *Faits et dits dignes de mémoire* 230
Hesiod 280
Hess, Andreas, printer 156, 159–60, 161
Heynlin, Johann 204, 236
Hieronymus Cunctator 175
Hippocrates, *De hominis structura* 77
Hita, count of *see* López de Mendoza, Íñigo, marquis of Santillana
Hobbes, Thomas 305
Homer 47, 76 , 251–52, 257, 376
Horace (Quintus Horatius Flaccus) 17, 81, 144, 249–50, 258
Hosius, Stanislaus (Stanisław) 139
Hrotswitha of Gandersheim 99
Humfrey, duke of Gloucester 82, 151, 240, 268–70, 272–76, 313, 315, 342, 372, 377, 379
Humfrey, Thomas, chaplain 297–98
Hunyadi family of Transylvania 154, 171
Hussowczyk, Mikołaj 146
Hutten, Ulrich von 101
Hypselas, Peter, scribe 65
Iacobus Diassorinos 66
Iamblichus 25
Inglis, Alexander 240
Ingolstadt 80, 82, 93, 94–96, 98
Innocent VIII, pope 135, 370
Irenicus, Franciscus 101
Isabella the Catholic, queen of Castile 180, 192, 194, 198, 343
Isabella Jagiełło, queen of Hungary 171
Ischadianos, Antoninus, scribe 65

Isidore, metropolitan of Kiev 43, 62
Islip, Simon, archbishop of
  Canterbury 293
Isocrates 25, 85
Jagiellon, Fryderyk, cardinal 361
James III, king of Scotland 249,
  255
James IV, king of Scotland 237
Jan Olbracht, king of Poland 133,
  145, 350
Janos II, king of Hungary 171
Janus Pannonius *see* Pannonius,
  Janus
Jean d'Angoulême 229
Jeanne de Laval, queen of Sicily 209
Jerome, St 273, 288
Joan of Arc 225
Johannes Sacranus *see* Oświęcimia,
  Jan z
John Corvinus of Hungary 354
John I Albert, king of Poland *see* Jan
  Olbracht
John II, king of Aragon 343
John II, king of France 210
John of Ludzisko (Jan z Ludziska)
  130, 131
John of Wiślica *see* Wyślicy, Jan z
John VIII Palaeologus, emperor of
  Byzantium 43
John, duke of Calabria 208
Jouffroy, Jean, cardinal 206, 211,
  352
Juan II, king of Castile 175, 180,
  181–83, 184, 191, 193, 194–96,
  198, 315, 360
Julius Caesar *see* Caesar, Julius
Juvenal (Decimus Iunius Iuvenalis)
  17, 249, 255, 258, 343
Karai, László 159
Karoch, Samuel 82
Katherine of Aragon 340
Köln *see* Cologne
Konstanz *see* Constance
Koper (Slovenia) *see* Capodistria

Kozlowski, Nicholas (Mikola)
  126–27
Kristeller, Paul Oskar xv, 5, 6, 7,
  17, 19, 28, 53, 195, 309, 325
Krzycki, Andrzej (Andreas Cricius)
  139, 145
La Spezia (Liguria) 344
Lactantius Firmianus 291
Ladislaus I, king of Hungary *see*
  Ladislaus III
Ladislaus II Jagiellon, king of
  Hungary 312, 343, 358
Ladislaus Posthumus, king of
  Hungary 150
Ladislaus III, king of Poland 122,
  126, 136
Lampoudes, Matthaius, scribe 63
Landriani, Gerardo, bishop of Lodi
  346
Langdon, John, monk 294–95, 298
Langenstein, Heinrich von 104
Lascaris, Alexander 65
Lascaris, Constantine 46, 61, 63,
  70
Lascaris, Janus 35, 47, 64, 70, 75
Latini, Brunetto 12–14, 18, 23
Lauer, Georg, printer 159–60
Lebègue, Jean 213, 235
Lefèvre, Jacques 241
Leipzig 80–82, 93
Leo X, pope 47
Leontares, Demetrius 61
Leontius Pilatus *see* Pilatus, Leontius
Leto, Giulio Pomponio *see*
  Pomponius Laetus
Libanius, *Declamationes* 353
Linacre, Thomas 286–89
Lincoln 295–96
Livy (Titus Livius Patavinus) 13,
  17, 205, 229, 230–31, 242, 245,
  246, 255, 260, 327, 351, 363
Logothetes, Antoninus, scribe 61
Lombard, Peter *see* Peter Lombard
London 79, 286, 312, 379

López de Mendoza, Iñigo, marquis of Santillana (1398 – 1458) 175–80, 183, 187–94
López de Mendoza, Íñigo, count of Tendilla (1440 – 1515) 373
Loredan, Leonardo, doge 366
Loreto (Marche) 342
Louis I, duke of Anjou 208
Louis II, king of Hungary 155, 170
Louis XI, king of France 211, 246, 348, 351, 354
Louis XII, king of France 361, 373
Louis, duke of Orleans 210, 226
Louvain 241, 248–49, 311, 346, 378
Lovati, Lovato dei 17–18
Lucan (Marcus Annaeus Lucanus) 249–50, 257
Lucca 357
Lucena, Juan de, *De vita beata* 192
Lucera (Apulia) 374
Lucian 26, 55, 73, 84, 85, 208, 353
Luder, Peter 81–82
Ludzisko, John of *see* John of Ludzisko (Jan z Ludziska)
Luna, Álvaro de, constable of Castile 180, 191
Lydgate, John 292
Lyra, de, Nicholas 249
Lysias 25
Lysis Pythagoricus, *Epistola ad Hipparchum* 73
Machet, Gérard 224–25
Machiavelli, Niccolò 180–81
Macres, Macarios 41
Magister, Thomas 52
Mainz 80, 91, 105–6, 108-9, 115–16
Mair, John 241, 258
Malatesta, Sigismondo Pandolfo 361
Malaxos, John, scribe 66
Malaxos, Manuel, scribe 67
Malaxos, Nicholas, scribe 67
Maleas, Michael, scribe 67
Malpaghini, Giovanni 24
Mamoukas, Pantaleon, scribe 68

Manetti, Giannozzo 348
Maniacutia, Nicolò 54
Manrique, Gómez 177, 184, 187
Mansel, Jean, *Fleurs des histories* 235
Mantegna, Andrea 354
Mantua 324, 342, 359, 361, 379
 Congress of 330, 338
Manuel, student of Constantine Lascaris 63
Manutius, Aldus 50, 330, 331, **339**
Manuzio, Paolo 339
Marcanova, Giovanni, merchant 326
Marcanova, Giovanni, humanist 326
Marcello, Jacopo Antonio 209
Margounios, Maximus, scribe 67
Mari, Cipriano de' 208
Marineo, Luca 194, **364**, 374
Marjoribanks, John, Scottish lawyer 257
Marliani, Raimondo 251–52
Marso, Pietro 266–67, 347, **372–73**, 376
Marsuppini, Carlo 367
Martial (Marcus Valerius Martialis) 18, 249, 258, 280, 368
Martianus Capella, *De nuptiis Philologiae et Mercurii* 226
Martin V, pope 206, 224, 362
Martire d'Anghiera *see* Pietro Martire d' Anghiera
Marzio, Galeotto 150, 156, 167, **354**, 360, 378
Matthias Corvinus, king of Hungary 104, 134, 137, 145, 147–53, 155–57, 166–71, 313, 342–43, 344, 351, 354, 358, 365–66, 374, 378
Mauromates, John, scribe 66
Maximilian I, Holy Roman Emperor 85, 103, 312, 358, 361

Maximilian II, Holy Roman
  Emperor 167
Medici family 348, 352
  Cosimo de' 340–41, 366, 368, 369
  Giuliano de' 376
  Lorenzo de' 157, 344, 351, 354, 366, 370, 375
  Piero de' 376
Mediolanensis, Stephanus 1
Meghen, Pieter, scribe 269
Mehmed II (the Conqueror) 44
Melampus, *De naevis corporis* 77
Meletius Monachus, *De natura hominis* 77
Melissenos, Sophianus, scribe 68
Mena, Juan de 178, 193, 196
Menander 74
Mendoza, Íñigo López de *see* López de Mendoza, Iñigo
Messina (Sicily) 46
Mesue, Johannes, *Opera medicinalia* 249
Michael, Greek scribe 67
Micyllus *see* Moltzer, Jakob
Migli, Ambrogio 210, 226, 232
Milan 19, 223, 314, 341, 348, 352, 354, 359, 360, 370, 373, 378
Mirandola, (Giovanni) Pico della 257, 260, 261, 339, 345, 350, 368, **369–70**, 376
Moccia, Giovanni 205, 231
Mohács, battle of (1526) 154, 159, 162, 164, 165, 166, 169
Mohammed, Life of (*Vita Machometi*) 74
Moltzer, Jakob (Micyllus) 91
Montagnone, Geremia da 17
Monte, Pietro del *see* del Monte, Pietro
Montefeltro, Federigo da, duke or Urbino 357, 379
Montefeltro, Oddantonio da, duke of Urbino 338
Montepulciano, Bartolomeo da 323
Montepulciano (Tuscany) 375
Montis Fasanorum, Iohannes 31
Montone, Braccio da 356
Montpellier, University of 21, 224–25
Montreuil, Jean de 205, 207, 212, 217, 220, 222-23, 226, 227–28, 232, 235
Monzón, Juan de 216, 220, 221
Morer, John 285–90, 292, 304
Morlage, Heinrich, canon 109
Moros, Manuel, scribe 67
Morton, John, cardinal 291–92
Moschos, Demetrius, scribe 64, 70
Moschos, George, scribe 64
Mourmouris, John, scribe 67
Mourmouris, Nicholas, scribe 67
Müller, Johannes of Konigsberg *see* Regiomontanus
Münster, Sebastian 101
Muret, Jean 205–6, 231–32
Murmellius, Johannes, schoolmaster 109
Murner, Thomas, friar 115
Murokephalites, Michael, scribe 67
Mussato, Albertino 17–18
Musurus, Marcus, scribe 64
Myllar, Andrew, printer 253
Nádasdy, Tamás 166
Nagonius, Johannes Michael 312, **360–61**
Naples 19, 307, 344, 351, 353, 355, 358
Narni (Umbria) 354
Nathanael, John, scribe 67
Nebrija, Antonio de 54, 185, 194, 196, 364
Negro, Francesco 140, 144, **353**
Neumarkt, Johann von 79
Niccoli, Niccolò 25, 89, 340–41, 352, 359, 362, **367–68**
Nicholas (Byzantios?), scribe 64

INDEX OF NAMES

Nicholas of Cusa, cardinal 356
Nicholas of Hussów *see* Hussowczyk, Mikołaj
Nicholas of Modrus, bishop 322
Nicholas V, pope 127–28, 338, 359, 363, 370
Nicodemos, Greek scribe 64
Norwich 291
Noto (Sicily) 355
Nouccios, Andronicus, scribe 65
Núñez, Hernán 196
Nuremberg 83, 90, 99, 104, 132
Oeglin, Erhard, printer 100
Ogilvie, Walter 244–46, 255, 263
Olahus, Nicolaus, archbishop of Esztergom 158, 165, 168, 171
Oleśnicki, Zbigniew, cardinal 119–24, 126–27, 129, 133
Olmedo, battle of (1445) 191
Opporinus, Johannes 167
Oradea (Transylvania) 153
Oresme, Nicole 233
Orosius 13, 251
Osiander, *Strategicon* 77
Oświęcimia, Jan z 144
Otto of Freising, *Gesta Friderici I Imperatoris* 100
Ovid (Publius Ovidius Naso) 13, 81, 142, 144, 217, 233, 257
Heroides 255; *Ibis* 18, 373; *Metamorphoses* 259
Oxford, University of 240, 269, 291, 311, 334, 346, 357, 378
Canterbury College 295
Corpus Christi College 265–66, 378
New College 287
Pacheco, Juan 191
Pachys, Nicholas, scribe 67
Padua 9, 18-19, 321, 342, 346, 351, 354, 358, 361, 362, 368–69, 371
University of 81–82, 84–85, 130, 148, 165, 326, 351, 354, 358, 361, 362, 368, 372, 379

Palaiologus, Manuel Rhaul, scribe 63
Palamas, Gregory 41
Palermo (Sicily) 364, 368, 374
Palmieri, Matteo 209, **367**
Paniter, Patrick 241, 245
Pannartz, Arnold, printer 250, 330, 356
Pannonius, Janus 142, 148–49, 156, 157, 161, 208–9, 317, 345, 354, 375
Panormita (Antonio Beccadelli) 84, 208–9, 344, 358, 359, 363, **368–69**, 374
Papulas, John, scribe 63
Paris 204–5, 210, 220, 222–24, 226, 241, 247, 259, 331, 333–34, 346, 348–49, 356, 358, 363
University of 104, 206, 213–14, 216–18, 220–21, 225–26, 257, 348–49, 359, 369
Collège de Montaigu 241
Collège de Navarre 213, 220–22, 224–25
Parma 157, 349, 378
Paul II, pope 278, 350, 357, 376
Paul of Krosno (Paweł z Krosna, Paulus Crosnensis) 132, 141
Paulus Diaconus, *Historia Romana* 251
Paulus, Greek scribe 65
Pavia 83, 354, 356, 360, 363, 369
Council of Pavia–Siena 322
Pavia, Girolomo da 219
Pazzi, Piero de' 348
Pécsi, Lukáes 167
Pera, Philip, Fra of *see* Philip, Fra of Pera
Peregrinus, Daniel 265
Perotti, Niccolò 46, 144, 326, 332, 347, 356, 360, **368**, 379
Persius (Aulus *Persius* Flaccus) 17, 249, 255, 257
Perugia 84, 356, 358
Pesaro (Marche) 349

Peter of Crete, scribe 64
Peter Lombard 288, 295–96
Peter of Warda (Varadi, Péter) 164
Petrarch (Petrarca, Francesco) 4, 14, 16, 19, 20–22, 33, 37, 46, 81, 84–85, 86, 97, 99, 102, 205, 207, 210, 214–19, 221–23, 226, 228–34, 258, 335
Petreius, Nicholas 64, 76
Petrus Hispanus 140
Peuerbach, Georg von 104–5, 156
Peutinger, Conrad 101
Phalaris, Ps., *Epistolae* 352
Philip the Good, duke of Burgundy 211
Philip, Fra of Pera 53
Philippos, Greek scribe 65
Philomusus (Locher), Jacob 100
Philoponus, *Commentaria in Aristotelis De generatione animalium* 77
Phroulas, John, scribe 67
Piazzola, Rolando da 17
Piccolomini, Æneas Sylvius (Pius II) 83, 85–86, 87, 102, 106, 119, 122–23, 151, 210, 238, 278, 310, 313–14, 324, **337–38**, 341, 356–57, 359
Pico della Mirandola *see* Mirandola, (Giovanni) Pico della
Pienza (Tuscany) 338
Pietramala, Galeotto Tarlatti da, cardinal 218, 222, 227, 232
Pilatus, Leontius 37, 45-46, 48, 60, 69
Pindar 25, 280
Pinturicchio (Bernardino di Betto) 238
Pirckheimer, Franz the Elder 83
Pirckheimer, Franz the Younger 83–84
Pirckheimer, Hans 84
Pirckheimer, Johann 85
Pirckheimer, Thomas 83–84
Pirckheimer, Willibald 85
Pisa 102
 Council of 322
Pitti, Buonaccorso 229
Pius II, pope, *see* Piccolomini, Æneas Sylvius
Pius III, pope 357
Pizan, Christine de 228–29, 234
Pizanos, John, scribe 67
Planudes, Maximus 41
Platina (Bartolomeo Sacchi) 376
Plato 26, 38, 56, 85, 187, 228, 274, 347, 351, 366
 Dialogues 25; *Laws* 75; *Letter to Axiochus* 74; *Epinomis* 75; *Parmenides* 75; *Republic* 76, 151, 273–75, 341, 370; *Sententia pulcherrima Socratis, verbis celebrata Platonis* (excerpt) 77; *Symposium* 55
Plautus (Titus Maccius Plautus) 257, 378
Pletho, George Gemistus 37, 52, 56, 62, 78, 358
Pliny the Elder (Gaius Plinius Secundus) 254, 280-84
Pliny the Younger (Gaius Plinius Caecilius Secundus) 107, 221, 355
Plotinus 25
Plousiadenos, John, scribe 63
Plutarch 25, 72, 78, 84, 85, 342, 348, 372
Poggio Bracciolini *see* Bracciolini, Poggio
Poitiers 312, 349
Polemon Periegetes, *Fragmenta* 77
Politian 54, 142, 260, 339, 347, 349, 369, 370, **375–76**, 378
Polona, Iacobina 119
Polybius, *De militia Romanorum* 75
Pomponius Laetus 93, 132, 155, 256–58, 347, 348, 350, 356, 358, 360, 365, 368, 373, **376–77**
Pomponius Mela, *Cosmographia* 257
Pontano, Giovanni 369

INDEX OF NAMES

Porphyry, *Isagoge* 75
Portico (Romagna) 340
Prague 79, 358
Premierfait, Laurent de 205, 231–34
Prendilacqua, Francesco 380
Probatares, Manuel, scribe 67
Proclus 25
Psellus, Michael 52, 56
Ptolemy 75, 104, 209
Publius Faustus *see* Andrelini, Fausto
Pulgar, Fernando de 183, 187, 198
Quintilian (Marcus Fabius Quintilianus) 17, 26, 129, 209, 218, 253, 256, 322, 363, 375, 378
Quintus Curtius, *Life of Alexander* 154
Raimondi, Cosma 224, **346–47**
Ramus, Petrus 170
Ranzano, Pietro 167, **374**
Regensburg, Diet of 94, 324
Regio, Raffaele 259
Regiomontanus (Müller, Johannes of Konigsberg) 104–5, 153, 156, 345
Reims 213
René of Anjou, king of Sicily 208, 223
Révai, Ferenc 166, 168
Rhenanus, Beatus 90–91, 101, 349
Rhentios, Theodore, scribe 68
Rhodios, Philippos, scribe 65
Rhosaitos, Michael, scribe 67
Rhosus, John 49–50, 63
Rhousanos, Pachomius, scribe 68
Rhousotas, Immanuel 51, 62
Richard III, king of England 239, 242–44
Ridolfi, Lorenzo 23
Rimini (Romagna) 361 Rinuccini, Cino 24
Rivulus, Adamatus xiii, 307, 337
Rome 39, 41, 132–34, 139, 205–6, 214-15, 259, 292–93, 303, 308, 320, 330, 335, 338–39, 342, 344, 346–53, 356, 257, 358, 359, 361, 363, 365, 368, 369, 372, 373, 374, 376
Collegio Greco 47, 57, 69
University of 346, 373, 376
Rood, Theodoric, printer 372
Rossi, Roberto de' 24
Rostock 80, 93
Roverella, Bartolomeo, archbishop of Ravenna 349
Rubiera (Emilia) 343
Rufinus, *Expositio symboli* 291
Rutherford, John, provost of St Salvator's 257
Russell, John, bishop of Lincoln 269, 281
Rusticci, Cencio de' 323
Sabellico, Marcantonio 99, 136, 254, 343, 347, **365–66**, 376
Salamanca, University of 364
Sallust (Gaius Sallustius Crispus) 12, 13, 144, 204, 235, 242, 245, 247, 250, 256
Salutati, Coluccio, chancellor of Florence 16, 22–25, 205, 207, 217, 218–20, 227, 292, 362, 367, 374
Saluzzo, Amedeo di, cardinal 205, 231
Sambucus, Joannes 149, 158, 165–74
San Concordio, Bartolomeo de 13
San Gimignano (Tuscany) 349
Sánchez de Arévalo, Rodrigo, bishop 199
Sanctamauras, John, scribe 68
Sandros, Bernardinus, scribe 65
Santillana, marquis of *see* López de Mendoza, Íñigo
Santo Domingo, La Hispaniola 340
Sartor, Cephas 203
Savonarola, Girolamo 366, 370
Scaranos, Demetrius, scribe 38, 61
Scarperia, Jacopo Angela da 209

Schedel, Hartmann 81, 85
Scheurl, Christoph 85
Scheves, William, archbishop of St Andrews 248–50
Scholarius, George *see* Gennadius II
Schurener de Bopardia, Johannes, printer 90
Scordulios, Zacharia, scribe 68
Scoutariotes, John, scribe 63
Secundinus, Nicholas 63, 77
Sellyng, William, prior of Christ Church, Canterbury 269, 281, 285, 286–89, 292–98, 301–4, 326, 327, 377
Seneca (Lucius Annaeus Seneca) 81, 142, 176, 221, 242, 355
  De Clementia 276; *Epistolae ad Lucilium* 230; tragedies 18
Serbopoulos, John, scribe 63
Serra, Juan, rhetorician 224–25
Servius (Maurus Servius Honoratus) 257
Severos Lacedaimenos, John 67
Seville 374
Sforza, Francesco, duke of Milan 352, 359–60
Sforza, Galeazzo Maria, duke of Milan 360
Sgouropoulos, Demetrius, scribe 61
Siena 9, 238, 337–339, 352, 369
  Council of *see* Pavia
Sigismund, Holy Roman Emperor 85, 150-52, 212, 309–10, 369, 371
  Sigismund I, king of Poland 138, 145
Sigismund III, king of Poland 125
Silius Italicus 26, 155, 266–67
Sixtus IV, pope 104, 134, 347, 352, 354, 357, 376
Sommerfeld *see* Aesticampianus, Johannes
Sophianos, Johannes 78
Sophianos, Michael 67, 76
Sophianos, Nicholas, scribe 67
Sophocles 25, 280

Sophopoulos, John, scribe 63
Sosipiades, *Septem sapientium praecepta* 74
Souliardos, Michael, scribe 64
Spengler, Lazarus 85
Spinola, Gian Giacomo, merchant 328–29
St Albans (Hertfordshire) 79, 292
St Andrews 241–42, 253
St Gall, monastery of 322
Statius 232, 242, 258
Strabo 25, 209, 211, 219, 359
Strasbourg 112, 113–16, 378
Strategos, Caesar, scribe 61
Strozzi, Palla 23–25, 340, 367
Strozzi, Tito Vespasiano 93
Subiaco, monastery of 330
Suetonius (Gaius Suetonius Tranquillus) 231, 245, 251–52, 254–55, 279
Suleiman I (the Magnificent), sultan 162, 170
Sulpizio, Giovanni 256
Surigone, Stefano 275–76, 292, 311–12, 327, 346, **377**
Sweynheym, Conrad, printer 250, 330, 356
Świdnica (Silesia) 141
Synesius 278, 279, 282
Syropoulos, Franciscus, scribe 66
Syropoulos, Silvester, scribe 64
Sziget, battle of (1566) 169
Tacitus (Publius Cornelius Tacitus) 88–92, 93–94, 98–99, 101, 109, 111–15, 349
Talayerus Martin 226
Talenti, Antonio 377
Talenti, Rolando 224, **377**
Tardif, Guillaume 223, 225, 235, 334, 358
Tübingen 82
Tedaldi, Francesco 325
Tenax, Christina 147
Tepl, Johann von 80

INDEX OF NAMES

Terence (Publius Terentius Afer) 17, 81, 142, 232, 257
Themistocles, *Letter to Chrysippus* 74
Theocritus 280
Theodorus, Greek scribe 64
Theoleptus, Greek scribe 68
Theophrastus 359
   De plantis 78; *Metaphysics* 73
Thucydides 211, 286, 363
Tifernate, Gregorio 225, **358–59**
Tinódi, Sebestyén 168–69
Tiptoft, John, earl of Worcester 89, 269, 271, 277–80, 284, 353, 360, 364–65
Tolentino (Marche) 351
Torda, Sigismundus 167
Toulouse 312–13, 349, 363, 379
   University of 224, 225
Tourrianos, Nicholas, scribe 68
Tragoudistes, Hieronymous, scribe 66
Traversagni, Lorenzo 290, 346, **362–63**
Traversari, Ambrogio 38, **340–41**, 352, 367
Trebizanos, Thomas, scribe 68
Trebizond, George of *see* George of Trebizond
Tribolis Michael, scribe 63
Trivizias, George, scribe 51, 62
Trivolis, Demetrius, scribe 51, 61
Troyes, Chrétien de 214
Tryphon, George, scribe 66
Tucher, Sixtus 94
Tunisia 314, 360
Turmair, Johannes *see* Aventinus, Johannes Turmair
Tzangaropoulos, George, scribe 62
Udine 365
Ugoleto, Angelo 157, 378
Ugoleto, Taddeo 157, **378**
Uniones, Pinus 337
Urban V, pope 214
Urban VI, pope 206

Urbino 338
Urceo, Antonio (Cortesi) 142, **343–44**, 347, 349
Vadianus *see* Watt, Joachim von
Valerius Flaccus 26
Valerius Maximus 13, 81, 230–31, 245, 292
Valla, Giorgio 63
Valla, Lorenzo 24, 54, 55, 85, 87, 192, 211, 219, 235-36, 256, 258, 278, 286–88, 333, 335, 344, 347, 352, 355, 358, **363–64**, 369, 375, 376 *De voluptate* 363; *Elegantiae linguae latinae* 144, 204, 236, 253, 333, 364; translation of Homer, *Ilias* 255; translation of Thucydides 211
Varadi, Péter *see* Peter of Warda
Varna, battle of (1444) 44, 122, 136
Vaus, John 253–56
Vegetius (Publius Flavius Vegetius Renatus) 229, 230
Vegio, Maffeo 255
Velasco, Pedro Fernández de *see* Fernández de Velasco, Pedro 197, 198
Velius, Caspar Ursinus 165
Venetus, Camillus, scribe 51
Venice 19, 25, 82, 90, 125, 133–34, 162, 249, 255, 339, 346, 347, 351–54, 359, 365, 378–79
   Biblioteca Marciana 35, 365
Verantius, Antonius 165, 167
Vergerio, Pier Paolo (the Elder) 85, 151, 152, 196–97, 218, 308–10, 312, 362, **371**
Vergil, Polydore 346
Verona 19, 81, 342, 345, 347, 359
Verona, Guarino da *see* Guarino da Verona
Vicenza 19, 365
Vicovaro (Lazio) 365
Vieillot, Pierre Paul 236
Vienna 79, 82, 83, 86, 93, 103, 143, 338, 350, 358, 363

University of 90, 104, 365
Collegium poetarum et mathematicorum 103–104
Sodalitas literaria Danubiana 164
Virgil 14, 17, 84–85, 132, 141, 142, 144, 226, 255, 257, 260
Æneid 21, 242–43, 245, 255, 256, 286; *Eclogae* 242; *Georgics* 217, 226
Visconti, Filippo Maria, duke of Milan 352, 360, 369, 370
Visconti, Galeazzo II, *signore* of Milan 210
Visconti, Valentina, duchess of Orleans 210
Vitelli, Cornelio 311, **346**, 348, 358, 371
Vitéz, Johannes 152, 153, 156–57, 159, 161–62
Vitri, Philippe de, *Dit de Franc Gontier* 234
Vitruvius (Marcus Vitruvius Pollio), *De architectura* 257
Vittorino da Feltre 342, 354, 356, 368, **379–80**
Walther, Bernhard, merchant 104
Wapowski, Bernard 124, 361
Wapowski, Pietr 361
Watt, Joachim von (Vadianus) 101
Wawan, William, cleric 253
Waynflete, William, bishop of Winchester 290–91, 363
Wechelus, Andreas 149
Weiss, Roberto xiii–xvi, 15–19, 28, 30, 79, 82, 87, 88, 89, 237, 243, 268–70, 272, 277, 284, 286
Weissenburg, Treaty of 171
Wells (Somerset) 281, 291, 299–302
Werken, Theoderic, scribe 269, 293, 304
Weyden, Rogier van der 345
Whethamstede, John, abbot 269, 292
Whitelaw, Archibald, archdeacon of Lothian 239, 242–44, 246, 250–51, 254, 263
Wimpheling, Jakob von 94, 114–16
Winterburg, Johann 90
Wipfeld (Franconia) 93
Wittenberg (Saxony) 80
Worcester, John Tiptoft, earl of *see* Tiptoft, John
Worcester, William 271, 280–85, 292
Würzburg (Franconia) 80
Wyle, Niklas von, town clerk 87
Wyślicy, Jan z 146
Xanthopoulos, Demetrius 61
Xenophon 25, 26, 55, 74, 85, 160, 375
Zabarella, Francesco, cardinal 323
Zacchia, Laudivius, *De vita beati Hyeronimi* 161
Zacharides, Emmanuel, scribe 64
Zanetti, Bartolomeo 51
Zanobi da Strada 102
Zápolya, János 170
Zel, Ulrich, printer 253
Zenos, Demetrius, scribe 66

www.ingramcontent.com/pod-product-compliance
Lightning Source LLC
Chambersburg PA
CBHW030516230426
43665CB00010B/638